Lecture Notes in Computer Science 8653

Commenced Publication in 1973
Founding and Former Series Editors:
Gerhard Goos, Juris Hartmanis, and Jan van Leeuwen

T0224064

Marijn Janssen   Hans Jochen Scholl
Maria A. Wimmer   Frank Bannister (Eds.)

Electronic Government

13th IFIP WG 8.5 International Conference, EGOV 2014
Dublin, Ireland, September 1-3, 2014
Proceedings

Springer

Volume Editors

Marijn Janssen
Delft University of Technology
Faculty of Technology, Policy and Management
Jaffalaan 5, 2628 BX Delft, The Netherlands
E-mail: m.f.w.h.a.janssen@tudelft.nl

Hans Jochen Scholl
University of Washington, The Information School
Mary Gates Hall, Seattle, WA 98195-2840, USA
E-mail: jscholl@u.washington.edu

Maria A. Wimmer
University of Koblenz-Landau, Faculty of Computer Science
Universitätsstr. 1, 56070 Koblenz, Germany
E-mail: wimmer@uni-koblenz.de

Frank Bannister
Trinity College, School of Computer Science and Statistics
Dublin 2, Ireland
E-mail: frank.bannister@tcd.ie

ISSN 0302-9743   e-ISSN 1611-3349
ISBN 978-3-662-44425-2   e-ISBN 978-3-662-44426-9
DOI 10.1007/978-3-662-44426-9
Springer Heidelberg New York Dordrecht London

Library of Congress Control Number: 2014945462

LNCS Sublibrary: SL 3 – Information Systems and Application, incl. Internet/Web
and HCI

Typesetting: Camera-ready by author, data conversion by Scientific Publishing Services, Chennai, India

Printed on acid-free paper

Springer is part of Springer Science+Business Media (www.springer.com)

Preface

The 13th annual international IFIP Electronic Government Conference (IFIP EGOV 2014) was organized by the International Federation for Information Processing Working Group 8.5 (Information Systems in Public Administration), or IFIP WG 8.5 for short. IFIP EGOV is the core scientific conference in the domain of ICT and public administration and attracts high-quality paper each year.

Each year, scholars from all over the world present their research and share their experiences in the fields of e-government and e-governance. Since the start in 2001, the EGOV conference has provided important guidance for research and development in this fast-moving domain of study.

The IFIP e-government conference brings together leading researchers and professionals from across the globe and from a number of disciplines. Together with IFIP ePart, the sister conference on electronic participation, the two conferences have attracted participants from all continents. International scholars with different disciplinary backgrounds meet to share and discuss innovative as well as solidly grounded theories, methods, concepts and solutions for the domain of study.

As in previous years, IFIP EGOV 2014 was co-located with IFIP ePart, the 6th International Conference on eParticipation (IFIP ePart 2014), which aims at presenting advances in both social and technological scientific domains, seeking to demonstrate new concepts, methods, and styles of e-participation. Co-location of both conferences intentionally allows for exchange and cross-fertilization between the two domains of study, and hence the chairs of both conferences are committed to continuing the co-location of IFIP EGOV and IFIP ePart. Many participants attend both conferences.

Papers at IFIP EGOV are notable for their scientific credibility and rigor as well as their high relevance to practice. Likewise the keynote speakers come from both practice and academia, which presents a fruitful combination as practice can drive research, and research is needed by practice.

The IFIP EGOV 2014 call for papers attracted a wide range of topics with 70 submissions, which included 27 (accepted) full research papers and 27 posters and ongoing research papers. In addition, a workshop on "Critical Success Factors for Open Data – From Policy to Participation and Innovation" was organized. The papers were grouped under the following parts:

- Foundations
- Services and Interoperability
- Policy and Stakeholders
- Open Data
- Design and Values

Ongoing research and poster as well as workshop abstracts were published in a complementary open access proceedings volume. In contrast to previous years, this has immediate visibility for others, which the organizers hope might result in more usage and impact and will drive multi-disciplinary research. The proceedings contain contributions to both IFIP EGOV and IFIP ePart conferences.

The Paper Awards Committee was again led by Committee Chair Olivier Glassey of IDHEAP, Lausanne/Switzerland. The Organizing Committee carefully reviewed the accepted papers and granted outstanding paper awards in various areas. The winners were awarded in the ceremony during the conference dinner, which has become a highlight of each IFIP EGOV conference. Their names were announced on the conference website: http://www.egov-conference.org/egov-conf-history/egov-2014/.

Many people are needed to make large events like this conference happen. We thank the members of the IFIP EGOV 2014 Program Committee and the additional reviewers for their great efforts in reviewing the submitted papers. Our particular thanks go to Frank Bannister and the conference organization of Trinity College Dublin, Republic of Ireland, who hosted the 2014 IFIP EGOV and IFIP ePart conferences on shortest notice. At the heart of Dublin lies Trinity College with its magnificent buildings and beautiful campus spanning 47 acres. Trinity College Dublin was created by royal charter in 1592. There were 16,646 registered students in 2012/13 and over 100,277 alumni (source: www.tdc.ie). Trinity College has a long history, whose ongoing traditions and enduring artifacts we were able to enjoy. The conference dinner was held in the marvellous eighteenth century dining hall. The welcome drinks were held in the atrium, which has a modern structure and is an obvious contrast to the more traditional dining hall.

We were grateful and had the greatest pleasure to hold IFIP EGOV 2014 at such a special place.

September 2014   Marijn Janssen
                                              Hans J. (Jochen) Scholl
                                                  Maria A. Wimmer
                                                   Frank Bannister

Organization

Executive Committee

Marijn Janssen — Delft University of Technology, The Netherlands

Hans J. (Jochen) Scholl — University of Washington, USA

Maria A Wimmer — University of Koblenz-Landau, Germany

Frank Bannister — Trinity College Dublin, Ireland

International Program Committee

Suha Alawadhi	Kuwait University, Kuwait
Vincenzo Ambriola	University of Pisa, Italy
Kim Andersen	Copenhagen Business School, Denmark
Renata Araujo	UNIRIO, Brazil
Karin Axelsson	Linköping university, Sweden
Frank Bannister	Trinity College Dublin, Ireland
Victor Bekkers	Erasmus University, The Netherlands
Lasse Berntzen	Vestfold University College, Norway
John Bertot	University of Maryland, USA
Dana-Maria Boldeanu	Bucharest Academy of Economic Studies/ E-CAESAR Centre, Romania
Laurence Brooks	Brunel University, UK
Wojciech Cellary	Poznan University of Economics, Poland
Antonio Cerone	United Nations University, China
Bojan Cestnik	Jožef Stefan Institute, Slovenia
Jean-Loup Chappelet	Swiss Graduate School of Public Administration, Switzerland
Yannis Charalabidis	National Technical University Athens, Greece
Wichian Chutimaskul	King Mongkut's University of Technology Thonburi, Thailand
Antonio Cordella	London School of Economics, UK
Flavio Corradini	University of Camerino, Italy
Ahmed Darwish	Ministry of State of Administrative Development, Egypt
Sharon Dawes	University at Albany/SUNY, USA
Rahul De'	Indian Institute of Management Bangalore, India
Yogesh Dwivedi	Swansea University, UK
Elsa Estevez	United Nations University, China
Enrico Ferro	Istituto Superiore Mario Boella, Italy
Leif Skiftenes Flak	University of Agder, Norway

Michael Räckers   European Research Center for Information
                           Systems (ERCIS), Germany
Peter Reichstaedter   Federal Chancellery of Austria, Austria
Nicolau Reinhard   University of São Paulo, Brazil
Reinhard Riedl   Bern University of Applied Sciences,
                           Switzerland
Øystein Sæbø   University of Agder, Norway
Rodrigo Sandoval   State Autonomous University of Mexico
                           Toluca, Mexico
Hans J Scholl   University of Washington, USA
Margit Scholl   TH Wildau, Germany
Jamal Shahin   Vrije Universiteit Brussel, Belgium
Henk Sol   Groningen University, The Netherlands
Mauricio Solar   Universidad Tecnica Federico Santa Maria,
                           Chile
Maddalena Sorrentino   University of Milan, Italy
Witold Staniszkis   Rodan Systems, Poland
Efthimios Tambouris   University of Macedonia, Greece
Yao-Hua Tan   Delft University of Technology,
                           The Netherlands
Lidwien Van De Wijngaert   University of Twente, The Netherlands
Mirko Vintar   University of Ljubljana, Slovenia
Jörn Von Lucke   Zeppelin Universität Friedrichshafen, Germany
Vishanth Weerakkody   Brunel University, UK
Maria Wimmer   Universität Koblenz-Landau, Germany
Petra Wolf   Technical University Munich, Germany
Adam Wyner   University of Aberdeen, UK
Chien-Chih Yu   National ChengChi University, Taiwan

Additional Reviewers

Gabriel Cavalheiro   Brazilian School of Public and Business
                           Administration, Getulio Vargas Foundation,
                           Brazil
Marcelo Fornazin   Brazilian School of Public and Business
                           Administration, Getulio Vargas Foundation,
                           Brazil
Laura Fortunato   University of Salento, Italy
Yiwei Gong   Nyenrode Business University, The Netherlands
Anton Joha   Whiteline Research and Delft University of
                           Technology, The Netherlands
Devender Maheshwari   Delft University of Technology,
                           The Netherlands
Eleni Panopoulou   University of Macedonia, Greece
Anneke Zuiderwijk   Delft University of Technology,
                           The Netherlands

Table of Contents

Foundations

The EGOV Research Community: An Update on Where We Stand 1
Hans J. Scholl

The Development in Leading e-Government Articles 2001 - 2010:
Definitions, Perspectives, Scope, Research Philosophies, Methods and
Recommendations - An Update of Heeks and Bailur 17
Christian Ø. Madsen, Jesper Bull Berger, and Mick Phythian

An Online Transparency for Accountability Maturity Model 35
Rui Pedro Lourenço and Leila Serra

Towards an Evaluation Model for Open Government: A Preliminary
Proposal 47
Rodrigo Sandoval-Almazan and J. Ramon Gil-Garcia

Contextual Factors Influencing Health Information Systems
Implementation in Public Sector – Investigating the Explanatory Power
of Critical Success Factors 59
Karin Axelsson and Ulf Melin

PA Meets IS Research: Analysing Failure of Intergovernmental
Information Systems via IS Adoption and Success Models 72
Lies Van Cauter, Monique Snoeck, and Joep Crompvoets

Services and Interoperability

Interconnecting Governments, Businesses and Citizens – A Comparison
of Two Digital Infrastructures 84
Bram Klievink, Anneke Zuiderwijk, and Marijn Janssen

The Role of Trust in the Prioritization of Channel Choices 96
Kai-Jo Fu and Chung-Pin Lee

Identifying a Public Sector Information Systems (PSIS) for E-service:
A Case of Land Records E-service in Bangladesh 106
Muhammad Shahanoor Alam and Laurence Brooks

Source and Channel Choices in Business-to-Government Service
Interactions: A Vignette Study 120
*Yvon Van den Boer, Willem Pieterson, Rex Arendsen, and
Manon De Groot*

Connecting People: Semantic-Conceptual Modeling for Laws and
Regulations   133
  Tom Van Engers and Sjir Nijssen

Modelling Process Intensive Scenarios for the Smart City   147
  Riccardo Cognini, Flavio Corradini, Andrea Polini, and Barbara Re

Shared Services: Maverick or Originator?   159
  Paolo Depaoli, Maddalena Sorrentino, and Marco De Marco

Policy and Stakeholders

Assessing Policy Making for ICT Innovation: A Decision Support
Research Agenda   171
  Ciara Fitzgerald and Frédéric Adam

Open Government Data: Facilitating and Motivating Factors for
Coping with Potential Barriers in the Brazilian Context   181
  Claudio Sonaglio Albano and Nicolau Reinhard

Analyzing Stakeholders in Complex E-Government Projects: Towards a
Stakeholder Interaction Model   194
  Vanessa Greger, Dian Balta, Petra Wolf, and Helmut Krcmar

LAN House* Implementation and Sustainability in Brazil:
An Actor-Network Theory Perspective   206
  Carla Danielle Monteiro Soares and Luiz Antonio Joia

Bridging the Digital Divide at the Regional Level? The Effect of
Regional and National Policies on Broadband Access in Europe's
Regions   218
  Pau Palop García, Basanta Thapa, and Björn Niehaves

Designing a Second Generation of Open Data Platforms: Integrating
Open Data and Social Media   230
  Charalampos Alexopoulos, Anneke Zuiderwijk, Yannis Charapabidis,
  Euripidis Loukis, and Marijn Janssen

Categorization of Brazilian Internet Users and Its Impacts on the Use
of Electronic Government Services   242
  Marcelo Henrique De Araujo and Nicolau Reinhard

A Decision Model for Data Sharing   253
  Silja M. Eckartz, Wout J. Hofman, and Anne Fleur Van Veenstra

Policy, Process, People and Public Data   265
  Ann-Sofie Hellberg

Is the Public Motivated to Engage in Open Data Innovation?   277
    Gustaf Juell-Skielse, Anders Hjalmarsson, Paul Johannesson, and
    Daniel Rudmark

Design and Values

Dialectics and Contradictions in Public Procurement of Information
Systems   289
    Carl Erik Moe and Maung Kyaw Sein

Strategic Aspects for Successful E-government Systems Design: Insights
from a Survey in Germany   301
    Catherine G. Mkude and Maria A. Wimmer

Proposing an Entrepreneurial Process for the Co-creation
of IT Value   313
    Hans Solli-Sæther and Leif Skiftenes Flak

Developing Value-Centric Business Models for Mobile Government   325
    Chien-Chih Yu

Author Index   337

The EGOV Research Community:
An Update on Where We Stand

Hans J. Scholl

University of Washington, Seattle, United States
jscholl@uw.edu

Abstract. The body of practical and academic knowledge in e-government has significantly grown over the past decade. New publication outlets in e-government have emerged, and the research agenda has deepened and widened. The paper assesses the current topical orientations and trends in e-government and also updates an earlier study, which profiled the researcher community. The paper documents the productivity and impact of the most prolific scholars in e-government. The center of gravity of e-government research in terms of the location of most prolific scholars has shifted away from North America.

Keywords: Electronic Government Research (EGR), EGR topics and themes, EGR disciplinary breakdown, leading EGOV scholars, preferred outlets of publication, Electronic Government Reference Library (EGRL), EGOV-LIST.

1 Introduction

Inspecting and assessing the "state of play" in any given academic study domain is beneficial to domain insiders and outsiders alike: It can, for example, provide both parties with insights about (a) where the domain is topically headed and what the major themes under investigation are, (b) who the major contributors are, (c) what the size of the academic community and its output is, and (d) what the most popular outlets for publication are, among a number of other aspects.

For domain insiders such inquiry helps identify and confirm trends in research and also gives feedback to an insider's own research interest and contribution relative to others in the same study domain. To domain outsiders such inquiry helps overview the domain along a range of criteria that make possible informed comparisons to other domains of study. In particular, in tenure and promotion situations with reviewers and review boards little familiar with the standards and norms of the particular study domain such inquiry and its findings can play an important informative role. For the study domain of Electronic Government this study updates in part the results and findings of earlier studies on the subject [9-12]. It also complements recent findings on "Forums for Electronic Government Scholars" [13].

As the "Release History" of the Electronic Government Reference Library (EGRL, http://faculty.washington.edu/jscholl/egrl/history.php – accessed 3/28/2014) shows, which records the peer-reviewed publications in the English language, the volume of

M. Janssen et al. (Eds.): EGOV 2014, LNCS 8653, pp. 1–16, 2014.

new entries into the EGRL has significantly increased in more recent years. While the worldwide output of peer-reviewed publications in the English language used to average around 300 in the previous reporting period, it more than doubled to an annual volume of over 640 publications between 2009 and 2013 (see Tables 1 and 2).

From its first recognizable beginnings as a new domain of study in the late 1990s through the better part of two decades Electronic Government Research (EGR) has emerged into a solidly multi-disciplinary academic endeavor at the intersection of research streams such as public administration, information systems, computer science, political science, and information science to name a few [8, 11]. As assessed before, the study domain has grown past its infancy [10]. However, except for a recent survey study, which reported on recent topical directions in EGR [12], no comprehensive inquiry on the topical distribution of EGR has been conducted in half a decade. In that way, it appears reasonable and timely to assess the "state of play" as it presents itself based on the entries in the most recent version of the EGRL (version 9.5 as of March 2014). Previous studies have topically portrayed the EGR study domain and also presented the domain's community structure in terms of geographical provenance, research productivity, and disciplinary breakdown. In this update, we also add the dimension of scholarly impact measured by means of citations (Google Scholar) as well as the Hirsch and I10 indices also reported at Google Scholar.

2   Literature Review

According to the data in the EGRL versions 9.5, by the end of 2008, the entire body of EGR knowledge amounted to 2974 publications in the English language, 42.3 percent of which represented journal papers, while 48.6 percent were published at conferences and the rest in monographs and chapters in edited books (see Table 1). With these numbers we update and correct some findings presented before [11], which were based on an earlier version of the EGRL (4.4), which had not yet included a number of publications that were added to the EGRL at a later date. However, as found before the study domain in its first decade used conferences as preferred outlets for publications slightly more frequently than journals. This might be owed also to the fact that during that period of time some journals were newly introduced, which have become EGR core journals since [11].

After the discovery and wide recognition of the multidisciplinary nature of contributions to EGR, early discourses from a solely single-disciplinary perspective ceded, and the study domain began accepting its disciplinary diversity as strength rather than a liability [8, 10].

Since 2008 a number of studies have appeared, which presented journal-related geographic, institutional, and academic profiles of the EGR community, mainly for single journals, for example, Electronic Government, International Journal of Electronic Government Research, and Transforming Government [2, 3, 6]. More comprehensive profiles, disciplinary backgrounds, and topical mainstays were presented and discussed based on the data found in the EGRL, which amounted the core group of EGR scholars to 55 individuals and the extended core (of less prolific) EGR scholars to 225 individuals [9, 10].

In 2010, the same study also presented the topical orientations in EGR in this order as mainly focused on

a) *Management, Organization, and Transformation* followed by topics such as
b) *Digital Democracy,*
c) *Electronic Services,*
d) *Design Studies and Tools,*
e) *Policy, governance, and law,*
f) *Infrastructure, Integration, and Interoperability,*
g) *Information Security,* and
h) *EGR Foundations and Standards of Inquiry* [10].

A more recent study [12], which was based on survey data from 206 EGR scholars, found a slightly different set of the topical interests, which might indicate that some shift in emphasis and focus might have occurred in EGR. When inspecting the topical areas it is apparent that some topics are new (for example, Social Media, Cloud Services, and Open Data/Big Data), while others are fused into different categories (for example, Digital Democracy into Open Government and Participation). The rank-ordered topical list in the more recent study included

a) *Open Government and Participation,*
b) *Transformational Government,*
c) *Services and Information,*
d) *Social Media and Social Networking in the Public Sector,* and less prominently on
e) *Policy, Governance, Ethics, and Law,*
f) *Cloud Services,*
g) *Enterprise Architecture,*
h) *Interoperability in the Public Sector* and
i) *Open Data/Big Data*

However, while the EGRL-based data reveal what actually has been studied and published, the survey data represent the individual scholarly interest at the time the survey was taken, which may or may not have resulted in actual studies and publications.

In summary, the study domain of EGR has remarkably thrived since the appearance of its initial contributions by the end of the 20th century. A sizable global community of scholars has formed around the topics of EGR, and EGR scholars apparently have embraced the multi-disciplinary composition of their domain. Topical interests and orientations in EGR might have slightly changed as a recent study suggests. However, this potential shift has not yet been documented on the basis of hard data from publication records.

3   Research Questions and Methodology

3.1   Research Questions

Taken the insights from the literature review, the current "state of play" in EGR can be assessed along three areas: Based on bibliographic data in the EGRL (version 9.5,

March 2014), it can be determined (1) which types of publication outlets are mostly used in EGR, (2) who are major contributors to the advancement of the study domain in terms of publication output, and what is the leading EGR Scholars' academic impact, and (3) what are the salient topics in EGR in recent years.

Research Question #1 (RQ #1): What types of publication outlets do EGR scholars preferably use (journals, conferences, and other)?

Research Question #2 (RQ #2): What publication output do the most prolific EGR scholars contribute, and what is their impact in terms of citations in Google Scholar and citation indices such as the h-index and the i10 index?

Research Question #3 (RQ #3): Based on the bibliographic data in EGRL version 9.5, what are major topics of interest in the reporting period of 2009 to 2013?

3.2   Data Selection and Analysis

Data Selection. The Electronic Government Reference Library (EGRL, version 9.5, March 2015) provided the data source for this study. The EGRL was first made publicly available in the fall of 2005 and has been semi-annually updated ever since (see http://faculty.washington.edu/jscholl/egrl/history.php). It originally contained 922 references of peer-reviewed academic publications in the English language, which met certain criteria (see http://faculty.washington.edu/jscholl/egrl/criteria.php). It has been estimated that the EGRL consistently captures and contains at least 95 percent of the eligible peer-reviewed EGR literature [11], which shields against potential topical, geographical, or author-related bias. Version 9.5 contained a total of 6,283 references, of which 6,242 were selected for data analysis, since they fell into the period from the early beginnings of EGR publication until the end of calendar year 2013.

Data Extraction and Preparation. The EGRL 9.5 EndNote X7.1 (Build 9529) reference manager version (see http://endnote.com) was used to export the references into the standard tagging Refman (RIS) file format, which is widely used to format and exchange references between digital libraries. By means of the tags, for example, "TY - JOUR" for publication type journal, "AU - Janssen" for an author's name, or "KW - social media," references were extracted and prepared for further processing and analysis. Data had to be harmonized. For example, author names were found in different forms with regard to first names (abbreviated or full). Also, spelling of certain keyword or title terms differed with regard to differences in US versus other spelling variants (for example, "organization" versus "organisation"). Keywords containing multiple terms were concatenated by double equal symbols (==) between the terms so to avoid separation in subsequent analyses of term frequencies. Pre-analysis data preparation and harmonization was performed in part with TextEdit version 1.9 (Build 310) and with Mac Excel 2008 version 12.2.3 (Build 091001). All terms were converted to lower case, the punctuation was removed except for dashes and double equal symbols, as were sparse terms and stop words.

Data Analysis. The analysis was mainly carried out using the R statistical package (version 3.0.3, GUI 1.63 Snow Leopard build (6660)). For text mining under R the tm package version 0.5-10 by Feinerer and Hornik [4, 5] was downloaded from the Comprehensive R Archive Network (CRAN) (see http://cran.us.r-project.org – accessed 3/12/2014) and used. Frequencies of author names were counted. For authors with frequency counts greater than 18, which represented the most prolific 51 scholars in EGR, an additional (manual) data collection was performed with regard to the individual author's Google Scholar entry. For each scholar in the list the citation count, the h-index, and the i10-index were recorded if publicly available (http://scholar.google.com/ - accessed April 15, 2014). Unlike other indices, which only count journal citations, the Google Scholar citation index includes citations of academic work published in journals and also at other outlets such as conferences. The Google Scholar citation index represents a more accurate account of scholarly impact in those study domains and fields, in which weight and value of academic conferences are rated higher than in other fields relative to journals as, for example, it is the case in EGR, where journals and conferences have been rated as equally high [12].

Also, frequencies of entry types (journals, conferences, books, book chapters, and other types) were counted per period (that is, prior to 2004, 2004 through 2008, and annually for the years 2009 through 2013). This portion of the frequency counting was performed in the aforementioned version of Excel.

For the analysis of topical orientations and directions in the publications, the keyword entries (tag "KW") and title entries (tag "TI ") were used. Document term matrices were created via R tm, which listed the frequency counts for each year from 2009 through 2010. Synonyms (for example, "internet voting" and "e-voting" as well as differential spellings such as "e-government" as opposed to "egovernment" or "electronic government" were clustered and frequency counts summed up.

4   Findings

In the following sections the findings are presented one research question at a time. The results regarding types of publication outlets are presented first (RQ #1) followed by findings with regard to scholarly productivity of the most prolific contributors in EGR (RQ #2), and topical interests and directions (RQ #3).

4.1   Types of Publication Outlets in EGR (RQ #1)

As earlier studies had already shown for the period up to the end of calendar year 2008 [10, 12], in terms of number of peer-reviewed publications, conferences had been highly popular outlets for publication of manuscripts among EGR scholars. In that capacity conferences were slightly more popular than journals (see Table 1), which underlines their relative weight and importance in EGR. However, what this study reveals, is that initially journals were more frequently used as outlets of preference: Before 2004 (and for the lack of respective conferences on the subject matter)

47 percent of EGR publications appeared in journals, while (only) 32.2 percent of EGR manuscript were presented at conferences (see Table 1). This ratio between conferences and journals dramatically changed after conferences such as dg.o, the HICSS e-Government Track, and DEXA (later IFIP) EGOV almost concurrently emerged as dedicated forums for the presentation of EGR. In the period between 2004 and 2008, the percentage share of conferences rose from 32.2 percent to 54.7 percent while the percent share of journals shrunk from 47.0 percent to 40.5 percent (see Table 1). By the end of the early growth phase in 2008, conference publications had an overall share of 48.6 percent of EGR publications, while journals represented 42.3 percent of EGR publications. Monographs (3.4%) and book chapters (4.5%) were less frequently used for the presentation of EGR (see Table 1). By the end of the early growth phase the annual volume averaged about 300 EGR contributions with a higher average (433) for the period from 2004 to 2008 (see Table 1). While these results are not entirely new, they present new details about the domain's inaugural (1998 through 2003) and early growth phases (2004 through 2008), which also help better assess the evolution of the domain in the years from 2009 to 2013.

Table 1. EGR Publications by Outlet Type Before 2009

Year	Journal Papers	Conference Papers	Books	Book Chapters	Other	Per-period Totals
Before 2004	381	261	63	91	14	810
Percentages (before 2004)	47.0%	32.2%	7.8%	11.2%	1.7%	100.0%
Averages (before 2004)	76	52	13	18	3	162
2004 through 2008	876	1183	39	44	22	2164
Percentages (2004 through 2008)	40.5%	54.7%	1.8%	2.0%	1.0%	100.0%
2004 to 2008 Averages	175	237	8	9	4	433
Before 2009 Totals	1257	1444	102	135	36	2974
Before 2009 Percentages	42.3%	48.6%	3.4%	4.5%	1.2%	100.0%
Before 2009 Averages	126	144	10	14	4	297

As Table 2 details, the number of EGR publications grew despite some year-over-year fluctuations and peaked in 2012 with 747 publications in that year alone. This second rapid growth phase in EGR produced more publications (3268) in the years from 2009 to 2013 than what had been published in total (2974) until then. In other words, when comparing the three periods, it becomes evident that the majority of EGR-based academic knowledge (or, 52.4%) was published in the second rapid growth phase. The average annual volume rose from 162 publications (prior to 2004), over 433 (2004 to 2008) to 654 (2009 to 2013) (see Table1 and Table 2).

While conference papers maintained the lead over journal publications (45% versus 44.1%), the gap shrunk to less than a percentage point, or just 29 publications (see Table 2 and Figure 1). When comparing the publication numbers of conferences and journals in a year-over-year fashion it becomes evident that the number of conference publications topped that of journal publications in every single year except for 2013 (see Table 2). In that year, the number of conference papers dropped from the year before by 104 (or, over 30%) – see also Figure 1.

Table 2. EGR Publications by Outlet Type in the Period from 2009 to 2013

Year	Journal Papers	Conference Papers	Books	Book Chapters	Other	Per-year Totals
2009	239	292	29	104	15	679
2010	285	311	21	17	9	643
2011	291	294	17	1	7	610
2012	326	338	47	28	8	747
2013	299	234	14	33	9	589
Totals	1440	1469	128	183	48	3268
Percentages	44.1%	45.0%	3.9%	5.6%	1.5%	100.0%
5-year Averages	288	294	26	37	10	654

It is noteworthy that the number of book chapters reached an all-time peak in 2009 (a fact mainly owed to the publication of two handbooks with a high number of chapters [1, 7]). Two years later the number of book chapter publications fell to an all-time low of one.

As observed for the period from the beginnings to 2008, so for the period between 2009 and 2013, with about 90 percent conference and journal publications account for the lion's share of all peer-reviewed academic publications in EGR.

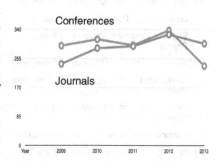

Fig. 1. Number of Conference and Journal Publications between 2009 and 2013

In summary, since its inception in the late 1990s the multi-disciplinary study domain of EGR has shown strong growth in peer-reviewed publication output indicating a rising interest in the domain and its phenomena. Despite a dip of publication numbers in 2013, the period of 2009 to 2013 has shown accelerated growth over the previous 5-year period. With 6242 publications the accumulated body of knowledge in EGR is significant in size, more than half of which appeared between 2009 and 2013, that is, most knowledge in EGR has been developed relatively recently.

Table 3. Top 51 EGR Contributors (1 to 29)

Rank	Name	# of Entries in EGRL v 9.5 (March 2014)	h-index (April 15, 2014)	i10-index (April 15, 2014)	# of Google Scholar Citations (April 15, 2014)
1	Marijn Janssen, TU Delft, The Netherlands	85	27	72	2570
2	Ramon Gil-Garcia, CIDE, Mexico City, Mexico	81	22	50	2103
3	Theresa A. Pardo, CTG, SUNY Albany, USA	78	25	56	2548
4	Hans Jochen Scholl, University of Washington, Seattle, USA	62	20	39	1591
5	Maria A. Wimmer, University of Koblenz, Germany	51	20	41	1654
6	Vishanth Weerakkody, Brunel University, Uxbridge, UK	50	23	48	1606
7	Sharon S. Dawes, CTG, SUNY Albany, USA	42	24	38	2302
8	Yannis Charalabidis, University of the Aegean, Samos, Greece	40	13	29	675
9	Ann Macintosh, University of Leeds, UK	37	n/a	n/a	n/a
10	Christopher G. Reddick, University of Texas, San Antonio, USA	36	15	26	1121
11	Luis F. Luna-Reyes, UDLA, Puebla, Mexico	34	16	23	961
12	Paul T. Jaeger, University of Maryland, College Park, USA	32	n/a	n/a	n/a
	Björn Niehaves, Hertie School of Governance, Berlin, Germany	32	19	38	1382
14	Kim N Andersen, Copenhagen Business School, Denmark	29	17	29	1405
	Yogesh K. Dwivedi, Swansea University, UK	29	27	59	2178
	Ake Grönlund, Örebro University, Sweden	29	n/a	n/a	n/a
17	Jörg Becker, University of Münster, Germany	28	38	141	7284
	John C. Bertot, University of Maryland, College Parl, USA	28	n/a	n/a	n/a
	Efthimios Tambouris, University of Macedonia, Thessaloniki, Greece	28	16	30	990
20	Miriam Lips, Victoria University of Wellington, New Zealand	26	n/a	n/a	n/a
	Konstantinos Tarabanis, University of Macedonia, Thessaloniki, Greece	26	n/a	n/a	n/a
22	Dimitrios Askounis, National Technical University of Athens, Greece	25	n/a	n/a	n/a
	Muhammad M. Kamal, Brunel University, Uxbridge, UK	25	11	12	426
24	Anthony Cresswell, CTG, SUNY Albany, USA	24	22	31	1396
	Euripidis Loukis, University of the Aegean, Samos, Greece	24	13	23	707
26	Donald F. Norris, University of Maryland, Baltimore, USA	23	n/a	n/a	n/a
27	Zahir Irani, Brunel University, Uxbridge, UK	22	n/a	n/a	n/a
	Ralf Klischewski, German University Cairo, Egypt	22	20	36	1305
29	Frank Bannister, Trinity College, Dublin Ireland	21	n/a	n/a	n/a

4.2   Core EGR Community Academic Contributions and Impact (RQ #2)

As in the aforementioned earlier study reported [9], a number of 8 publications sufficed in late 2008 to make it into the top group of 55 most prolific contributors in EGR. Five years later it took at least 18 publications to make it into the then smaller group of 51 most prolific contributors in EGR (see Table 4). In the previous study, 19 publications were enough to make the top group of 10 most prolific EGR scholars; 5 years later 36 publications were needed to make the top 10 (see Table 3). Interestingly, the top group remained relatively stable, that is, 7 of 10 of the previously most prolific contributors appeared again in this group 5 years later (Janssen, Gil-Garcia, Pardo, Scholl, Wimmer, Dawes, and Mactintosh).

As mentioned above, for this study and to the extent they were made publicly available by the authors themselves, the citation indices for the most prolific contributors to EGR were collected from Google Scholar for documenting the relative academic impact of each scholar and the top group collectively..

Table 4. Top 51 EGR Contributors (29f to 45) Continued from Table 3

Rank	Name	# of Entries in EGRL v 9.5 (March 2014)	h-index (April 15, 2014)	i10-index (April 15, 2014)	# of Google Scholar Citations (April 15, 2014)
	Lemuria Carter, North Carolina A & T State University, Greensboro, USA	21	15	17	2041
	Soon Ae Chun, City University of New York, USA	21	18	33	1041
	Ramzi EL-Haddadeh, Brunel University, Uxbridge, UK	21	n/a	n/a	n/a
	Tomasz Janowski, United Nations University, Macao, China	21	n/a	n/a	n/a
	Alberto Polzonetti, University of Camerino, Italy	21	n/a	n/a	n/a
	Yao-hua Tan, TU Delft, The Netherlands	21	n/a	n/a	n/a
36	Enrico Ferro, Enrico Ferro, Istituto Superiore Mario Boella, Italy	20	13	14	489
	M.P. Gupta, Indian Institute of Technology, Dehli, India	20	n/a	n/a	n/a
	Taewoo Nam, Myungji University, Seoul, Korea	20	n/a	n/a	n/a
	Reinhard Riedl, Berner Fachhochschule, Bern, Switzerland	20	n/a	n/a	n/a
	Roland Traunmüller, University of Linz, Austria	20	n/a	n/a	n/a
	Anne Fleur van Veenstra, TU Delft, The Netherlands	20	n/a	n/a	n/a
	Mirko Vintar. University of Ljubljana, Slovenia	20	11	13	526
43	Leif S. Flak, University of Agder, Norway	19	11	11	514
	Olivier Glassey, IDHEAP, Lausanne, Switzerland	19	7	5	176
45	Natalie Helbig, CTG, SUNY Albany, USA	18	9	9	430
	Helle Z Henriksen, Copenhagen Business School, Denmark	18	3	3	45
	Bram Klievink, TU Delft, The Netherlands	18	n/a	n/a	n/a
	Albert Meijer, Utrecht University, The Netherlands	18	16	30	890
	Gregoris Mentzas, National Technical University of Athens, Greece	18	25	51	1960
	Rodrigo Sandoval-Almazan, State Autonomous University of Mexico Toluca, Mexico	18	7	3	161
	Eric W. Welch, Arizona State University, Phoenix, USA (as of 1/26/2014)	18	19	27	1678

For 31 of the top-51 EGR scholars the information was found and recorded. Also, for 9 of the top-10 EGR contributors this information was publicly available, which provides a sound foundation for assessment of this particular subgroup. The inspection of the citation indices revealed that several authors had relatively high citation indices, while they had relatively low numbers of EGR publications. Upon inspecting the citation counts of these individual authors, one extreme case was found (Becker/Münster/Germany-see Table 3), where the EGR-related citations were low, while the overall citation count (7284) overwhelmingly corresponded to work produced in other fields of study. For preventing undue skewness of EGR-related results, this case was disregarded when calculating the descriptive statistics.

As Table 5 and Figure 2 reveal, with 67 the range in number of publications for the top 51 EGR scholars is quite significant, and the top-10 scholars in EGR make a relatively large overall contribution to the domain in terms of output. However, also in terms of impact, these scholars make a difference: With two exceptions the 10 most prolific EGR scholars have higher numbers of citations than the mean (1229) and the median (1213); they also have higher h-indices than the mean (16.8) and the median (16.5) as well as higher i10-indices than the mean (29.9) and the median (29.5) in the sample–see Table 5.

Table 5. Descriptive Statistics of Top 50 EGR Contributors' Publication Entries and Citation Indices (One Case Intentionally Omitted)

Descriptive Statistics	# of Entries in EGRL v 9.5 (March 2014)	h-index (April 15, 2014)	i10-index (April 15, 2014)	# of Google Scholar Citations (April 15, 2014)
Min	18	3	3	45
Max	85	27	72	2570
Range	67	24	69	2525
Mean	29.4	16.8	29.9	1229.0
Median	23	16.5	29.5	1213
Mode	21	20	38	n/a
Std Dev	16.1197	6.2279	17.4884	734.5843

In the aforementioned earlier study [9], the geographic provenance of the most prolific EGR contributors based on the location of their academic affiliations was also analyzed. When comparing the numbers of the two samples in the earlier study and in this study, some noteworthy changes have occurred, while other relationships have remained stable. As Table 6 shows, the vast majority of most prolific EGR contributors (90.2%) still comes from either Europe or North America; other geographic areas are either not or only minimally represented. No scholar from South America appeared among the top scholars anymore, while at least one scholar from Africa was still represented in the top group. While no scholar located in Asia made it into the top group in the earlier study, in this study three scholars were found in this group.

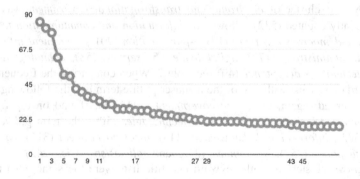

Fig. 2. Distribution of Number of Publications of Top 51 EGR Contributors

· However, the most striking change occurred in the ratio between contributors from Europe and North America; while the two groups were of almost equal size in 2008 (Europe= 27; North America=26), the European contingent has grown to 31, while at the same time the North American subgroup of most prolific scholars shrank by 9 to a mere 15, which is less than half the size of its European counterpart (see Table 6).

Table 6. Geographic Provenance of Top EGR Contributors

Provenance of Top 51 EGR Contributors	2009 to 2013		Before 2009	
Geographic Area	Number of Contributors	Percentage	Number of Contributors	Percentage
Europe	31	60.8%	27	49.1%
North America	15	29.4%	26	47.3%
Asia	3	5.9%	0	0.0%
Africa	1	2.0%	1	1.8%
South America	0	0.0%	1	1.8%
Oceania	1	2.0%	0	0.0%
Totals	51	1	55	1

4.3   Topics of Focus/Interest in 2009 through 2013 (RQ #3)

As pointed out in the methods section, the manuscript keywords and manuscript titles were used to obtain clues about the topical directions and scholarly interests in the study domain. The keywords were seen as most significant indicators, since they give authors an opportunity to pinpoint their work within a topical range, while manuscripts titles were seen as only ancillary indicators, since titles provide authors with high degrees of freedom and a range of options with regard to exactly specifying or not specifying at all the respective topics.

The keyword cluster of *electronic and transformational government* was by far most frequently counted (532) followed by *information and communication technologies* (160), *e-democracy/e-voting* (112), *e-participation* (90), *government information* (81), *public administration* (77), *digital divide* (65), *services* (58), *technology adoption* (51), and *technology acceptance* (49)-see table 7. When comparing the frequencies of the keyword cluster list with that of the manuscript title term list, the following cluster rankings emerged: again, *electronic government* (1414) was found on top followed again by *information and communication technologies* (509), the term *public* (394), *services* (382), *information & knowledge* (346), *local government* (316), *case/cases* (264), *participation* (257), *development* (242), and *policies/strategies* (242).

The top-two clusters in both keyword and title lists were the same, also in their ranking, while *services*, *information*, *public*, and *participation* appeared in both lists albeit at different ranks. In other words, six keyword clusters were also found among

Table 7. Most Frequent Topical Clusters based on Keywords (2009 to 2014)

	Keyword/Cluster	Frequency 2009	Frequency 2010	Frequency 2011	Frequency 2012	Frequency 2013	Frequency 2009 to 2013	Frequency Charts 2009 to 2013
1	e-government, electronic government, internet in public administration, transformational government	67	42	132	145	146	532	
2	information & communication technologies	5	21	43	43	48	160	
3	democracy, digital democracy, e-democracy, e-voting, internet voting	13	2	42	30	25	112	
4	participation, e-participation, political participation, civic engagement, citizen engagement	5	3	34	28	20	90	
5	information, government information, electronic-government information, public-sector information	12	9	21	27	12	81	
6	government, public administration	3	6	17	13	38	77	
7	access to information, accessibility, digital divide	3	7	17	19	19	65	
8	services, information services, web services, public services, service delivery	2	9	14	20	13	58	
9	adoption, technology adoption, diffusion	2	4	13	16	16	51	
10	acceptance, user acceptance, technology acceptance model	2	3	21	14	9	49	

the top topical clusters in the manuscript titles, which indicates a relatively high degree of correspondence between the two. It is also noteworthy that nine of the top-ten topical keyword clusters show trend lines with a positive slope (see the mini-charts embedded in Table 7). When compared with the findings of the 2013 survey-based study [12], it appears that *transformational government* (including open government), *participation, services, information and communication technologies* (in terms of *cloud services, institutional architecture, and interoperability* as a proxy) and *digital divide* form the intersection of topical foci in the respective top-ten focal areas in either study. However, topics such as social media and open/big data, which ranked prominently in the survey-based results, do neither appear in the top rankings of the keyword cluster list nor those of the title cluster list.

In summary, the topical directions of EGR in the period of 2009 to 2013 have mainly focused on *electronic and transformational government, information and communication technologies* in all its vices, *participation, services,* and the *digital divide*. Newer topics such as social media use in and in contact with government, open/big data, and smart government have not made it into the top list of topics.

5   Discussion, Future Research, and Concluding Remarks

The study's object has been to update and in part triangulate previous studies on the state of play in EGR. This includes the study of the overall numbers of publications in EGR and of the type of publication outlets used (e.g., conferences and journals). Furthermore, individual scholarly output was investigated, the geographic provenance of the most prolific scholars was analyzed, and moreover, this study presented for the first time findings on scholarly impact in terms of citations and citation indices. Finally, the major topical directions in EGR in the period of 2009 through 2013 were analyzed. The three perspectives incorporated in this study help provide a detailed profile of the EGR study domain and its current state of play. Along with the recent study on "Forums for Electronic Government Scholars" [13], this study complements the findings on preferred outlets for presenting EGR and the relative academic weight of these outlets.

5.1   Some Key Observations

Ranking of Publication Outlet Types. Quite a few disciplines rank order publication outlet types in terms of the outlet type's relative weight and appreciation, when considering the value of the contributions. In some fields, conference contributions are more highly valued than journal contributions (for example, in computer science), or vice versa (for example, in public administration or MIS), or the discipline values books the highest (for example, in philosophy). In EGR journal and conference contributions appear to be on a par in weight. This is not surprising given the multidisciplinary nature of the study domain. As an indicator, with regard to conference and journal publications also the numbers of these two outlet types are on a par in EGR. The low republishing counts consistently found in the EGRL (that is, for example, same or similar author lists, similar title and keywords, same or consecutive years of publication), when searching for duplicates or near-duplicates in EGRL maintenance, are another indicator that the two types overwhelmingly account for original work. As other research [13] found the top-rated conferences were the HICSS e-Government Track, the IFIP EGOV conference, and the dg.o conference whereas the top-rated journals in EGR were Government Information Quarterly (GIQ), Information Polity (IP), Journal of Information Technology and Politics (JITP), Transforming Government (TGPPP), and the International Journal of Electronic Government Research (IJEGR). These outlets appear to attract the lion's share of EGR publications.

Core EGR Community. The most prolific contributors have also been referred to as the core community of EGR. While 8 contributions qualified for a spot in the list of 55 top EGR contributors in 2008, the same number was counted for a total of 179 EGR contributors in this study; and with respect to the extended core community, that is, scholars with at least 5 contribution (by the end of 2008), when using the same criterion in this study a list of 396 EGR contributors was produced. In other words, not only has the inner core group significantly increased in size but also the extended core group: when applying the same criteria as in the previous study [9], then the inner group grew by 225%, and the extended core group increased by 76% in the period of 2009 to 2013. These numbers also explain the overall growth in the number of publications in EGR.

However, the decreased number of scholars from North America in the EGR domain's inner core group presents a serious concern; as seen in the findings section, while the number of scholars in this core group located in Europe and Asia went up during the same period, the number of scholars from North America went down by 42.3%. When scanning the names of North American colleagues who are no longer listed among the most prolific EGR scholars, two circumstances can help explain their absences, that is, (1) lack of EGR-related funding (in the cases of about 8 US scholars), and (b) retirement, either from academia or from work life (in the cases of at least 2 US scholars). Paradoxically, while the Obama Administration has successfully introduced numerous technology-based innovations in government, it also displayed a serious lack of interest in research on the subject. Digital Government as an area of focused research funding by the National Science Foundation was abandoned in 2010 altogether. As a consequence, unlike Europe and other world areas, in which EGR remained to be well funded serving as a driver for continued administrative innovation, the lack of funding of EGR, particularly in the USA, appears to have stifled the scholarly production as well as the academically supported progress of e-government practice in this part of the world. This may over time also impact the attractiveness of conference venues in this geographic area, since local contributions as the backbone of conference attendance may remain relatively low, and it needs to be seen, how well contributions from other parts of the world can make up for the gap. However, the numbers may indicate a shift in the centers of gravity in EGR, which appears to become less North America-oriented and more Europe-based.

Topical Directions. It was most surprising that in the topical analysis of both keywords and manuscript titles the terms "social media," "cloud computing," "open/big/linked data," and even "open government" were relatively infrequently found. In the list of keywords, the term "social media" did not make it into the top 20, while in the list of title terms it appeared at rank #15, although with a steep positive slope in its trend line. A future inquiry might find the more recent topical areas of focus more prominently ranked.

5.2   The Way Ahead in EGR

In summary, the multi-disciplinary domain of EGR has grown significantly in recent years, and its core scholarship is strong and stable. The study domain has attracted a high number of new contributors from all over the world. As an academically pluralist and global undertaking, EGR may see shifting centers of gravity in its scholarship in the years to come despite the fact that many of its premier outlets for publication remain located in North America.

With a now strong and well-recognized cluster of EGR publication forums [13] tenure and promotion should increasingly become attainable to EGR scholars also in disciplines and institutions, in which EGR is seen as a specialty or niche domain of study. While the acceptance of multidisciplinary research undertakings appears to have grown over recent decades, even making it a necessity for the effective investigation of many phenomena in both natural and social sciences, the evaluation of scholarly performance might still be influenced more by discipline-internal criteria than criteria reflective of cross-disciplinary achievements. Therefore, for future research it might be interesting to analyze how the career paths of some 400 scholars who represent the EGR core community have actually unfolded over the years. It appears appropriate to reproduce and extend this study in another five years' time.

References

1. Chadwick, A., Howard, P.N. (eds.): Routledge Handbook of Internet Politics. Routledge, London (2009)
2. Dwivedi, Y., Weerakkody, V.: A Profile of Scholarly Community Contributing to the International Journal of Electronic Government Research. International Journal of Electronic Government Research 6(4), 1–11 (2010)
3. Dwivedi, Y.K., Singh, M., Williams, M.D.: Developing a demographic profile of scholarly community contributing to the Electronic Government. An International Journal. Electronic Government, an International Journal. 8(2/3), 259–270 (2011)
4. Feinerer, I.: tm: Text Mining Package. R package version 0.5-7.1 (2012)
5. Meyer, D., Hornik, K., Feinerer, I.: Text mining infrastructure in R. Journal of Statistical Software 25(5), 1–54 (2008)
6. Rana, N.P., Williams, M.D., Dwivedi, Y.K., Williams, J.: Reflecting on E-Government Research. International Journal of Electronic Government Research 7(4), 64–88 (2011)
7. Reddick, C.G. (ed.): Handbook of Research on Strategies for Local E-Government Adoption and Implementation: Comparative Studies, Hershey, PA, London, UK. Information Science Reference (2009)

8. Scholl, H.J.: Discipline or interdisciplinary study domain? Challenges and Promises in Electronic Government Research. In: Chen, H., Brandt, L., Gregg, V., Traunmüller, R., Dawes, S., Hovy, E., Macintosh, A., Larson, C.A. (eds.) Digital Government: E-Government Research, Case Studies, and Implementation, pp. 19–40. Springer, New York (2007)

9. Scholl, H.J.: Profiling the EG Research Community and its Core. In: Wimmer, M.A., Scholl, H.J., Janssen, M., Traunmüller, R. (eds.) EGOV 2009. LNCS, vol. 5693, pp. 1–12. Springer, Heidelberg (2009)

10. Scholl, H.J.: Electronic Government: A study Domain Past Its Infancy. In: Scholl, H.J. (ed.) E-Government: Information, Technology, and Transformation, vol. 17, pp. 11–32. M.E. Sharpe, Armonk (2010)

11. Scholl, H.J.: Electronic Government: Introduction to the Domain. In: Scholl, H.J. (ed.) E-Government: Information, Technology, and Transformation, vol. 17, pp. 3–10. M.E. Sharpe, Armonk (2010)

12. Scholl, H.J.: Electronic Government Research: Topical Directions and Preferences. In: Wimmer, M.A., Janssen, M., Scholl, H.J. (eds.) EGOV 2013. LNCS, vol. 8074, pp. 1–13. Springer, Heidelberg (2013)

13. Scholl, H.J., Dwivedi, Y.K.: Forums for Electronic Government Scholars: Insights from a 2012/2013 Study. Government Information Quarterly 31(2), 229–242 (2014)

The Development in Leading e-Government Articles 2001-2010: Definitions, Perspectives, Scope, Research Philosophies, Methods and Recommendations: An Update of Heeks and Bailur

Christian Ø. Madsen[1], Jesper Bull Berger[2], and Mick Phythian[3]

[1] The IT University of Copenhagen, Copenhagen, Denmark
chrm@itu.dk
[2] Roskilde University, Roskilde, Denmark
jbberger@ruc.dk
[3] Centre for Computing & Social Responsibility,
De Montfort University, Leicester, UK
mick.phythian@gmail.com

Abstract. This paper presents a study of the development in leading e-government papers from 2001-2010. Inspired by a study by Heeks and Bailur, the analysis uses a different sampling method, adds new themes, and focuses on changes over time. Through an iterative process known as template analysis the five most cited papers from each year are analyzed according to themes such as perspectives on the impact and impact causes of e-government, methods used, underlying research philosophies and recommendations. Findings indicate that the papers are still somewhat optimistic regarding the impact of e-government, but no longer as technologically deterministic. Discussions of research philosophies start to appear, as do social constructionist studies, although most papers are still positivistic. There is an increase in the use of primary data, and some movement in focus from infrastructure and services towards citizens. There is little development in the discussions of generalization of results and recommendations offered.

Keywords: E-government, literature review, template analysis.

1 Introduction

Heeks and Bailur [22] reviewed e-government literature from 2001-2005 and state that narrow and poor research practice predominates [22, p. 260]. Yildiz [50] – from a literature review in the same period – finds e-government research to be of a 'deductive, outside-in approach' and states that these exploratory and descriptive studies 'do not tell us what is happening inside the black box of e-government'. According to Ndou [37, p. 3], 'one of the reasons why many e-government initiatives fail is related to the narrow definition and poor understanding of the e-government concept, processes and functions'. The need for a thorough understanding of e-government is thus perhaps even more salient now.

M. Janssen et al. (Eds.): EGOV 2014, LNCS 8653, pp. 17–34, 2014.
© IFIP International Federation for Information Processing 2014

Having stated a need for more in-depth knowledge of e-government the authors have conducted an e-government literature review from 2001-2010 as an update of Heeks and Bailur [22] to reveal how the e-government research field has changed. This paper examines the most cited papers' perceptions of what e-government is, what e-government is about and how e-government is performed. This is done by adopting the scales from Heeks and Bailur (e-government impact, impact causes, research philosophy, methods and recommendations) and adding the researchers' own scales of e-government content, which we believe has changed over time, at least within the most cited papers.

2   Related Work

The initial analysis for this literature review showed a major growth in papers using the term 'e-government' around 2001, which was also when two of the most cited works in the field were published; Layne and Lee's article on the development of e-government stage models [32], and Jane Fountain's study of the interaction between IT and institutions [58]. These works differ in many of the aspects that we analyze. Layne and Lee's work is mostly conceptual and is technologically deterministic and optimistic [32]. It outlines a fixed path for e-government and the changes it will bring to organizations. Fountain presents three in-depth case studies and 'the technology enactment framework', a theory with a socio-technical standpoint that information technologies are changed by institutions, but also cause changes in these institutions as they are applied. Fountain argues that technologies are not always used the way the producers had intended [58]. This is a case often made outside the e-government field [72] but one that does not fit well with stage models or adoption models, where citizens' actions are typically limited to either adopting or rejecting the technology in question.

Previous literature reviews of e-government have focused on specific journals [22, 62] developing countries [13, 78], individual countries [73], or specific themes such as adoption [61, 75] or trust [51]. Others [50] did not base their review from a set sample of papers but instead focused on an in-depth discussion of certain themes. An alternative approach is found in bibliographical reviews which include several hundred papers but cover only certain areas available either from abstracts [65] or analyzing data from bibliographic databases [54].

None of these studies measure the papers in their literature reviews according to how frequently they have been cited. However, in one study [77], authors apply a network approach to literature review by aggregating results of studies that used the Technology Adoption Model (TAM) [57] to predict citizens' adoption of e-government. This approach provides an overview of how frequently certain hypotheses were tested and validated. A similar meta-analysis has been conducted by Rana et al. [70].

Heeks and Bailur [22] analyzed eighty four articles published between 2001 and 2005 with 'e-government', 'e-governance' or 'digital government' in the title. The articles were chosen from three sources 'identified as the leading e-government-specific research outlets' [22] Government Information Quarterly, Information Polity and conference proceedings from European Conference on e-Government. They used template analysis [63] to analyze five main aspects of the articles 'whose selection was influenced but not determined by earlier research analyses in information systems and in public administration.' [22, p. 246]: Perspectives on impacts and impact causes, research philosophies, theory, methods, and recommendations.

Heeks and Bailur criticized the e-government field for being too optimistic and technologically deterministic, lacking theoretical basis and references to research philosophy, poor treatment of generalization, and lacking practical recommendations [22, p. 243]. Further, many authors were criticized for staying in their offices and thinking about how the development within e-government could, or worse, should take place, rather than actually conducting empirical studies [22, p. 257]. This led to articles suffering from 'naïve optimism'. Heeks and Bailur did find, however, that around half the authors criticized some of the positive statements about e-government, and a majority did not have an entirely technologically deterministic view on the impact causes of e-government [22, p. 249].

None of the literature reviews since Heeks and Bailur were based on in-depth analysis of the development over time across the e-government field. One of the primary purposes of this study was to see if the criticisms of Heeks and Bailur [22] had made an impact and whether there had been any development in the areas they mentioned. It was decided to use citation intensity as the primary selection criterion since the authors wanted to study papers from across the field that were frequently acknowledged through references. As a partly interpretative analysis was conducted, the researchers could not be sure that their interpretations were the same as Heeks and Bailur [22], it was therefore decided to include papers from both before and after the Heeks and Bailur study.

3   Theory

Template analysis (TA) [63] is a technique for analyzing texts using a template, which may contain initial themes for analysis but is developed through several iterations of reading and coding. King recommends that scholars start by coding a segment of the total texts and discuss areas of disagreement to develop the template. Through these iterations the development of the template becomes part of the analysis [63]. TA offers structure to an analytical process, but also flexibility in developing the template to suit the study. It has been applied for both quantitative and qualitative analysis by researchers with different epistemological positions [64].

Heeks and Bailur [22] based the perspectives notion on Rowe and Thomson [71]; so the authors returned to that source, where researchers' perspectives on the implications of IT are placed on a continuum from optimistic and technologically deterministic to pessimistic and socially deterministic.

The technological determinists regard technology as 'an autonomous force which compels society to adapt to it' [71, p. 20] and brings positive changes such as economic benefits and improved living conditions. Historical periods are classified by technology (Bronze Age, Information Age etc.) with technological revolutions in between. They typically study the long-term societal impact of technology.

Around the middle of the continuum are authors who regard technology as neutral, and study how political, cultural and other factors influence technology use and development. Rowe and Thomson [71] describe these authors using terms as 'socio-technical', 'social shaping' and 'social constructionist'. Although different 'they all examine the way boundaries between the 'social' and 'technical' are negotiated, rather than accepting them as given.' [71, p. 24]. They emphasize peoples' and societies' choice in how technologies are used, and focus at the institutional level.

The social determinists regard technology as a social product, and often mention negative effects such as unemployment, pollution and surveillance. Instead of revolutions they believe in incremental change [49], and 'argue that technologies are found because they are sought; and are adopted, designed, released, applied and controlled by those trying to protect their own interests.' [71, p. 27].

Heeks [60] and Heeks and Bailur [22] developed Rowe and Thomson [71] separating it into two continua, thereby creating a two-dimensional field on which to place authors according to their value statements on the impact and impact causes of e-government. The first dimension measures the potential perspectives on introducing e-government from purely optimistic to purely pessimistic; the other dimension measures the causes of the impact from technological determinism to social determinism. The midpoints consist of a neutral perspective with statements about both positive and negative impacts and a socio-technical perspective on impact causes with 'value statements about IT enabling or supporting outcomes that are also guided by human agency' [22, p. 247]. The researchers note that it is the potential impacts of introducing e-government that are measured, issues such as failed implementation or lack of adoption are not taken into account.

In their analysis of how the policymakers' perception of e-government has evolved Chadwick and May [10] present three models labeled as:

- Managerial – An offspring of e-commerce and New Public Management this model regards e-government as a tool to improve the 'business' of governance, to make it faster, cheaper and increase customer (citizen) satisfaction.
- Consultative – According to the consultative model governments can use IT to 'pull' information and opinions from citizens in order to improve policymaking. This is the first step towards improving democracy through the use of IT.
- Participatory – Chadwick and May [10] describe the participatory model as having 'utopian leanings' in its description of a 'cyber civil society' (p. 277) where citizens participate in democratic processes facilitated by IT.

4   Method

Citation intensity was chosen as the sampling criterion to study the papers with largest impact in the e-government field. It was drawn from Google Scholar using Publish or Perish. Employing Scholar included more sources, but limited triangulation due to unknown search algorithms, a similar search in Web of Science, for example, resulted in a narrower search base. Due to the Google search robot control constraints, the search was extended over several days.

The same starting year was used as Heeks and Bailur [22]. Analysis of citation intensity from 2012 (when the analysis was begun) showed that a paper had passed its inauguration period after two years, making 2010 the latest possible end year. Citation history analysis of the most cited papers from each year showed that they tended to stay in their position, due to the Matthew-effect [69]; papers keep getting cited because they have been cited previously or appear in certain journals [66].

The search criterion was that 'e-government' should be in the title. 'e-government' is the predominant notion (compared to 'e-governance', 'eGovernment' etc.). Due to resources available, only the five most cited papers every year were included. The sample is given in the 'Literature review sample references'.

The sample of fifty papers (see appendix B) included forty nine papers from 23 peer reviewed journals (nineteen from GIQ and seven from PAR). Thirty four would have appeared if Web of Science had been used. The papers that would not have appeared are generally those with the least amount of citations. All the papers with most and second most citations were included in the Web of Science sample.

The authors do not claim that citation intensity is equal to high quality research, only that it is an indicator for commonly acknowledged research, thus impact research. Scholars, however, do not necessarily reference all of their influences [67] and they also may cite research that they are not influenced by [66]. An extended scan of key words could validate this claim.

TA provided structure to the analysis and also encouraged the inclusion of new themes from the papers analyzed. From the coding of the first batch, it was discovered that the definition and type of e-government had evolved over time; hence these items were included. The definition type was taken from [10] and later collapsed into two values (managerial and consultative/participatory) due to unclear use in papers. A change in e-government application, level and practice emerged, thus we included these. [22] was included in the sample as one of the top five cited in 2007. It was discussed whether this paper which worked as a template for our analysis should be excluded for blocking the existence of a 'real' e-government research paper, but decided to stick to the method and keep the paper. A scale to distinguish between research on research and research *per se* was created. Some researchers employed very optimistic statements about the impact of e-government' [31], whilst other researchers were less optimistic, but more due to adoption and implementation issues than to e-government impact as such [e.g. 46]. The authors introduced Heeks to this and he agreed that this could make the comparison difficult, on this basis a scale was created stating whether 'not so optimistic' impact was due to adoption or implementation issues.

The coding was done in four iterations by two of the authors. Each iteration was finalized during whole-day meetings, where results were discussed and coding guidelines adjusted accordingly. The template was uploaded as an online questionnaire and adjusted after each iteration; adding scales after the first two iterations and deleting scales after the third and fourth. The first two batches (15 papers) were re-coded after the second iteration due to added scales and updated coding guidelines.

The researchers strived to achieve data simplicity by using single-value coding; for eleven scales such as data collection methods multiple choice answers were necessary. The use of single choice coding had implications. A coding as 'neutral' on the optimism/pessimism scale can either stem from a paper having no value statements, [e.g. 20] or expressing both optimism and pessimism in the same paper [e.g. 3, p. 243]. The final template contained twenty three scales in total (see appendix A); fourteen scales from [22], (e-government perspectives, philosophy, method and recommendations), three that supported [22] and six new scales (e.g. e-government definition type, application and level).

The online template included space for coders' comments. After the first iteration it was discovered that these comments were not precise enough to recall reflections from reading the papers. It was then decided to add text citations to every coding. This led to shorter and more text focused arguments and increased discussion speeds significantly.

Initially the intention was to reach agreement on all scales through discussion, argument and reflection. An almost systematic deviation in coder differences on perspectives was revealed after the first iteration. One coder (with a natural science background) coded papers as more optimistic and technology deterministic than the other coder (with a humanities background). Reflecting on the statement from Heeks and Bailur that 'the same particular impact can be perceived by one stakeholder as positive while perceived by another stakeholder as negative' [22, p. 248] and after long discussions about perspectives, it was decided to accept a deviation of one point on the five point scale, and use the mean instead. For all papers, the scales for perspectives and research philosophy (considered the ones with highest degree of interpretivism), were discussed for agreement.

For the first two iterations (15 papers) coding was discussed and mutual agreement reached. For the last two iterations, the work was distributed and each coder elicited the common coding from the written argument and citations. After the third iteration there were 142 disagreements from coding of 15 papers (59% intercoder reliability); after the fourth iteration, there were 70 disagreements from coding 20 papers (85% intercoder reliability).

5   Results

This section describes the results of the analysis of the fifty most cited e-government papers in 2001-2010 by comparing the results to what Heeks and Bailur [22] found and by examining the evolution from the first five-year period to the next, if any.

5.1   Perspectives on e-Government

Impact from e-government (from optimistic to pessimistic) and impact causes (from technological determinism to social determinism) in the two five-year periods and average, are depicted in Figure 1. Papers were mostly optimistic during the whole period, with a tendency towards less optimism in the late period. A change is seen in impact causes from mostly technological determinism in 2001-2005 to a more balanced socio-technological view in 2006-2010, but with increased deviation.

No papers were found to be wholly pessimistic and only one was slightly pessimistic, the rest were coded neutral to optimistic. The statements ranged from full scale 'cyber-optimism' [12] where the impact is inevitable and unquestionable, e.g. that the second e-government stage 'is the beginning of the e-government as a revolutionary entity, changing the way people interact with their government.' [32, p. 128] to a slightly more reserved, but still positive outlook. The potential negative impact, e.g. privacy, security and the digital divide are treated more like barriers for adoption than regular drawbacks.

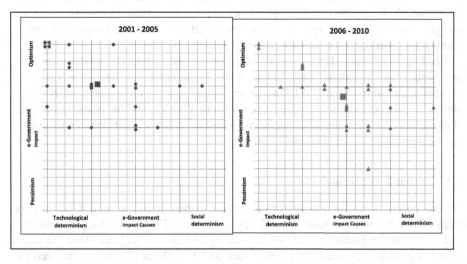

Fig. 1. Perspectives of impacts and impact causes of introducing e-government: left, 2001-2005; right 2006-2010

Coursey and Norris [12] criticize e-government stage models, Schuppan [40] is critical of e-government treated as a universal phenomenon that can easily be applied to developing countries, Heeks and Bailur [22] and Yildiz [50] criticize the research field. The digital divide hinders certain groups in society from achieving the benefits of e-government, resulting in 'long-lasting and widening economic gaps' [4, p. 117]. Coursey and Norris [12] state that e-government may 'simply reinforce existing power arrangements.' [12, p. 534]. The most critical group of papers concerns developing countries, e.g. increased corruption [40]. However, these papers also recognize positive impacts from e-government.

There was a notable development in impact causes from mostly technological determinism in 2001-2005 to socio-technical in 2006-2010. Where technology determinism rules, the Internet is the force that transforms the public sector [23, p. 434]. For the social determinists, it is use that shapes technology, which is regarded as an empty shell that carries the values of those that have chosen to have developed it, and those that use it in their everyday life. Moreover, the authors argue that these interests carried by technology are enacted by public sector organizations in their daily actions and routines [58], so that the outcome of e-Government reforms is shaped by the e-Government policies' aims and goals, the technological characteristics shaped by these policies and the organizational practices which ultimately shape the actual outcomes of the reforms.' [11, p. 2].

Thirty two papers contain a definition of e-government. The increase in papers without definitions over time could be regarded as higher certainty of the central notion and increased maturity. Although not all papers have explicit definitions, there was an underlying understanding of e-government as 'the use of the Internet to deliver services and information to citizens and businesses [39, p. 52]. Sometimes e-government plays an active transformational role, e.g. 'as a tool to achieve better government' [45, p. 288]. Actors are mostly defined as citizens (and businesses) although a more exhaustive range is sometimes used, e.g. 'citizens, business partners, employees, other agencies, and government' [32, p. 123].

Chadwick and May [10] saw a predominance of the managerial model over time and argue that 'the democratic potential of the Internet has been marginalized' Chadwick and May [10, p. 271]. The authors found signs of the managerial model in almost all papers; forty nine of fifty papers included 'efficiency' or 'costs' in the text. Half the papers still contained statements regarding e-government as citizens empowerment or enhanced democracy [15, p. 211].

5.2   What Is the Scope?

Several papers from the second period concern papers from the first. Three papers from 2006-2010 were meta-studies. Heeks and Bailur [22] and Yildiz [50] analyzed and criticized the research field, while Coursey and Norris [12] criticized the stage model approach [32] extended by Andersen and Henriksen [3] and synthesized by Lee [34].

Half the papers have government and four of ten had citizens as object of study. Only one paper investigates interaction with businesses [39]. Even though, many papers include government employees in the e-government definition, only one paper studies employees and government institutions [11].

Ten papers study e-government in developing countries [4, p. 4]. Another group of studies (eight papers), are concerned with the stage model view to e-government [32, 36, 39, 48, 49], a synthesis of models [34] and criticism of stage models [3, 12]. Although some papers state that the study is about 'local government', 'government' is mostly treated generically with few characteristics except for size.

Forty eight of fifty papers include 'citizen' in the text. Factors that impact citizens' perception of e-government services (the demand side) are reported in one-fifth of the papers; trust [8] and risk [24] together with factors of the behavioral models constitute an almost archetypical form of statistical treatment of survey data to test hypotheses. Citizens are typically treated generically as well e.g. 'The term 'citizen' is used in this paper to indicate all constituents of e-Government, including resident aliens, businesses and other potential users of e-Government.' [46, p. 162], and with a few exceptions [42] include demographic and geographic variables and political affiliation.

Services are an integral element of the e-government definition and it appears in the vast majority of the studies. The underlying assumption is that services are something that governments offer and that citizens can choose to use as stated by AlAwadhi and Morris [1] 'e-government services are highly voluntary'. This view makes the adoption process pivotal to e-government. Adoption is investigated using services as a general notion to be adopted by citizens [e.g. 1, 5, 24, 33, 42]. Other studies investigate specific services; tax filing [5, 8, 26, 46], automobile registration [5, 6, 8] and use of e-mail communication [17, 49]. Studies deduce from either the general 'service' concept or from one or (in one case) two specific services to conclusions about e-government as such; e.g. Lean et al. [33] concludes from the general notion for services that 'perceived usefulness, perceived relative advantage and perceived image have significant positive relationship with citizens' intention toward using e-government services'. Carter and Bélanger [8] note that 'Clearly, the answers were influenced by the nature of the online services selected', recognizing the influence of the specific service that is investigated.

Examples of services are given: 'business license' [e.g. 32] or an exhaustive service taxonomy: payments, communications, licenses etc. [e.g. 29], however, only one definition of service has been found: 'Features were defined as 'services' if the entire transaction could occur online' [49]. Types of services are mainly derived by the e-government stage model as information or transaction. Kumar et al. [31] find service quality crucial for adoption and presents five critical service quality factors.

The e-mail responsiveness study by West [49] is the only study of e-government services in use, the rest are studies of – at best – description of use, intention to use or purely conceptual.

Many of the early papers described e-government at a conceptual level; they would present e-government, discuss potential impacts, or predict its adoption. Only a few of the most recent papers [11, 17, 40] contained in-depth analysis of actual use.

The political development in recent years has also created new areas for study. E-government services are now becoming mandatory in several countries. How does this affect citizens, both users and non-users?

Recognizing that e-government is multivariate and complex, it is surprising that little attempt to elaborate on, detail or dissect these often stated assumptions – or to even question the assumptions are seen, at least not within the most cited papers.

No in-depth studies of 'government', 'citizen' or 'service', either on a conceptual, theoretical or practical level are found. Scholars have argued that e-government applies to many domains and that no one model can be found [e.g. 56], yet no studies investigate or compare e-government in different domains. E-government is governed by legislation, politics and economy, yet, we see no studies of national government impact on how e-government is enacted in different public domains, institutions or levels. Organizational adoption can be tricky [68, 76]; the role of top and middle managers are key [55, 59], however, none of the most cited papers deals with organizational issues within e-government. Acquisition- and tender processes, vendor relations, platforms or technology don't have the focus of the most cited papers. There are few studies that strive to encompass an overall model of e-government, e.g. an Enterprise Architecture view [14] or relevant internal and external technological, organizational, human themes etc. [18, 37]. These studies provide a starting point for more detailed analysis.

Finally, none of the studies in the sample investigate the participatory, democratic or empowering element of e-government at all even though half of the papers refer to this in the definition of e-government or consider for the negative impact of e-government.

5.3   How Is e-Government Investigated?

Heeks found that in only one of seven papers it was clear 'that the researchers had left their own offices and ventured out to do their research' [22, p. 257]. Only in five studies (one of ten) in the sample, researchers had left their offices to collect qualitative data from interviews, observations and focus groups.

As Heeks and Bailur [22] noted in 2007: 'This might, for example explain the absence from some research of the human, social, and political elements that more easily become apparent during direct contact with data subjects and settings' [22, p. 257]. We can repeat this seven years later; further, we can state as Heeks and Bailur [22]: 'those who had clearly left their office took a balanced sociotechnical perspective on e-government [22, p. 257].

The use of primary data increased over time. Twelve papers from 2001-2005 used primary data, compared to seventeen from 2006-2010. Further, five papers in the first period did not present any data compared to only one paper from the second period.

Four of the fifty papers contained longitudinal studies. Chadwick and May [10] studied e-government agendas across a decade, West [49] examined budget data from 1998-2000 and the development of content on US state and federal web sites from 2000-2001, Norris and Moon [38] analyzed results from two surveys on local governments' adoption of e-government, and Tolbert et al. [44] examined the development of e-government in US states from 2000-2004. Note that these studies covered the supply side of e-government. There were no longitudinal studies of e-government use by the demand side. There was a slight increase in studies that describe methods for data collection and analysis. Few papers, however, provide constructs for the research field to validate, criticize etc. Less than half the papers had discussions of validity and generalizability and there was no development in this over time.

Heeks and Bailur [22] found practical e-government recommendations in half their sample and 'three-quarters gave a few single sentence or, at best, single paragraph recommendations. Only four gave any specific guidance on how practitioners should take action' [22, p. 258]. In contrast, two thirds of the authors' sample gave recommendations; one third only provided recommendations of *what*, [34]. One third provided recommendations of *how*, [37]. Few studies contained comprehensive recommendations, other than Carter and Bélanger [8, p. 19].

In line with Heeks and Bailur (2007) we found that recommendations are seldom comprehensive. Further, we found fewer studies with specific *how* recommendations and more studies with *what* recommendations over time. Besides being sparse, recommendations point in many different directions (economy, website design, human skills etc.). No studies offer reflections on *applying* recommendations; i.e. political, strategic or tactical concerns, thus being of limited value for practitioners.

Heeks and Bailur found no references to research philosophies, although they labeled them. In contrast, the authors' study found that the field has developed and polarized since. In line with their findings, there was no reference to research philosophy in the 2001-2005 sample. However, five papers from 2006-2010 did contain brief references to research philosophy. They were either labeled as 'murky middle' or social constructionist.

Almost three quarters of our sample were labeled positivist. Eight papers included definitions of independent and dependent variables and contained statistical testing of hypotheses. Five papers (one from 2003, four from 2006-2010) were labeled social constructionist, even if more than one quarter of the papers refer to Fountain, primarily 'The virtual state' [58], This may imply that researchers try to balance their work by citing a constructionist scholar. We find only one study, however, that states the specific impact of Fountain's work on the specific research [11].

The study shows the following regarding the most cited papers from 2001-2010:

- They remain positive about the impact of e-government, but have become less technologically deterministic. Many authors still attribute the impact of e-government to technology alone
- The hypothesized benefits are mostly within the 'managerial model': reduced costs as a result of increased effectiveness and efficiency and better customer service
- The scope has changed from conceptual to a larger focus on actors e.g. citizens
- Government, service and citizen (the core of e-government) remain undefined
- Many e-government internal issues remain uninvestigated
- An increase in research maturity; more meta-studies, more primary data, more use of research methods, and more references to research philosophy over time
- A lack of descriptions of methods and generalizability of results. Very few studies use longitudinal methods, and there is little development in this area.
- Recommendations are sparse, more 'what to do' than 'how' to do.
- The underlying research philosophy in vast majority of studies remains positivistic.

6   Implications

Longitudinal studies can provide answers to questions and insights that are unattainable through cross-sectional studies [53]. Methods such as panel studies or time series [53] could be used to gain insight into citizens' or employees' actual and continued (or discontinued) use of e-government services, and what happens after adoption. Moreover, longitudinal studies can provide some directions to the path of e-government. Transaction data has been recommended as suitable data for this purpose [3]. Another option could be to analyze the publicly available data from surveys of enterprises' and households' use of IT and e-government by the UN, OECD, and EU. Without longitudinal studies we are left with limited knowledge of the impact of and on e-government, and the underlying drivers.

The vast majority of papers in the sample represent an optimistic and positive view on e-government ranging from improved efficiency [29], reduced costs [37], faster services and enhanced quality [21], accountability and transparency [4], increased citizens' trust in government etc. The 'executive managerial model' [10] is by far the most predominant view; forty nine of the fifty papers include 'efficiency' or 'costs' in the text. Apart from the case studies from developing countries [e.g. 30, 37, 40], no paper offers any proof of e-government actually delivering the often claimed benefits.

In this study the researchers have analyzed the five most cited papers from each year from 2001 to 2010 with 'e-government' in the title. Would the picture have been different if ten papers had been selected? It is not known if the trend has changed since 2010. Has big data strengthened the focus towards specific domains or has social media introduced another view of the citizen? Both tendencies may be due to their novelty but may introduce more exploratory studies and move the focus away from positivism. A bias may have been introduced into the sample by only using 'e-government' as search criterion, especially as 'e-governance' may have included more papers with the participatory/democratic scope. The authors consider that this study compares to Heeks and Bailur [22] despite the same sample collection method not being used. The first five years in the sample coincided with the predecessors and the same patterns were seen. The relatively small amount of papers in this study is a limitation, especially as it compares results over time, meaning there are only 25 papers in each group. The authors have tried to account for this limitation by comparing the results to other literature reviews, where possible, and by conducting an in-depth analysis with detailed examples from the papers studied.

7   Conclusions

The most cited papers on e-government have matured since the study by Heeks and Bailur [22]. There is more rigorous use of methods for data collection and analysis; more creation of primary data. Apart from this, we found pretty much the same patterns as they did, in some regards, we even saw a less diversified research field, including an overly optimistic e-government view based on strong technology determinism; a more positivistic approach and very few researchers that actually engaged in contact with data subjects and settings. E-government is agreed upon as governments delivering services to primary citizens through the internet. In this paper it is shown that the key notions in e-government, being governments, services or actors, all are treated rather vaguely, unsystematically and with no reasoned motivation, thus the e-government research scope seems unfocused. The most cited papers within e-government research do not distinguish between types of government/public institutions or types/form of services and mostly ignores actors other than citizens, i.e. other public institutions or businesses; employees (that perform e-government) are entirely invisible; even citizens are treated evenly, no distinction between different segments of citizens' different needs and capabilities. This could explain why researchers' recommendations were consistently vague, unsystematic and unfocused.

Technology has matured, national e-government strategies and e-government initiatives are now part of the everyday political agenda, governments and institutions implement these initiatives and there are examples of states making government' digital services mandatory along with fiscal consequences, central government reducing state funding according to anticipated enhanced efficiency from implemented e-government initiatives. Cases where citizens have missed important information from public institutions because new e-government initiatives have emerged (a case in Denmark was settled on appeal and the public institution had to change e-government practice and treat citizens' cases differently [74]) and cases, where civil servants express serious fatigue and stress due to performance pressure in combination with poorly aligned e-government technology and work practices that lead to low quality and errors in case handling, also have emerged [52].

The authors consider that there is a need for more balanced, qualitative and quantitative studies, more longitudinal studies and more contact with practice together with a further maturing of e-government research and not least a greater self-awareness from researchers of underlying perspectives and philosophy along with a more critical approach may move the research field to be better able to match the current e-government practice, thus ensuring the research fields' raison d'etre.

References

Literature Review Sample

1. AlAwadhi, S., Morris, A.: The Use of the UTAUT Model in the Adoption of E-government Services in Kuwait. In: 41st Hawaii International Conference on System Sciences (HICSS-41), Waikoloa, Big Island, Hawaii, p. 219 (1-11) (2008)
2. Almarabeh, T., AbuAli, A.: A general framework for e-government: definition maturity challenges, opportunities, and success. European Journal of Scientific Research 39(1), 29–42 (2010)
3. Andersen, K.V., Henriksen, H.Z.: E-government maturity models: Extension of the Layne and Lee model. Government Information Quarterly 23(2), 236–248 (2006)
4. Basu, S.: E-Government and Developing Countries: An Overview. International Review of Law, Computers & Technology 18(1), 109–132 (2004)
5. Bélanger, F., Carter, L.: Trust and risk in e-government adoption. The Journal of Strategic Information Systems 17(2), 165–176 (2008)
6. Bélanger, F., Carter, L.: The impact of the digital divide on e-government use. Communications of the ACM 52(4), 132–135 (2009)
7. Bertot, J.C., Jaeger, P.T., Grimes, J.M.: Using ICTs to create a culture of transparency: E-government and social media as openness and anti-corruption tools for societies. Government Information Quarterly 27(3), 264–271 (2010)
8. Carter, L., Bélanger, F.: The utilization of e-government services: citizen trust, innovation and acceptance factors *. Information Systems Journal 15(1), 5–25 (2005)
9. Carter, L., Weerakkody, V.: E-government adoption: A cultural comparison. Information Systems Frontiers 10(4), 473–482 (2008)
10. Chadwick, A., May, C.: Interaction between states and citizens in the age of the internet: "e-government" in the United States, Britain, and the European Union. Governance-an International Journal of Policy and Administration 16(2), 271–300 (2003)
11. Cordella, A., Iannacci, F.: Information systems in the public sector: The e-Government enactment framework. Journal of Strategic Information Systems 19(1), 52–66 (2010)
12. Coursey, D., Norris, F.: Models of E-Government: Are They Correct? An Empirical Assessment. Public Administration Review 68(3), 523–536 (2008)

13. Dada, D.: The failure of e-government in developing countries: A literature review. The Electronic Journal of Information Systems in Developing Countries, 26 (2006)

14. Ebrahim, Z., Irani, Z.: E-government adoption: architecture and barriers. Business Process Management Journal 11(5), 589–611 (2005)

15. Evans, D., Yen, D.C.: E-Government: Evolving relationship of citizens and government, domestic, and international development. Government Information Quarterly 23(2), 207–235 (2006)

16. Fang, Z.: E-government in digital era: concept, practice, and development. International Journal of the Computer, the Internet and Management 10(2), 1–22 (2002)

17. Gauld, R., Goldfinch, S., Horsburgh, S.: Do they want it? Do they use it? The 'Demand-Side' of e-Government in Australia and New Zealand. Government Information Quarterly 27(2), 177–186 (2010)

18. Gil-Garcia, J.R., Pardo, T.A.: E-government success factors: Mapping practical tools to theoretical foundations. Government Information Quarterly 22(2), 187–216 (2005)

19. Gilbert, D., Balestrini, P., Littleboy, D.: Barriers and benefits in the adoption of e-government. The International Journal of Public Sector Management 17(4/5), 286–301 (2004)

20. Guijarro, L.: Interoperability frameworks and enterprise architectures in e-government initiatives in Europe and the United States. Government Information Quarterly 24(1), 89–101 (2007)

21. Gupta, M.P., Jana, D.: E-government evaluation: a framework and case study. Government Information Quarterly 20(4), 365–387 (2003)

22. Heeks, R., Bailur, S.: Analyzing e-government research: Perspectives, philosophies, theories, methods, and practice. Government Information Quarterly 24(2), 243–265 (2007)

23. Ho, A.T.K.: Reinventing local governments and the e-government initiative. Public Administration Review 62(4), 434–444 (2002)

24. Horst, M., Kuttschreuter, M., Gutteling, J.M.: Perceived usefulness, personal experiences, risk perception and trust as determinants of adoption of e-government services in The Netherlands. Computers in Human Behavior 23(4), 1838–1852 (2007)

25. Howard, M.: E-government across the globe: how will'e'change government. e-Government 90, 80 (2001)

26. Hung, S.-Y., Chang, C.-M., Yu, T.-J.: Determinants of user acceptance of the e-Government services: the case of online tax filing and payment system. Government Information Quarterly 23(1), 97–122 (2006)

27. Jaeger, P.T.: The endless wire: E-government as global phenomenon. Government Information Quarterly 20(4), 323–331 (2003)

28. Jaeger, P.T., Thompson, K.M.: E-government around the world: lessons, challenges, and future directions. Government Information Quarterly 20(4), 389–394 (2003)

29. Kaylor, C., Deshazo, R., Van Eck, D.: Gauging e-government: A report on implementing services among American cities. Government Information Quarterly 18(4), 293–307 (2001)

30. Kim, S., Kim, H.J., Lee, H.: An institutional analysis of an e-government system for anti-corruption: The case of OPEN. Government Information Quarterly 26(1), 42–50 (2009)

31. Kumar, V., et al.: Factors for successful e-government adoption: a conceptual framework. Electronic Journal of e-Government 5(1), 63–76 (2007)

32. Layne, K., Lee, J.W.: Developing fully functional E-government: A four stage model. Government Information Quarterly 18(2), 122–136 (2001)

33. Lean, O.K., et al.: Factors influencing intention to use e-government services among citizens in Malaysia. International Journal of Information Management 29(6), 458–475 (2009)

34. Lee, J.: 10 year retrospect on stage models of e-Government: A qualitative meta-synthesis. Government Information Quarterly 27(3), 220–230 (2010)
35. Mecella, M., Batini, C.: Enabling Italian e-government through a cooperative architecture. Computer 34(2), 40-+ (2001)
36. Moon, M.J.: The evolution of e-government among municipalities: Rhetoric or reality? Public Administration Review 62(4), 424–433 (2002)
37. Ndou, V.: E-government for developing countries: opportunities and chal-lenges. In: The Electronic Journal of Information Systems in Developing Countries, p. 18 (2004)
38. Norris, D.F., Moon, M.J.: Advancing E-Government at the Grassroots: Tortoise or Hare? Public Administration Review 65(1), 64–75 (2005)
39. Reddick, C.G.: A two-stage model of e-government growth: Theories and empirical evidence for U.S. cities. Government Information Quarterly 21(1), 51–64 (2004)
40. Schuppan, T.: E-Government in developing countries: Experiences from sub-Saharan Africa. Government Information Quarterly 26(1), 118–127 (2009)
41. Silcock, R.: What is e-Government? Parliamentary Affairs 54(1), 88–101 (2001)
42. Thomas, J.C., Streib, G.: The new face of government: Citizen-initiated contacts in the era of E-government. Journal of Public Administration Research and Theory 13(1), 83–102 (2003)
43. Tolbert, C.J., Mossberger, K.: The Effects of E-Government on Trust and Confidence in Government. Public Administration Review 66(3), 354–369 (2006)
44. Tolbert, C.J., Mossberger, K., McNeal, R.: Institutions, Policy Innovation, and E-Government in the American States. Public Administration Review 68(3), 549–563 (2008)
45. Verdegem, P., Verleye, G.: User-centered E-Government in practice: A comprehensive model for measuring user satisfaction. Government Information Quarterly 26(3), 487–497 (2009)
46. Warkentin, M., et al.: Encouraging citizen adoption of e-government by building trust. Electronic Markets 12(3), 157–162 (2002)
47. Welch, E.W.: Linking Citizen Satisfaction with E-Government and Trust in Government. Journal of Public Administration Research and Theory 15(3), 371–391 (2005)
48. Wescott, C.G.: E - Government in the Asia - pacific region. Asian Journal of Political Science 9(2), 1–24 (2001)
49. West, D.M.: E-Government and the Transformation of Service Delivery and Citizen Attitudes. Public Administration Review 64(1), 15–27 (2004)
50. Yildiz, M.: E-government research: Reviewing the literature, limitations, and ways forward. Government Information Quarterly 24(3), 646–665 (2007)

Other References

51. Akkaya, C., Wolf, D., Krcmar, H.: The role of trust in e-government adoption: A literature review (2010)
52. Astrup, T.P., Flensburg, T., Olsen, M.: Heavy workload and slow IT frustrate civil servants. Politiken (2013) (in Danish)
53. Blaikie, N.W.H.: Designing social research: the logic of anticipation (2010)
54. Bolívar, M.P.R., Muñoz, L.A., Hernández, A.M.L.: Trends of e-Government Research. Contextualization and Research Opportunities. International Journal of Digital Accounting Research 10(1) (2010)
55. Braun, J., Ahlemann, F., Mohan, K.: Understanding Benefits Management Success: Results of a Field Study (2010)

56. Carbo, T., Williams, J.G.: Models and Metrics for Evaluating Local Electronic Government Systems and Services. Electronic Journal of e-Government 2(2), 95–104 (2004)
57. Davis, F.D.: Perceived usefulness, perceived ease of use, and user acceptance of information technology. MIS Quarterly 13(3), 319–340 (1989)
58. Fountain, J.E.: Building the virtual state: information technology and institutional change, vol. xii, 251 p. Brookings Institution Press, Washington, D.C. (2001)
59. Gallivan, M.J.: Organizational adoption and assimilation of complex technological innovations: development and application of a new framework. ACM Sigmis Database 32(3), 51–85 (2001)
60. Heeks, R.: Reinventing Government in the Information Age. International Practice in IT-Enabled Public Sector Reform, p. 362. Routledge, New York (1999)
61. Hofmann, S., Räckers, M., Becker, J.: Identifying Factors of E-Government Acceptance – A Literature Review. In: 33rd International Conference on Information Systems (ICIS 2012), Orlando, Florida, USA (2012)
62. Joseph, R.C.: A structured analysis of e-government studies: Trends and opportunities. Government Information Quarterly 30(4), 435–440 (2013)
63. King, N.: Template analysis (1998)
64. King, N.: Doing template analysis. Qualitatve Organizational Research: Core Methods and Current Challenges, pp. 426–450 (2012)
65. Kræmmergaard, P., Schlitcher, B.R.: A Comprehensive Literature Review of the E-Government: Research Field over a Decade. In: tGov Workshop 2011 (tGOV 2011) (2011)
66. Larivière, V., Gingras, Y.: The impact factor's Matthew Effect: A natural experiment in bibliometrics. Journal of the American Society for Information Science and Technology 61(2), 424–427 (2010)
67. MacRoberts, M.H., MacRoberts, B.R.: Problems of citation analysis: A study of uncited and seldom - cited influences. Journal of the American Society for Information Science and Technology 61(1), 1–12 (2010)
68. Markus, M.L., et al.: Organizational and Institutional Arrangements for E-Government: A Preliminary Report on Contemporary IT Management Approaches in US State Governments. In: 46th Hawaii International Conference on System Sciences (HICSS-46). IEEE Computer Society, Wailea (2013)
69. Merton, R.K.: The Matthew effect in science. Science 159(3810), 56–63 (1968)
70. Rana, N.P., Dwivedi, Y.K., Williams, M.D.: A meta-analysis of existing research on citizen adoption of e-government. Information Systems Frontiers, 1–17 (2013)
71. Rowe, C., Thomson, J.: People and chips: the human implications of information technology (1996)
72. Silverstone, R., Hirsch, E., Morley, D.: Information and communication technologies and the moral economy of the household. Consuming Technologies: Media and Information in Domestic Spaces, 22 (1992)
73. Snead, J.T., Wright, E.: E-government research in the United States. Government Information Quarterly (2014)
74. The Council of Appeal on Health and Safety at Work. It was wrong to cancel child payment. Principle Decisions 2014 (Feburary 17, 2014) (cited March 29, 2014)
75. Titah, R., Barki, H.: E-government adoption and acceptance: a literature review. International Journal of Electronic Government Research 2(3), 23–57 (2006)
76. Tyre, M.J., Orlikowski, W.J.: Windows of opportunity: Temporal patterns of technological adaptation in organizations. Organization Science 5(1), 98–118 (1994)

77. van de Wijngaert, L., Bouwman, H., Contractor, N.: A network approach toward literature review. Quality & Quantity, 1–21 (2012)
78. Wahid, F.: The current state of research on eGovernment in developing countries: A literature review. In: Scholl, H.J., Janssen, M., Wimmer, M.A., Moe, C.E., Flak, L.S. (eds.) EGOV 2012. LNCS, vol. 7443, pp. 1–12. Springer, Heidelberg (2012)

Appendix A: Template with Coding Scales

1	What is the impact of introducing e-government?
5 Optimistic, 4 Mostly optimistic, 3 Neutral, 2 Mostly pessimistic, 1 Pessimistic	
2	What are the impact causes?
5 Technological determinism, 4 Slightly Technological deterministic, 3 Socio - Technical, 2 Slightly social deter., 1 Social determinism	
3	Have adoption/implementation been used as explanation for missing impact from e-Government?
1 Yes, 2 No, 3 Not applicable	
4	Does the paper present a definition of e-government?
1 Yes, clearly, 2 Yes, vaguely, 3 No	
5	Which interaction type(s) of e-government is/are discussed?
1 Managerial, 2 Consultatory/e-Democracy, 3 Not applicable	
6	What is the scope?
1 Meta, research on research, 2 Research, 3 Conceptual	
7	On what level does the paper describe e-government?
1 Global, 2 National, 3 Local, 4 Domain, 5 Other	
8	Where does the study/paper take place?
1 Develop countries, 2 Developing countries, country list	
9	What is the object of study?
1 Infrastructure, 2 Actors, 3 Services, 4 Concepts	
10	Who are yhe actor(s) of study?
1 Citizens, Comments, 2 Employees, 3 Managers, 4 Business, 5 Governments, 6 Supra governments, e.g. EU, 7 Researchers, 8 Others, 9 Not applicable	
11	What is the time dimension of the paper?
1 Present, 2 Historical, 3 Future, 4 Other	
12	How many times have the paper been cited according to Google Scholar (January 1st 2014)?
13	How many references does the paper contain?
14	What is the underlying research philosophy?
1 Positivism, 2 Murky middle, 3 Constructivism, 4 Not applicable	
15	Are there any references to research philosophy?
1 Yes, 2 No	
16	What is the data level?
1 Primary, 2 Secondary, 3 Tertiary, 4 Not applicable	
17	Which method(s) is/are used for data collection?
1 Questionnaire, 10 No method used, 11 Other, Comments, 2 Document analysis, 3 Interview, 4 Web content evaluation, 5 Literature review, 6 Reflection on project experience, 7 Observation	
18	Is there description of data collection methods?
1 Yes, 2 No, 3 Not applicable	
19	Are questions, constructs etc. presented?
1 Yes, 2 No, 3 Not applicable	
20	Which method(s) is/are used for data analysis?
1 Quantitative analysis, 2 Qualitative analysis, 3 Statistic modelling, 4 Descriptive analysis, 5 No method used, 6 Other, 4 Web content evaluation, 5 Literature review, 6 Reflection on project experience, 7 Observation	
21	What is the time dimension of studies conducted?
1 Cross sectional, 2 Longitudinal, 3 Other, 4 Not applicable	
22	Isresearch validity (generalization) discussed?
1 Yes, 2 No	
23	What kind of recommendations are made to e-government practitioners?
1 What, 2 How, 3 No	

Appendix B: Most Cited e-Government Research 2001-2010, Elected Scale Value

Year	Paper	12	1	2	3	4	5	6	13	14	15	16	18	21	22	23
2001	Layne and Lee [32]	1481	4	4	2	1	1	2	11	1	2	1	2	1	2	1
	Silcock [41]	290	4	5	2	1	1	2	14	1	2	3	2	1	2	1,2
	Howard [25]	121	5	5	2	1	1	2	0	1	2	3	1	1	2	1
	Mecella and Batini [35]	111	3	2.5	2	3	1	2	12	1	2	1	2	1	2	1
	Wescott [48]	116	4	3.5	2	1	1	2	74	1	2	4	2	1	1	1,2
2002	Moon [36]	1131	3	4	1	1	1	2	35	1	2	2	1	1	1	1
	Warkentin et al. [46]	359	4.5	4.5	1	1	1	2	24	1	2	4	3	1	2	1,2
	Ho [23]	773	5	3.5	2	1	1	2	52	2	2	1	2	1	2	1
	Kaylor et al. [29]	256	3	4.5	2	1	1	2	14	1	2	1	1	1	1	3
	Fang [16]	295	5	5	2	1	1	2	21	1	2	4	2	1	2	1
2003	Chadwick and May [10]	440	4	1.5	2	1	1	2	73	3	2	1	2	2	2	3
	Thomas and Streib [42]	337	3	3	2	3	1	2	19	1	2	1	1	1	1	1
	Gupta and Jana [21]	294	4	2	1	3	1	2	31	2	2	1,3	1	1	2	1,2
	Jaeger and Thompson [28]	260	3	3	2	3	1	1	22	2	2	4	3	1	2	1
	Jaeger [27]	255	4	4	2	1	1	2	46	1	2	4	3	1	2	1
2004	West [49]	687	4	3	2	1	1	2	24	1	2	1,2	1	2	1	1,2
	Ndou [37]	308	5	5	2	1	1	2	44	2	2	1	2	1	2	1,2
	Gilbert et al. [19]	243	3.5	3	2	3	1	2	46	1	2	1	1	1	1	1,2
	Reddick [39]	207	4.5	4.5	2	1	1	2	49	1	2	2	1	1	1	3
	Basu [4]	222	4	4	2	1	1	2	41	1	2	3	2	1	2	1,2
2005	Norris and Moon [38]	344	3.5	5	2	1	1	2	55	1	2	2	1	2	1	3
	Carter and Bélanger [8]	685	4	4.5	1	1	1	2	44	1	2	1	1	1	1	1,2
	Gil-Garcia and Pardo [18]	333	5	5	2	1	1	2	84	2	2	1	1	1	1	1,2
	Welch [47]	323	4	3	2	3	1	2	29	1	2	2	1	1	1	3
	Ebrahim and Irani [14]	262	5	4.5	2	3	1	2	67	1	2	3	2	1	2	3
2006	Tolbert and Mossberger [43]	288	4.5	4	1	1	1	2	80	1	2	2	1	1	1	1
	Andersen and Henriksen [3]	294	3	2.5	2	2	1	2	32	2	2	1	2	1	2	3
	Hung et al. [26]	223	3.5	3	1	3	1	2	52	1	2	1,3	1	1	1	1,2
	Dada [13]	158	2	2.5	2	1	1	2	28	3	1	3	2	4	2	1
	Evans and Yen [15]	151	4	4.5	2	1	1	2	42	1	2	2,3	2	1	2	3
2007	Heeks and Bailur [22]	420	3	2.5	2	3	3	1	35	2	1	1	1	1	1	3
	Yildiz [50]	382	3.5	2	2	1	1	1	83	2	1	1	2	1	2	3
	Horst et al. [24]	177	3	3	2	3	3	2	18	1	2	1	1	1	2	3
	Guijarro [20]	150	3	3	2	3	1	2	28	1	2	1	2	1	2	1
	Kumar et al. [31]	153	5	5	2	1	1	2	79	1	2	2	2	1	2	3
2008	Coursey and Norris [12]	228	3.5	3	1	1	1	1,2	24	1	2	2	1	1	1	3
	Bélanger and Carter [5]	288	4	3	1	3	1	2	62	1	2	1	1	1	2	1,2
	Carter and Weerakkody [9]	145	4.5	4.5	2	3	1	2	60	1	2	1	1	1	1	1,2
	Tolbert et al. [44]	92	4	2	2	1	1	2	92	1	2	1,2,3	1	2	1	3
	AlAwadhi and Morris [1]	123	4	2	2	1	1	2	40	1	2	1	1	1	2	1
2009	Verdegem and Verleye [45]	153	4	4	1	1	1	2	92	1	2	1	1	1	1	1
	Schuppan [40]	110	3	2	2	3	2	2	54	3	2	1	1	1	1	1
	Kim et al. [30]	103	4	2.5	2	1	1	2	53	3	1	1	1	1	1	1
	Bélanger and Carter [6]	72	4	3.5	2	3	1	2	12	1	2	1	1	1	1	1,2
	Lean et al. [33]	89	4.5	4.5	2	1	1	2	79	1	2	1	1	1	2	1,2
2010	Bertot et al. [7]	231	3.5	3	2	3	1	2	111	2	2	4	2	1	2	1
	Gauld et al. [17]	59	4	2.5	1	3	1	2	56	1	2	1	1	1	1	1
	Cordella and Iannacci [11]	64	3.5	1	2	3	1	2	90	3	1	1	1	1	1	3
	Lee [34]	50	4	3.5	2	1	1	2	39	1	2	3	1	1	2	1
	Almarabeh and AbuAli [2]	53	5	5	2	1	1	2	18	1	2	3	2	1	2	1,2

An Online Transparency
for Accountability Maturity Model

Rui Pedro Lourenço[1,2] and Leila Serra[2,3]

[1] INESC Coimbra, Portugal
[2] Faculty of Economics, University of Coimbra, Portugal
{ruiloure@fe.uc.pt}
[3] Universidade Federal do Maranhão, Brazil
{leila.maria@ufma.br}

Abstract. Online transparency for accountability assessment exercises reported in the literature rely solely on the analysis of public entities' individual web sites, measuring the data disclosed and the way it is disclosed, and not taking into consideration the context in which these 'target' entities operate. This paper aims at identifying key contextual elements that may influence the way data is disclosed by public entities in their individual web sites, and therefore should be taken into consideration when designing the assessment models and exercises. The contextual elements identified were organized into an online transparency for accountability maturity model that may be used on its own to assess the overall level of sophistication of a country or region ('context'), or it may be used in a stage-gate approach to define the appropriate type of entities assessment model. Researchers wanting to assess a set of 'target' entities should therefore begin by analyzing the context in which they operate (using the proposed maturity model) and then define their assessment model according to the recommendations proposed in this paper for the corresponding maturity level.

Keywords: Transparency, accountability, assessment, maturity model.

1 Introduction

The subject of *Open Government* has been emerging as a top topic of interest in Electronic Government Research over the last few years [1]. Meijer et al. [2] emphasize that *openness* includes both the possibility of citizens to monitor governmental action ("vision": *transparency*), but also to influence government processes through access to decision-making arenas ("voice"). As one of the *Open Government* objectives [3], *transparency*, in particular, has also received attention from both academics and practitioners, the later confirmed by the emergence of Open Government Data Portals (such as Data.Gov) worldwide[1].

---

[1] See https://www.data.gov/open-gov/ for a list of such initiatives (last consulted in 13-03-2014).

M. Janssen et al. (Eds.): EGOV 2014, LNCS 8653, pp. 35–46, 2014.

With respect to transparency in the open government context, Linders and Wilson [3] further distinguish between the disclosure of government data aiming to promote its reuse for social or economic value, and data openness with the intent to support accountability of public officials. While the former is more closely associated with the creation of high-profile Open Government Data Portals, this work aims at addressing the latter (*transparency for accountability*).

The concept of *accountability* is very complex and may be understood from many different perspectives. Bovens [4] not only advances a very synthetic description for accountability ("the obligation to explain and justify conduct"), but also proposes several perspectives from which the concept of accountability may be analyzed. From the "To Whom is Account to be Rendered" perspective emerges the concept of *political accountability*, whereby citizens (among others) are the recipients of governmental disclosure efforts as a counterpart for the power delegation which characterizes representative political systems [4]. Open Government in general, and transparency in particular, may be considered an important prerequisite for political accountability because they allow citizens to access the information they need to assess the conduct of public officials responsible for managing the resources at their disposal [4].

While transparency has been associated for a long time with 'traditional' (paper based) freedom of information, the technological transformations of the last decades, the Internet in particular, have impacted profoundly the disclosure processes and access possibilities to government information [5]. The relevance of online transparency has led to several assessment exercises reported in the literature (see, for instance, [6] for a list of examples). In these exercises, researchers usually select a set of 'target' public entities, define a set of transparency requirements (assessment model) and analyze those individual entities' web sites to assess in what extend they meet the requirements. The result is usually expressed as a disclosure index, a "single-figure summary indicator" [7] which is considered as a proxy for the entity transparency level.

However, such online assessment models and exercises, by analyzing the individual entities web sites in isolation, do not consider the context in which the entities operate. Such context (country, federal state/region, ...) might condition the assessment models applicable to them. The importance of the context may be illustrated by the emergence of open government dataset portals, and their impact on the way transparency is 'traditionally' assessed: data concerning a particular public entity (under assessment) may no longer be disclosed solely at the entity web site. This, and other characteristics of the entities context, creates new challenges to online transparency assessment exercises and 'traditional' assessment models may no longer be totally adequate for the purpose. In sum, online transparency assessment exercises can no longer rely solely on entities' individual web sites analysis and need also to consider the context in which they operate.

Although some maturity models have been proposed in the context of open government (see following section) they do not establish any connection with 'traditional' individual entities online transparency assessment models. The goal of this paper is then to close this gap. It starts by identify key contextual elements which may influence the way 'target' entities assessing models are defined and applied, and then proposes an online transparency for accountability maturity model based upon them ('context maturity model'). Instead of just computing a single-figure summary indicator (index) for each entity, with a one-size fits all assessment model that disregards the context in which the entities operate, we propose to use a stage-gate approach: in a first step, the model is used to assess the context maturity level from an internet-enabled transparency perspective (common to all individual entities under assessment); then, depending on the maturity of the context, a specific (more detailed) assessment model ('entities assessment model') is used to provide an index value for each entity. In the end, both indicators (context level and entity index) will form a global assessment of each entity efforts concerning online transparency for accountability. Alternatively, the proposed context maturity model may be used in a standalone basis to assess and compare the development of countries, federal states, regions or any other contextual entities.

The remainder of this paper is organized as follows. The next section will reflect upon some of the maturity models already proposed in open government related literature. This will be followed by a section where a set of key context characteristics relevant to individual public entities online transparency assessment exercises is presented. Then, section 4 presents and characterized the proposed maturity model. The paper will end with some conclusions and reflections about further developments.

2   Previous Research on Maturity Models

Maturity models are commonly used to describe or represent the "anticipated, desired, or typical evolution path" [8] of an entity (such as an organization or country) or class of objects (such as processes) over time. In this context, maturity is considered as a synonym of "competency, capability, or level of sophistication" on a particular domain [9]. Although such development path may be represented by a continuous index, usually it is modelled by a discrete staged maturity model [10] and a set of criteria is used to assign each entity to a particular stage at a particular moment ("a snap-shot of the organization regarding the given criteria" [8]). Stages in maturity models are also commonly considered as cumulative, that is, "higher stages build on the requirements of lower stages" [9] as entities progress from the lower stages to top ones. This one-dimensional linear approach to maturity assessment, although simpler, may not be fully adequate to the complexity of the relevant domain. An alternative is to use a stage-gate approach where separate assessment models are used for each of the 'main' maturity model stages [9].

Maturity (stage) models have been proposed for a long time both in the field of eGovernment [11-15], eDemocracy/eParticipation [16, 17], and eGovernance [18]. However, these models focused mainly on the sophistication of online service provision and/or citizens' engagement and participation, reserving a secondary role for information provision and were therefore not aligned with the current Open Government initiatives who put transparency and participation at the heart of eGovernment and eDemocracy.

Recently, an Open Government Data stage model [19] was proposed to address the shortcomings of the previous eGovernment maturity models with respect to online information provision. This model focus specifically on data integration and consists of four stages ranging from 'Aggregation of Government Data' to 'Integration of Government Data with Non-Gov Formal data and Social data'.

In the same context, Lee and Kwak [20] proposed an Open Government Maturity Model to assess and guide the development of open government initiatives with a special attention to the way social media may contribute to increase public engagement. The model follows closely the three main open government objectives (transparency, participation and collaboration [3]) by making them correspond to the three intermediary stages between 'initial conditions' (level 1) and the more sophisticated 'ubiquitous engagement' (level 5).

Despite these efforts, none of the two previous models specifically address the global aspects of online transparency for accountability assessment, but rather focus on particular aspects of data provision. The proposed maturity model will not only address contextual online transparency (when used in a 'standalone mode'), but will also serve as a bridge to 'traditional' individual entities online transparency assessment models by adopting a stage-gate approach: in the first step the maturity model will analyze the context in which these entities operate and, depending on this first assessment, will then serve as a guidance to develop and apply the appropriate entities assessment procedure. This approach will result in an index value for each entity within the maturity level of the overall context. This way it is possible to avoid unnecessary analysis concerning 'advanced aspects' when the overall context is still characterized by a low maturity level.

The next section will present the key context characteristics considered to develop the proposed model.

3   Key Context Characteristics

The proposed maturity model is based on the identification of key characteristics associated with the context in which public entities operate which were derived from literature analysis. These characteristics concern both technological and organizational aspects, and the way they influence and relate to each other.

3.1   Technological Infra-structure

The first major contextual characteristic which is deemed relevant to the type of online transparency assessment model applicable to individual public entities is a technological one: technical infra-structure. Since online transparency assessment exercises tend to be performed in developed (or, at least, developing) countries, it is almost always taken for granted that a technical infra-structure exists, namely the Internet, over which public entities disclose their data. Moreover, it is usually assumed that most (if not all) entities addressed have a web presence of some sort and that they use such presence to disclose (more or less) relevant accountability data.

Beside the infra-structure itself, other aspects that might be used characterize the context include broadband internet adoption rate by citizens (the ultimate recipients of accountability data), for instance.

3.2   Dataset Portals and Web Sites

An important element that may influence the way individual entities disclose accountability information is related to the existence of external (global) dataset portals and web sites, corresponding to what Kalampokis et al. [21] refer to as "direct data provision"[2]. As part of Open Government initiatives, many generic open data portals, such as Data.gov, were created as aggregators of data that is usually reported by entities on a voluntary basis.

A different type of thematic (more specific) portals has also emerged, such as Recovery.gov [22] or European national sites disclosing data concerning the projects and beneficiaries of the European Regional Development Fund (ERDF) and the European Social Fund (ESF) [23].

Still in this category, another type of portals may be considered, stemming from the way public entities in modern States are organized into *sectors*: clusters of entities grouped together according to their similar legal status (regime), type of services provided, goals pursued, or administrative autonomy. Sometimes these sectors have dedicated portals, curated by a particular supervising entity that collects, processes and discloses data concerning all public entities from that sector. In sum, data portals, either generic, thematic or sectorial, changed the relevant context for accountability data disclosure and should be taken into consideration when performing assessment exercises.

3.3   Accountability Networks

In the last decades the structure and organization of modern States changed profoundly as a result, among others, of privatizations and New Public Management inspired reforms [24]. This resulted in a more complex and fragmented State, with a blurred frontier among private and public entities, therefore making it more difficult for ordinary citizens to "comprehend, map and record" the resulting constellations of public entities [24]. These structural changes had also an impact on existing *accountability regimes* ("the sum of a series of interconnected accountability arrangements and relationships regarding a particular actor") [25], thus leading to dense and complex "networks of accountability" [26].

Under these *accountability regimes*, individual public entities are subjected to administrative and financial supervision and control from auditors, inspectors, controllers and other supervising entities. The existence of such internal (not public), administrative *accountability networks* changed the relevant context for accountability data

---

[2] From the perspective of the entities to which the data belongs, publishing it in a global portal rather than on their own web sites would perhaps better qualify as an "indirect data provision".

disclosure since entities are now subjected to mandatory data internal disclosure regimes.

This new reality should also be taken into consideration when performing assessment exercises, namely in what concerns the type and amount of data expected to be disclosed publicly on entities individual web sites (at least a subset of that reported through the accountability network, for instance).

3.4   Overall Structure and Organization of Information

An important element of context characterization is related to the existence of overall structures that increase the visibility and access to information, facilitate the organization of the disclosed data by individual entities, and provide the necessary framework and guidelines to such disclosure procedures.

An example of such structures would be Public Sector Information (PSI) catalogues [27], which may include the identification and characterization of public sectors in which the State entities are clustered, and the identification and characterization of all entities belonging to each sector. Other catalogues may exist to list and describe information resources (including open government data portals and individual entities web sites), thus increasing their visibility and facilitating the access to accountability related data.

From a more technical perspective, an example of an overall structure would be the existence of common ontologies which individual entities may use to describe the disclosed datasets (metadata), thus facilitating their search, retrieval and analysis. Yet another contextual element would be the existence of a global Linked Data framework designed to facilitate publishing data on the Web "in such a way that it is machine-readable, its meaning is explicitly defined, it is linked to other external data sets, and can in turn be linked to from external data sets" [28]. With such a framework in place, individual entities would then be able to use it in a more effective way.

In sum, these technological transformations have also changed the relevant context for accountability data disclosure and should be taken into consideration when performing assessment exercises.

4   The Online Transparency Maturity Model

According to De Bruin et al. [9], maturity models may be applied for descriptive, prescriptive or comparative purposes. The proposed maturity model aims to be descriptive in the sense that it could be used to assess (describe) the as-is situation of online transparency development of a particular context for a set of public entities, such as a country or federal state. Similarly, the model may be used to provide a benchmarking baseline among countries (a typical 'context', for instance), and as a prescriptive model in the sense that it may be used to provide a framework to develop and implement an online transparency policy. The model assumes that the public entities operate in a political democratic context, whereby a legal and Constitutional

framework exist that protects freedom of information and general access to administrative documents.

Rather than simply using a one-dimensional standalone maturity model, we propose to adopt a global stage-gate assessment approach to structure online transparency
assessment exercises in two steps:

- In the first step we take advantage of the simplicity of a maturity model by
  using it in a preliminary evaluation of the context in which 'target' public
  entities operate;
- Then, a specific assessment model is used to complete the analysis of the
  'target' entities. Such model considers the potential and limitations of the
  context, as expressed by the evaluation resulting from the maturity model.

Figure 1 presents the cumulative stages of the proposed online transparency maturity model.

Level 4 – Overall structure and organization
Level 3 – Accountability networks
Level 2 – Data portals
Level 1 – Initial conditions
Level 0 – No technical infra-structure

Fig. 1. The Online Transparency Maturity Model

Each stage will be characterized below using the contextual elements identified in
the previous section. Also, some of the major implications for online transparency
assessment models appropriate for each context maturity level will be discussed.

4.1   Maturity Level 0 – No Technical Infra-structure

According to Becker et al. [8], "the bottom stage [of a maturity model] stands for an
initial state that can be, for instance, characterized by an organization having little
capabilities in the domain under consideration." From the perspective of this maturity
model, this means that the context in which the 'target' entities operate is characterized by a poorly developed internet infra-structure with few public entities having its
own web site. If so, it is perhaps meaningless to conduct online (internet-enabled)
transparency exercises and therefore to define and apply any online transparency assessment model. If, however, such assessment is to be performed anyway, the model
and procedure used should focus on simple characteristics of online disclosure.

4.2 Maturity Level 1 – Initial Conditions

Once the internet infra-structure is in place and entities (both public and private) generally have their own web site, we may consider that the context in which public entities operate has reached its 'initial conditions'. Other elements to consider when assigning 'contexts' to this stage may include the level of broadband access rate by citizens and entities, and other similar indicators.

At this context maturity level, online transparency assessment models should consider solely the data disclosed in each entity web site as each public entity independently discloses accountability related data. 'Traditional' assessment models, as described earlier in this paper, fall into this category and therefore should be considered adequate to assess entities functioning in this level of context maturity. Furthermore, such models should not expect individual entities to adopt sophisticated technological approaches, such as the ones associated with Linked Data [28], for instance, to disclose data. Rather, data might be disclosed in a simpler spreadsheet format. Other dimensions of the entities assessment models should also adopt a conservative perspective in what concerns technological and organizational sophistication.

4.3 Maturity Level 2 – Data Portals

The existence of open government data portals in the context in which 'target' entities operate is a pre-condition for the maturity of such a context to be considered in this level. The Open Government movement has contributed to the emergence of both generic (such as Data.gov) and thematic (such as Recovery.gov) portals. Sector portals have also been created in some countries, but they depend much more on the internal organization of States. Generic data portals usually depend on individual entities voluntary disclosure of data, while thematic and sector dedicated portals are usually associated with some kind of supervising entity (theme or sector) to which individual public entities are obliged to report accountability data. In this case it is up to the entities responsible for these thematic or sector dedicated portals to publish some (or all) of the reported data. From a technological point of view, establishing such data portals does not present a major technical challenge since many open source platforms (such as the widely used CKAN[3]) are currently available.

At this maturity level, online transparency assessment models must take into consideration the existence of these external/contextual data portals, and that entities may use them to disclose some (or all) relevant datasets (either voluntarily or not). Therefore, some of the characteristics of the portals themselves (dataset format, downloading possibilities, …) must be considered in the individual assessment models corresponding to this stage. In particular, such models should consider how is the data published in such portals visible and referred to (linked) from the entities web sites (that is, the way individual web sites relate to external portals) and how do they deal with the possibility of duplicated data (inconsistency).

---

[3] www.ckan.org

4.4   Maturity Level 3 – Accountability Networks

This stage presupposes not only that an internal (administrative) accountability network exists for the different types of public entities (even stretching beyond the public sector 'supervising' entities) but also that such network is explicit and visible: it is well known exactly what entities are part of the network and what is their role in it. It should also be clear what type of accountability relevant data is reported by each type of public entities through their accountability network.

At this maturity level, online transparency assessment models must take into consideration the existence of such networks and the way they might influence how data is disclosed. In general, such models should consider the accountability network of a particular entity as a reference to what should be available and how by:

- Defining a minimal set of data individual entities should disclose to the public (political accountability), considering that such data is already being produced for internal (network) reporting purposes (administrative accountability);
- Considering that part (or all) of that data is disclosed by the 'supervising' entities of the network and not directly in the target entities individual web site.

4.5   Maturity Level 4 – Overall Structure and Organization

For a certain context to be considered at this top level maturity, the requirements of all previous levels should be fulfilled. However, to reach this level, there needs also to exist an overall structure that gives coherence and connects all the individual elements that characterize the levels so far. This may include a catalogue of all resources relevant for online transparency assessment purposes (according to previous levels), a global ontology and a Linked Data infra-structure.

At this maturity level, online transparency assessment models must take into consideration whether or not individual entities take advantage of these technological elements provided by the context. For instance, each entity, its web site, and relevant data resources disclosed in it, should be visible in the global catalogues mentioned (almost like a Google search engine visibility). Furthermore, individual entities should use the global transparency for accountability ontology to provide standardized metadata for the datasets disclosed which, in conjunction with the adoption of Linked Data principles, should facilitate data search, retrieve and processing.

5   Conclusions

In the last few years the context in which public entities function has suffered the impact of both organizational and technological transformations. The complexity of accountability networks in which entities are inserted, and the emergence of Open Government Data portals, for instance, pose new challenges to the way individual entities may be assessed concerning how they use the Internet to disclose accountability related data. This means 'traditional' online transparency assessment methods that focus solely on the characteristics of individual entities web sites, thus ignoring such transformations in the context, may no longer give an accurate picture of the transparency panorama. Also, since different entities might operate in different contexts (with diverse technological and organizational characteristics), it is not adequate to use a one-size fits all assessment model.

This paper proposes an online transparency maturity model, based on some of the most prominent context characteristics (from an internet-enabled perspective on transparency), which may be used in a standalone manner to assess the context in which entities operate or, in a stage-gate approach, as a first step to define an adequate assessment model for the 'target' entities (depending on the maturity of their context).

Like any other maturity model, the advantage of its simplicity may be subjected to criticism. The model steps sequence and cumulativeness represent a certain desired evolution path of sophistication that may not correspond entirely to the reality of some contexts. For instance, a particular country being assessed might exhibit characteristics of several stages or even develop the elements of a top level before the developing the ones in the levels below. Nevertheless, the sequence in which the levels are proposed took into consideration the complexity, (global) scope and impact of the technological and organizational characteristics considered in each level.

The proposed model is intended not only to provide a macro assessment tool applicable to contexts such as countries or federal and regional states, but also to close the gap between this and other micro level (entity level) 'traditional' assessment exercises. Therefore, those wanting to initiate individual entities assessment exercises should consider first the level of maturity of the surrounding context, and then adapt the appropriate assessment model according to the suggestions made. In the end, the overall analysis should help both academics and public officials to develop better online transparency for accountability systems both at macro and micro level.

As this maturity model focus on internet-enabled transparency, further research might consider the possible impacts of proactive open government legal frameworks on online transparency maturity. Such proactive policy and legal structures extend beyond the general protection of freedom of information that constitute the hallmark of modern western-like democracies.

Acknowledgements. This work has been partially supported by the Portuguese Foundation for Science and Technology under project grant PEst-OE/ EEI/UI308/2014.

References

1. Scholl, H.J.: Electronic Government Research: Topical Directions and Preferences. In: Wimmer, M.A., Janssen, M., Scholl, H.J. (eds.) EGOV 2013. LNCS, vol. 8074, pp. 1–13. Springer, Heidelberg (2013)
2. Meijer, A.J., Curtin, D., Hillebrandt, M.: Open government: connecting vision and voice. International Review of Administrative Sciences 78, 10–29 (2012)
3. Linders, D., Wilson, S.C.: What is Open Government? One Year after the Directive. In: 12th Annual International Conference on Digital Government Research (Dg.o 2011), pp. 262–271. ACM, College Park (2011)

4. Bovens, M.: Analysing and Assessing Accountability: A Conceptual Framework. European Law Journal 13, 447–468 (2007)
5. Jaeger, P.T., Bertot, J.C.: Transparency and technological change: Ensuring equal and sustained public access to government information. Government Information Quarterly 27, 371–376 (2010)
6. Lourenço, R.P.: Data disclosure and transparency for accountability: A strategy and case analysis. Information Polity 18, 243–260 (2013)
7. Coy, D., Dixon, K.: The public accountability index: crafting a parametric disclosure index for annual reports. The British Accounting Review 36, 79–106 (2004)
8. Becker, J., Knackstedt, R., Pöppelbuß, J.: Developing Maturity Models for IT Management. Business & Information Systems Engineering 1, 213–222 (2009)
9. De Bruin, T., Freeze, R., Kaulkarni, U., Rosemann, M.: Understanding the Main Phases of Developing a Maturity Assessment Model. In: 16th Australasian Conference on Information Systems (ACIS), Australia, New South Wales, Sydney, pp. 8–19 (2005)
10. Klimko, G.: Knowledge Management and Maturity Models: Building Common Understanding. In: Second European Conference on Knowledge Management, pp. 269–278. Bled School of Management Bled, Slovenia (2001)
11. Andersen, K.N., Medaglia, R., Vatrapu, R., Henriksen, H.Z., Gauld, R.: The forgotten promise of e-government maturity: Assessing responsiveness in the digital public sector. Government Information Quarterly 28, 439–445 (2011)
12. Andersen, K.V., Henriksen, H.Z.: E-government maturity models: Extension of the Layne and Lee model. Government Information Quarterly 23, 236–248 (2006)
13. Layne, K., Lee, J.: Developing fully functional E-government: A four stage model. Government Information Quarterly 18, 122–136 (2001)
14. Lee, J.: 10 year retrospect on stage models of e-Government: A qualitative meta-synthesis. Government Information Quarterly 27, 220–230 (2010)
15. Siau, K., Long, Y.: Synthesizing E-government Stage Models - a Meta-synthesis Based on Meta-ethnography Approach. Industrial Management & Data Systems 105, 443–458 (2005)
16. Tambouris, E., Liotas, N., Tarabanis, K.: A Framework for Assessing eParticipation Projects and Tools. In: 40th Annual Hawaii International Conference on System Sciences (CD/ROM), p. 90. IEEE Computer Society (2007)
17. Macintosh, A.: Using information and communication technologies to enhance citizen engagement in the policy process. In: Promises and Problems of E-Democracy: Challenges of Citizen Online Engagement, pp. 19–142. OECD, Paris (2003)
18. Lourenço, R.P.: From e-Government and e-Democracy to e-Governance: a unified view. In: Janssen, M., et al. (eds.) Electronic Government and Electronic Participation: Joint Proceedings of Ongoing Research and Projects of IFIP EGOV and ePart 2011, vol. 37, pp. 345–351. Trauner Verlag (2011)
19. Kalampokis, E., Tambouris, E., Tarabanis, K.: Open Government Data: A Stage Model. In: Janssen, M., Scholl, H.J., Wimmer, M.A., Tan, Y.-H. (eds.) EGOV 2011. LNCS, vol. 6846, pp. 235–246. Springer, Heidelberg (2011)
20. Lee, G., Kwak, Y.H.: An Open Government Maturity Model for social media-based public engagement. Government Information Quarterly 29, 492–503 (2012)
21. Kalampokis, E., Tambouris, E., Tarabanis, K.: A classification scheme for open government data: towards linking decentralized data. International Journal of Web Engineering and Technology 6, 266–285 (2011)
22. Huijboom, N., den Broek, T.V.: Open data: an international comparison of strategies. European Journal of ePractice 12, 1–12 (2011)

23. Reggi, L., Ricci, C.A.: Information Strategies for Open Government in Europe: EU Regions Opening Up the Data on Structural Funds. In: Janssen, M., Scholl, H.J., Wimmer, M.A., Tan, Y.-h. (eds.) EGOV 2011. LNCS, vol. 6846, pp. 173–184. Springer, Heidelberg (2011)

24. Heald, D.: Why is transparency about public expenditure so elusive? International Review of Administrative Sciences 78, 30–49 (2012)

25. Bovens, M., Curtin, D., 't Hart, P.: Towards a More Accountable EU: Retrospective and Roadmap. Amsterdam Centre for European Law and Governance (2010)

26. Scott, C.: Accountability in the Regulatory State. Journal of Law and Society 27, 38–60 (2000)

27. Shadbolt, N., O'Hara, K., Berners-Lee, T., Gibbins, N., Glaser, H., Hall, W., Schraefel, M.C.: Linked Open Government Data: Lessons from Data.gov.uk. IEEE Intelligent Systems 27, 16–24 (2012)

28. Bizer, C., Heath, T., Berners-Lee, T.: Linked data – the story so far. International Journal on Semantic Web and Information Systems 5, 1–22 (2009)

Towards an Evaluation Model for Open Government:
A Preliminary Proposal

Rodrigo Sandoval-Almazan[1] and J. Ramon Gil-Garcia[2]

[1] Universidad Autónoma del Estado de México, Mexico
rsandovala@uaemex.mx
[2] Center for Technology in Government, University at Albany, USA
Centro de Investigación y Docencia Económicas, Mexico
jgil-garcia@ctg.albany.edu

Abstract. Open government implementation connects to several actions: public policy design, software implementation, website development, policy informatics, and the development of new regulations. Despite this important progress, very little has been done to measure the impact of open government and provide feedback in terms of the next steps for implementation. Furthermore, very few models intend to explain the functions, characteristics, or the future of this new trend toward openness. Our research from 2006 to 2012 uses a multi-component model to measure open government websites in the 32 Mexican state governments. However, the website model could become obsolete as a result of technology advancements. This paper analyzes some knowledge gaps and potential problems with this type of model and proposes a new approach to open government portals based on four conceptual pillars: wikinomics, open data, new institutionalism, and the fifth state (Network State).

Keywords: open government, models, transparency, e-government, open data.

1   Introduction

Parks [1], who first introduced the term open government, did not imagine the repercussions of his idea within the next century. Today governments around the world implement ideas of open government through corresponding policies [2–5]. However, open government initiatives currently face several problems related to a lack of clarity, including the conceptualization of the term, its functions and limitations, and in the research models used to understand it.

Open government has evolved along several paths. The Freedom of Information Act (FOIA) become the first step to building this concept; Richardson [6] states the "right to know" was the initial idea for this path, which other scholars also describe as a key starting point [7–9]. A different path pursues open data, in which government data must be transparent, reusable, standardized, and updated, among other aspects. The concept of open data introduced the importance of collaboration and information sharing [10].

M. Janssen et al. (Eds.): EGOV 2014, LNCS 8653, pp. 47–58, 2014.
© IFIP International Federation for Information Processing 2014

This kind of conceptual path has led to the belief that the worldwide "open government initiative would establish a system of transparency, public participation, and collaboration" [11]. For this paper, open government is conceived "as an institutional and technological platform that transforms government data into open data to allow citizens' use, protection, and collaboration in public decisions, accountability, and improvement of public services" [12]. This definition allows for several interpretations, such as: (1) open government can be understood as a platform that translates government data into the citizen's language; (2) these transformations allow citizens to protect, reuse, collaborate, or interact with data in several forms; and (3) as a result of this transformation, citizens are empowered to scrutinize public officials' decisions and actions to enhance accountability and to then propose different alternatives for public services and other government actions. However, discussion about the open government concept and the development of theoretical frameworks for it are underdeveloped in this field of research [13–15].

A second problem the open government trend faces is related to the delineation of its functions and limitations. Dawes [16] identifies some limits to open government with respect to the concept of stewardship and usefulness of the data. When looking at the functions of open government, it can be understood as a tool that allows public officials to release data from the government for the general public's use. And it has several dimensions, like open data visualization tools [17] and open data [18], which combined could be seen as the Big Data perspective [19, 20]. Open government's limitations are linked to information policies [21], cultural resistance from public officials [22], and the problem of trust in government agencies [23]. Some scholars are pursuing research agendas to address these issues. In contrast, we want to focus specifically on the development of models to assess open government initiatives.

The purpose of this paper is to propose a new assessment model for open government portals and it is organized into five sections, with this introduction as the first. Section two includes a literature review focused on models for assessing open government websites. The third section describes an older assessment model that was used for six years of continuous evaluation of Mexican portals, while section four explains the advantages, weaknesses, and limitations of that previous model. Section 5 proposes a new model, based on recent theoretical developments and current technologies, after which we make a few concluding remarks.

2 Literature Review: Open Government Assessment Models

One of the problems of open government is changing the government paradigm in order to introduce it and really allow the disclosure of government information [24]. This paradigm change could be reformulated by the construction of a model to facilitate understanding of open government implementation and offer recommendations to guide open government development [25–27]. However, the purpose of this paper is more limited. It is based on assessment models of e-government efforts. Researchers have created preliminary models to analyze the maturity of e-government and open data [28], which we can group them in two main categories: (1) models that assess systemic changes of open government and (2) models that assess open data achievements. In the first category, three models are included: the Kalampokis [29] stage model, the Scholl and Luna-Reyes [33] systemic model, and the Open Government Implementation Model (OGIM) [26]. The second category includes the implementation framework for Open Data in Colombia [30] and the model to assess open data in public agencies from Solar [31]. This section will briefly describe each of these models as they provide some of the conceptual basis for the model we developed in 2007.

Research models are important ways to frame reality and try to provide rational explanations about phenomena; however, it is not easy to find such models and they are usually ongoing projects because they required permanent update and feedback. One of the first models related to open government was developed by an international team [28]. This e-Government Maturity Model has three dimensions: information criteria, IT resources, and domains. This proposal has some additional variables that go beyond IT, such as e-Strategy, IT Governance, Process Management, and People and Organizational Capabilities. The purpose is to understand the integrated process of e-government through maturity. This early model is important to our research for two reasons: it reflects the introduction of a rational model to the e-government assessment perspective and it shares the integrated concept of evaluation from our original model, although we discard the idea of maturity because open government portals are mostly regulated by law and technological trends rather than an evolution in maturity [32].

Kalampokis [29] developed a second model in 2011 to assess open government data, which has two main dimensions: the first one is related to organizational and technological complexity and the second one is related to added value for data consumers. This proposal is more operational and focused on one section of the open government process—the data.

A different proposal with a more integrated perspective is the Open Government Implementation Model (OGIM) [26], which is a stage model that guides government agencies on their journey to open government. The model defines four main implementation stages and describes the deliverables, benefits, challenges, best practices, and metrics for each stage. The goal of Stage 1 is increasing data transparency; stage 2's objective is moving on to improving open participation (like open collaboration). Stage 3 is focused on realizing ubiquitous engagement and finally stage 4 harnesses the power of social media in order to engage the public. The OGIM model is closer to our research because it intends to measure the global outcomes of an open government implementation through the four stages. However, our research model is more focused only on open government websites rather than other implementations of this trend.

The last model was developed by Scholl and Luna-Reyes [33] and it uses dynamic systems theory to introduce more actors and variables into the implementation of open government, such as elected officials, executive power, and regulations and norms, to better understand the maturity and evolution of open government applications. From this review of four models we can conclude the following: (1) there is no single model to assess open government implementation; (2) models for assessing complete implementation of open government exist, but not specifically for open government websites; and (3) maturity is a constant in many models, but may not apply to this research area.

3   Assessment Model for Open Government Portals (2007-2012)

The main purpose of this model was to assess the progress of open government implementation among state web portals in Mexico. It is focused on the development of websites to introduce open government functions; it does not measure the impact of open government in other areas of state public administration. The model was built from two sources: a survey and then interviews with webmasters of Mexican state open government websites, with the interviews held during a professional meeting in October 2005. Once the data was collected, we identified different components of open government websites, which were validated with concepts from academic literature. We presented a first proposal in April 2006 to the webmasters who participated in the earlier data collection and used their opinions to refine the model. The final model has seven components:

1. Trust
2. Information value
3. Accountability
4. Constant innovation and change
5. Law accomplishment
6. Internal agency transparency
7. Information systems or search engines

1. Trust. This component was proposed to achieve the goal of measuring trust in public information. It measures three related questions focused on perception of information: (1) Information is trustworthy, (2) Information is validated by other sources, and (3) Website (interface) seems trustworthy.

2. Information value. This component answers the question: does this information produce value for citizens? Examples of when information has value include whether it is reusable, easy to find, helps inform decision-making, and is clear and understandable to the average person.

3. Accountability. The purpose of this component was to assess tools and functions that allow for individual and organizational accountability. The way that organizations enable citizens' claims, feedback, or accusations of misconduct from public officials were measured here.

4. Constant innovation and change. This component measures ongoing innovations or changes in the actual interface that could be considered valuable for users.

5. Law accomplishment. The Information Access Law, published in 2002, requires all Mexican government agencies to have open government websites and establishes minimum information standards, including the capability for citizens to ask for information and data disclosure. This component assesses the degree of compliance with these basic regulations.

6. Internal agency transparency. A constant request from webmasters in 2005 was to devise a way to force internal agencies to deliver government information on time. This component assesses state government efforts to deliver information in a timely fashion, such as publishing a ranking for internal agency performance on open government information.

7. Information systems or search engines. The objective of this component is to assess the search engine capabilities to retrieve information and the internal development of software to manage and capture data for the open government website.

The idea of this seven component model was to integrate legal regulations, interface standards, open government practices such as release information, accountability, and standards like information value and user trust in this first stage of open government implementation in Mexico. Several state governments used this research, which was published in a national magazine every year [34–36], to make decisions and design improvements for their portals.

In order to test this model we conducted a pilot test in 2006 and adjusted some questions and components. The first evaluation was conducted in 2007 and was continued annually until 2012, during February and March. The goal was to evaluate the 32 state government websites within two visits of 30 minutes maximum and collect the data to elaborate a ranking among the state governments.

4   Challenges and Problems of the 2007 Assessment Model

The assessment model for the open government portals was based on the technological trends of the first decade of the 21st Century; however, several important changes in technology (which Friedman describes [37]) forced adaptations to the model, At least three technological changes had a direct impact on the assessment model and two institutional changes indirectly impacted the model.

The first technological change is the speed of computational devices. Most powerful processors enable the development of software to support simultaneous operations. These changes allow government organizations to interact with larger databases and develop software to personalize search and use data more efficiently. This change affects the components of information value, information systems, and search engines.

The second technological change is the Web 2.0 trend [38]. The widespread use of Twitter, Facebook, blogs and wiki platforms to create content, exchange ideas, or interact with information creates new conditions for citizens to share, publish, and collaborate with information. The frequent use of this technology by government organizations and citizens transforms the use of government data and the relationship government has with its constituents [24]. Web 2.0 indirectly impacted all components of the assessment model.

The last technological change was the introduction of big data technologies to analyze, collect, and systematize large amounts of government data, usually stored in government data warehouses. The introduction of this capacity to handle a large volume of data increases the potential uses of government data and transforms the processes by which governments disseminate, publish, and share data [18, 19]. This change positively affected information sharing, diffusion of the data, and improved collaboration using new and more reliable data.

An important institutional change that transformed open government portals in Mexico was the introduction of the National Information Access Law that creates more protections for personal data and provides for sanctions against governments that do not comply with the publication of basic data required in the law. These new regulations increase with the second institutional change: the creation of the Open Government Partnership in September 2012. From the beginning, Mexico became a member of this partnership and assumed responsibilities and commitments with specific objectives and dates to accomplish them in the short term [39]. These two conditions forced the federal and state governments of Mexico to change their portals, which affected the utility of the previous open government assessment model.

5   New Assessment Model: A Proposal

Following our review of the literature surrounding different models related to open government and an analysis of previous assessment models, we propose a new model for open government website assessment based on five components: (1) Legal Obligations; (2) Open Data; (3) Collaboration; (4) Co-production; and (5) Institutional Arrangements (see Table 1).

Table 1. Open government research model proposal

Component	Description	Variables
Legal Obligations	Assess public policies at all government levels	Rules, agency relations, public policies
Open Data	Assess degree of advancement in open data and use of technology to organize and disseminate data	Open government data principles, cloud government, mobile government.
Collaboration	Assess tools and initiatives to promote collaboration among citizens	Collaboration tools with the use of Web 2.0
Co-production	Assess peer production, tools, process, and policies to promote feedback and accountability	Tools, apps, processes that enable peer production
Institutional Arrangements	Metrics on changes in internal processes, institutional relationships with power that facilitate open government	Information costs, transaction costs, agreements, rules and processes for open government

These components are directly linked to four theoretical pillars that summarize and combine previous empirical and theoretical research. Following, we describe the four pillars and their link to the proposed model.

5.1   First Pillar: Wikinomics

A very interesting example of open government in the U.S. has been the change to the patent system by including collaboration from the scientific community. This revolution was based on the ideas of peer collaboration, sharing information, and the use of technology in a process called Wiki Government [40]. These principles come from

Tapscott and Williams's [41] perspective that wikinomics demonstrates the principles of the so-called new economy: collaboration, co-production, peer sharing, and exchange of information. At least two components of open government websites are related to this principle: collaboration and co-production. We understand that openness with citizens—or the users of information—cannot be possible without considering both horizontal and vertical collaboration between producers and users of information, as well as the constant need to update and review government information using technological means. The Wiki Government concept promotes this kind of behavior and improves the release of the data. Peer-to-peer activities are possible using a common platform of collaboration and co-production in which users, both public officials and citizens, can be seen as prosumers (in the words of Tapscott and Williams)--people who produce and consume information at the same time.

5.2   Second Pillar: Open Data

This pillar is directly related to the second component of the model with the same name. We realize that open government implementation processes align with open data practices. Geiger and Von Lucke [18] establish that open data are all stored data that can be accessible to the public without any kind of restriction on use and distribution. Since 2007, O'Reilly has operated the Open Government Working Group that proposes eight principles of open data [42] that complement Geiger and von Lucke's ideas. From this perspective, open data will be the best complement for the organizational tasks of opening government processes, files, and procedures and is the main outcome directly related to citizens' information needs. We believe that part of an integrated measurement of open government portals must be the degree to which open data is available, as well as their quality and usefulness.

5.3   Third Pillar: The Network State or Intelligent Government

The idea of the fifth state by Dutton [43] proposes the Internet as a platform for new relationships between citizens and government. This complements Castells's [44] perspective on changing the legal perspective of the state and transforming it on a state related to nodes, links, and interrelations in a network. This new state is more the consequence rather than the cause of open government, in which the use of Web 2.0 forms the basis for Government 2.0 where policy makers and citizens collaborate to create data and share responsibility for government decision-making. It represents a new characterization of a smart state, which uses artificial intelligence, sensors, and other information technologies and reduces time, processes, and distances for citizens and government officials,[45]. The model components that measure this pillar over time and along transparency tasks are institutional arrangements and legal obligations.

5.4   Fourth Pillar: New Institutionalism and Sociotechnical Theory

Two theoretical frameworks explain the emergence of the network state. First, new institutionalism suggests that the introduction of open government will yield new ways to arrange relationships and coordination among institutions, which can be seen in the release process for data and updates to the websites. Secondly, sociotechnical theory links technology with human perspectives and the organizational background [46]. If we conceived that individuals behave and interact inside institutions [47] and these institutions are now open and without boundaries in terms on information, we must try to assess change and maturity in these behaviors along the different implementations of open government.

5.5   Connections Across the Pillars

More research on the relationships among the pillars and the more specific components of the model is needed to make the proposed model feasible and operational. However, some initial relationships are shown in Figure 1. For example, the first pillar, Wikinomics, is related to the collaboration and co-production components. The second pillar, Open Data, is related to the component with the same name, but also relates to co-production as one of the main avenues to produce and release data. The pillar called Network State and Intelligent Government is related to the development of institutional arrangements and collaboration opportunities. Finally, the fourth

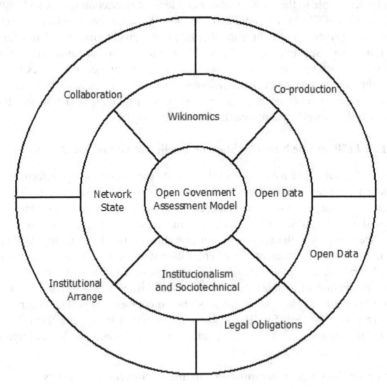

Fig. 1. O-Government Assessment Model

pillar of New Institutionalism and Sociotechnical Theory is related to the production of legal obligations and institutional arrangements.

In order to solve the problems confronting assessment models as described in the previous section, we intend to solve the first two technological problems, the speed of change and the adoption of Web 2.0, with the first pillar of Wikinomics. The model components from this pillar are collaboration and co-production as the main tools to facilitate the Wikinomics concept. The next technological problem of big data will be addressed using the open data strategies that governments now develop and will be reflected in the open data model component. The institutional challenges from the National Information Access Law and the Open Government Partnership are addressed using the Network State framework and New Institutionalism and Sociotechnical Theory in order to stabilize the legal platform and create broad objectives for the open government implementation.

6   Final Remarks

Assessment of open government websites must be standardized, but also constantly changing and adapting to new conditions. Evaluation tools should be able to produce modifications and improvements to the actual websites in order to help citizens in the task of understanding open government data, processes, and information. Our 2007 model helped to accomplish this task in Mexican transparency portals, since many state CIOs were paying attention to the variables and particular technologies included in the assessment and they modified and aligned their own portals to make them consistent with the evaluation tool. However, a new model is needed now; a model that captures new contexts, new technological trends, and a more IT-savvy citizen.

This new model will begin to fill three existing gaps in open government research. The first one is to promote better and more systematic metrics for the design and implementation of open government initiatives. Second, this paper should help to improve our current understanding of the impacts—positive or negative—of open government on other important concepts in public administration such as transparency, accountability, co-production, and institutions. Third, this study contributes to the development of models to assess maturity and evolution of these open government portals, but also to broadly understand the progress that has been made in this field of research.

The proposed new model has to be tested and analyzed using real open government and transparency portals. In order to do this work based on the new theoretical pillars and their related specific concepts, our next steps should be to develop a questionnaire to measure the components, to perform a pilot test, and to collect the necessary evidence from Mexican portals. This first data collection effort could then produce better explanations and theoretical insights about the impact of open government as a way to interact with and engage citizens, businesses, and other stakeholders.

References

1. Parks, W.: The Open Government Principle: Applying the Right to Know under the constitution. George Wash. Law Rev. 26, 1–22 (1957)
2. Alanazi, J., Chatfield, A.: Sharing Government-Owned Data with the Public: A Cross-Country Analysis of Open Data Practice in the Middle East. In: 18th Americas Conference on Information Systems (AMCIS 2012), pp. 1–10 (2012)
3. Lucke, P.D.J., von, G.K.: Open Government Collaboration. In: Gascó-Hernández, M. (ed.) Open Government, pp. 189–204. Springer, New York (2014)
4. Bertot, J.C., Jaeger, P.T., Grimes, J.M.: Promoting transparency and accountability through ICTs, social media, and collaborative e-government. Transform. Gov. People Process Policy 6, 78–91 (2012)
5. Bertot, J.C., Jaeger, P.T., Hansen, D.: The impact of polices on government social media usage: Issues, challenges, and recommendations. Gov. Inf. Q. 29, 30–40 (2012)
6. Richardson, E.L.: Freedom of Information. Loyola Law Rev 20, 45 (1973)
7. Drachsler, D.A.: Freedom of Information Act and the Right of Non-Disclosure. The. Adm. Law Rev. 28, 1 (1976)
8. Bayne, P.: Freedom of Information. Leg. Serv. Bull. 9, 121 (1984)
9. Birkinshaw, P.: Freedom of information and its impact in the United Kingdom. Gov. Inf. Q. 27, 312–321 (2010)
10. Lathrop, D., Ruma, L.: Open Government: Collaboration, Transparency, and Participation in Practice. O'Reilly Media (2010)
11. McDermott, P.: Building open government. Gov. Inf. Q. 27, 401–413 (2010)
12. Sandoval-Almazan, R.: La larga marcha del Gobierno Abierto. Teoría, medición y futuro. INAP, Mexico City (2013)
13. Fishenden, J., Thompson, M.: Digital Government, Open Architecture, and Innovation: Why Public Sector IT Will Never Be the Same Again. J. Public Adm. Res. Theory 23, 977–1004 (2013)
14. Scholl, H.J.: Five trends that matter: Challenges to 21st century electronic government. Inf. Polity Int. J. Gov. Democr. Inf. Age 17, 317–327 (2012)
15. Prieto, L.M., Rodríguez, A.C., Pimiento, J.: Implementation framework for open data in Colombia. In: Proceedings of the 6th International Conference on Theory and Practice of Electronic Governance, pp. 14–17. ACM, New York (2012)
16. Dawes, S.S.: Stewardship and usefulness: Policy principles for information-based transparency. Gov. Inf. Q. 27, 377–383 (2010)
17. Graves, A., Hendler, J.: Visualization tools for open government data. In: Proceedings of the 14th Annual International Conference on Digital Government Research, pp. 136–145. ACM, New York (2013)
18. Geiger, C.P., von Lucke, J.: Open Government and (Linked) (Open) (Government) (Data). JeDEM - EJournal EDemocracy Open Gov. 4, 265–278 (2012)
19. Keiser, B.E.: Big Data, Open Government, and Sunlight. Inf. Today 30, 1–33 (2013)
20. Bertot, J.C., Choi, H.: Big data and e-government: issues, policies, and recommendations. In: Proceedings of the 14th Annual International Conference on Digital Government Research, pp. 1–10. ACM, New York (2013)
21. Dawes, S.S., Helbig, N.: Information strategies for open government: challenges and prospects for deriving public value from government transparency. In: Wimmer, M.A., Chappelet, J.-L., Janssen, M., Scholl, H.J. (eds.) EGOV 2010. LNCS, vol. 6228, pp. 50–60. Springer, Heidelberg (2010)

22. Bertot, J.C., Jaeger, P.T., Grimes, J.M.: Using ICTs to create a culture of transparency: E-government and social media as openness and anti-corruption tools for societies. Gov. Inf. Q. 27, 264–271 (2010)
23. Bannister, F., Connolly, R.: Trust and transformational government: A proposed framework for research. Gov. Inf. Q. 28, 137–147 (2011)
24. Newsom, G., Dickey, L.: Citizenville: How to Take the Town Square Digital and Reinvent Government. Penguin Press HC, The (2013)
25. Sandoval-Almazan, R.: The Two Door Perspective: An Assessment Framework for Open Government. J. E-Democr. 3, 29–45 (2011)
26. Lee, G., Kwak, Y.H.: Open government implementation model: a stage model for achieving increased public engagement. In: Proceedings of the 12th Annual International Digital Government Research Conference (dg.o 2011), pp. 254–261. ACM, College Park (2011)
27. Lee, G., Kwak, Y.H.: An Open Government Maturity Model for social media-based public engagement. Gov. Inf. Q. 29, 492–503 (2012)
28. Iribarren, M., Concha, G., Valdes, G., Solar, M., Villarroel, M.T., Gutiérrez, P., Vásquez, Á.: Capability Maturity Framework for eGovernment: A Multi-dimensional Model and Assessing Tool. In: Wimmer, M.A., Scholl, H.J., Ferro, E. (eds.) EGOV 2008. LNCS, vol. 5184, pp. 136–147. Springer, Heidelberg (2008)
29. Kalampokis, E., Tambouris, E., Tarabanis, K.: Open Government Data: A Stage Model. In: Janssen, M., Scholl, H.J., Wimmer, M.A., Tan, Y.-H. (eds.) EGOV 2011. LNCS, vol. 6846, pp. 235–246. Springer, Heidelberg (2011)
30. Prieto, L.M., Rodríguez, A.C., Pimiento, J.: Implementation Framework for Open Data in Colombia. In: 6th International Conference on Theory and Practice of Electronic Governance, pp. 14–17. Association for Computing Machinery, Albany (2012)
31. Solar, M., Concha, G., Meijueiro, L.: A Model to Assess Open Government Data in Public Agencies. In: Scholl, H.J., Janssen, M., Wimmer, M.A., Moe, C.E., Flak, L.S. (eds.) EGOV 2012. LNCS, vol. 7443, pp. 210–221. Springer, Heidelberg (2012)
32. Hewson, C., Laurent, D.: Research Design and Tools for Internet Research. In: The SAGE Handbook of Online Research Methods, pp. 58–78. Sage (2008)
33. Scholl, H.J., Luna-Reyes, L.F.: Transparency and openness in government: a system dynamics perspective. In: 5th International Conference on Theory and Practice of Electronic Governance (ICEGOV 2011), pp. 107–114. ACM (2011)
34. Sandoval-Almazan, R.: Ranking de Portales de Transparencia: La medición 2010 (2010)
35. Sandoval-Almazan, R.: Midiendo la Transparencia en Internet: Ranking de las páginas web de los Institutos de Transparencia en Mexico. Federalismo Y transparencia en Mexico: seis estudios de Caso, pp. 219–247. Alianza Civica-Comunidad Europea, Ciudad de Mexico (2009)
36. Sandoval Almazan, R.: Portales de transparencia: La evolución (2013)
37. Friedman, T.L.: The World Is Flat: A Brief History of the Twenty-first Century. Farrar, Straus and Giroux (2005)
38. Chun, S.A., Shulman, S., Sandoval, R., Hovy, E.: Government 2.0: Making connections between citizens, data and government. Inf. Polity 15, 1–9 (2010)
39. OGP: Open Government Declaration | Open Government Partnership, http://www.opengovpartnership.org/open-government-declaration
40. Noveck, B.S.: Wiki Government: How Technology Can Make Government Better, Democracy Stronger, and Citizens More Powerful. Brookings Institution Press (2009)
41. Tapscott, D., Williams, A.D.: Wikinomics: How Mass Collaboration Changes Everything. Portfolio Hardcover, New York (2006)

42. Open Government Working Group: 8 Principles of Open Government Data - OpenGovData.org, http://www.opengovdata.org/home/8principles
43. Dutton, W.H.: The Fifth Estate Emerging through the Network of Networks. Prometheus 27, 1–15 (2009)
44. Castells, M.: Comunicación y Poder. Alianza Editorial, Madrid, España (2009)
45. Gil-Garcia, J.R.: Towards a smart State? Inter-agency collaboration, information integration, and beyond. Inf. Polity Int. J. Gov. Democr. Inf. Age 17, 269–280 (2012)
46. Powell, W.W., DiMaggio, P.J. (eds.): The New Institutionalism in Organizational Analysis. University Of Chicago Press (1991)
47. Senge, K.: The "New Institutionalism" in Organization Theory: Bringing Society and Culture Back In. Am. Sociol. 44, 76–95 (2013)

Contextual Factors Influencing Health Information Systems Implementation in Public Sector – Investigating the Explanatory Power of Critical Success Factors

Karin Axelsson and Ulf Melin

Department of Management and Engineering,
Linköping University, SE-581 83 Linköping, Sweden
{karin.axelsson,ulf.melin}@liu.se

Abstract. In this paper, we approach the field of critical success factors (CSF) by analyzing a successful case of IT implementation within the public health sector. The purpose of the paper is to gain further understanding of if and how well CSFs can explain a successful case. The main conclusion drawn is that even though the studied organization shows signs of common CSFs, this alone cannot explain the success. An important contribution from this study is thus the focus on contextual factors when trying to understand what makes an implementation project successful.

Keywords: health information system, IT implementation, public sector, critical success factors, contextual factors, project success.

1   Introduction

In this paper[1], we approach the field of critical success factors (CSF) by analyzing a successful case of IT implementation within the public health sector. We have studied a University Hospital's implementation of an integrated health information system (HIS). During the longitudinal case study we came across one clinic which implementation process seemed to differ from many of the other clinics and care units [2]. This clinic was described by practitioners within the organization as very successful compared to many other units at this hospital. The impression of a success story made us curious to study this clinic in more detail to find out what made the process and result so different there. By understanding reasons behind the success we can analyze if CSFs potentially can explain the success, or if there are other explanations in this case. Based on our findings we discuss and question the maybe overestimated belief in CSFs as a "silver bullet" for success performance.

Heeks [13] discusses that many studies of HIS implementation have focused on successful cases and, thus, missed to learn from failures. We agree with Heeks' argument that there is a difference between design of HIS and the practice in a care

---

[1] This paper builds partially upon a conference paper [2] presented at European Conference on Information Systems in 2011, but the present paper has a somewhat different focus.

M. Janssen et al. (Eds.): EGOV 2014, LNCS 8653, pp. 59–71, 2014.

unit that can relate to several aspects; such as information, technology, processes, objectives and values, staffing and skills, management systems and structures, and other resources [13]. These are examples of the contextual circumstances that we have to address when discussing success and failure in implementation processes [2]. Contextual factors are often addressed in information systems (IS) research as for instance situational, organizational, environmental, task, and technology characteristics that influence the outcome of an IS development project [15], and are emerging in CSF research [24]. A similar discussion about the importance of the context in HIS implementation is emphasized by Yusof et al. [32], who suggest an evaluation model for HIS that focus alignment between human, organization and technology. Important conditions for and barriers to the adoption of healthcare technology is also investigated and discussed [10], [28]. Despite Heeks' [13] call for studies of failures, we take a successful case as our point of departure in this paper, as we aim to compare this case and the reasons we find to explain the success with existing knowledge on CSFs. In order to focus on contextual factors, we apply a benefit perspective [9] when analyzing the case. We are not aiming to formulate CSFs from our case, as most studies of success stories do. The purpose of the paper is instead to gain further understanding of if and how well CSFs can explain a successful case. After this introduction, the paper is organized in the following way: In Section Two we discuss previous research on CSFs in IT implementation projects. The research approach is reported in Section Three. Empirical findings from our case are presented in Section Four and discussed in Section Five the findings are discussed. The paper is concluded in Section Six.

2   Previous Research on Critical Success Factors

One of the pioneers in CSF research, Rockart [26], describes critical success factors , as a guiding approach in the IS domain for managers to define the information needs in order to reach the objectives of the organization. Later on, CSFs were focused on identifying key factors important for successful behaviour [18], which is e.g. emphasized by a quote from Boynton and Zmud [6 p. 17]: "The CSF methodology is a procedure that attempts to make explicit those few key areas that dictate managerial or organizational success." Many authors have focused on describing and recommending certain actions and conditions under which success is more likely to occur. In parallel, CSFs have been criticized as offering over-simplified solutions that are difficult to realize in practice, since many contextual circumstances also influence the outcome [2], [5], [20], [29].

As described in [2], literature in the area of public sector IT projects as well as IT projects in general [23] reports on several sets of success factors. Gil-García and Pardo [11] as well as Ho and Pardo [14], have carried out extensive literature reviews of CSFs of IT projects in the public sector. Success factors mentioned are, for example, top management commitment, linkage to business, technical alignment, knowledgeable personnel, and user involvement [14]. The need to involve users in a sustainable way is also pointed out as a key issue by e.g. Chan and Pan [7]. Other scholars are focusing on CSFs in HIS implementation projects [21] and their findings are of a similar kind. CSFs, independently of source and context, tend to be alike. Thus, it does not seem to be evident differences between CSFs suggested for public or private sector. One interesting difference between public and private organizations, highlighted by Rosacker and Olson [27], is however that public organizations are considered as less competitive. This fact might be an important difference when discussing CSFs, since this implies that short-term incitements for change and innovation are lower in public organizations. This may be elaborated more on, but they argue that when applying CSFs in public sector each factor's dominance differs from findings in private sector (ibid.). Findings presented by Rocheleau and Wu [25] show that higher competition in private sector forces organizations to invest more resources in IT, compared to public organizations, in order to gain competitive advantage. However, they also find that public and private organizations rate IT as equally important, even though they spend fewer resources in IT (ibid.). This implies that despite varying degrees of competition between sectors, both public and private organizations aim to realize similar goals, such as increased coordination and efficiency, by implementing IT.

Berg [5] claims existing CSF lists to be challenging since success can be judged and structured in many dimensions; such as effectiveness, efficiency, organizational attitudes and commitment, employee satisfaction, and patient satisfaction. This is also discussed by Melin and Axelsson [20] investigating different images on HIS implementation challenging existing CSFs. This makes the guidance of successful practice more complex and CSF lists often offer a more simplified solution than what is actually needed in a "messy" real-life project. In order to illustrate the complexities of HIS implementation processes, Berg [5] investigates three myths related to such processes; implying that: (1) HIS implementation is a technical realization of a planned system in an organization, (2) HIS implementation can be left to the IT department, and (3) the implementation including the required organizational redesign can be planned. By scrutinizing these myths, Berg [5] concludes that HIS implementation is a mutual process where both organization and technology influence each other; a mutual process which has to be supported by both management and future users. The management of a HIS implementation process also implies an act of balance between initiating organizational change and using the HIS as a change agent without specifying and controlling this process too far [5].

CSF research includes identification and assessment of factors that might explain an organization's or a project's success [19]. In practice, CSF studies are often delimited to the identification of such factors, though [16]. There is a lack of CSF research which adopts a more holistic approach and analyzes how these factors can be handled in different contexts [24]. Remus and Wiener [24] imply that CSF research contributions to practice can be discussed and questioned, especially quantitative studies of success as the dependent variable. The authors are critical towards the idea of marketing CSFs as objective knowledge that is possible to adopt in any organization in order to easily handle challenges and reach goals. Remus and Wiener [24] argue that CSFs cannot be treated as instrumental, causal or objective. Instead, they view CSFs as being conceptual constructs that research and practice need to have dialogues about to find new perspectives (ibid.). Lau et al. [17] propose a framework of benefit evaluation where contextual factors that influence HIS adoption by clinicians are highlighted. They focus on the importance of handling people, organizational change and HIS implementation in a coherent way. Obviously, there are studies focusing contextual factors' relation to CSFs, but this kind of CSF research is still rather unusual [24].

An exception from this lack of a contextual focus is presented in an article by Doherty et al. [9], in which the authors claim that success in IT projects should be measured by its actual ability to deliver meaningful benefits, rather than applying factors that are said to facilitate successful outcome from IT projects. Doherty et al. [9] examined actionable factors that might lead to effective realization of benefits by studying three organizations. Benefit realization and benefit management is a vast research field [1], [31] which we do not intend to fully explore in this paper. Instead we use the findings from Doherty et al. [9] in order to investigate our case from a *benefit perspective*. Thus, we acknowledge the context when discussing success factors in our case. Doherty et al.'s result shows that a subset of traditional CFS might be improved in order to make them more focused on benefits realization. Their contribution is also formulated in a set of coherent principles [9]: (1) Benefit orientation – Explicit focus upon delivery of benefits in the organization is needed, (2) Organizational change – Benefits primarily come from organizational change rather than directly from technology, (3) Tailor to context – Every project is unique which implies that the specific organizational context must be acknowledged, (4) Factors are interdependent constructs – Success factors are not delivering success independently of each other but have to be managed altogether, (5) Investments have a lifecycle – Projects' success might be realized long after the implementation project is ended, and (6) Portfolio focus – Success factors need to be applied to an organization's all systems, not only to one individual system, in order to be actionable (ibid.).

Doherty et al. [9] claim that these principles can be seen as themes upon which successful practices and factors can be established. We will, thus, return to these key principles later in the paper when discussing the empirical findings. We identify several reasons for using these key principles in our discussion. Doherty et al. [9] give voice to problems with CSFs which we also find relevant; (1) system development projects are seen as a static process neglecting the fact that factors may have varying importance in different phases of the project, (2) the context is often forgotten or assumed to be identical for many projects, (3) CSFs are seen as discrete independent variables which makes us miss interrelations between factors, and (4) CSFs are focused on a project which ends when a technical artefact is delivered (ibid.). Since Doherty et al.'s key principles try to handle these identified problems we find them useful to apply to our case. By doing so, we also contribute with an independent examination of the principles.

3   Research Approach

In this paper we analyzed a case study [2] performed in the public health sector. We have conducted a qualitative, interpretive study [30] of an implementation process of a HIS in a Swedish public health provider organization. The findings discussed in this paper are part of a larger longitudinal study of this implementation process that started in 2008 and ended in 2011 [20]. The theme (contextual factors and CSFs) focused in this paper was highlighted empirically during the summer 2010. The findings regarding this particular theme within the larger case are generated from two dedicated qualitative, face-to-face, semi-structured interviews. The interviews were audio recorded and each interview lasted for two hours. A qualitative interview guide was used, with a mix of pre-defined open questions and open ended questions, topics and informal communication [22]. We asked questions about the respondents' experiences before, during and after the change and implementation process as well as what aspects they found to be most important in this context. During the interviews we focused why this case is perceived as much more successful than the rest of the organization. The two respondents are both organization developers employed by the studied public health provider. The two persons were selected as they possess much information about the focused case. The first respondent works at the hospital's care process centre (CPC), which is the organizational unit responsible for the HIS implementation process, and the second respondent was involved in the process change and HIS implementation project at the studied clinic. The second respondent was suggested during the first interview, i.e., we used a snowball sampling method [22] to find this respondent.

The empirical data might seem limited in the above description, but it is important to remember that we have studied the organization longitudinally. Consequently, the empirical context of the focused interviews is informed by other interviews, studies of documents, field work and systems studies. We have conducted over 25 interviews in this organization. In this larger study the respondents were located in the CPC, in two public health centres and in two other hospital clinics. We have also studied documents; e.g. the health provider's website with information to patients, internal project documentation, budgets, external evaluation reports, and media's coverage of the project. This data triangulation implies that we have a thorough understanding of the organizational context as we have had access to the University Hospital for a long time.

4   Empirical Findings

The following presentation of empirical findings is based on a part of an earlier publication covering this case [2]. The implemented HIS comprises a widely integrated medical record for all care units in the University Hospital which implied an important change in the entire organization. Internally the project was characterized as the largest change project ever initiated. The specialist healthcare centres located at the hospitals in the region did not have any IT based medical record system before. They have had disparate systems before handling, e.g., schedules, lab results, etc., but no integrated HIS. The implementation process of the integrated COSMIC system (Compliant Open Solutions for Modern Integrated Care) started with a pilot involving a few care units and was then continued to all units in a rather fast pace. The implementation project followed a "big bang" approach from the perspective of each organizational unit, but a step by step initiative from the overall perspective. Thus, time was apprehended as the most important project goal to meet (compared to system functionality and cost).

The unit focused in this paper is the orthopaedics clinical department at the University Hospital. The clinic had changed the process for handling referrals prior to the implementation of the HIS. The main motive for this process change was the need to improve usage of resources and planning, but also an ambition to increase patient focus. Identified problems in the old process were huge volumes of patients combined with unsatisfactory routines, high degree of randomness, and lack of sufficient planning. Very persistent hierarchical levels and roles between professional groups are some reasons for change inertia in the organization until this process change was conducted. Much focus had been put on certain professions and organizational issues instead of focusing the patients and their needs for care. Prior to the HIS implementation there was also a lack of central governing instruments in the organization. The implementation of process changes followed by the HIS have resulted in a very successful integration of the system's prescribed functions for referral management and the new work processes, according to our respondents.

The change process started in a conflict between an organization developer (one of our respondents) at the studied clinic and one of her managers. The identified problems, mentioned above, were obvious to the respondent, but the manager did not agree about the problem definition. Nevertheless, the organization developer was asked to estimate possible capacity to handle patient referrals in better ways with existing resources. When she presented her results she did not receive any approval from the organization, but she continued her assignment anyway (like a skunk work process). More or less by a coincidence, the respondent also started to cooperate with a researcher specialized in optimization. The cooperation resulted in a thorough plan for capacity and resource optimization for the referral management at the clinic. Because of severe resistance the organization developer started working with manual referral management based on rough sorting of referrals. In parallel, clear guidelines for referral management and assessment were established. The critical voices in the organization did not stop, but our respondent continued to defend the new process. She also became responsible for controlling that the new guidelines for referral management were followed.

This process change took place before the implementation of COSMIC. The developed manual workflow model for the referral management process was later integrated in COSMIC without any problems, as the process logic in COSMIC were very similar to the manual process. This is regarded as an important reason for the successful ending of the change process; the system supporting institutionalization of the process. As the process was changed prior to the HIS implementation this cannot be seen as a planned result. The organization developer decided to act on her own initiative, following her own belief and step out of her formal role, addressing the needed process changes by direct facilitation on an operational level. The ideas behind the new process are not particularly innovative in general, but rather straight forward to implement and use. The notable fact is that the need to be innovative within the healthcare sector was acknowledged. Prior to the process change, the studied clinic's routines for referral management were unstructured and uncoordinated. Without process changes, the referral management built into the HIS would not have supported the organization. One of the organization developers describes this as: "We had to some extent already simulated COSMIC by manually distributing referrals and assessment responsibility between plastic boxes. When COSMIC was implemented, the system did function in exactly the same way."

The plastic boxes, used for sorting and distribution of referrals based on medical diagnosis, were at a later stage easily modelled and implemented in the HIS and, hence, proved to be a successful alignment between the changed business process and the HIS functionality. Obviously, the studied clinic had started to think in new directions and question conditions that had been taken for granted before. The notion of overlapping competencies leading to efficiency, which has been a common view in the healthcare sector for a long time, was for example challenged. Instead, it was seen as more important to use existing resources in the most suitable way and actively recruit certain competencies. One of the most influencing changes in the studied process was the introduction of an explicit coordinator role. The coordinator is responsible for controlling the flow of referrals through the HIS and distributing them to the correct part of the clinic depending on required expert skills. This is put forth as an important new role by one of the organization developers: "We have introduced coordinators, this is very, very important. Now there are persons who are appointed to have this assignment."

Of course it might be easier to see positive changes afterwards, but it is obvious that the coordinator role is very important for the outcome of this change. Another critical factor is the distinct and in some aspect firm control that the clinic's management has conducted, as indicted by one of the organization developers: "The management has been really supportive – they have been very determined and told everybody that this is the way we shall handle the referrals from now on [...] please, staff each section according to this decision."

During the change process, conflicts related to the strict hierarchical organization and power structures associated with professional healthcare roles have been a recurrent challenge. The coordinator role was questioned since a "business generalist" got control of the flow instead of a skilled physician. This can, together with previous lack of central control instruments and unwillingness to change, be seen as inertia factors. The distinct change inertia might also be explained by lack of previous change processes. There was no experience of earlier change projects and many employees reacted negatively when the studied changes were presented. Our interpretation is that the organization was not ready to accept the change arguments in which positive consequences of increased patient focus and cooperation were emphasized. The hospital management used economic terms as incentives to handle this situation. If parts of the organization did not accept the new goals and processes they would be financially "disfavoured", as one of the organization developers expresses: "It is all about money – it always comes first. And it takes a strong leadership to have the courage to carry the ideas through. It is about understanding that we are responsible for a production that must be satisfying – it is not the resources in such that are going to be satisfied. You have to think the other way around."

5   Discussion

In table 1, below, we use Doherty et al.'s [9] key principles for successful benefit realization as a point of departure when discussing explanations of success in the studied case.

Table 1. Mapping empirical success explanations to Doherty et al.'s [9] key principles

Key principles	Explanation of the principle	Empirical success explanations in the case
Benefit orientation	Explicit focus upon delivery of benefits in the organization.	The organization developer was a very *committed key actor* who believed in the process changes longitudinally. She continuously worked with and had the courage to fight for issues that she hoped would be beneficial for the organization. She was strongly supported by top and middle management, as they also *focused on benefit realizations* rather than e.g. to institutionalize power relations between actors within professional hierarchies.
Organizational change	Benefits primarily come from organizational change rather than directly from technology.	The new referral process and the implemented HIS were aligned thanks to the fact that the *organizational change* took place before the HIS implementation. Organizational change was obviously explicitly emphasized as the main priority in the organization. The HIS implementation later took advantage of the process changes (the IT-process fit), and benefits were realized to a very high extent.
Tailor to context	Every project is unique which implies that the specific organizational context must be acknowledged.	The persons controlling the referral flow made systematic assessments based on high expertise and good overview of the organizational processes and contexts. This process was designed thanks to the organization developer's deep understanding of the *organizational context*, which she and others in the project acknowledged during the process changes and HIS implementation. The fact that a rewarding, although rather ad hoc, cooperation with an external expert on optimization took place, is another example of how contextual aspects have been handled successfully in this case.
Factors are interdependent constructs	Success factors are not delivering success independently of each other but have to be managed altogether.	The persons involved in the project got an explicit change authority and were able to make decisions and approach problematic situations in the entire organization, in order to find a new way of handling the referral flow. As the case illustrates, several of the success explanations above are *interlinked*; e.g. the management support, the personal commitment and persistence to conduct changes that the organization would benefit from and the external expert knowledge that was brought into the project.
Investments have a lifecycle	Projects' success might be realized long after the implementation project is ended.	Since the process changes in this case took place prior to the HIS implementation, one could argue that some benefits were realized already *before* the HIS was introduced. At least, this shows that the organization did not define the organizational change as a project with a pre-defined end. However, the real benefits from the HIS implementation occurred afterwards, when all personnel at the clinic used the HIS. If the referral process had not been redesigned before the HIS implementation, the benefits would have been limited due to a misfit between the process and the HIS.
Portfolio focus	Success factors need to be applied to an organization's all systems, not only to one individual system, in order to be actionable.	In this case, the HIS was an integrated and enterprise-wide system which implied that the process and system changes truly influenced the whole organization. The successful approach was in that sense applied in the entire organization, even if dimensions also were left out in other implementation contexts within the organization.

As mentioned earlier, these principles focus themes that can be usable when formulating successful practices and factors [9]. In this paper we do not intend to formulate any CSF. Instead, we apply the principles to our case in order to structure our findings around these themes. As can be seen in the table, the key principles cover our success explanations well. This illustrates that the usefulness of Doherty et al.'s theoretical construct is supported by the findings in our case.

The benefit orientation and the explicit focus upon delivery of benefits in the organization [9] are important aspects in this case. The studied organization succeeds in realizing substantial benefits from their HIS implementation thanks to recently made process changes. However, neither because of the software solutions in such nor because of the way the implementation project is carried out. The process change is not driven by or initiated in coherence with the HIS implementation. Nevertheless, this case is highlighted as a very successful example of HIS implementation in the studied University Hospital. An image of success is surrounding the case [20], and this image is not false as the case indeed shows a successful outcome. The results were not reached by following any CSF list to success. Instead, this situation can be compared to one of the myths that Berg [5] discusses; the belief that the HIS implementation including required organizational redesign can be completely planned. Berg proposes a balance act between initiating organizational changes and using the HIS as a change agent [5].The statement that benefits primarily come from organizational change rather than directly from technology [9] corresponds well to the role the HIS had in this case. The HIS did not have the role of a driving change agent, but it had a very important role for realizing the benefit of the change process in the end. The change process was driven by one person, but without support from strategic intentions in the organization. Thus, the reached fit between organization, human and technology [32] was not explicitly planned, it rather occurred during the process.

Every project is unique which implies that the specific organizational context must be acknowledged [9]. The case indicates that implementation of a HIS is not automatically creating success just by following a list of important fulfilment measures or CSFs. On the contrary, if the process of referral management had not been changed prior to the HIS implementation, the system would not have fitted into this organization. Croll [8] shows that for a HIS implementation to be successful it is of utmost importance that the HIS is accepted by the clinical users. In our case the improved referral process and its coherence with HIS led to system acceptance among the user groups. From the case, we cannot say that common CSFs such as top management commitment, linkage to business, technical alignment, knowledgeable personnel, and user involvement [14] alone would have led to success, even though we find signs of these dimensions in the case. Instead, the success can be explained by individual key persons' deep organizational understanding of the situation and commitment to their assignment, persistence and strong beliefs to achieve change [3] and to achieve this also challenging the barriers of implementing HIS in professional and hierarchical organizations with strong norms [10]. This is in line with Ashurst et al.'s (2008) conclusion that effective benefits realization demands an on-going commitment. This combined with a growing demand for organizational control and patient focus as well as top management's thorough governance was very important factors for performing successful change management.

The claim that success factors are not delivering success independently of each other but have to be managed altogether [9] stands in contrast with the ambition to help organizations to succeed in their daily tasks by creating road maps for success. Such lists of CSF have been very much adopted and appreciated in practice, but have also been criticized [24], [29]. The goal of standardizing and determining successful behaviour is not aligned to the notion of situational uniqueness and contextual differences as pointed out by many scholars [5], [9], [12], [13], [17], [24], [32].

Projects' success might be realized long after the implementation project is ended [9] which implies that patience is an important feature in this kind of project. This also relates to Doherty et al.'s [9] last principle, meaning that success factors need to be applied to an organization's all systems, not only to one individual system, in order to be actionable. In the studied case process development was conducted, which challenged established and institutionalized hierarchies and powerful professional groups. Without being able to handle the hierarchical conflicts between professions or overcoming the change inertia in the studied organization, no set of CSFs would have solved the situation. One could argue that handling these challenges was part of this organization's unique signature [12] that made it successful. Understanding the uniqueness of each organizational unit is critical in order to succeed transferring this success to other care units in the future. What worked in this case does not necessary have to be the key to success in next case.

6   Conclusions

In this paper we have examined if and how well CSFs can explain a successful case of HIS implementation. CSFs have been criticized by many as neglecting the contextual circumstances, which we have discussed earlier in the paper. We adhere to these raised objections and have therefore applied Doherty et al.'s [9] key principles when structuring and analyzing findings from the case. At a first glance one might think that these key principles are yet another set of success factors. However, Doherty et al. [9] are aware of the mentioned problems with CSFs and have formulated their principles in a way that acknowledges contextual factors when evaluating benefit realization.

Our main conclusion is that even though our case shows signs of common CSFs, this alone cannot explain the success. The implemented HIS offered the appropriate functionality, but the organization would not comply voluntarily. The success in our case can instead be explained by the fact that contextual circumstances were handled in a beneficial way by a strongly committed and persistent organization developer who, in a way, created her own implementation plan as a skunk work and proved to be strong enough to contest the old professional hierarchies. This encourages us to argue that contextual factors are very critical to understand and acknowledge during HIS implementations. This is supported by Beeuwkes Buntin et al.'s [4] literature review of HIS benefits, where human aspects are critical to successful HIS implementation. A similar reasoning is made by Remus and Wiener [24] who call for further studies of CSFs from this wider perspective. We also believe that key factors in this case have been a history of local empowerment and organizational stability [2]. The lack of organizational change experience might, to a great extent, have caused employees to react negatively on change initiatives whatever the cause was.

Even though we have studied HIS implementation in this paper, we argue that our findings could be expanded to other IT implementation settings and sectors as well. Of course there are some characteristics that may distinguish the health sector from other sectors; such as strong professional roles, explicit hierarchies, specialized expertise, and certain laws and regulations, but we argue that the result to some extent is valid also when implementing other IT systems than HIS. However, since our main point in this paper is the importance of understanding contextual circumstances, it is important to acknowledge such uniqueness. The contextual circumstances might differ between sectors (otherwise they would not be contextual) and particular organizations and settings within them, but we argue that the context needs to be acknowledged in any IT implementation process. The fact that our explanations of success in the studied case were possible to map to Doherty et al.'s [9] key principles is another argument for the claim that our results could be useful also in other IT implementation situations outside the healthcare sector, and that analytical generalization potentially can be done.

This paper reports from a single case study. We have used the case to understand if and how well CSF can be used to explain success. In order to develop a complete picture we will study and compare further cases, preferably implementation, IT and organizational cases with a large variation.

Acknowledgements. This study has been financed by the Swedish Council for Working Life and Social Research. We are also grateful to Fredrik Söderström for his data collection effort.

References

1. Ashurst, C., Doherty, N.F., Peppard, J.: Improving the impact of IT development projects: the benefits realization capability model. European Journal of Information Systems 17(4), 352–370 (2008)
2. Axelsson, K., Melin, U., Söderström, F.: Analyzing best practice and critical success factors in a health information system case - are there any shortcuts to successful IT implementation? In: Tuunainen, V., Nandhakumar, J., Rossi, M., Soliman, W. (eds.) Proceedings of the 19th European Conference on Information Systems, Helsinki, Finland, pp. 2157–2168 (2011)
3. Beath, C.M.: Supporting the information technology champion. MIS Quarterly 15(3), 355–372 (1991)
4. Beeuwkes Buntin, M., Burke, M.F., Hoaglin, M.C., Bluemnthal, D.: The benefits of health information technology: a review of the recent literature shows predominantly positive results. Health Affairs 30(3), 464–471 (2011)
5. Berg, M.: Implementing information systems in health care organizations: myths and challenges. International Journal of Medical Informatics 64(2-3), 143–156 (2011)
6. Boynton, A.C., Zmud, R.W.: An assessment of critical success factors. Sloan Management Review 25(4), 17–27 (1984)
7. Chan, C.M.L., Pan, S.L.: User engagement in e-government systems implementation: a comparative case study of two Singaporean e-government initiatives. Journal of Strategic Information Systems 17(2), 124–139 (2008)

8. Croll, J.: Testing for usability is not enough: Why clinician acceptance of health information systems is also crucial for successful implementation. In: Takeda, H. (ed.) E-Health 2010. IFIP AICT, vol. 335, pp. 49–60. Springer, Heidelberg (2010)

9. Doherty, N.F., Ashurst, C., Peppard, J.: Factors affecting the successful realization of benefits from systems development projects: findings from three case studies. Journal of Information Technology 27(1), 1–16 (2012)

10. Fichman, R.G., Kohli, R., Krishan, R.: The role of information systems in healthcare: current research and future trendes. Information Systems Research 22(3), 419–428 (2011)

11. Gil-García, J.R., Pardo, T.A.: E-government success factors: mapping practical tools to theoretical foundations. Government Information Quarterly 22(2), 187–216 (2005)

12. Gratton, L., Ghoshal, S.: Beyond best practice. MIT Slone Management Review 46(3), 49–57 (2005)

13. Heeks, R.: Health information systems: failure, success and improvisation. International Journal of Medical Informatics 75(2), 125–137 (2006)

14. Ho, J., Pardo, T.A.: Toward the success of e-government initiatives: mapping known success factors to the design of practical tools. In: Proceedings of the 37th Hawaii International Conference on Systems Sciences, pp. 1–6. IEEE (2004)

15. Kearns, G.S., Sabherwal, R.: Strategic alignment between business and information technology: a knowledge-based view of behaviors, outcome, and consequences. Journal of Management Information Systems 23(3), 129–162 (2006)

16. Kuang, J., Lau, J., Nah, F.: Critical factors for successful implementation of enterprise systems. Business Process Management Journal 7(3), 285–296 (2001)

17. Lau, F., Price, M., Keshavjee, K.: From benefits evaluation to clinical adoption: making sense of health information system success in Canada. Healthcare Quarterly 14(1), 39–45 (2011)

18. Leidecker, J., Bruno, A.: Identifying and using critical success factors. Long Range Planning 17(1), 23–32 (1984)

19. Leimeister, J.M., Sidiras, P., Krcmar, H.: Success factors of virtual communities from the perspective of members and operators: an empirical study. In: Proceedings of the 37th Hawaii International Conference on System Sciences (HICSS), Hawaii, USA (2004)

20. Melin, U., Axelsson, K.: Implementing Healthcare Information Systems - Mirroring a Wide Spectrum of Images of an IT Project. Health Policy and Technology 3(1), 26–35 (2014)

21. Øvretveit, J., Scott, T., Rundall, T.G., Shortell, S.M., Brommels, M.: Improving quality through effective implementation of information technology in healthcare. International Journal for Quality in Health Care 19(5), 259–266 (2007)

22. Patton, M.Q.: Qualitative evaluation methods. Sage Publications, Beverly Hills (1980)

23. Reel, J.S.: Critical success factors in software projects. IEEE Software, 18–23 (May/June 1999)

24. Remus, U., Wiener, M.: A multi-method, holistic strategy for researching critical success factors in IT projects. Information Systems Journal 20(1), 25–52 (2010)

25. Rocheleau, B., Wu, L.: Public versus private information systems: do they differ in important ways? A review and empirical test. The American Review of Public Administration 32(4), 379–397 (2002)

26. Rockart, J.F.: Chief executives define their own data needs. Harvard Business Review 57(2), 81–93 (1979)

27. Rosacker, K.M., Olson, D.L.: Public sector information system critical success factors. Transforming Government: People, Process and Policy 2(1), 60–70 (2008)

28. Venkatesh, V., Xiaojun, Z., Sykes, T.A.: 'Doctors do too little technology': a longitudinal field study of an electronic healthcare system implementation. Information Systems Research 22(3), 523–546 (2011)
29. Wagner, E., Scott, S., Galliers, R.: The creation of 'best practice' software: myth, reality and ethics. Information and Organization 16(3), 251–275 (2006)
30. Walsham, G.: Doing interpretive research. European Journal of Information Systems 15(3), 320–330 (2006)
31. Ward, J., Daniel, E.: Benefits management – delivering value from IS and IT investments. John Wiley and Sons Ltd, Chichester (2006)
32. Yusof, M.M., Kuljis, J., Papazafeiropoulou, A., Stergioulas, L.K.: An evaluation framework for health information systems: human, organization and technology-fit factors (HOT-fit). International Journal of Medical Informatics 77(6), 386–398 (2008)

PA Meets IS Research: Analysing Failure of Intergovernmental Information Systems via IS Adoption and Success Models

Lies Van Cauter[1], Monique Snoeck[2], and Joep Crompvoets[1]

[1] KU Leuven, Public Governance Insitute, Leuven, Belgium
{Lies.VanCauter,Joep.Crompvoets}@soc.kuleuven.be
[2] KU Leuven, Research Centre for Management Informatics, Leuven, Belgium
Monique.Snoeck@kuleuven.be

Abstract. When comparing success rates of information systems in the public and private sector, governments generally lag behind. Information system failure received limited coverage in public administration: not much research examines whether private sector IS success or acceptance models can be applied in a public sector context. This paper aims to contribute to this research gap.

We investigate if two IS acceptance or success models can be applied to study the causes of failure of an e-government system. The first model is 'the Unified Theory of Acceptance and Use of Technology'; the second 'the Updated Information System Success Model'. Our results, based on an exploratory case study analysis, demonstrate that both models have value to analyse intergovernmental information system failure. The combination of IS lenses in a more comprehensive model might be a valuable future contribution to e-government studies.

Keywords: failure, IS acceptance/ success models, intergovernmental IS.

1   Introduction

During the last 15 years public organizations have shifted from a model emphasizing information protection to one of information sharing [33]. Intergovernmental information sharing has become a powerful strategy to improve governmental services and operations. As a result, the implementation of intergovernmental information systems (IS) has been attracting increasing amounts of resources and of research interest and is believed to represent one of the most significant IT implementation and organizational challenges for the next decade [20], [26]. Intergovernmental collaboration in IS knows however a long history of conflict, friction and failure [26] and specific guidance for implementing intergovernmental IS successfully is lacking [2].

Realizing the benefits of IS requires governments to understand and overcome causes of failure. In the context of this paper, we consider success and failure as the level to which system acceptance, usage and experienced benefits meet the

M. Janssen et al. (Eds.): EGOV 2014, LNCS 8653, pp. 72–83, 2014.

expectations (or not) that motivated the development or acquisition of the software. In the past there has been already quite some research on IS failure focusing on aspects such as utility, ease of use, acceptance and IS success in general. In this stream of literature, success and failure are the flip side of each other and it is assumed that by paying attention to success factors, failure will be avoided. In this line of reasoning, it is worthwhile to explore the causes of failure, since this information may be useful in averting future failures [7].

On the other hand, much of the existing literature focuses primarily on the private sector [28], [10]; little research identifies measures that determine intergovernmental IS failure. To investigate intergovernmental IS failure, two possible approaches can be considered. On the one hand, a bottom up, inductive approach, similar to e.g. in [17], can be followed to identify root causes of intergovernmental IS failure in different cases. These can be generalized to a specific theory for intergovernmental IS failure. On the other hand, we can follow a top-down, deductive approach to examine whether IS acceptance and success models mainly resulting from research in business information systems can be extended to examine intergovernmental IS failure [2], [27]. Several authors have already advocated that using private sector models in a public sector context might provide new insights on management of intergovernmental IS. First, when comparing the success rates of IS in the public and private sector, governments generally lag behind [12], which indicates that there is room for public sector to learn from the private sector. Second, despite differences between both sectors in terms of access, structure, accountability and mandatory relationships, there are enough similarities to successfully apply private sector models to investigate factors affecting the implementation of IS in the public sector [14]. Finally, public management and IS studies can be coupled, this coupling might strengthen both domains [7], [18]. In this paper, we investigate whether research on IS success factors can be leveraged for the domain of intergovernmental IS. Hence, the main research question is: *Can traditional IS acceptance and success models be applied to study the causes of failure of intergovernmental information systems?*

For reasons of space limitations, this paper is limited to the investigation of one IS acceptance and one IS success model. The remaining sections are organised as follows. Section 2 explains the selection of the theoretical models and briefly presents the Unified Theory of Acceptance and Use of Technology and the updated Information System Success model. Next, section 3 presents the failed public management case and the method for data collection. Section 4 examines if these models can be applied to study the causes of failure of the road sign database case. Discussion on this applicability and on future research can be found in section 5. We conclude in section 6.

2   Investigated Models

2.1   Selection of the Theoretical Models

In the search to measure IS success in the private sector, nearly as many measures as studies were developed [6]. IS theorists are still grappling with the question of which constructs best represent IS success and failure [6], [10]. Despite this multitude of studies and measures, the TAM, UTAUT and the DeLone & McLean IS success model surface as leading IS acceptance/success models [16].

Before 2003, the Technology Acceptance Model (TAM) was the most widely utilized theory to study IS/IT adoption within the IS discipline [7]. Different variants of the TAM were created, one being the Unified Theory of Acceptance and Use of Technology (UTAUT) [30]. Today, research on technology adoption shows that the UTAUT has the highest power in explaining behaviour intention and usage: the UTAUT explains 70% of acceptance while other models explain about 40% [31]. We therefore prefer the UTAUT above the TAM.

This paper therefore focuses on the UTAUT and the updated IS Success Model to study intergovernmental IS failure. Both models see success or failure as brought about by causally linked factors. Underlying is the assumption that IS success and failure can be identified by the presence or absence of these factors [14]. For UTAUT, the use of an IS presents an early sign of success [9]. Acceptance of an IS is seen as a possible precursor of success [21]. UTAUT has a personal user focus: it takes into account human factors such as individual expectations (on performance/efforts/ease of use), personal characteristics (age, gender, experience, voluntariness) and interaction of stakeholders (social influence). The updated IS success model, views success from a rationalist managerial perspective. Service quality, information quality and system quality are seen as key determinants of user satisfaction and (intention to) use [16]. In the next paragraphs both models are briefly discussed.

2.2   The Unified Theory of Acceptance and Use of Technology

Research in technology acceptance models culminates with UTAUT. It integrates eight models used in IT acceptance research. Venkatesh et al [30] distinguish four direct factors of user acceptance and usage behaviour: *Performance expectancy* is the degree to which an individual believes that using the system will help him to gain in job performance. Second, *effort expectancy* is the degree of ease associated with the use of the system. Third, *social influence* is the degree to which an individual perceives that important others believe he should use the new system. Finally, *facilitating conditions* are the degree to which an individual believes that an organizational and technical infrastructure exists to support the use of the system [32]. Facilitating conditions determine use. Social influence, performance and effort expectancy determine the intention to use a system. Behavioural intention in turn determines use [22].

The moderating factors are gender, age, experience and voluntariness of use. The UTAUT suggests the following: (1) gender and age moderate the effect of performance expectancy on behavioural intention; (2) gender, age and experience moderate the effect of effort expectancy on behavioural intention; (3) gender, age, experience and voluntariness moderate the effect of social influences on behaviour intention and (4) age and experience moderate the effect of facilitating conditions on behavioural intention [1].

The level of actual use of UTAUT is lower than the citation level may suggest [30]. Some criticise that after years of researching TAM, UTAUT brings us back to TAM's origins as it is not so different from the Theory of Planned Behavior [3].

2.3   The Updated Information System Success Model

In 1992 DeLone and McLean [5] introduced an alternative taxonomy to understand the dimensions of IS success. The taxonomy provided a scheme for classifying the multitude of IS success measures in the literature . Ten years after the publication of their first model and based on the evaluation of the contributions to it, DeLone and McLean (D&M) proposed an updated IS success model. Now, the majority of IS researchers has switched to the updated D&M success model published in 2003 [6]. A recent meta-study has shown that most of the updated D&M model's propositions explaining the success of an IS are actually supported [21].

A first dimension of the updated D&M model is *system quality* which measures the quality of information processing within the system in terms of ease of use and learning, system flexibility and reliability etc. *Information quality*, secondly, focuses on IS output and looks to desirable characteristics of system outputs such as relevance of information, meaningfulness, accuracy, completeness... A third dimension is *service quality*, the quality of system support that users get from the IT department such as responsiveness, accuracy or technical competence from staff... *Intention to use and use* fourthly measure the user attitude. Use is seen as a behaviour, the manner in which staff and customers use the capabilities of an IS e.g. amount and frequency of use, extent and purpose of use. *User Satisfaction*, a fifth dimension, describes the users level of satisfaction. *Net benefits* finally are the extent in which IS contributes to the success of the individuals that use the system e.g. improved decision making, productivity & efficiency [5], [6], [11], [21].

Political and managerial factors are underrepresented in this model, researchers must keep this in mind if they use it for the analysis of e-government systems [1].

3   Methodology

3.1   Research Methodology

Zikmund (1984) suggests that the degree of uncertainty about the research problem determines the research methodologies. As mentioned little research has examined whether IS acceptance/ success models can be used to study intergovernmental IS failure [27]. An exploratory case study investigates, mainly in a qualitative manner, distinct phenomena characterized by a lack of detailed preliminary research [24]. This form of case study often is applied to explore a relatively new field of scientific investigation [19].

The research under study is framed in behavioural science. This paradigm seeks to verify theories that explain / predict human or organizational behaviour surrounding the analysis, design, implementation, management and use of IS. *"Such theories ultimately inform researchers and practitioners of the interactions among people, technology and organizations that must be managed if an information system is to achieve its stated purpose"* [13]. By verifying if two theoretical models are applicable to study causes of intergovernmental IS failure we aim to inform if this is possible and on what might be causes of failure during the implementation of an IS.

Since we are investigating causes of failure, a *failed* case study will be taken as starting point. The analysis of the case study is performed in the following way. Both the UTAUT and the IS success model define a number of factors that determine IS success. We first collected data about the case by means of open ended interviews by telephone. The advantage of standardized open ended interviews is that these provide a richness of details, may give the researcher perspectives he did not consider before and reduce the risk that the respondent is lead in a certain direction. Telephone interviews may reduce interviewer bias because there is no face-to-face contact [1]. All interviews were transcribed. Subsequently, the texts of the interviews were matched against the factors of each model, in search for evidence of a positive or negative influence on ultimate IS success.

3.2   Selected Case Study

The road sign database was selected from an inventory of 100 intergovernmental IS in Flanders [29]. The case was selected because: (1) it exists since 2008 and added value of an IS only reveals itself after a number of years. (2) It was an innovating project with a cost of 20 million euro (which is a high amount for the Flemish government) and large innovating projects are likely to fail [12]. (3) Municipalities are asked to deliver data to the Flemish government voluntarily, getting municipalities there is in practice a hot topic and knotty problem. Scientifically little is known about the voluntary use of systems [9]. An explorative case study of the road sign database was conducted at the beginning of this research. In order to prevent being influenced by a theoretical lens, we explored the case by interviewing 130 municipalities with open questions. Legislation and policy documents were collected too.

The road sign database contains all road signs, their main characteristics and positions on Flemish roads. The opportunity to launch this was a huge traffic obstruction in Bruges. A bridge was hit by a truck as there was no road sign about the bridge's height. The Flemish government created the database and inventoried the road signs. It then asked its 308 municipalities and the Department of Mobility and Public Works for the Flemish roads to keep the database up-to-date but they do not.

3.3   Data Collection

In order to explore the reasons for not using the road sign database, we interviewed 23 pioneering users. 18 of them did not use the database. As we wondered if this low adoption rate counted for other municipalities, additionally 107 municipalities were questioned by telephone. In total 130 of the 308 Flemish municipalities were questioned in a systematic way. At Flemish level, we interviewed the project managers of the Flemish Agency for Roads and Traffic, the Flemish Department of Mobility and Public Works and the Agency for Geographical Information face-to-face.

During the telephone interviews municipalities were asked how frequent the database was used. If they did not (often) use it, we asked why and if they employed any alternatives. Non-users were asked if they desired to get (back) on board. Municipalities who used the system were questioned for what purpose and if they kept the database up-to-date. Table 1 summarizes the usage results.

Table 1. Road Sign Database: Frequency of use (N= 130)

Never used	Non use	Use once or few times/year	Monthly use
26	66	31	7

Four groups can be distinguished. A first consists of municipalities that never tried to use the database. Seven never started because they possess their own database. The other nineteen did not have the time or personnel to start with the database or categorize it as 'not useful'. The second group enrolled but currently does not use the database. This is the case for 66 of the 130 interviewed municipalities. The third group consists of 31 municipalities that use the database once or a few times a year and the fourth group of 7 municipalities utilizes it at least once a month.

We interviewed more than one third of the Flemish municipalities. Possibly, the results could be slightly different for the whole population. We believe that the chosen municipalities are representative in size and geographical distribution. The Department of Mobility and Public Works confirmed that our results correspond to the situation of other municipalities: they do not keep their data up-to-date. Neither does the Agency for Roads and Traffic. As a result of the low usage, the database got spoiled.

4   Results of the Case Study Analysis

4.1   The UTAUT and the Road Sign Database

UTAUT allows to study the causes of failure from a personal lens. Table 2 provides an overview of the results of the interviews for each factor of this model. Each factor is concluded with the identification of main causes of failure identified according to this perspective.

The analysis of the different factors suggest a negative influence on behaviour intention and use behaviour. The interviews indeed confirm that because of social influence, a low performance and effort expectancy 26 municipalities never started with the database. For others, behavioural intention dropped shortly after the launch of the database. Ultimately, a dropping behaviour intention combined with poor facilitating conditions made 66 municipalities stop using the database. The Flemish Agency for Roads and Traffic stopped updating the regional roads and created its own ' road database'. Only 7 of the 130 questioned municipalities use the database minimally once a month.

To which extent does a personal oriented lens give insight in the causes of failure? By analysing the interviews through the lens of the determinants of the UTAUT, we were able to detect six causes of failure of the road sign database. As we did not explicitly ask respondents about moderating determinants, we are not able to investigate the role of these factors.

Table 2. Analysis of the road sign database through the lens of UTAUT

Performance expectancy	Some municipalities hoped to save time by using the database, they soon got disillusioned. The database could not enhance their job performance. Cheap and quick alternatives made it less attractive. Promised applications on legislation were never built. → Performance expectancy scores badly because of a low time performance (C1), cheap and quick alternatives (C2) and a lack of purpose (C3)
Effort expectancy	Respondents who followed a traineeship remarked it was cancelled several times as the teacher could not enter the system. Municipalities often experienced log-in problems and the system crashed from time-to-time. The more users entered the system, the slower it functioned. → The poor effort expectancy can be linked with two causes of failure: low time performance (C1) and technological issues (C4).
Social influence	At a certain point the reputation of the database was so poor that municipalities who did not use database yet, heard the stories and decided not to use it. Other municipalities experienced problems and stopped. → A bad reputation (C5) troubled the database, the many flaws became a justification for abandonment.
Facilitating conditions	Municipal hard- or software investments were not needed as the database was a web-based application. The weak technical infrastructure did not facilitate civil servants during their task, the system was time intensive and data got lost because of crashes. →Analysis along this factor reveals poor end-user support (C6) and technological issues (C4).
Moderating determinants: Gender, age, experience, voluntariness	The use of the database is voluntary: the Flemish government just asked to keep it up-to-date. In our explorative research, gender, age and experience were rarely spontaneously mentioned by interviewees. Gender appeared to influence usage in one municipality: during a pregnancy leave the database was not used. Age seemed to play a role for three interviewees: they would soon retire and leave the start-up of the database to their replacing colleague. Experience was mentioned briefly by several respondents: *'for municipalities who use the database fulltime, inputting should go more easily'*. →Because the exploratory interviews only delivered a few remarks about moderating determinants, we can't make any further statements

4.2   The Information System Success Model and the Road Sign Database

The updated IS success model allows to study the causes of failure of the road sign database from a rational managerial lens.

Table 3 provides an overview of the results of the interviews for the factors of this model. Each factor is concluded with the identification of main causes of failure identified according to this perspective.

Table 3. Analysis of the road sign database through the lens of the updated IS success model

Information Quality	92 of the questioned municipalities do not use the database (any more). For 90 of these 92 the data is outdated and incomplete. Remarkably two municipalities who do not use it for their own decision making, keep it up-to-date once a year. On the other hand, one could expect that the 38 municipalities who use the database keep it up-to-date. Only 12 of 38 users do. There are no alternatives, if a municipality does not keep track of its road signs, no other party will. The overall information quality is low. → Rather than acting (only) as a factor for IS success, Information Quality turns out to be mainly a result of the lack of usage.
System Quality	Reliability of the system appears to be low as it crashes often. The system flexibility is limited, and the more users enter the system, the slower it functions. Respondents who do not use the system on a monthly basis claim they have to figure out how it works over and over again. The overall system quality is low. →Technical issues (C4) and low time performance (C1) cause a low system quality.
Service Quality	The Flemish government has a competent staff that supports the database. But municipalities find this staff difficult to reach when experiencing problems. A few municipalities who never started with the database remarked they asked to join a training course or receive a log in code but never received an answer. →Service quality appears to be low and can be attributed to a lack of technical end-user support (C6)
Intention to Use	Intention to use is determined by the three previous factors and by net benefits (see further). Yet some respondents remarked that they intended to use the database until they heard how bad functioning it was. The Flemish government does not have legal or financial resources to encourage the updating of the database. Easy alternatives for gathering road sign information decreased the benefits of maintaining the road sign database. → A lack of purpose (C3), cheap and quick alternatives (C2) and a bad reputation (C5) caused a decrease in intention to use.
Use	Less than 1/3 of the questioned municipalities uses the system. For those who do, the frequency of use is partly dependent on the number of new road signs.
User Satisfaction	User satisfaction is determined by the three previous factors and by net benefits (see further). Respondents who still use the database find it supportive for their mobility plans, to localise road signs or to advice the municipal council, this indicates the presence of some benefit for users. Yet the interviews also indicate that low system quality (slow time performance) caused many users to abandon the ship. →Most municipalities who once used the system, believe user satisfaction to be low because of a slow time performance (C1).

Analysis of the factors suggests a negative influence on net benefits. The interviews confirm that the majority of the municipalities does not experience the IS as a tool that makes their work more efficient. Time investments appear to outweigh net benefits. A lack of net benefits appears to be mainly caused by a lack of purpose (C3), a bad reputation (C5) and the option for cheap and quick alternatives (C2).

By filling in the factors of the D&M IS success model, six main causes of failure could be detected. This model not only gives insight in six causes, it also seems to point out the consequences of this failure: a poor information quality and low actual use. Unlike UTAUT it pays attention to information quality. The road sign database seems to be subjected to an implosion effect: municipalities left the database, because of that information quality drops, this makes the database even less used which in turn further deteriorates information quality.

5   Discussion

This paper explored two IS acceptance/ success models to study a failed intergovernmental IS. Two IS theoretical lenses were studied via an exploratory case study analysis. In total the models exposed six main causes of failure for the database:

1. Slow time performance (C1) is a reason for not using the database. Inputting or deducting data soon appeared to be time-consuming. About 1/3 of the questioned municipalities claim they do not desire to invest in a slow functioning system.
2. Secondly, many cheap and quick alternatives (C2) make the slow bad functioning database less attractive. Popular alternatives to detect a road sign are google street view, looking on the streets, searching its own register or asking the local police.
3. A third cause is a lack of purpose (C3). An overview of road signs is interesting for the Flemish government. Municipalities seem only interested in signs on their territory. Most do not use the database for maintenance purposes. Little municipalities do not feel the need to map their signs electronically. As a respondent stated: *"We are four square kilometres large, I know every road sign by heart"*. Others have an own more adapted register. The Flemish government asked to re-enter their data, it was not possible to transfer. This call did not seem very appealing.
4. A fourth cause of failure (C4) is related to technological issues. The database was plagued by severe log in troubles and frequent system crashes.
5. Fifthly, a bad reputation (C5) negatively influenced the intention to use of municipalities who considered the database.
6. A final cause of failure is lack of end user support (C6). Local governments with technological problems, could not reach the Flemish government.

In most impaired projects failure is due to several different factors which are often interrelated [7]. Here too, we see that failure is not only caused by technical failure [12], also non-technical factors and their interplay need to be taken into account [7], [24]. Using multi-measures is valuable to catch the multifaceted nature of failure [22]. Via the personal theoretical lens of UTAUT, six causes of failure could be detected. The same counts for the rational managerial lens, the updated IS success model.

Remarkably these different lenses detect the same causes of failure: *Time perform-ance* (C1) was detected in 'performance and effort expectancy' (UTAUT) and in 'sys-tem quality and user satisfaction' (IS success model). *Cheap and easy alternatives* (C2) as a cause of failure was uncovered by both models via 'performance expec-tancy' (UTAUT) and 'intention to use' (IS success model). The overall cause, *lack of purpose* (C3) was detected via 'performance expectancy' (UTAUT) and 'intention to use' (IS success model). *Elements of technical issues* (C4) could be found via 'effort expectancy' and 'facilitating conditions' for UTAUT and via 'system quality' for the IS success model. *A bad reputation* was pictured by social influence (UTAUT) and intention to use (IS success model). *The lack of end user support* (C6) became clear via 'facilitating conditions'(UTAUT) and 'service quality' (IS success model).

This case study suggests that the user perspective in the UTAUT and the rational managerial lens of the updated D&M model are not competing views concerning intergovernmental IS failure. Al Khatib [1] also finds that these models can serve as antecedents. An integration can help build a conceptual bridge [1], [33]. Combining both approaches might provide a richer understanding of failed intergovernmental IS. The results of the case study indicate that although the applied theoretical models are called IS 'acceptance' or 'success' models, they can be used to study intergovernmen-tal IS 'failure'. Previously we mentioned that both models see success or failure as brought about by causally linked determinants. Underlying is the assumption that IS success and failure can be identified by the presence or absence of certain determi-nants [14]. The six causes of failure point out that the road sign database scores low on the factors of the studied IS acceptance/success models:

- For UTAUT, the combination of a bad reputation, a poor performance expec-tancy and effort expectancy made the behavioural intention to use the road sign database drop. Facilitating conditions and behavioural intention determine use. The absence of these conditions because of poor end-user support and technical problems and a dropping behavioural intention made 67 users abandon the ship. We can speak of failed case as the IS was not able to meet the expectations of many stakeholders [7] and as the many flaws became a justification for aban-donment.

- By following the causal logic of the updated IS success model we also come to a diagnosis of failure. The road sign database scores low on service quality and system quality. These negatively influence user satisfaction and (intention to) use. Combine this with a bad reputation and slow time performance and users drop out, they chose alternatives to collect and store their road sign data. Which in turn creates a lack of purpose of the road sign database. The absence of net benefits will affect user satisfaction and intention to use [3].

6   Conclusion and Future Research

Electronic intergovernmental information sharing is the new goal in the public sector. The implementation thereof is an IT and organisational challenge for the next decade. There is a need to examine whether traditional IS acceptance and success models can be applied to intergovernmental IS and to study their causes of failure. In this paper we contributed to this research gap.

The applicability of two IS acceptance/ success models, the UTAUT of Venkatesh et al (2003) and the updated IS success model of Delone and Mc Lean (2003), was tested via an explorative case study of the failed road sign database project. Both lenses have value to detect causes of failure, hence their completeness in analysing the case is not proven. Part of the intellectual challenge of studying intergovernmental electronic collaboration is blending multiple theoretical and research perspectives to obtain a complete picture [23]. The combination of different IS lenses in a more comprehensive model might be a valuable future contribution to e-government studies.

Exploratory research is broad in focus and rarely provides definite answers to specific research issues [19]. The findings are therefore limited and cannot be generalized. Hence, this study needs to be replicated in the future to see if testing IS acceptance/success models on other failed intergovernmental IS yields the same results.

In future research we will also consider the use of more theory fitting, less open questions. As such, variables like the moderating determinants of the UTAUT can be questioned more explicitly. Another limitation of the study is that other lenses on failure exists such as an IS constructivist narrative and socio material approach of failure. We could test them in an e-government context [14].

References

1. Abdelsalam, H., Reddick, C.G., El Kadi, H.A.: Success and Failure of Local E-Government Projects: Lessons Learned from Egypt. In: Aikins, S.K. (ed.) Managing E-Government Projects. Concepts, Issues and Best Practices, pp. 242–261 (2012)
2. Al Khatib, H.: E-government systems success and user acceptance in developing countries: The role of perceived support quality. Brunel Business School Thesis, 1–10 (2013)
3. Benbasat, I., Barki, H.: Quo vadis, TAM? Journal of Association for Information Systems 8(3), 211–218 (2007)
4. DeLone, W.H., McLean, E.R.: The D&M Model of Information Systems Success: A Ten-Year Update. Journal of Management Information Systems 19(4), 9–30 (2003)
5. DeLone, W.H., McLean, E.R.: Information Systems Success: The Quest for the Dependent Variable. Information Systems Research 3(1), 60–95 (1992)
6. Dörr, S., Watlher, S., Eymann, T.: Information Systems Success - A Quantitative Literature Review and Comparison. In: 11th International Conference on Wirtschaftsinformatik, Leipzich, pp. 1813–1827 (2013)
7. Dwivedi, Y.K., Henriksen, H.Z., Wastell, D., De', R. (eds.): TDIT 2013. IFIP Advances in Information and Communication Technology, vol. 402. Springer, Heidelberg (2013)
8. Dwivedi, Y.K., Williams, M.D.: Demographic Influence on UK Citizens' E-Government Adoption. Electronic Government, An International Journal 5(3), 261–274 (2008)
9. Elbanna, A., Linderoth, H.C.J.: Tracing Success in the Voluntary Use of Open Technology in Organisational Setting. In: Dwivedi, Y.K., Henriksen, H.Z., Wastell, D., De', R. (eds.) TDIT 2013. IFIP AICT, vol. 402, pp. 89–104. Springer, Heidelberg (2013)
10. Floropoulos, J., Spathis, C., Halvatzis, D., Tsipouridou, M.: Measuring the success of the Greek Taxation Information System. International Journal of Information Management 30, 47–56 (2010)
11. Gable, G.G., Sedera, D., Chan, T.: Re-conceptualizing IS Success: The IS-Impact Measurement Model. Journal of the Association for Information Systems 9(7), 377–408 (2008)
12. Goldfinch, S.: Pessimism, Computer Failure and Information Systems Development in the Public Sector. PAR 67(5), 917–929 (2007)
13. Hevner, A.R.: Design Science in Information Systems Research. Management of Information Systems Quarterly 28(1), 75–105 (2004)

14. Kautz, K., Cecez-Kecmanovic, D.: Sociomateriality and Information Systems Success and Failure. In: Dwivedi, Y.K., Henriksen, H.Z., Wastell, D., De', R. (eds.) TDIT 2013. IFIP AICT, vol. 402, pp. 1–20. Springer, Heidelberg (2013)
15. Lai, C.S.K., Pires, G.: Testing of a Model Evaluating e-Gov Portal Acceptance and Satisfaction. The Electronic Journal Information Systems Evaluation 13(1), 35–46 (2010)
16. Landeweerd, M., Spil, T., Klein, R.: The Success of Google Search, the Failure of Google Health and the Future of Google Plus. In: Dwivedi, Y.K., Henriksen, H.Z., Wastell, D., De', R. (eds.) TDIT 2013. IFIP AICT, vol. 402, pp. 221–239. Springer, Heidelberg (2013)
17. Lehtinen, T.A.O., Mäntylä, M.V., Vanhanen, J., Itkonen, J., Lassenius, C.: Perceived causes of software project failures – An analysis of their relationships. Information and Software Technology 56(6), 623–643 (2014)
18. Lips, M., Bekkers, V., Zuurmond, A. (eds.): ICT en openbaar bestuur; Implicaties en uitdagingen van technologische toepassingen voor de overheid, pp. 1–749. Uitgeverij Lemma, Utrecht (2005)
19. Mills, A.J., Durepos, G., Wiebe, E.: Encyclopedia of case study research. Sage Publications (2010)
20. Pardo, T.A., Gil-García, J.R., Burke, G.B.: Information Sharing and Public Health: A Case-based Look at the ICT Expectations-Reality Gap. In: Meijer, A., et al. (eds.) ICTs, Citizens and Governance: After the Hype!, pp. 180–197. IOS Press, Amsterdam (2009)
21. Petter, S., DeLone, W., Mclean, E.: Measuring Information Systems Success: Models, Dimensions, Measures and Interrelationships. European Journal of Information Systems 17(3), 236–264 (2008)
22. Rana, N.P., Williams, M.D., Dwivedi, Y.K., Williams, J.: Theories and theoretical models for examining adoption of e-government services. E-Service Journal, 26–56 (2012)
23. Rigg, C., O'Mahony, N.: Frustrations in collaborative working: Insights from institutional theory. Public Management Review 15(1) (2013)
24. Sekaran, U., Bougie, R.: Research Methods for Business: A Skill Building Approach. John Wiley & Sons, UK (2010)
25. Scholl, H.J., Kubicek, H., Cimander, R., Klischewski, R.: Process integration, information sharing, and system interoperation in government: A comparative case analysis. Government Information Quarterly 29(3), 313–323 (2012)
26. Scholl, H.J., Klischewski, R.: E-Government Integration and Interoperability: Framing the Research Agenda. International Journal of Public Administration 30, 899–920 (2007)
27. Scott, M., DeLone, W., Golden, W.: Understanding net benefits: a citizen based perspective on e-government. In: 30th ICIS Conference, Phoenix, pp. 1–11 (2009)
28. Sørum, H., Medaglia, R., Normann Andersen, K., Scott, M., DeLone, W.H.: Perceptions of Information System Success in the Public Sector: Webmasters at the Steering Wheel? Transforming Government People, Process and Policy 6(3), 239–257 (2012)
29. Van Cauter, L., Snoeck, M., Crompvoets, J.: Flemish intergovernmental data collections: an inventory. Technical report. SBOV Leuven. 1-127 (2013)
30. Venkatesh, V., Morris, M.G., Davis, G.B., Davis, F.D.: User acceptance of information technology: towards a unified view. MIS Quarterly 27(3), 425–478 (2003)
31. Venkatesh, V., Thong, J.Y.L., Xu, X.: Consumer Acceptance and Use of Information Technology: Extending the Unified Theory of Acceptance and Use of Technology. MIS Quarterly 36(1), 157–178 (2012)
32. Williams, M.D., Rana, N.P., Dwivedi, Y.K.: A Bibliometric Analysis of Articles Citing the Unified Theory of Acceptance and Use of Technology. In: Dwivedi, Y.K., et al. (eds.) Information Systems Theory, pp. 37–58. Springer (2012)
33. Wixom, B.H., Todd, P.A.: A Theoretical Integration of User Satisfaction and Technology Acceptance. Information Systems Research 16(1), 85–102 (2005)

Interconnecting Governments, Businesses and Citizens – A Comparison of Two Digital Infrastructures

Bram Klievink, Anneke Zuiderwijk, and Marijn Janssen

Delft University of Technology, Delft, The Netherlands
{A.J.Klievink,A.M.G.Zuiderwijk-vanEijk,
M.F.W.H.A.Janssen}@tudelft.nl

Abstract. Public and private organizations in various areas are setting up digital Information Infrastructures (IIs) for interconnecting government, businesses and citizens. IIs can create value by sharing and integrating data of multiple actors. This can be the basis for value added services and especially collaborations of public and private partners can make IIs thrive. Easier access to integrated services and products (jointly) offered by government and businesses may stimulate transparency and innovations. IIs are under development in many domains, including for open data and international trade. However, there are notable differences in the design, characteristics and implementation of the IIs. The objective of this paper is to compare two diverse IIs in order to obtain a better understanding of common and differing elements in the IIs and their impact. Among the differences are the roles of government, businesses and users, in driving, developing and exploitation of the IIs.

Keywords: public-private networks, digital infrastructure, information infrastructure, platforms, information exchange, broker, e-government.

1 Introduction

Governments around the world are in the stage of setting-up digital information infrastructures (IIs) to enhance the fulfillment of their public tasks and enhance collaboration with businesses and citizens. Actors have a diverse set of associated components or services and IIs interconnect them and support connecting a variety of users and providers to each other. These digital IIs may interconnect governments with businesses and citizens to support collaboration between them.

Collaborating in digital infrastructures alters the relationship between government, businesses and the public. For government this is a recent phenomenon added to traditional information sharing approaches. Budget cuts, increased interdependence among a multitude of actors in networks and with blurring boundaries between governments, businesses and the public have led scholars to emphasize that governments need to collaborate with the private sector and other actors to organize public action [1-6]. This has resulted in a plea for governments to change the way they collaborate. The solution here is concerted action by a variety of actors by leveraging existing ICTs and re-use of the original information that already exists somewhere. This goes

M. Janssen et al. (Eds.): EGOV 2014, LNCS 8653, pp. 84–95, 2014.

beyond just connecting the IT and information systems of actors to each other and includes socio as well as technical aspects of great heterogeneity [7, 8].

Digital information infrastructures are interconnected system collectives [9], through which information existing within organizations can be used and shared, also across organizational boundaries [8, 10]. Although these infrastructures often have (in some form) already been available for decades, this often concerns 'closed' systems that are used by a limited number of users and governed by a single actor. Inspired by web-based social media and business platforms, recently the focus is on opening up systems and seeking value in using them for connecting organizations and people.

Information infrastructures are used to describe shared, heterogeneous systems that are continuously evolving as actors generate new functionalities based on the information infrastructures, which are in turn also shared [8]. Information infrastructures can be used by a wide variety of actors, with both usages, roles and types of actors evolving over time [11]. Consequently, there is not a single owner or controller of digital IIs and they should be flexible enough to include new services and functionality to adapt to the changing customer needs.

Since recently, digital IIs are also being developed for their potential to support the re-use of data and functionality of private sector infrastructures by government and for sharing and integrating data of the actors involved in the II [12, 13]. This could result in easier access to integrated public and private services and products for citizens and increased transparency and innovations in both the public and private sector.

Various types of IIs can be identified, including open data IIs and IIs for logistics and trade. In these types, the type of actors that play a role, the functionalities and the institutional and technical designs all vary. This raises the question in which respect they are different and if and how they can learn from each other.

These differences may indicate that these digital IIs can be used for public action in different ways, and this could provide opportunities for learning from each other. Comparing digital IIs on various aspects is useful in order to obtain a better understanding of the common and differing elements in the IIs and to identify the factors that affect the variation in IIs and which factors influence their impact. This understanding could contribute to the development of new IIs and the improvement of existing IIs. The objective of this paper is to develop a framework for comparing IIs and to use the framework for comparing two digital information infrastructures.

This paper is organized as follows. In the following section we describe our approach. Subsequently, we assess relevant literature as a first step for developing a framework. We then compare two digital information infrastructures and in the process provide further detailing of the framework. One II concerns a business infrastructure also supporting government tasks, the other is a government infrastructure focused on the general public. We end with conclusions and a future research agenda.

2   Research Approach

This research contributes to the existing literature and digital government practice offering first steps towards developing a framework for comparing IIs, based on literature a comparison of two digital information infrastructures. In this section we describe the research approach for attaining this objective. The main components of our approach are:

1. A literature review for identifying II characteristics. There we describe various articles to identify aspects that play a role in government use of digital information infrastructures. We describe literature related to infrastructures, information infrastructures, digital infrastructures, boundaries between the public and the private sector, and network effects.
2. A case comparison. As the objective is enhancing our understanding of digital information infrastructures in the context of interconnecting government, businesses and citizens, a qualitative, case study-based approach was used [14]. A qualitative approach was employed to get an in-depth understanding of the cases. Theoretical sampling was used to select the cases, which is appropriate since we aim to explore a relatively new field and stimulate the extension of emergent theory and provide examples [15]. To sample the cases, a list of criteria for case characteristics was developed:

   • The cases employ established digital information infrastructures;
   • The cases represent various levels of openness and maturity;
   • The cases represent digital IIs on various geographical levels;
   • Case study information should be available and accessible.

We opted for comparing platforms with varying degrees of openness, maturity and geographical coverage, as much can be learned from a comparison of these contexts. A multiple-case design is used, since this is preferred over single-case designs, as multiple cases provide more compelling evidence [16]. Furthermore, the use of multiple cases from different contexts could expand the external generalizability of the research findings compared to a single case study. Based on the criteria, the following two cases were selected:

• European open government data II; focussed on connecting and engaging data publishers (governments) and users of open data (businesses and citizens). The infrastructure is open for both providers and users. It connects to services and functionalities provided by others and enables new actors to connect to it. The development started in 2011, and the first phase is currently being finalized. The geographical coverage is worldwide and is currently available in nine languages (including English, Chinese, German, French and Bahasa Indonesia).
• Global trade data II; focuses on exchanging trade data amongst business actors. The infrastructure can be used to gather data for government (needed for performing key government functions), but government cannot provide the infrastructure functionality directly. This is a business II, in which the degree of openness depends on the role of each actor. The development also started in 2011, and the II is continuously being refined and expanded. It has global coverage.

By exploring different types of cases, we were able to compare them and identify common and different aspects. The two cases were investigated by using a variety of research methods, including interviews, user group discussions, observations in project meetings, reading reports and investigating publicly available documents and websites. A data collection protocol covered the purpose, the multi-sided user base, the functionality and services, decision-making, and the role of government. Table 1 displays the sources of data for the two cases.

Table 1. Overview of the information sources that were used in the case studies in this research

Methods used	Case 1: Open data II	Case 2: Logistics data II
One-to-one interviews	1	11
User group discussions	5	9
Project meetings	7	15
Reports and documents	19	35
Websites	2	2

3   Towards a Framework for Comparing Digital Information Infrastructures

This section provides background information derived from investigating the literature. There is not much literature in which digital IIs are related to their roles in the interconnections between government, citizens and businesses. We therefore identify characteristics of IIs that are core to the concept and relevant to this domain. A key characteristic of infrastructures is that "they are used by many different users, with the usage evolving over time, as may the type of users" [11]. Digital infrastructures can be viewed as socio-technological systems that emerge and evolve through the interplay of technology, users, providers, and policy-makers [11]. In the context of this research, digital infrastructures can also be viewed as (part of) IIs. From a broad perspective an II includes technological and human components, networks, systems and processes that contribute to the functioning of a specific information system [17]. Hanseth and Lyytinen [7] define an II as "a shared, open (and unbounded), heterogeneous and evolving socio-technical system (which we call installed base) consisting of a set of IT capabilities and their user, operations and design communities" (p. 4). Following this definition, IIs comprise both the IT and (inter-)organizational structures (e.g. networks). Furthermore, IIs typically also comprise the users of the infrastructure, network operators, and other actors and components. These technological and social structures are the basis for facilities and services, which in turn can be used by actors, society and economies for key functions [8]. IIs offer a potential for transformation of the way actors interact and organize (economic) activity. Although often used to describe the evolving nature of technology from a business or common perspective, IIs also impact and even reshape the organizations and their services in the public sector [11]. Especially the large amounts of data that are accessible through them offer tremendous potential for innovation in the public and private sector. Examples of IIs are the internet and wireless service infrastructures, which have shown considerable benefits for individuals, businesses and society [7].

With regard to the interconnection and networks of governments, businesses and citizens, the literature shows that many operations of government transcend the boundaries between the public and the private sector [e.g. 18]. As governments cannot themselves realize all public action, they will have to organize public action instead. The main challenge for this is that the private sector business models should be aligned with the action and values that have to be created by government organizations [19]. As value is not created by a single actor in the network but by coordinating the organisations in the public-private network, public value creation is not exclusively the domain of the government [20]. Since business focus on making money and profitability is essential for their long-term survival, public values like equal access might clash with private sector values like competition and efficiency [21]. Only at relatively high costs access can be given to all, which reduces the profitability. Private sector actors might therefore not be interested in providing equal access to all service consumers. In connecting to other parties in platforms, a balance should be struck between enabling businesses to find a business model, and government's values.

Therefore, responsibilities for the development, operations and maintenance of the II should be defined carefully. Development of infrastructures and governance are intertwined. Managing the interdependencies between parts of the infrastructure is crucial for ensuring stable operations. Furthermore, since various actors are involved in the development, maintenance and governance of digital IIs, network effects are crucial to make an infrastructure work. Network effects or network externalities refer to the dependence of the value of a good or service on the number of other people who use it [22]. Key in IIs is that they are shared; various actors can extend the infrastructure and integrate it with their own operations and thereby facilitate II emergence [13]. Through the II, actors can connect to systems of other actors in the network, and these systems become part of the infrastructure as well. As this happens over multiple tiers, this adds to the complexity. An important characteristic of IIs is the installed base; this is both an additional factor complicating the development of IIs (as the installed base includes a variety of (legacy) systems), and is necessary for the II to add value, as the benefit of connecting to an II becomes bigger the larger the installed base is. This concerns users, developers, and providers of data and services. The characteristics following from the foregoing are summarized in Table 2.

Table 2. Elements for a framework for the comparison of digital information infrastructures

Characteristic of (digital) (information) infrastructures	Source
Emerge and evolve through the interplay of technology, users, providers, and policy-makers	[11, 13]
Used by many different users	[8, 11]
Usage evolving over time	[8, 11]
Type of users evolving over time	[11]
Socio-technological systems	[7, 11]
Networks, systems and processes that contribute to the functioning of a specific information system	[17, 23]
Installed base and critical mass, including (strategies) for expansion and cultivation	[7, 23, 24]
Facilities and services based on II, that actors use to function	[8, 13]
Interactions between public and private sector	[25]
Decision and governance structures	[23, 25]

4 Framework and Findings from the Case Study Comparison

The II in the first case has been developed approximately two years ago and is focused on connecting and engaging data publishers and users of open government data. The II is used to make government data mainly from the social sciences and humanities domain available to citizens, businesses and other stakeholders in Europe to contribute to the realisation of open data advantages, such as increased transparency [26, 27], strengthened citizen engagement [28] and improved policy and decision making [26, 27]. The II interconnects governments, businesses and citizens by integrating data derived from many European open government data portals with services and functionalities developed by businesses to analyse, curate and visualise these data and the use of these data and services by citizens. The II is open in the sense that any organization, business or person can use the II and contribute to it by adding datasets and applications that are not available in the II yet or by connecting extended (e.g. cleansed) datasets and the results of data use to the original dataset. It is available worldwide, and is localized in (currently) nine languages, including many of the world's biggest languages. This greatly enhances the usability for citizens all over the world. The open data II can be found via http://www.engagedata.eu/. More information about the project in which this II was created is available at http://www.engage-project.eu/.

The second case concerns a private information infrastructure for exchanging global trade and logistics data amongst business actors for government supervision and control purposes. In the domain of global supply chains, innovations are currently undertaken to enhance data sharing and the timely availability of accurate data in global trade networks. This concerns business information infrastructures, but given the strong role of regulation and compliance (e.g. tax, security) this also requires intensive information exchange with, among others, customs authorities. The infrastructure is designed for enhancing information sharing between business actors involved in global trade, but can also be used to combine data for government purposes and thereby support compliance. This is a business platform, in which the degree of openness depends on the role of each actor. The government is one of the stakeholders, but cannot steer or provide the II nor its functionality directly. This II is not directly publicly accessible. More information about the project in which this II was created is available at http://www.cassandra-project.eu/.

Table 3 provides an overview of the main results, in the form of an application of the characteristics mentioned in Table 2. Table 3 includes the theoretical characteristics of the framework in direct application to the cases, and is the basis for comparison. Some characteristics also follow from the cases and the comparison, thereby further developing the comparison framework. Given the nature of IIs as a socio-technical concept, both technical and non-technical elements are part of the comparison. The table provides background to the qualitative comparison of the two information infrastructures, which follows after the table.

Table 3. Comparing the two cases of digital information infrastructures

II characteristics	Case 1: Open data II	Case 2: Logistics data II
Actors involved in the design	9 initiating project partners (university and research, and businesses) from various European countries	Consortium of 26 partners (government, universities, IT providers and logistics providers, from various European countries
Actors involved in the use	Open government data suppliers and users	Business involved in trade or logistics, IT solution providers, government inspection agencies
Number of actors involved in the use	1000+	Actors from seven global trade flows (each spanning two continents) involved
Type of users and usage evolving over time	Yes, as the II and its services change, the type of users and usage also changes	Yes, starts with including data sources, systems and functionality of core group of users (traders and customs), expanding over time (other businesses and government agencies)
Interactions between public and private sector	Yes, the II provides tools for the private and public sector to interact (e.g. requests for data provision; discussing about what can be learned from data use)	Yes, government agencies re-use business data from the II for assessments of trade lanes. Businesses use added value functionality for compliance purposes
Openness and costs	Free to use. Open for anyone to publish and use raw or processed open government data	Distributed architecture with interface based on global open standard; can be implemented directly or via IT solution with added services
Strategies for creating critical mass and for attracting and connecting users	Social media (Twitter, LinkedIn, Facebook), workshops, websites, blogs, video, hackathons, education and tutorials, newsletters, networks of project partners, presentations, brochures	Individual exploitation plans for all partners, including value propositions by IT solution providers ('hubs' in the II). Active dissemination through video, newsletters, presentations, brochures and demo's.

Actor involvement and interaction

Table 3. (*continued*)

	Role of software developers	*Extending functionalities*	*Large: opening up diverse actor communities and making dispersed systems accessible via the II; building of value-added functionality*
Design and services	Socio-technical components, systems, processes and networks	Technical components and systems (e.g. forums, Wiki's and data quality rating systems) enable social interaction between users	Part of control structures and procedures of businesses; part of key government processes (e.g. pre-arrival risk assessment, import, export)
	Services provided	Diversity of services for open data publishing (e.g. publishing original and extended datasets and linking these datasets to each other) and use (e.g. visualisation, contextual metadata, analysis, discussion)	Data capture and exchange services. Diverse services for opening up legacy systems. Data quality assessment and improvement (e.g. meta-data). Compliance services. Supply chain control services.
	Integration with other platforms and systems	Yes, services can be developed by various parties, possible to connect to other open data repositories and other platforms with data use services (e.g. visualisation and infographic applications)	Yes, II exists by integration in (existing) multiple platforms offered by the IT solution. Also integration in business and government systems is possible and has been demonstrated
Management and governance	Decision structures	User-driven development	Stakeholder representation for standard selection; IT solution providers comply to standard; businesses adopt compatible IT solution
	Governance structure	(Semi-)Public-private governance by founding organizations and governance by users of the II, both aiming at shared functionality, data requirements and data and service exchange.	Public-private governance for shared functionality, data requirements and exchange.

In the first case, the II is operated by a semi-public organization, while in the second case the II is operated by a variety of business actors, each controlling a part of the II, joined-up by using open standard based interfaces. In both cases, the information infrastructure is designed in collaboration with various other (semi-) public and private organizations. Both digital infrastructures make use of data and information provided by government agencies. Moreover, in both cases governments do not only provide data and information, but they can also be users of the digital information infrastructure. Yet, they are not involved in its development. The functionalities provided by the infrastructure are not key government functions and this enables innovative use of public data, without governments having to do it themselves. The government, however, has an interest to steer the business development in a way that leads to a solution that is also able to serve the public function (invisible hand).

Not only government agencies can use the IIs. Both IIs have functionalities that are shared between and can be used by both (semi-) public and private parties. In the first case these functionalities can also be used by citizens. For instance, there are functionalities to discuss what can be learned from the use of open government data. Governments, private organizations and citizens can all use this one functionality in different ways. Governments can use it to adapt their data publishing strategies and policies, while companies can use it to find out how one can innovate with these open data, and citizens can use it to make more informed decisions in everyday life. The second case also has functionalities that can be used by both public and private parties, but citizens cannot directly use the functionalities of this II.

Salient differences are also attributed to the governance. A significant difference between the two cases is that the digital II in the first case is user-centric, whereas the second case is driven by IT solution providers and logistics service providers. Those parties need to make value propositions to other parties involved in global trade (buyers, sellers, inspection agencies) to have them join as well, which is vital as they are important providers of data and users of services. This is necessary to ensure a critical mass and make it interesting for government agencies to gather information from the II. In turn, the fact that governments can also use it, is relevant for businesses in their decision to adopt it, as this opportunity supports compliance and is capable of reducing the administrative burden for the business community. The II in the first case cannot function without contributions of its users, since its value depends on social interaction between and collaboration of users. For example, if users would not share data, services and what can be learned from these with each other, the II becomes less valuable to other users. For this infrastructure it is very important to create strategies for obtaining a critical mass and for attracting and connecting users. While the European Commission currently funds the infrastructure, finding a self-sustainable model for the infrastructure is challenging, since it is not desirable to sell open government data. One of the core principles of open government data is that they should be available for free [e.g., 29, 30, 31]. A potential solution for this could offer business models in which users do not pay for the data, but for the use of data services, such as data curation and analysis.

Finally, a key difference can be found in the actors involved in the design of the infrastructure. The first case involved nine project partners who designed the II based on requirements that were identified in the literature, interviews a survey and workshops. Three private organizations were involved, but the design of the II was not based on the way that they already used open data in practice or on the way that they wanted to use open data in the future. The private organizations were mainly involved in the II design to explore the open data field rather than to deliver an II that they aimed to use themselves. In contrast, the second case of 26 partners employed a 'Living Lab' methodology in which existing trade lanes of the project partners were used to implement, test and refine the development of the infrastructure [32]. In this way, for each trade lane, a host of business partners got involved that were not part of the project consortium, but play a key role in providing the data required, and in using the functionality based on it. In this case, the involved private organizations were also interested in the use of the II themselves.

5   Conclusions and Discussion

In this explorative study, we have compared various characteristics of IIs that are used to interconnect government organizations, businesses and citizens. As a next step in our research we will compare more IIs, selected based on varying characteristics on the key dimensions we identified in this study (both the theoretical characteristics and those found in the case comparison). In future research, we will further refine the key characteristics of digital infrastructures we found in this study to come to a definitive framework and testable propositions, which we will use in a comparison of more IIs.

Among the key characteristics we found in this study are that governments can 'connect' to these infrastructures and steer those parts that need to be steered (e.g. with incentives or via regulations) to ensure that effective public action is realized and that public values are respected or created. Also, it is important to acknowledge that IIs consist of emerging parts. This makes it impossible to fully predict and design the direction of the development in advance. The type of uses that are enabled by the II, as well as the types of actors that are involved, can evolve in unforeseen ways. Actors will attempt to steer it in a direction that suits them, but have limited means for doing so. Therefore, a key challenge for IIs is establishing in what form quality and development directions will be determined and governed, whilst catering for the requirement that IIs need to be flexible to adapt to events that shape their evolution. Still, as actors change their ways of working based on the II, robustness and stability are required, which means that these have to be accommodated by the technological design (e.g. via open standards) and the organizational design (clear responsibility and governance structures), especially related to accountability in case of errors. Some of these characteristics are similar to those playing a role in open source software [33].

There are various notable differences in the design, characteristics and implementation of digital IIs that interconnect government, businesses and citizens. For instance, some IIs are user driven, while others use more formal consultations for their design, and the type of data and services involved may vary. If digital infrastructures do not arise bottom-up (e.g. from a community of businesses or others), governments may have to create or facilitate an environment in which businesses take up the functionality, for example by providing key information that can form the basis of the infrastructure. This requires businesses to have some kind of revenue model or other incentives. Depending on the functionality, governments need to warrant that certain (public) values are met. The policy implications of this should be amongst the key topics for further research.

Finally, governments may operate some components of the information infrastructure itself. This can for example happen with components of the vital infrastructures of society, including digital and information infrastructures. This can help ensuring critical mass. However, to meet the efficiency and effectiveness requirements of government, businesses need to operate most of it.

Acknowledgements. This paper results from the CASSANDRA project (FP7; SEC-2010.3.2-1, grant agreement no. 261795) and the ENGAGE project (FP7; INFRA-2011-1.2.2, grant agreement no: 283700), which are supported by funding from the 7th Framework Programme of the European Commission. Ideas and opinions expressed by the authors do not necessarily represent those of all project partners.

References

1. Dunleavy, P., Margetts, H., Bastow, S., Tinkler, J.: New Public Management Is Dead–Long Live Digital-Era Governance. Journal of Public Administration Research and Theory 16, 467–494 (2006)
2. Fountain, J.E.: Paradoxes of Public Sector Customer Service. Governance 14, 55–73 (2001)
3. Milward, H.B., Provan, K.G., Fish, A., Isett, K.R., Huang, K.: Governance and Collaboration: An Evolutionary Study of Two Mental Health Networks. Journal of Public Administration Research and Theory 20, i125–i141 (2010)
4. Pollitt, C., Bouckaert, G.: Public Management Reform: a Comparative Analysis. Oxford University Press, Oxford (2004)
5. Salamon, L.M. (ed.): The Tools of Government: A Guide to the New Governance. Oxford University Press, Oxford (2002)
6. Stoker, G.: Public Value Management: A New Narrative for Networked Governance? The American Review of Public Administration 36, 41–57 (2006)
7. Hanseth, O., Lyytinen, K.: Design theory for dynamic complexity in information infrastructures: the case of building internet. Journal of Information Technology 25, 1–19 (2010)
8. Tilson, D., Lyytinen, K., Sørensen, C.: Digital Infrastructures: The Missing IS Research Agenda. Information Systems Research 21, 748–759 (2010)
9. Henfridsson, O., Bygstad, B.: The Generative Mechanisms of Digital Infrastructure Evolution. Mis Quarterly 37 (2013)
10. Gal, U.: Boundary Matters: The Dynamics of Boundary Objects, Information Infrastructures, And Organisational Identities, vol. PhD. Cape Western Reserve University (2008)
11. Janssen, M., Chun, S.-A., Gil-Garcia, J.R.: Building the next generation of digital government infrastructures. Government Information Quarterly 26, 233–237 (2009)
12. Tan, Y.-H., Bjørn-Andersen, N., Klein, S., Rukanova, B. (eds.): Accelerating Global Supply Chains with IT-Innovation. ITAIDE Tools and Methods. Springer, Berlin (2011)

13. Klievink, B., Van Stijn, E., Hesketh, D., Aldewereld, H., Overbeek, S., Heijmann, F., Tan, Y.-H.: Enhancing Visibility in International Supply Chains: The Data Pipeline Concept. International Journal of Electronic Government Research 8 (2012)
14. Benbasat, I., Goldstein, D.K., Mead, M.: The Case Research Strategy in Studies of Information Systems. MIS Quarterly 11, 369–386 (1987)
15. Eisenhardt, K.M.: Building Theories from Case Study Research. Academy of Management Review 14, 532–550 (1989)
16. Yin, R.K.: Case study research. Design and Methods. SAGE Publications, Thoasand Oaks (2003)
17. Braa, J., Hanseth, O., Heywood, A., Mohammed, W., Shaw, V.: Developing health information systems in developing countries: The flexible standards strategy. MIS Quarterly 31, 381–402 (2007)
18. Milward, H.B., Provan, K.G.: Managing the Hollow State: Collaboration and Contracting. Public Management Review 5, 1–18 (2003)
19. Janssen, M., Kuk, G., Wagenaar, R.W.: A Survey of Web-based Business Models for e-Government in the Netherlands. Government Information Quarterly 25, 202–220 (2008)
20. Jørgensen, T.B., Bozeman, B.: Public values an inventory. Administration & Society 39, 354–381 (2007)
21. Rosenau, P.V.: Introduction. The Strengths and Weaknesses of Public-Private Policy Partnerships. American Behavioral Scientist 43, 10–34 (1999)
22. Katz, M., Shapiro, C.: Network Externalities, Competition and Compatibility. American Economic Review 75, 424–440 (1985)
23. Constantinides, P.: Perspectives and implications for the development of information infrastructures. Information Science Reference (2012)
24. Hanseth, O., Monteiro, E., Hatling, M.: Developing information infrastructure: The tension between standardization and flexibility. Science, Technology & Human Values 21, 407–426 (1996)
25. Klievink, B., Janssen, M., Tan, Y.-H.: A Stakeholder Analysis of Business-to-Government Information Sharing: the Governance of a Public-Private Platform. International Journal of Electronic Government Research 8 (2012)
26. Bertot, J.C., Jaeger, P.T., Grimes, J.M.: Using ICTs to Create a Culture of Transparency: E-government and Social Media as Openness and Anti-Corruption Tools for Societies. Government Information Quarterly 27, 264–271 (2010)
27. Janssen, K.: The Influence of the PSI Directive on Open Government Data: An Overview of Recent Developments. Government Information Quarterly 28, 446–456 (2011)
28. Huijboom, N., van den Broek, T.: Open Data: an International Comparison of Strategies. European Journal of ePractice, 4–16 (2011)
29. http://assets.sunlightfoundation.com/policy/OpenDataPolicyGu idelines/OpenDataPolicyGuidelines_V2.pdf (accessed April 8, 2014)
30. http://opengovdata.io/ (accessed April 8, 2014)
31. http://opendefinition.org/ (accessed April 8, 2014)
32. Klievink, B., Lucassen, I.: Facilitating adoption of international information infrastructures: A living labs approach. In: Wimmer, M.A., Janssen, M., Scholl, H.J. (eds.) EGOV 2013. LNCS, vol. 8074, pp. 250–261. Springer, Heidelberg (2013)
33. Gallivan, M.J.: Striking a balance between trust and control in a virtual organization: a content analysis of open source software case studies. Information Systems Journal 11, 277–304 (2001)

The Role of Trust in the Prioritization
of Channel Choices

Kai-Jo Fu[1] and Chung-Pin Lee[2]

[1] Shanghai University of Finance and Economics, China
kaijofu@gmail.com
[2] Tamkang University, Taiwan
chungpin@mail.tku.edu.tw

Abstract. The role of trust is a significant element in the digital channel. While most studies have examined how the idea of trust has affected users' behaviors and developed integrative models of e-government, little attention has been paid to its critical role as a factor affecting citizens' preference toward certain service channels. There is no systematic investigation to compare different types of channel choices by differentiating between primary public service deliveries such as government information, application and transaction, and e-participation. Therefore, the purpose of this study is to explore how to perceive the role of trust as a possible determinant of service choice, in terms of different types of government services. Using survey data collected in Taiwan 2011, this study utilized a multinominal logistic analysis to examine the proposed models. The findings suggest that the different types of channel choices can be influenced by certain critical elements such as, political trust, trust in the Internet, and risk concern.

Keywords: e-governance, trust, citizen preference, channel choice.

1   Introduction

The promise of e-government can expand the scope for citizens' interaction with governments and reduce the cost of democratic participation. As a result, many countries have swiftly embraced the Internet as a means to improve the quality of public service delivery and to contribute to the legitimacy of governance [7], [18]. However, even though growing investment in e-government appears have made it the perfect channel choice for the public, research has found that citizens are not fully exploiting the use of Internet services [14], [16]. Recent studies reveal that one of the most significant missing links in the implementation of e-government is the understanding of the role trust plays in the digital channel [5], [19]. A great deal of research has demonstrated that trust is an influential variable which affects citizens' willingness to use e-government services [2], [6], [13]. While most studies have examined how the idea of trust affects users' behaviors and develops integrative models of e-government [4], [5], [12], [17], little attention has been paid to its role as a critical factor which affects citizens' preference toward service channels.

M. Janssen et al. (Eds.): EGOV 2014, LNCS 8653, pp. 96–105, 2014.

Despite the emphasis placed on significant facets of e-government, research has found that most of these Web contacts have been limited to information searching and retrieval, instead of employing citizen-initiated contacts [15], [18]. When compared with other service channel choices, recent studies reveal that the use of traditional channels (e.g., telephone and face-to-face) still remains higher than the use of Internet services [9], [14]. The results demonstrate that channels have different characteristics, which make them useful for purposes with different requirements. However, there is no systematic investigation to compare different types of channel choices by their delivery of different primary public services such as, information, application and transaction, and e-participation. In other words, there is a need to develop fundamental knowledge to uncover the determinants of channel choices.

Therefore, the aim of this study is to explore the role of trust as a possible determinant of service choice, which differentiates and prioritizes different types of e-government functions. First, we review the literature in relation to trust and various intentions for the use of e-government services across different lines of disciplines. Next, this study proposes the research model and hypotheses in terms of the theoretical foundation. We test three types of public service delivery, including, knowing government information, government service application, and E-voting. This study utilizes a multinominal logistic analysis, in the analysis of a large sample collected in Taiwan, to examine these models. Finally, the results and the implications of these findings are discussed.

2   A Framework of Trust in e-Government

2.1   The Concept of Trust

As more and more concerns are uncovered by the current research on e-government, researchers and practitioners have emphasized how the idea of trust affects e-government adoption and the role of trust in electronic environments [4, 5], [20]. Drawing from e-commerce literature, most e-government researchers point to two essential factors that can affect citizens' adoption of digital services, trust in e-service vendor and trust in service delivery technology. In other words, we can find that there are two types of trust which are often discussed in the literature of e-government, they are trust in technology and trust in organization [6], [17].

Recently, researchers have integrated technology acceptance model (TAM) and Diffusion of Innovation (DOI) into e-governance study. These models are applied in a variety of e-government adoption research [6], [10]. In particular, the concept of trust in some studies stresses the trust in e-government, which is indicated as the successful carrying out of on-line transactions and the establishment of a reliable system [1].

From the perspective of information system study, introducing a new technology can mean an increase in benefits gained, as well as an increase in risks, for the end-user. Trust in Internet and technology can affect citizens' willingness to use e-government services. Moreover, from the perspective of political science and public administration, scholars argue that citizens have a higher probability of accepting and supporting public policies, and higher willingness in using e-government services, if they trust in governments. Since people have multiple channels at their disposal to interact with governmental agencies, the purpose of our study is to identify what role of trust plays in the prioritization of channel choices. Therefore, we propose three fundamental types of trust production mechanisms in e-governance, including government-based trust, technology-based trust, and e-government-based trust. In addition, perceived risks and privacy concerns are expected to hinder the use of e-government services [19].

2.2   Satisfaction with e-Government Services

Cyber consumer satisfaction represents a predominant concept in e-commerce success [8] and e-loyalty [3]. The contentment of the customer, with respect to his/her prior purchasing experience, can affect his/her psychological state and potential to develop a close relationship with the e-commerce firm. Likewise, prior studies have empha-sized that citizens' satisfaction with e-government services can, in turn, increase pub-lic trust in government [11], [20]. Apparently, satisfaction with e-government services can be applied in predicting citizens' preferences toward service channels, where the interaction could be in favor of the e-government service. On the contrary, dissatisfied citizens are more likely to resist attempts to use e-government services and search for alternatives.

2.3   Models

Based on the aforementioned literature, we propose the following model involving factors anticipated to influence citizens' preference toward channel choice.

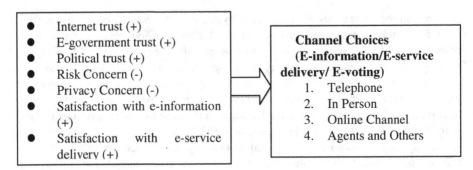

Fig. 1. Factors Anticipated to Influence Citizens' Preference toward Channel Choices

3   Research Method

3.1   Case Background

In recent years, reforming government has become a global trend. In line with these developments, Taiwan has built four phases to implement a comprehensive program of e-government. The major goals of e-government are to simplify the administrative process, improve government efficiency, and increase citizens' satisfaction. In order to accomplish the e-government plan, the central government has raised e-government spending to expand the scope of the program implementation. According to the assessment of the World Economic Forum Readiness Index in 2013, the e-government in Taiwan has not only stayed ahead of the world average, but also demonstrates high readiness and usage around the world[1].

3.2   Data and Methodologies

Data for this study are derived from a random sampling telephone interview survey conducted from August 30 to September 6 in 2011 in Taiwan. The unit of the survey was the household, that is, one person per household was interviewed. A total of 2243 persons were successfully interviewed. With a 95% confidence interval, the sampling error was ±2.07%. We first employ a multinominal logistic analysis to investigate the probability that citizens would prefer a particular type of service channel to contact with the government. This study involves four types of service channels including telephone, in person, online, agents and others. In addition, two types of citizen engaging governmental services are examined: governmental service application (GSA) and knowing governmental information (KGI)[2]. The second level of analysis examines the use of e-voting system. We use logit maximum likelihood estimates to predict when a citizen will choose electronic voting system. Voting behavior is considered to be a dichotomous dependent variable and coded one if adopting E-voting and zero if not.

4   Findings

We first analyze what factors are associated with citizen preference of channel choices by three types of government services. Table 1 displays the multinominal logistic maximum likelihood estimates for different types of channels including telephone, in person, agents and others of GSA, with the online channel as the reference group[3]. The LR chi-square showed statistically significance, since it is less than .001, suggesting a good model fit.

---

[1] http://www.weforum.org/reports/global-information-technology-report-2013

[2] Types of service channels are considered to be a nominal dependent variable. The dependent variable is coded as 0 for Online, 1 for telephone, 2 for in person, 3 for agents and others. The multinominal logistic analysis has a reference group as its category of Online channel (0).

[3] Before utilizing multinominal logistic estimates, we employ LR tests to examine the combined alternatives. In the original questionnaire, five types of channel choices were provided including on-line, telephone, in person, agents, and others. The results found that there is no difference whether 'agents' and 'others' were combined or not. In order to simplify the model, we involve four types of channel choices including telephone, online, in person, and others. We then test the IIA assumption with the use of a Small-Hsiao test. The results indicate that the final model does not violate the IIA assumption.

Table 1. Multinomial Logistic Model of Government Service Application (GSA)

GSA model	Tele-phone/online	In Person/online	Others/online	Wald test
	β	β	β	
Income	-.006	.099	-.199*	11.59*
Age	.019*	.030***	.034**	15.97***
Education	-.188*	-.329***	-.363**	17.15***
Gender	-.185	.160	.361	5.26
ITUSE	.064	.463	.452	3.36
Risk concern	-.048	-.035	-.037	.81
Privacy	-.035	-.021	-.043	1.43
Egov_trust	.077	-.104	.049	5.93
Political trust	-.293***	-.311***	-.494***	24.18***
Internet trust	.082	-.096	-.080	.85
Contact with gov	.401***	.238**	-.165	18.01***
Satisfaction with egov info	-449+	-.242	-.173	3.60
Dissatisfaction with egov info	-.426	-.039	-.636	2.56
Satisfaction with egov service	-.606**	-.712***	-.060	15.76***
Dissatisfaction with egov service	-.1.726**	-1.730***	-.055	17.81***
Intercept	1.802	2.657	2.433	
N	1008			
LR X²(45)	204.41***			
PueudoR²	.080			

Note:
+ p<.1; * p<.05; **p<.01; ***p<.001.

Table 2 presents the results of know government information (KGI) by three types of channels[4].

Table 2. Multinomial logistic model of knowing Government Information (KGI)

GSA model	Telephone/online	Others/online	Wald test
	B	β	
Income	-.088	-.113	3.871
Age	.019*	.026***	13.167***
Education	-.029	-.343***	15.941***
Gender	-.491*	.149	7.245*
ITUSE	.493	.836***	10.591**
Risk	-.019	-.012	.118
Privacy	.012	.003	.107
Egov_trust	.096	.053	1.351
Political trust	-.097	-.365***	19.949***
Internet trust	-.068	-.342	2.949
Contact with gov	.296*	.223*	8.398**
Satisfaction with egov info	-.413	-.501	6.240*
Dissatisfaction with egov info	-.232	-.423	1.747
Satisfaction with egov service	-.346	-.562*	6.494*
Dissatisfaction with egov service	-.951	-.706	3.458

---

[4] Again, we use LR tests to detect the difference when alternatives are combined. The results discovered that three types of service channels can be combined together, including in person, agents, and others. We further examine Small-Hsiao test of IIA assumption with no violation. In order to simplify the model, the KGI model involves three types of service channels including telephone, online, and others.

Table 2. (*continued*)

Intercept	-2.240	.808
N	1013	
LR X^2(30)	184.07***	
PueudoR^2	.103	

Note:
+ p<.1; * p<.05; **p<.01; ***p<.001.

In terms of what citizens prefer to use voting system, we use logistic regressions in our analysis. The logistic results are shown in Table 3.

Table 3. Logistic model of E-voting

Evoting model/ variables	B	Evoting model/ variables	β
Income	.015	Egov_trust	.012
Age	-.023**	Political trust	-.106
Education	.200**	Internet trust	.384**
Gender	-.216	Contact with gov	-.180 *
ITUSE	-.482	Satisfaction with egov info	.017
Risk	-.095*	Dissatisfaction with egov info	.162
Privacy	.051*	Satisfaction with egov service	.121
		Dissatisfaction with egov service	.054
Intercept	-.509	LR X^2(30)	70.05***
N	1022	PueudoR^2	.055

5   Discussion of Results

On the basis of our data analysis, it reveals that trust is definitely significant for e-government adoption. This study indicates that the concept of trust plays different roles in different types of service functions. Our results discovered that political trust, but not trust in the Internet and e-government, is significantly associated with channel choices in both GSA and KGI models. Political trust is the fundamental mechanism to underpin government legitimacy and the policy-making process. As citizens have higher level of political trust, they are more willing to pay taxes, follow the laws, engage in the public affairs and be in favor of new public policies. As a result, whether e-government can be citizens' preferable channel choice depends on the level of political trust.

Additionally, our findings suggest that higher level of trust in the Internet can increase citizens' willingness to adopt the electronic voting system. Trust in the Internet indicates an individual's perception of the digital surroundings that makes an environment safe. As ICTs becomes a popular and common phenomenon, people naturally feel comfortable in browsing government information and utilizing online applications. Yet, the design of e-voting systems requires complex technologies and knowledge, resulting in most people feeling unfamiliar and uncomfortable with the e-voting environment. As people feel distrust in the digital environment, they tend to favor voting in person or using traditional ways that they are most comfortable with. It would be difficult to undo the damage once citizens have decided not to adopt the e-voting system. Similarly, the level of risk perceptions can reduce citizens' willingness to use e-voting systems, because of the lack of control and the feelings of uncertainty associated with new technology.

In the examination of satisfaction with e-government services, the results illustrated, interestingly, that certain findings were opposite to what was predicted. Naturally, citizens who feel higher level of satisfaction with e-government services are more likely to choose online government application compared to the other traditional ones. However, citizens who are dissatisfied with e-government services, still have a high probability in choosing digital channels to complete government applications. Dissatisfaction with e-government services will not stop citizens from adopting digital channels. The findings imply that citizens would rather employ online service applications instead of other traditional ones, once they have begun using it. In other words, citizens will continue using e-service delivery once they have used it for the first time. As a result, governments need to make an effort to promote e-government and encourage citizens to use it in order to change their behavior pattern.

6   Conclusion

This study investigated the role of trust in e-governance, by comparing e-government to traditional service delivery channels, using data collected across Taiwan. Our results indicated that different service functions of e-government can be influenced by different types of trust. This study discovered that the assessment of e-government functions needs to be differentiated from the traditional models. E-government has many different functions offering a variety of public services such as information, online application, and electronic participation. Few empirical studies have been conducted to examine citizens' preference toward service channels by the diversity of government services. This study proposed and tested a multinominal logit and logistic model to explain the concept of trust by different types of government services.

In addition, this exploratory study contributes to the trust in e-government literature by uncovering the dimensions of trust's role in influencing channel choices. Our findings highlight the fact that the role of trust unfolds different angles in the e-government services. Contrary to our expectations, trust in Internet and trust in e-government were not significant. Political trust, on the other hand, in both functions of public services (KGI and GSA), wielded   great influence on the usage of e-government. As in the electronic voting system, the trust in Internet becomes prominent in its ability to affect citizens' willingness to use new technology.

The results indicated that e-government is worth pursuing as a means of service delivery channel, whether citizens are satisfied or dissatisfied with e-government service. Interaction through online transactions, applications or question services could be especially important for increasing e-government utilization.

References

1. Abdelghaffar, H.: Citizens' Readiness for E-Government in Developing Countries (CREG). In: Kamel, S. (ed.) E-Strategies for Technological Diffusion and Ddoption: National ICT Approaches for Socioeconomic Development, pp. 215–233. IGI Global, Hershey (2010)
2. Alsaghier, H., Ford, M., Nguyen, A., Hexel, R.: Conceptualising Citizen's Trust in E-government: Application of Q Methodology. Electronic Journal of E-Government 7(4), 295–310 (2009)
3. Anderson, R.E., Srinivasan, S.S.: E-Satisfaction and E-Loyalty: A Contingency Framework. Psychology & Marketing 20(2), 123–138 (2003)
4. Bélanger, F., Carter, L.: Trust and Risk in E-Government Adoption. The Journal of Strategic Information Systems 17(2), 165–176 (2008)
5. Carter, L., Bélanger, F.: The Utilization of E-Government Services: Citizen Trust, Innovation and Acceptance Factors. Information Systems Journal 15(1), 5–25 (2005)
6. Carter, L., Weerakkody, V.: E-Government Adoption: A Cultural Comparison. Information Systems Frontiers 10(4), 473–482 (2008)
7. Dawes, S.S.: The Evolution and Continuing Challenges of E-Governance. Public Administration Review 68(s1), 86–102 (2008)
8. DeLone, W.H., McLean, E.R.: Measuring E-Commerce Success: Applying the DeLone & McLean Information Systems Success Model. International Journal of Electronic Commerce 9(1), 31–47 (2004)
9. Ebbers, W.E., Pieterson, W.J., Noordman, H.N.: Electronic Government: Rethinking Channel Management Strategies. Government Information Quarterly 25(2), 181–201 (2008)
10. Horst, M., Kuttschreuter, M., Gutteling, J.M.: Perceived Usefulness, Personal Experiences, Risk Perception and Trust as Determinants of Adoption of E-Government Services in The Netherlands. Computers in Human Behavior 23(4), 1838–1852 (2007)

11. Morgeson Iii, F.V., Van Amburg, D., Mithas, S.: Misplaced Trust? Exploring the Structure of the E-Government-Citizen Trust Relationship. Journal of Public Administration Research & Theory 21(2), 257–283 (2011)
12. Parent, M., Vandebeek, C.A., Gemino, A.C.: Building Citizen Trust Through E-Government. Government Information Quarterly 22(4), 720–736 (2005)
13. Pieterson, W., Ebbers, W., van Dijk, J.: Personalization in the Public Sector: An Inventory of Organizational and User Obstacles towards Personalization of Electronic Services in the Public Sector. Government Information Quarterly 24(1), 148–164 (2007)
14. Pieterson, W., van Deursen, A.: The Internet as a Service Channel in the Public Sector. Paper Presented at the ICA, Dresden Germany (2006)
15. Reddick, C.G.: Citizen Interaction with E-Government: From the Streets to Servers? Government Information Quarterly 22(1), 38–57 (2005)
16. Reddick, C.G., Turner, M.: Channel Choice and Public Service Delivery in Canada: Comparing E-Government to Traditional Service Delivery. Government Information Quarterly 29(1), 1–11 (2012)
17. Teo, T.S.H., Srivastava, S.C., Jiang, L.: Trust and Electronic Government Success: An Empirical Study. Journal of Management Information Systems 25(3), 99–131 (2008)
18. Thomas, J.C., Streib, G.: The New face of Government: Citizen-Initiated Contacts in the Era of E-Government. Journal of Public Administration Research and Theory 13(1), 83–102 (2003)
19. Warkentin, M., Gefen, D., Pavlou, P.A., Rose, G.M.: Encouraging Citizen Adoption of E-Government by Building Trust. Electronical Markets 12(3), 157–162 (2002)
20. Welch, E.W., Hinnant, C.C., Moon, M.J.: Linking Citizen Satisfaction with E-Government and Trust in Government. Journal of Public Administration Research and Theory 15(3), 371–391 (2005)

Identifying a Public Sector Information Systems (PSIS) for E-service: A Case of Land Records E-service in Bangladesh

Muhammad Shahanoor Alam and Laurence Brooks[*]

School of Information Systems, Computing and Mathematics,
Brunel University, Uxbridge, Middlesex, UB8 3PH, UK

Abstract. This paper aims to identify the need for Public Sector Information Systems (PSIS), a particular field of the IS discipline dealing with the design, redesign and evaluation of E-services in public sector organizations. A longitudinal and empirical study of an E-service project in a public sector organization in Bangladesh reveals that without addressing underlying organizational problems, taking account into organization contexts, statutes and practices and considering the organizational reality and users' capability; it is difficult to implement E-services in public sector organizations. This paper argues that a particular information system (public sector information systems (PSIS)) has the potential to lead to better design and implementation of successful E-services in public sector organizations.

Keywords: land records management, public sector information systems, Bangladesh.

1 Introduction

With the advancement of information technology (IT) and increasing use of IT for business and organizational purposes, electronic service (E-service) has become a widely used concept across disciplines and academic fields [26], [32]. For example, from buying a book on eBay to online dating or from booking an air ticket to paying council tax can be performed through E-services. However, the forms, process and nature of E-services are vary widely. For example, an email enquiry can be resolved in a few minutes in a business organization while it might take two weeks in the contexts of a public sector organization. According to the nature of an organization, Lindgren and Jansson [26] have categorized E-services into two distinct types: private and public. Private E-services deal with business organizations in particular private sector organizations, whereby clients are considered as customers and profit is the main goal. On the other hand, public E-service is delivered from public sector organizations whereby clients are treated as citizens and services are regulated by organizational and bureaucratic rules. Notably, ensuring citizens' easy access to services is the

---

[*] Corresponding author.

M. Janssen et al. (Eds.): EGOV 2014, LNCS 8653, pp. 106–119, 2014.

main goal rather than profit. Thus, significantly, E-services for public sector organizations differ from E-services for private sector organizations. Consequently, designing E-services for public sector organization requires a particular focus on specific features and contexts of public sector organization. The process, volume and complexity of public E-service is distinct from private E-services. Since public sector organizations are guided by a number of regulations, statutes, and processes; it takes a longer time and its process is more complicated. Therefore, this paper seeks to understand what a Public Sector Information System (PSIS) offers in terms of designing E-services for public sector organizations.

The public sector managers and consultants are often inspired by E-services in private sectors while they only focus on technology; not on the underlying contexts. Consequently, although E-services in public sector organizations have expanded very rapidly; it has remained largely unattainable in the public sector organization in developing countries [3], [14], [23], [32]. More importantly, it is inevitable to understand the information systems and underlying contexts in of public sector organization in order to design E-service for public sector organization. Thus, this paper aims to identify the role of public sector information systems (PSIS) in designing and implementing E-service in public sector organizations.

Efforts of introducing effective service delivery in public sector organization can be traced from New Public Management (NPM) to more recent Electronic Governance (E-Governance). However, Dunleavy [11] claims that NPM is dead; public sector organizations need digital era governance which is synonymous to E-governance. More recently, Lips [27] asserts that E-government is also dead because it is unable to manage transformational change with the use of IT in public sector organizations. E-governance is not a panacea for enhancing service delivery in public sector organization because designing electronic service delivery without tracing underlying contexts cannot ensure effective service delivery in public sector organizations. Evidently, the rate of E-governance as well as E-service failure is very high. Notably about 85% of E-governance projects have been failed in the context of developing countries [17]. However, it is not the aim of this paper to identify limitations of E-governance or identify the best approach for designing and implementing E-service in public sector organizations; rather, this paper aims to identify the role of public sector information systems (PSIS) as a complementary approach in designing and implementing E-service in public sector organizations. Although PSIS is not new it is potential approach for designing and implementing E-service in public sector organizations.

E-service in public sector organization is a complex task. It involves organizational contexts, legal statutes, decision making authority, organizational hierarchy, routines, skills and innovations at work [3], [30], [37]. A PSIS is inevitable to trace underlying organizational processes and contexts of public sector organizations. Public sector organizations are wide and complex, with its core task as service delivery to citizens. More importantly, E-service from public sector organizations is not the same as E-service in private organizations [26]. E-service from public sector organization involved rules, regulations, bureaucracy, legal statutes, routines and traditions, for example, NHS – National Health Service in the UK, social security service in the US and passport and driving license authorities in almost every country.

A number of disciplines and fields including E-governance, information systems, management, organization studies and computer science are relevant in designing and implementing E-service applications. However, focuses on the context of public sector organizations and process of service delivery in public sector organization require particular attention due to the nature and wide of public service delivery. Particularly, public sector organizations in many developing countries carry thick bureaucratic processes and heritage from colonial legacies, vested interests of staff and decision makers, rigidity in statutes and structure of organizations [2], [5], [20], [21]. Consequently, designing and implementing E-service in public sector organizations demands more in-depth and wider approach, tools and skills. This paper aims to identify the role of PSIS in designing and implementing E-service in public sector organizations, particularly with a focus on developing countries contexts and illustrated with a case of E-service of land records in Bangladesh, a developing country.

The rest of the paper comprises four sections. The following section describes the methodology of data collection and background to the case. This is followed by a brief literature review on public sector information systems (PSIS). The next section illustrates the case of land records E-service delivery in Bangladesh. Finally the paper is concludes by identifying the significance of PSIS in designing and implementing E-service in public sector organizations.

2   Methodology and Background

This paper is the outcome of an interventional and longitudinal study. The authors were involved in designing and evaluating an E-service project in a public sector organization in Bangladesh over the last three years. This study has been conducted through an action design research (ADR) [4], [44] framework which allows the researchers to conduct multiple iterations from problem formulation to designing solution to implementation and evaluation of E-service of land records in a public sector organization.

Thus the ADR methodology has provided the opportunity for conducting close observations of the organizational processes and contexts. Thus researchers chose participant observation, ethnographic and semi-structured interviews methods for data collection. They have conducted participant observation on organizational processes and contexts relating this service delivery. Besides, ethnographic and semi-structured interviews have been conducted with four clerical staff, two managers and six citizens, the service recipients. Since an author was a former employee in the organization and a current researcher, this dual role allowed them to apply interventional and observational methods and approaches.

Throughout, researchers close observation and intervention within this complex organizational context help in problem formulation, implementation and evaluation processes of E-service. Data from this study has been analyzed using a thematic approach, with themes derived both from literature, theories, observation, interventions and interviews. The nature of this study finding is qualitative and findings have been presented with thematic and descriptive style. Thus, the study findings has been reported and narrated by the researchers.

This study has been conducted in a public sector organization, namely the District Record Room (DRR) that is responsible for issuing land records to citizens in Bangladesh. The DRR issued certified copies of land records on the basis of citizens' applications. Thus it is called 'land records service'. The land records service in Bangladesh is a core service from the public sector organization for the citizens and every day about 15,000-20,000 citizens need land records. However, this service has a bad reputation for being overly complex, corruption and public suffering which has brought it to the attention of policy makers and development partners. Thus the government has been trying to address these problems through implementing E-service of land records.

3   E-service Efforts in Public Sector Organization: NPM –E-Governance –Public Sector Information Systems (PSIS)

Public sector organizations carry a list of distinctive features: labor intensive; broad scope; organizational legacy; bounded with legal statutes, guided by rules and regulations; thick bureaucratic processes and merely any reward for innovation rather risk in innovation and change. Consequently, access to the services of public sector or deliver effective service delivery from public sector has never been easy. Thus a number of studies and evaluation reports suggested that in order to design and implement E-service for public sector organizations requires tracing underlying contexts of the service; increasing collaboration and cooperation and transforming productivity and efficiency [6], [13], [19], [46]. A number of efforts have been employed in transformation of public sector organization as well as service delivery from public sector organization. This paper mainly focuses on New Public Management (NPM) and E-governance, whereby service delivery as well as E-service is the main attraction. NPM brought a wave of reform in services in public sector organizations with a view to providing effective and efficient service delivery to citizens [11]. NPM engaged in deliberate changes of structures and processes in public sector organizations to ensure better service delivery [38]. It was mainly management led tools, techniques and strategies. However, NPM failed to keep pace with the dynamism of organizational change and trace the changes relating to technological inducement in public sector organizations [10], [11], [27].

Consequently, NPM was blended with public administration in planning and organizing of management functions and services to achieve quality service through using human and technological resources. Thus, it also focused on decentralization to reduce bureaucratic hierarchy and complications. Further, it introduced competition and ensured rewards and specific performance measures through reforming complicated processes and employing resources. However, NPM brought mechanistic concepts and tools from the ideology of the management of private sector organizations and these were hardly applicable to public sector organizations [12], [29]. Moreover, NPM followed linear directions in designing services from public sector organizations but changes in of public sector services is often dynamic and unpredictable. Changes in public sector organization take place through dynamic relations between technology and organizational contexts. Therefore, NPM has failed to integrate its tools and processes into the practice relating to technology and public sector organizations [11]. Electronic governance (E-governance) emerged with the expansion of IT in public sector organization. Therefore, gradually NPM has been replaced by E-governance.

E-governance has become a catchphrase, a discourse and a catalyst to ensure better service delivery to citizens through employing IT in public sector organizations [49]. E-governance refers to interactions between government, citizens, business processes and actors using electronic means with a view to achieving citizens' easy access to public services and ensuring transparency and efficiency in public sector organizations [11], [27], [48], [49]. However, E-governance focuses on governance that refers to the act of governing which include role and interactions between government, private sector and civil society for enhancing service delivery, increasing participation, accountability and transparency. Further, governance is just interstices across private, public and civic sectors and aims to steer the processes that influence decisions and actions across the sectors [33]. E-Governance seeks to provide public services for the ease and option of citizens, keep citizens informed, and solicit their voice in the functioning of government. The ultimate goal is to ensure citizens' stake, to put citizen at the heart of public administration, without any exclusion. However, E-governance cannot harness the advantages of IT implementation without organizational change, legal reforms, participation of staff and resources and citizens' preparedness and engagement. Consequently, the rate of failures of E-governance initiatives is very high [16], [17].

Furthermore, since inception E-governance has been suffering with maintaining the balance between designing organizational processes and employing information technology. Until now, the main focus of E-governance has remained on IT implementation instead of designing and redesigning the organizational processes for effective service delivery. As a result, E-governance failed to take into account the role of organizational contexts. Similarly, Yildiz [48] asserts that E-governance research suffers with oversimplifying of organizational contexts and processes.

Designing E-service in public sector organizations requires understanding of organizational contexts and processes. Since public sector organizations carry thicker bureaucratic processes and complex organizational contexts, E-service cannot be designed in public sector organization rationally, predictably, straightforward and as a linear process, rather it is unpredictable, dynamic and complex [22]. Thus, E-governance is incapable of tracing dynamic change because it predominantly focuses on technological capabilities and leads with a linear perspective on the usage of E-service and its impacts and outcomes [27]. Consequently, Lips [27] argues that it is inevitable to think of an alternative stream in E-government [27].

Thus, success and failure of E-governance mainly relies on the design and redesign of organizational processes (legal statutes, regulations, organizational behavior, attitudes, alliances, networks, readiness and participation) along with the technological design. In order to understand organizational processes and contexts of public sector organization, particularly public sector information systems (PSIS) offers potential lens. Designing E-service is not only technological design rather it requires taking into account the organizational processes and context.

This paper, thus, seeks relevance of public sector information systems (PSIS) in designing E-service. PSIS is not new but so far it is also not well established. Thus this paper has identified the potential benefits of PSIS in designing and implementing E-service in public sector organizations.

4   Designing E-services in Public Sector Organizations and PSIS

Inherently, IS focuses on public sector organization from a holistic view that captures contexts, nature, dynamism and unpredictability in technology and organization. Although information systems (IS) emerged in the 1950s; as a distinct field it developed in the 1970s but it has 'exploded' in the 1990s and it is increasingly expanding with the use of IT in organizational applications [8], [18]. The core of IS is that it acts as the interface between organizational the contextual relations and the use of IT. Thus IS seeks human behavior and technology in relation to understand multifaceted interactions between changing technologies and changing human tasks, goals, preferences and dynamics [31]. Thus, IS can be seen as a bedrock of using IT in public sector organization [18].

The centrality of the IS discipline is to deal with IT in everyday life rather than deeply engaging with purely technical aspects of information technology [36]. Evidently, IS deals with IT and organizational contexts with equal emphasis. More importantly, IS reveals organizational culture, contexts, norms and process that play a trivial role in designing technology for public sector organizations and service delivery for public sector organization [41], [42]. Similarly, Walsham [47] finds that there is strong link between technological processes and contexts of public sector organization in developing countries. However, there is little of agreement on how the technology interacts with organizations [35].

Since the inception of IS discipline, public sector information systems (PSIS) has focus on public sector organizations with inherent characteristics: continuous monitoring, controlling and evaluating (reporting), intervening on the basis of evaluation and applying operational and management [18]. Thus PSIS deals with public sector accounting, human resources, taxation, and public service delivery. In order to manage and monitor public services from public sector organizations, PSIS plays a vital role. For example, while the NHS in UK tries to control costs and simultaneously improve service delivery standards, it does so though PSIS. The role of PSIS is remarkable to accelerate of public service in the UK. Consequently, although in the UK E-government program ended in 2006; the expenditure behind PSIS has been increased [24].

Identifying the significance of PSIS, Rocheleau [39] suggests that although public sector organizations spend much money on IT, it might appear that the organization suffers from a lack of motivation while IS in the public sector organization plays a vital role in identifying the factors underlying this. Heeks [18] identified the role of PSIS in dealing with four important aspects: monitoring and controlling information about what has happened and what is happening instead of what will happen;

evaluating through simple techniques; feeding evaluation reports into decision making processes and focusing on operational and tactical aspects. Thus, although PSIS is an underutilized field, it has the potential to deal with organizational contexts and service delivery design [7]. Evidently, a large volume of E-service design relied on E-service framework or models for private sector. Rosacker and Olson [40] note that PSIS have more distinctive features than private sector information systems and therefore while designing information system for public sector organization the role of PSIS is inevitable.

4.1   PSIS for E-service in Public Sector Organization

With the expansion of IT in citizens' expectations about services from public sector organization have increased in terms of quality i.e. convenience, accessibility and affordability; and it terms of quantity i.e. more services within a short span of time and at a 'one stop shop'; and in terms of availability i.e. 24/7. To meet citizens' expectations, every public sector organization has been designing IT applications known as E-service initiatives with view to citizens' easy access [28], [43]. Thus E-service has emerged as a potential field, focusing on designing and redesigning IT and organizational processes of public sector organization. Although every government is striving to deliver E-services successfully, many developing countries have failed to provide effective and efficient E-service for their citizens [1], [2], [28], [45].

In the main, E-service in public sector organization aims to provide citizens' with easy access to services, reduce costs and time and make the service more convenient. It is not merely a technological issue; rather it is closely connected with organizational, social, economic and user contexts [15]. Thus, designing E-Service applications in public sector organizations is complex and involves many phases, processes, actors, roles and practices [15], [25], [34]. Consequently, technological design alone cannot ensure effective and efficient public services [9].

The range and nature of E-services is very wide, including unidirectional broadcasting to highly interactive communication involving clients, staff, workflow systems, data-bases and specially designed interaction software [15]. E-services include kiosks, telecentres, call centers, web portals and front offices or other means. However, designing and managing E-services requires citizens' familiarity with the services, convenient, flexibility in choices; easy accessibility; equality between e-service and non e-services and effective use of information [9]. Taken together, this paper argues that PSIS offers potential as a lens to understand organizational processes, contexts, users' capability and attitude of organizational staff in order to design E-services for public sector organizations. Therefore, this paper applies PSIS to designing E-service for land records in Bangladesh public sector organizations.

5   E-service for Land Records in Bangladesh

Bangladesh is a least developed country located between India and Myanmar. It is the most population dense country in the world with a total of 160 million people; it has high rates of illiteracy, very low electronic literacy and access to technology. It is mainly agro–based country with a visible land scarcity; an average land per person is 0.22 acre only. In addition to, its 80% of people live in rural areas; a total 70% of people agriculturists and agriculture contributes to 60% of total GDP. Thus land and land records related services are significant. Land records services are delivered from public sector organizations. Land records are inevitably needed for legal, financial, welfare services, development planning, and transfer of land ownership, determination of ownership and size of land parcels and resolving of land litigations. Thus service delivery of land records has become a core service to citizens from the public sector organizations.

Service delivery of land records refers to issuing a certified copy of a land records from the District Record Room (DRR) to citizens. Daily about 20,000-30,000 applications are received by public sector organizations, the DRRs, for service delivery of land records. The district under study receives about 300-400 applications per day.

This service has been identified as ineffective, corruptive, cause of public sufferings and middlemen dependent. Consequently, designing and implementing E-service has been identified as an important mechanism for making this service effective, bringing this service at the citizens' door step and removing complicacy and middlemen from this service.

5.1   Organizational Context for Land Records E-service

Although Bangladesh gained independence from Pakistan in 1971, it had previously been under British Colonial Rule from 1757 to 1947. The land records and its service delivery was introduced by the Colonial government in the country, thus it inherited and to some extent still relies on the colonial rules, regulation and statues in particular related to land services. In addition, land records services has been identified as the top ranked sector for corruption; a major source of litigation and a sector for intolerable public suffering [21]. Further, this service follows archaic service delivery processes, dilapidated conditions of the printed land records and registers; complicated systems land records and this service delivery is controlled by strong bureaucratic processes. Together, these have given rise to rampant rent seeking vested interests of staff and middlemen's corruption network for mediating this service.

Thus with a view to ensuring easier access for citizens to the land records service, the government of the day has launched E-service for land records. The government designed a flagship program, 'Access to Information (A2I)', directed from the Prime Minister's office. A2I has designed three electronic access points to ensure citizens easy access to the land record service. These are telecentres known as Union Information Service Center (UISC), front desk known as E-service Center (ESC) and District Web Portal (DWP) (See figure-1). Thus, the E-service for land records has designed a country wide technological network comprising 4501 telecentres, 64 front desks (one in each district) and 64 district web portal (one in each district), aiming to ensure citizens' easier access this service. However, the organizational contexts and processes, merely accepts the technological design of the E-service of land records.

The land records service evolved from printed land records, which appeared during the British colonial regime at the end of the 20th century. The DRR is entrusted with the responsibility for preserving land records and providing service delivery of land records. In 1950, the feudal system (Landlords - Zamindars) was abolished. Thereafter, the tenants, the cultivators, became the land owners. Consequently, land records turned into valuable documents for the citizens. A certified copy of a land record is required proof of ownership and land records become a compulsory element for related services: land purchase, sales, mortgages, taxation, land litigation, infrastructural planning and development.

From the colonial regime to now, there are up to three versions of land records for each plot of land. The first version was prepared by the British colonial rulers in 1920s. When land ownership changed from landlord to tenants in the 1950s during Pakistan's regime, another version of land record was prepared. Bangladesh gained its independence from Pakistan in 1971. Thereafter the third version of land records preparation started and it is not completed yet. As a result, each plot of land may have three versions of records and surprisingly, all of the versions are active records for proof of ownership of a plot of land. Notably, the majority of the population is illiterate. So they do not know their land records ID numbers and the versions of land records. Consequently, citizens cannot submit their application through the E-service access points. During the interviews one staff member mentioned, "The E-service has designed this E-service which can be compared with a nice garden with several entrance points but its visitors are blind".

As a result, out of the three access points, telecentres and DWPs remain underutilized (see figure -1). The front desk, the ESC was designed to receive online application, but as citizens could not submit their online application, the ESC has turned to paper based applications, similar to the previous systems. Consequently middlemen and corruption network between staff and middlemen remain same. Eventually the E-service has increased corrupt processes.

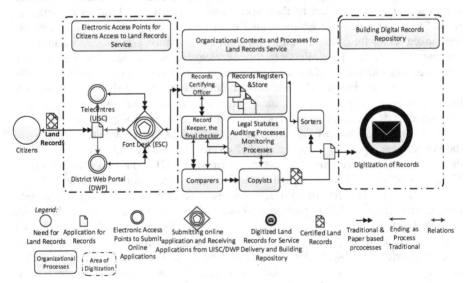

Fig. 1. E-service contexts and processes in the District Record Room (DRR) - a public sector organization

On the other hand, although each rural local Union Council has telecentres that are connected to the DRR and citizens could submit their applications from the telecentres to the DRR. However, citizens rarely accessed to the land records service to the telecentres. Because of, citizens found that traditional middlemen who are based at district headquarters have strong network with the DRR staff to expedite this service delivery.

Thus, setting multiple access points for citizens' easy access to this service is technologically possible. However, the organizational contexts interpreted the technological design of the E-service its own way. The E-service of land records in the organizational contexts every application requires printed copy of online application along with adhesive stamps as fees. Therefore, after electronic submission of applications from a telecentre or citizens needs to print online submitted application form and send it to the DRR along with appropriate fees. Consequently, although from technological point of view, telecentres are easy accessible to the E-service of land records, it has become most difficult due to organizational processes and contexts.

In addition to, citizens have no middlemen network to pay 'bribes' or 'speed money' to the DRR staff to expedite this E-service while they submit applications through the telecentre and the DWP. Moreover, DRR staff do not take 'bribes'/ 'speed money' except from the middlemen networks. Thus without a 'bribe' or 'speed money' applications submitted by citizens through a telecentre or DWP for the E-service land records are either delayed or are found to be missing from the DRR. It is open secret that without a 'bribe' or speed money, this service will not be processed. Furthermore, the organizational processes and required information for submitting application for E-service of land records are so complex that citizens must rely on middlemen to mediate the land records E-service.

6   Implications for PSIS in Designing Land Records E-service

From the case discussed above, the following implications can be drawn for designing E-service for land records whereby the role of PSIS is inevitable.

6.1   Absence of Organizational Contexts

This E-service has been designed without taking into account of the organizational contexts. The land records are complicated and have many different versions. Citizens are often not aware about the ID numbers for land records and the differing versions of land records. Consequently, it is difficult for citizens to apply for land records through E-service.

6.2   Statutes and Practices

Legal statutes and practices cannot be designed and changed overnight, but it is possible to design IT. In this case, the E-service has been designed without changing legal statutes. Although this service has designed online application submission process, it requires manual fees submission process i.e. stamps. Besides, for the auditing purpose it needs printed copy of online applications.

Moreover, this design also has failed to account behavioral resistance from the staff and middlemen. Thus without removing the middlemen and corruption network between the middlemen and the staff, the E-service network has been deployed.

Furthermore, the staff have been receiving bribes or speed money for this service for a long time. Consequently, only setting of E-service network cannot remove their relations with the middlemen who manage the 'speed money' (bribes) from citizens. Thus, without excluding the processes that provide opportunities for speed money, designing the E-service is practically worthless. Although the telecentres and the DWP have been designed for citizens' access to this service, citizens found that these are not effective to receive 'speedy service'. Thus, they return to the traditional processes, which is the middlemen network. Finally middlemen have adapted themselves through submitting citizens' application through the 'Front Desk' known as E-service Center (ESC) to continue mediation of this service. It has become possible because the organizational processes are in favor of the middlemen and any other methods of submissions are resisted by the staff.

6.3   Users' Capability and Organizational Reality

The users of the E-service are mostly farmers who are mainly illiterate. Thus filling online applications with appropriate land records ID numbers, understanding different versions of land records and the jurisdiction number for land records are difficulties for them. Besides, setting of website, DWP, for submitting online land records applications is unrealistic where only 0.35% of the population has internet access. In addition, the low literacy and electronic literacy and limited connectivity and accessibility to computer and internet are prevalent across the country. Consequently, the E-service has hardly made any improvement in citizens' access to this service. This E-service has been designed from technological viability any change in organizational contexts. As a result, although electronic access points have been setup, they did not remove the organizational problems; rather the organizational problems have reshaped the E-service.

6.4   Monitoring and Evaluation

Although the DWP has failed to ensure citizens' easier access to the DRR, the advantages of this access point has been harnessed by the organizational staff and middlemen to provide better services to their clients who provide bribes. Because of, the staff have good internet connections and printers, so they use it for submitting online applications via DWP on behalf their middlemen.

On the other hand, unsurprisingly, although the aim of the E-service centers (the front desk) was to be an access point for those citizens visiting the district headquarters. However, instead it has become the access point for middlemen who submit paper based application via this service. Thus, the underlying organizational contexts and practices have been continuously redesigning the E-service. Finally, this E-service has no means continuous monitoring and evaluation.

7   Conclusion

This paper has illustrated the case of E-services in public sector organizations in a developing country. Successful implementation of E-services in general is difficult and in developing countries is a great challenge. The failure rate for E-service projects in developing countries is very high and existing E-governance approaches have largely failed to address the problems. Many scholars have already looked at finding alternative streams or alternatives to E-governance for designing and implementing E-services in public sector organizations. This paper has argued that there is need for public sector information systems (PSIS), as a dedicated field of IS for designing and evaluating E-services for public sector organizations. One of the defining characteristics for this is the strong emphasis on taking into account the organizational context during the design and implementation process.

In conclusion it can be said that E-service in public sector organization cannot succeed without taking into account the organizational contexts, statutes and practices. PSIS has become an inevitable part of the design, monitoring and evaluation of E-service in public sector organizations. More recently public sector E-service organizations are modelling themselves on private sector E-services. Since the context of the public sector organization is significantly different from private sector organizations, a public sector information systems (PSIS) offers the potential to deal with the contexts, practices, users, organizational reality, resources, rules, regulations and statutes of the public sector organization in designing E-service.

References

1. Alam, M.S., Brooks, L., Abbott, P.: Action Design Ethnographic Research - in Search of a Rigorous Methodology for IS Research (2012)
2. Alam, M.S., Brooks, L., Khan, N.I.: Action Design Ethnographic Research (ADER): Vested Interest Networks and ICT Networks in Service Delivery of Land Records in Bangladesh. In: Bhattacherjee, A., Fitzgerald, B. (eds.) Shaping the Future of ICT Research. IFIP AICT, vol. 389, pp. 51–67. Springer, Heidelberg (2012)
3. Axelsson, K., Melin, L., Lindgren, I.: Public e-Services for Agency Efficiency and Citizen Benefit — Findings from a Stakeholder Centered Analysis. Government Information Quarterly 30, 10–22 (2013)
4. Beck, R., Weber, S., Gregory, R.: Theory-Generating Design Science Research. Information Systems Frontiers 15, 637–651 (2013)
5. Bhuiyan, M.S.H.: Public Sector eService Development in Bangladesh: Status, Prospects and Challenges. Electronic Journal of e- Government 9, 15–29 (2011)
6. Chen, Y., Khosrow-Pour, M.: Digital Government Development. In: Khosrow-Pour, M. (ed.) Encyclopedia of E-Commerce, E-Government, and Mobile Commerce, pp. 203–209. IGI Global, Hershey (2006)
7. Cordella, A., Iannacci, F.: Information Systems in the Public Sector: The e-Government Enactment Framework. The Journal of Strategic Information Systems 19, 52–66 (2010)
8. Davis, G.B., Olson, M.H.: Management information systems: Conceptual foundation, structure and development, 2nd edn. McGraw-Hill, New York (1985)

9. Donnelly, P., McGuirk, T.: Electronic Delivery of Public Services in the United Kingdom: The Case of the Merseyside Fire Service and Fire Service Direct. Asian Journal of Public Administration 25, 185–208 (2003)

10. Dunleavy, P.: Organisation and state organisation in digital era. In: Mansell, R., Avgerou, C., Quah, D., et al. (eds.) The Oxford Handbook of Information and Communication Technologies, Oxford University Press, Oxford (2007)

11. Dunleavy, P., Margetts, H., Tinkler, J.: New Public Management is dead—long Live Digital-Era Governance. Journal of Public Administration Research and Theory 16, 467–494 (2005)

12. Farazmand, A.: Privatisation Or Reform? Public Enterprise Management in Transition. International Review of Administrative Sciences 65, 551–567 (1998)

13. Gershon, P.: Releasing Resources to the Front Line: Independent Review of Public Sector Efficiency (2004)

14. Gil-Garcia, J.R., Martinez-Moyano, I.J.: Understanding the Evolution of e-Government: The Influence of Systems of Rules on Public Sector Dynamics. Government Information Quarterly 24, 266–290 (2007)

15. Gronlund, A.: Managing electronic services: A public sector perspective. Springer, London (2000)

16. Heeks, R.: Most E-Government for Development Project Fail: How can Risk be Reduced? iGovernment Working Paper Series, Paper no. 14 (2003)

17. Heeks, R.: Information System in Developing Countries: Failure, Success and Local Improvisations. The Information Society 18, 101–112 (2002)

18. Heeks, R.: Public Sector Management Information Systems (1998)

19. Heeks, R.: Reinventing government in the information age: International practice in IT-enabled public sector reform. Routledge (2002)

20. Imran, A., Gregor, S.: Uncovering the Hidden Issues in E-Government Adoption in a Least Developed Country: The Case of Bangladesh. Journal of Global Information Management 18, 30–56 (2010)

21. Imran, A., Gregor, S.: Vested Interests Obstructing Information Systems use: Land Administration in a Least Developed Country, pp. 1–24 (2011)

22. Institute for Government: System error: Fixing the flaws in government IT. Institute for Government, London (2010)

23. Irani, Z., Love, P.E.D., Montazemi, A.: E-Government: Past, Present and Future. European Journal of Information Systems 16, 103–105 (2007)

24. Jones, S.: Social Dimension of IT/IS Evaluation: Views from the Public Sector. In: Irani, Z., Love, P.E.D. (eds.) Evaluating Information Systems: Public and Private Sector, pp. 236–256. Butterworth-Heinemann, Oxford (2008)

25. Liikanen, E.: Backflap. In: Gronlund, A. (ed.) Managing Electronic Services: A Public Sector Perspective. Springer, London (2000)

26. Lindgren, I., Jansson, G.: Electronic Services in the Public Sector: A Conceptual Framework. Government Information Quarterly 30, 163–172 (2013)

27. Lips, M.: E-Government is Dead: Long Live Public Administration 2.0. Innovation in the Public Sector 20, 30–41 (2013)

28. Lofstedt, U.: E-Government - Assessment of Current Research and some Proposals for Future Directions . International Journal of Public Information Systems 1, 39–52 (2005)

29. McCourt, W.: New public management in developing countries. In: McLaughlin, K., Osborne, S.P., Ferlie, E. (eds.) New Public Management: Current Trends ands Future Prospects, Routledge (2002)

30. Melin, U., Axelsson, K.: Managing E-Government Projects: A Comparative Case Study of Two Inter- Organizational E-Service Development Initiatives, pp. 1716–1727 (2008)
31. Niederman, F., March, S.T.: Design Science and the Accumulation of Knowledge in the Information Systems Discipline. Journal ACM Transactions on Management Information Systems 3 (2012)
32. Nygren, K.G., Axelsson, K., Melin, U.: Public e-Services from Inside: A Case Study on Technology's Influence on Work Conditions in a Government Agency. International Journal of Public Sector Management 26, 455–468 (2013)
33. O'Leary, R., Gerard, C., Bingham, L.B.: Introduction to the Symposium on Collaborative Public Management. Public Administration Review 66 (2006)
34. OECD: Service Delivery in Fragile Situations: Key Concepts. Findings and Lessons Journal of Development 9 (2008)
35. Orlikowski, W.J.: The Duality of Technology: Rethinking the Concept of Technology in Organizations. Organization Science 3, 398–427 (1992)
36. Orlikowski, W.J., Iacono, C.S.: Research Commentary: Desperately Seeking the 'IT' in IT Research–A Call to Theorizing the IT Artifact. Information Systems Research 12, 121 (2001)
37. Persson, A., Axelsson, K., Melin, U.: E-Government Challenges – Exploring Inter-Organisational Aspects of e-Service Development, pp. 1419–1430 (2006)
38. Pollitt, C., Bouckaert, G.: Public management reform. Oxford University Press, Oxford (2004)
39. Rocheleau, B.: Evaluating Public Sector Information Systems: Satisfaction Versus Impact. Eval. Program Plann. 16, 119–129 (1993)
40. Rosacker, K.M., Olson, D.L.: Public Sector Information System Critical Success Factors. Transforming Government: People, Process and Policy 2, 60–70 (2008)
41. Sahay, S.: Implemenation of Information Technology: A Time-Space Perspective. Organisation Studies 8, 229–260 (1997)
42. Sahay, S., Robey, D.: Organizational Context, Social Interpretation, and the Implementation and Consequences of Geographic Information Systems. Accounting, Management and Information Technologies 6, 255–282 (1996)
43. Scholl, H.J.: Introduction to the Electronic Government Cluster of Minitracks (2004)
44. Sein, M.K., Henfridsson, O., Purao, S., et al.: Action Design Research. MIS Quarterly 35, 37–56 (2011)
45. Sleeman, B.: Recent Literature on Government Information. Journal of Government Information 30, 20–41 (2004)
46. Varney, D.: Service Transformation: A Better Service for Citizens and Businesses, a Better Deal for the Taxpayer (2006)
47. Walsham, G.: Interpreting information systems in organizations. Wiley, Chichester (1993)
48. Yildiz, M.: E-Government Research: Reviewing the Literature, Limitations, and Ways Forward. Government Information Quarterly 24, 646–665 (2007)
49. Yildiz, M., Saylam, A.: E-Government Discourses: An Inductive Analysis. Government Information Quarterly 30, 141–153 (2013)

Source and Channel Choices in Business-to-Government Service Interactions: A Vignette Study

Yvon Van den Boer[1], Willem Pieterson[2], Rex Arendsen[3], and Manon De Groot[4,*]

[1] University of Twente,
Center for e-Government Studies,
Enschede, The Netherlands
y.vandenboer@utwente.nl
[2] Syndio Social, Chicago, United States
willem@syndiosocial.com
[3] Delft University of Technology, Delft, The Netherlands
rex.arendsen@gmail.com
[4] Netherlands Tax and Customs Administration (NTCA),
The Research and Marketing Department
Utrecht, The Netherlands
im.de.groot@belastingdienst.nl

Abstract. To deal with tax matters, businesses have various potential sources (e.g., Tax Office, advisor, industry organization, friends/family) in their environment. Those sources can be coupled with an increasingly wide variety of channels (e.g., telephone, face-to-face, website, e-mail) through which information can be obtained. This has led to an increasingly complex information flow between governments and businesses. This paper provides new directions for public service delivery strategies by studying both source and channel choices of businesses using the vignette method. The findings indicate that source and channel choices are determined in different ways (i.e., positive or negative) by different factors. Furthermore, we found that source and channel choices are interrelated. It is concluded that that sources and channels fulfil different roles for information seekers. It is advisable for government to anticipate these roles in the design of their service delivery strategies.

Keywords: Source Choice, Channel Choice, Interrelation, Business-to-Government Service Interactions, Information seeking.

1 Introduction

In the Netherlands, over a million small and medium-sized businesses (SMEs) regularly have to deal with various types of complex government requirements. One of the most well-known examples in this context involves managing tax problems. For several decades, governments have sought suitable service delivery strategies to

---

* Views and recommendations expressed in this paper are those of the individual author and do not necessarily reflect official positions or opinions of the NTCA.

M. Janssen et al. (Eds.): EGOV 2014, LNCS 8653, pp. 120–132, 2014.

interact with businesses regarding these matters as efficiently and effectively as possible. For example, research on e-government and multichannel management has contributed to current strategies. The primary aim of these strategies is to guide information seekers to electronic channels, such as a website, which are assumed to be less expensive than traditional channels such as the telephone and face-to-face communication. At present, however, the use of the more costly channels remains high [e.g., 1,2]. This calls for new insights to develop revised strategies for efficient and effective service delivery.

To cope with tax matters, SMEs have various potential information sources in their environment from which to choose. The myriad sources can be coupled with an increasingly wide variety of channels through which information can be obtained. The growing number of available channels and the increasing role of other information sources have made the information flow between governments and businesses increasingly complex. As a result, it will become more difficult for governments to maintain high levels of service. This will particularly be the case if businesses do not primarily rely on the government for accurate and reliable information but instead turn to other sources because they are now easier to access than before (i.e., through the rise of new and social media) [3]. Furthermore, the increasing availability of service channels limits the efficiency with which governments can provide services to their clients (i.e., citizens and businesses). These considerations lead to the question of how governments should address the availability of numerous information sources and channels.

This situation is further complicated by a lack of theories that can help us to understand a) why businesses use certain available sources and channels and b) whether and how source and channel choices are interrelated (i.e., do businesses always use the same source-channel combination?). Although theories exist that can help us to understand a) why individuals use certain communication channels (or 'media') [e.g., 4,5] and b) the processes by which information sources are selected (e.g., Byström and Järvelin's model of information seeking [6]), there are only a few studies that clearly distinct between the source and channel and recognize their interaction, but provide no detailed explanations or determinants [e.g., 7, 8].

This paper aims to fill this gap in the current knowledge by providing insights into a) which sources and channels businesses select in business-to-government (B2G) service interactions, b) differences and similarities between source and channel choice processes by including some of the potential influencing factors for both types of choices, and c) the interrelation between source and channel choices (i.e., the channels that are used to contact various kinds of sources). With this, the paper provides new directions for public service delivery strategies as well as for future research that integrate source and channel choices.

The paper starts with a theoretical discussion about definitions of the source and channel as well as relevant theories for studying source and channel choices, followed by an elaboration of the research method. Subsequently, the results will be discussed. The paper ends with the discussion, conclusions and implications.

2   Theoretical Background

This section discusses the definitions of the source and channel we use throughout this paper as well as which influencing factors for source and channel choices are recognized by theories in the media choice and information-seeking domain.

2.1   Definitions of the Source and Channel

For reasons of clarity, we make a clear distinction between the information source and communication channel. The source is defined as the person or organization storing the information, from whom (or which) that information can be obtained from by the seeker (adapted from Christensen & Bailey [8]). Examples of sources are governmental agencies, advisory organizations, friends, family and colleagues. The channel refers to the means by which information is transferred between the source and seeker (adopted from [9]). Channels are viewed as equivalent to media, such as the telephone, e-mail, websites and face-to-face communication.

2.2   Relevant Theories on Source and Channel Choices

Theories of channel choice are primarily rooted in the media choice and use literature (e.g., Media Richness Theory [4,5], the Social Influence Model [10], and the Channel Expansion Theory [11, 12]). Theories that provide insight into source choices (and sometimes channel choices) are primarily rooted in the domain of information seeking (e.g., Byström and Järvelin's model of information seeking [6], Leckie's model of information seeking [13]). The theories in both research domains identify a wide variety of factors that have been found to be important in the selection processes of sources and channels. However, apart from the lack of definitions in many studies [e.g., 14-18], the concepts media, channels, and sources are often explained differently and seem conflated with one another [e.g., 19-21]. This hinders the determination of which exact factors influence source choices and which channel choices.

Nevertheless, the most widely recognized influencing factor, across both research areas, for source and channel choices is formed by *task characteristics* [e.g., 6, 9, 10, 13]. The impact of *personal aspects* (e.g, age, gender, education) as well as *situational factors* (e.g. time, distance) is recognized in several theories in both domains [e.g., 6, 9, 10, 22]. However, Baldwin and Rice [19] argue that *personal aspects* are only marginally of influence compared to *organizational factors* (e.g. organization size). Media choice theories recognize some forms of contextual influences such as *social influences* [10-12] and *cultural norms* [22]. Conversely, theories of information seeking behavior consider the context as the shaping mechanism for the entire information seeking process. Examples of contextual aspects are *established interaction patterns* and the *information environment* of organizations [7], *staff and organization size, type* and *location* of the organization and *general use* of sources and channels [19]. The latter seems to be equal to norms of channel use as proposed by the media choice theories. But also *awareness of available sources* in the environment of the seeker seems of importance [13]. Other influencing factors exist, but are beyond the scope of this paper since we are not able to incorporate them in the vignettes (e.g., *perceived source and channel characteristics, relationship characteristics*).

3   Research Method

Design. We used the vignette method in this study. Vignettes are short descriptions of a particular situation in which the respondents need to empathize [23]. For each vignette the respondents were asked which information source and which channel they should use in the given situation. One of the advantages of a vignette study is that it approaches reality. It is not unconceivable that the respondent is or will be confronted with such a situation and is or will be faced with such a decision [e.g., 24, 25]. A disadvantage of a vignette study is that, due to the many factors included, the amount of unique vignettes can rise quickly [26]. As a consequence we included only a few variables. Furthermore, it was chosen to confront the participants with an acceptable number of the vignettes by creating a split. This method is called the incomplete block design [26]. The unique vignettes are divided into groups and each respondent is designated to a particular group. For the current study 32 unique vignettes were formulated (five factors with each two values (2^5) were included in each situation). Each respondent was given 4 vignettes. The manipulated variables (see table 1) were associated with *characteristics of the task* (i.e., complexity, importance, specificity), *available time* as a *situational factor*, and *social influence* (i.e., getting advice).

Table 1. Manipulated Variables in the 32 Vignettes

Factor	Variables	Manipulation	As expressed in vignettes
Task	Complexity	1. Simple	...*it seems a rather simple question*
		2. Complex	...*it seems a complex question*
Task	Specificity	1. General	... *all companies use the same*
		2. Specific	.. *it can be quite different*
Task	Importance	1. Unimportant	... *the important seems not high*
		2. Important	... *the importance is high*
Situational	Available Time	1. In a hurry	...*there is little time*
		2. Plenty of Time	... *no hurry, there is plenty of time*
Social Influence	Getting Advice	1. None	...*someone in your direct*
		2. Getting advice	*environment recommends you*

An example of a vignette is presented below. The manipulated variables are in bold, but were of course invisible to the respondents.

> Your company is doing well. Plans exist to expand the company. It could be relevant to change the legal form of your company in such a situation, however, this **can be quite different** from company to company. You are planning to deepen out this **complex question**. It is of **high importance**, since a change in the legal form has major consequences. Fortunately there is no hurry, because you have **plenty of time** to deepen out this question. Someone in your direct environment **recommends you** to visit an advisor to discuss the various possibilities.

Sample and Response. The study was conducted among Dutch SMEs (self-employed and businesses up to fifty employees). For an efficient and effective sampling we choose to use disproportionate stratified random sampling [27]. Underlying reason is the skewed distribution of organization size in the population. We invited $n=21000$ businesses to participate. The letters were addressed to the management of a business. They were asked to pass it on to the person in the business who is responsible for dealing with tax matters. All respondents were randomly selected from the database of the Netherlands Tax and Customs Administration (NTCA). This database was updated just before we carried out our sample survey in January 2013 and contains all registered businesses in the Netherlands. After two weeks we sent out a reminder to the businesses that had not responded yet. Finally, 6% of all invited participants completed the survey. 68.3% of the respondents were men and 31.4% were women. 54.5% of the respondents were higher educated, 33.5% medium educated, and 12.0% low. Slightly over 80% were managing directors (43.1% self-employed and 40.0% in a business with employees). The rest of the respondents were the specialists in the business (e.g., administrative assistant, financial employee, controller).

4 Results

4.1 Selected Source-Channel Combinations

Table 2 shows which sources are selected in throughout all vignettes. The advisor is by far the most chosen source in the given situations (62.6%). With 20.7% the NTCA is the second most consulted source. All other potential sources are selected less often. In 5.9% of the presented vignettes the respondents did consult no source.

Table 2. Overview of chosen sources in the 32 vignettes of this study

	n	%
NTCA	984	20.7
Another governmental organization than NTCA	26	.7
Advisor/Advice organization	2976	62.6
A colleague within organization	81	1.7
An external contact who I know personal	143	3.0
Family or a good friend	126	2.7
Association (e.g., Chamber of Commerce, Industry Organization)	127	2.7
I consult no source	284	5.9
Total	4747	100.0

Figure 1 shows which channels are used to contact various kinds of sources. The sources are shown on the horizontal axis, the channels on the vertical axis. Except for contact with family/friends and the NTCA, the telephone is the most used channel for all kinds of sources. With regard to family and friends face-to-face is the most used channel (56.1%). Colleagues are also often consulted via face-to-face (40.2%). In approximately a quarter of the cases, contact with the advisor (25.4%) and association (24.9%) occurs face-to-face. E-mail is mostly used to consult the advisor (21.9%) and external contacts (28.5%). The NTCA and associations are often approached via their websites (respectively, 52.7% en 18.5%).

To study the interrelation between source and channel choice in more detail we executed a chi-square test. The results show that there is a significant association between the selected source and the chosen channel $\chi^2(42)=6916.12$, $p<.001$. The values of the standardized residuals are used to interpret the results. Agresti and Finlay [28] argue that a value greater than 3 or lower than −3 reflects a true effect. The strongest significant underrepresentations (i.e., significantly lesser selected than other combinations) were found for the combinations NTCA with face-to-face ($z=-11.3$), advisor with the website ($z=-18.1$), and NTCA with e-mail ($z=-8.8$). Significant, but less strong underrepresentations exist for the combinations NTCA with the telephone ($z=-3.8$), external contact with the website ($z=-3.9$), and family/friends with website ($z=-3.4$) and with e-mail ($z=-3.6$). The most strong overrepresented combination (i.e., significantly more often selected) is NTCA with the website ($z=36.9$). Other strong overrepresentations concern the advisor with e-mail ($z=8.1$), with telephone ($z=5.8$), and with face-to-face ($z=5.4$) as well as the combinations colleague with face-to-face ($z=6.8$), family/friends with face-to-face ($z=9.2$).

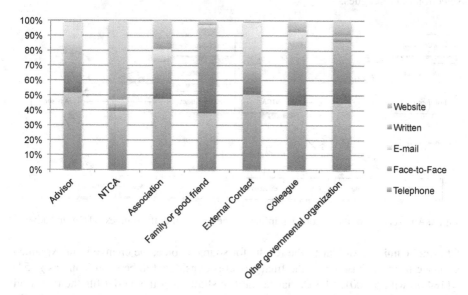

Fig. 1. An overview of the chosen source-channel combinations in the 32 vignettes

4.2   Influencing Factors of Source and Channel Choices

We executed two multinomial logistic regression analyses (NOMREGs) to study the influence of the manipulated factors on source and channel choices. This section starts with the discussion of the results regarding source choices, followed by the results for channel choices.

Source Choices. The change in unexplained variance from the baseline to the final model is considered to be significant, as χ^2 (63) =1467.84 with p<.001, which implies that the final model shows a better fit than the original model. For assessing model fit the Deviance statistic is preferred over the Pearson Statistic [29]. The Deviance statistic shows that the model fits the data well (p=1.000). The pseudo R-square values of Cox and Snell and Nagelkerke show decently-sized effects with values of R^2=.27 and R^2=.30, respectively.

Figure 2 shows only the results for the two most selected sources NTCA and advisor. Table 3 in the appendix provides an overview of the results for all sources. Despite the fact that we found some similar results for both sources there are some contrasting results as well. When the task becomes more general (i.e., less specific) it is more likely that the NTCA is chosen (b=2.51, p<.001), but less likely that the advisor is selected (b=−.86, p<.05) . Furthermore, while *organization size* and *educational level* are significant predictors for the selection of the NTCA, they do not exert significant influence on the selection of the advisor. Comparing the predictors of other sources (e.g., colleagues, associations) also brings differences to light. For instance, when as a task becomes less specific, it becomes less likely that family or friends are chosen (b=−.90, p<.001), but *task specificity* has no influence on the selection of colleagues.

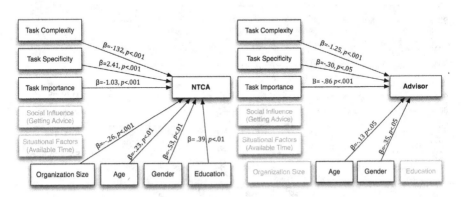

Fig. 2. An overview of the factors that influence the selection of the sources NTCA and advisor

Channel Choices. Similar to the results for source choice, the change in unexplained variance from the baseline to the final model is considered to be significant, as χ^2(54) =1184.98 with p<.001. The Deviance statistic shows that the model fits the data well (p=1.000). The pseudo R-square values of Cox and Snell and Nagelkerke are R^2=.22 and R^2=.24, respectively.

The website channel and the telephone channel were most selected in the vignettes. The results are presented in figure 3. Table 4 in the appendix provides an overview of the results for all channels. When comparing the results of the website and telephone we obviously found that the selection of the website depends on more aspects than the telephone. For instance, *task specificity* ($b=2.17$, $p<.001$) and *social influence* ($b=-.49$, $p<.01$) are found to be significant predictors for the selection of the website, but exert no influence on the selection of the telephone. Furthermore, while *gender* influences both the website and telephone channel, *organization size, age* and *education* are found to be significant predictors for only the selection of the website channel and not for the telephone channel. Again, we found differences between the other channels as well. For example, When a task becomes more general (i.e., less specific) it becomes more likely that the e-mail is chosen ($b= .40$, $p<.05$, but less likely that face-to-face is selected ($b=-1.38$, $p<.001$).

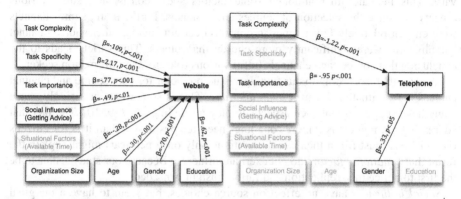

Fig. 3. An overview of the factors that influence the choice for the website and telephone

5   Discussion and Conclusions

The practical reason for conducting this study is the notion that despite implementing various types of strategies, the use of more costly public service channels is still high [e.g., 1,2]. Research on, for example, e-government and multichannel management, has contributed to current strategies. However, governments have failed to design effective and efficient service delivery strategies that are based on the research. We argue that a reasonable approach to tackle this issue could be to broaden the focus of current multichannel strategies by paying attention to the role of the information source related to a particular channel. Therefore, this paper examined source and channel choices in a single study, using the vignette method. This section addresses the limitations of the conducted study, followed by a discussion of findings as well as the conclusions. The paper ends with providing several implications.

Limitations. Although the vignette method provides the opportunity to ask participants about their choices in realistic situations, a number of limitations should be noted with respect to this study. The most important limitation is that not all (potential) predictors were manipulated and incorporated in the vignettes. So, further research is needed to study the influence of other factors as well. Another issue that is not addressed is whether the participants wanted to consult a second source or channel because we only asked for their first source-channel combination. Insights into other choices throughout the information-seeking process are still needed. Further, we studied the situation in one country and in the context of B2G service interactions. This hinders the generalizability of the results to other countries and contexts.

Discussion and Conclusions. One of the more significant findings to emerge from this study is that the significance, strength and type of relationship (e.g., positive or negative) between the influencing factors and the various source and channel choices vary. This indicates that although some factors show consistent results, various aspects influence the selection of sources and channels. Furthermore, some channels were chosen relatively fewer times to consult a certain source, other source-channel combinations were significantly more chosen than others. This variety leads to the conclusion that sources and channels fulfill various roles for the information seeker.

A factor that, according to our findings, is no predictor for both source and channel choices is the situational aspect *available time*. This is somewhat surprisingly, since many have suggested that such aspects do play a role [e.g., 6, 7, 9, 10]. The fact that addressing tax matters is a more 'ongoing' need for businesses than it is for citizens (i.e., citizens must fill in their tax declarations only once per year) might explain the result that *situational factors* do not exert an influence. Because our study seems to be the first to notice this, replication and further insight is needed.

Social influences have no effect on source choices, but seem to have a marginal effect on channel choice. Although the understanding and perceptions related to the vignettes were pre-tested, the lack of influence might be due to issues in the manipulation of the *social influence* factor (i.e., it might be difficult for respondents to imagine themselves in such a situation). Nevertheless, our conclusion that *social influences* have (at least) a marginal effect on channel choice seems plausible because it is in line with the findings of many others [e.g., 10, 30- 32]. The effect of *social influences* on source choice seems less studied [e.g., 7], which might underline our finding that source choices are not affected by *social influences*.

In general, our findings indicate that *task characteristics* play a major role in the selection processes of source and channel choices. This result generally does not divert from other research findings [e.g., 6, 9, 10, 13, 22]. However, our contribution to the existing knowledge is the finding that the characteristic *task specificity* particularly determines which source and which channel will be selected, whereas the task characteristics *importance* and *complexity* are found to be action triggers (i.e., to start an information-seeking process). Furthermore, given the observed differences in the direction of the influence of *task specificity,* the results indicate that sources and channels fulfill various roles (i.e., some are selected for general/orientation purposes while others are selected for specific, interpretation purposes).

The largest predictor concerning *personal* and *organization characteristics* is *education*, followed by *organization size*. Baldwin and Rice [19] argue that *organizational characteristics* exert more influence than *personal characteristics*. They even argue that individual characteristics have no influence at all. In contrast, several studies in the context of channel-choice behavior argue that these basic personal characteristics (e.g., gender, age, and education) are reliable predictors [33, 34]. Our study found that people that are higher educated are more likely to use electronic channels and consult formal sources. Larger organizations are less likely to choose the website and face-to-face. Only the advisor is independently chosen from the size of an organization, for all other sources it is observed that larger organizations are less likely to consult a source compared to no source.

Implications. The primarily starting point of current service delivery strategies is the channel of a single information source. However, our findings suggest that information seekers have many sources at their disposal to obtain information. This finding again calls for a change to incorporate the users' perspectives. Governments should realize that they act in a networked setting with various other potential sources from which businesses can obtain information. It is advisable for governments to anticipate the role of source-channel combinations. Governments can accomplish this by gaining an overview of relevant key sources in their network and determine their own role as one of those information sources in that network. The division of roles among the various sources should be considered when designing service delivery strategies. It is also important to link the role of an information source to the role of the channels that are at the disposal of that particular source. Box 1 illustrates this.

Box 1—Illustration: Implications for the NTCA website

Our findings have shown that the NTCA in combination with the website channel is primarily selected for general tasks. It would be relevant for the NTCA to consider this when developing its website. Thus, it could decide to give general information a more prominent place on the website and put more specific information in the background. Visitors are still able to obtain detailed information, but in the first instance, information overload is avoided by providing only general information. 'Decision trees' may help in structuring general and specific information. They assist visitors in selecting and finding only information that is relevant to their specific situations.

However, what if the determined roles of an information source and its channels are not the desired ones? For example, what if the findings indicate that the NTCA is often consulted to solve specific tasks, which require interpretation because the answers differ from business to business, but the NTCA primarily offers general information? In such situations, it is important to start the debate about what role the government should fulfill. What expectations should SMEs have for public service delivery? What are the responsibilities of SMEs themselves? Debating these aspects would help governments to formulate service-delivery strategies that incorporate both their own role and the advisor's role in a networked setting. Therefore, we suggest that governments should implement strategies that guide information seekers to desired source-channel combinations, which we call multisource and multichannel management. Cross-referrals should help guiding the seeker to another channel or other source-channel combinations. Box 2 illustrates how cross-referrals may be used in service delivery processes.

Box 2—Illustration: Implementing cross-referrals

The provided information on the website of the NTCA about how to change the legal form of a business is inadequate because there are many specific details to consider. The website can provide only general information that is applicable to every business (e.g., explanations of rules or declaration deadlines). The NTCA can add the simple sentence, 'If you want specific information whether changing the legal form would be appropriate for your business, please call or visit an advisory organization. There, they can help you with making a decision'. Also call-center employees can do this by simply telling information seekers to obtain advice from another source or via another channel.

The results of this paper indicate that sources and channels fulfil various roles for the information seekers (i.e., businesses). Despite the promising results and implications for public service delivery strategies, future research is needed to increase and refine our understanding of source and channel choices in B2G service interactions.

References

1. Pieterson, W., Ebbers, W.: The use of service channels by citizens in the Netherlands: implications for multi-channel management. International Review of Administrative Sciences 74(1), 95–110 (2008)
2. OECD: Forum on Tax Administration: Working smarter in revenue administration—Using demand management strategies to meet service delivery goals. Organization for Economic Co-operation and Development, Paris (2012)
3. Agichtein, E., Castillo, C., Donato, D., Gionis, A., Mishne, G.: Finding high-quality content in social media. In: Proceedings of the International Conference on Web Search and Data Mining, pp. 183–194 (2008)
4. Daft, R.L., Lengel, R.H.: Information richness: a new approach to managerial behavior and organizational design. In: Cummings, L.L., Staw, B.M. (eds.) Research in Organizational Behavior, vol. 6, pp. 191–233. JAI Press, Homewood (1984)
5. Daft, R.L., Lengel, R.H.: Organizational information requirements, media richness and structural design. Management Science, 554–571 (1986)
6. Byström, K., Järvelin, K.: Task complexity affects information seeking and use. Information Processing & Management 31(2), 191–213 (1995)
7. Saunders, C., Jones, J.W.: Temporal sequences in information acquisition for decision making: A focus on source and medium. Academy of Management Review, 29–46 (1990)
8. Christensen, E.W., Bailey, J.R.: A Source Accessibility Effect on Media Selection. Management Communication Quarterly 10(3), 373–387 (1997)
9. Pieterson, W.: Channel choice: Citizens' channel behavior and public service channel strategy. Enschede, Gildeprint B.V. (2009)

10. Fulk, J., Schmitz, J., Steinfield, C.W.: A social influence model of technology use. In: Fulk, J., Steinfield, C.W. (eds.) Organizations and Communication Technology. Sage Publications, London (1990)
11. Carlson, J.R., Zmud, R.W.: Channel Expansion Theory: A Dynamic View of Medial and Information Richness Perceptions (1), 280–284 (1994)
12. Carlson, J.R., Zmud, R.W.: Channel expansion theory and the experiential nature of media richness perceptions. Academy of Management Journal, 153–170 (1999)
13. Leckie, G.J., Pettigrew, K.E., Sylvain, C.: Modeling the information seeking of professionals: a general model derived from research on engineers, health care professionals, and lawyers. The Library Quarterly, 161–193 (1996)
14. Wilson, T.D.: On user studies and information needs. Journal of Documentation 37(1), 3–15 (1981)
15. Wilson, T.D.: Models in information behavior res. Journal of Documentation 55(3), 249–270 (1999)
16. Krikelas, J.: Information-seeking behavior: patterns and concepts. Drexel Library Quarterly 19, 5–20 (1983)
17. Savolainen, R.: Everyday life information seeking: Approaching information seeking in the context of "way of life". Library & Information Science Research 17(3), 259–294 (1995)
18. Johnson, J.D.: On contexts of information seeking. Information Processing & Management 39(5), 735–760 (2003)
19. Baldwin, N.S., Rice, R.E.: Information-Seeking Behavior of Securities Analysts: Individual and Institutional Influences, Information Sources and Channels and Outcomes. JASIS 48(8), 674–693 (1997)
20. Boyd, A.: Multi-channel information seeking: a fuzzy conceptual model. Aslib Proceedings 56(2), 81–88 (2004)
21. Julien, H., Michels, D.: Intra-individual information behaviour in daily life. Information Processing & Management 40(3), 547–562 (2004)
22. Sitkin, S.B., Sutcliffe, K.M., Barrios-Choplin, J.R.: A dual capacity model of communication media choice in organizations. Human Communication Research 18(4), 563–598 (1992)
23. Morrison, R.L., Stettler, K., Anderson, A.E.: Using vignettes in cognitive research on establishment surveys. Journal of Official Statistics-Stockholm- 20(2), 319–340 (2004)
24. Wason, K.D., Cox, K.C.: Scenario Utilization in Marketing Research. In: Strutton, D., Pelton, L.E., Shipp, S. (eds.) Advances in Marketing. Texas: Southw. Marketing Association, pp. 155–162 (1996)
25. Barnett, T., Bass, K., Brown, G.: Ethical ideology and ethical judgment regarding ethical issues in business. Journal of Business Ethics 13(6), 469–480 (1994)
26. Graham, M.E., Cable, D.M.: Consideration of the Incomplete Block Design for Policy-Capturing Research. Organizational Research Methods 4(1), 26–45 (2001)
27. Foreman, E.K.: Survey sampling principles. Marcel Dekker, New York (1991)
28. Agresti, A., Finlay, B.: Statistical Methods for the Social Sciences, 4th edn. Pearson Prentice Hall, New Jersey (2009)
29. Menard, S.: Applied logistic regression analysis, 2nd edn. Sage Publ., Thousand Oaks (2002)
30. Turner, J.W.: Exploring the Dominant Media: How Does Media Use Reflect Organizational Norms and Affect Performance? Journal of Business Communication 43(3), 220–250 (2006)

31. El-Shinnawy, M., Markus, M.L.: Acceptance of communication media in organizations: richness or features? IEEE Transactions on Professional Communication 41(4), 242–253 (1998)
32. Haythornthwaite, C., Wellman, B.: Work, friendship, and media use for information exchange in a networked organization. Journal of the American Society for Information Science 49(12), 1101–1114 (1998)
33. van Deursen, A., van Dijk, J., Ebbers, W.: Why e-government usage lags behind: explaining the gap between potential and actual usage of electronic public services in the Netherlands. In: Wimmer, M.A., Scholl, H.J., Grönlund, Å., Andersen, K.V. (eds.) EGOV 2006. LNCS, vol. 4084, pp. 269–280. Springer, Heidelberg (2006)
34. van Dijk, G., Minocha, S., Laing, A.: Consumers, channels and communication: Online and offline communication in service consumption. Interacting with Computers 19(1), 7–19 (2007)

Annex

Table 3. An overview of the (in)significant influence of various factors on source choices

Factors	NTCA	Advisor	Colleague	External Contact	Family/ Friends	Association
Task complexity	+/-	+/-	+/-	+/-	-	+/-
Task specificity	+	+/-	-	+/-	+/-	+/-
Task importance	+/-	+/-	-	+/-	+/-	+/-
Available time	-	-	-	-	-	-
Social influence	-	-	-	-	-	-
Organization size	+/-	-	-	+/-	+/-	+/-
Age	+/-	+/-	+/-	-	+/-	-
Education*	+	-	+	+	-	-
Gender**	+/-	+/-	-	-	-	+/-

Table 4. An overview of the (in)significant influence of various factors on channel choices

Factors	Telephone	Face-to-Face	E-mail	Written	Website
Task complexity	+/-	+/-	+/-	+/-	+/-
Task specificity	-	+/-	+	-	+
Task importance	+/-	+/-	+/-	-	+/-
Available time	-	-	-	-	-
Social influence	-	-	-	-	+/-
Organization size	-	+/-	-	-	+/-
Age	-	-	+/-	-	+/-
Education	-	-	+	-	+
Gender	+/-	-	+/-	-	+/-

Note for both tables. + significant predictor (positive effect), +/- significant predictor (negative effect),

- insignificant predictor

* reference category was "high education level" , ** reference category was "women"

Connecting People: Semantic-Conceptual Modeling for Laws and Regulations

Tom Van Engers[1] and Sjir Nijssen[2]

[1] University of Amsterdam, Leibniz Center for Law, The Netherlands
vanEngers@uva.nl
[2] PNA Group, The Netherlands
Sjir.Nijssen@pna-group.com

Abstract. Working on building large scale information systems that have the job to serve their clients in a client friendly way and at the same time have to comply with the rules that regulate their behavior, including their (legal) decision-making processes, we observed that designing these systems is still more an art rather than a result of systematic engineering. We have been working on a method allowing stakeholders to systematically analyze the rules and their meaning (i.e. their effect in practical cases) in such way that it supports systems designers and (legal) experts in making sense out of the legal sources, and use this understanding of the regulatory system at hand when designing information systems that supports both the (administrative) organizations and their clients. In this paper we will elaborate on our proposed analysis approach, show how to systematically use the patterns explicitly but often implicitly available in laws and regulation. The Hohfeld conceptual model is very helpful. The Hohfeld model needs extension in our view and thus we have specified the semantic-conceptual model for Hohfeld as a solid base to add time travel aspects.

Keywords: Formal model of Hohfeld legal relations, analysis of law constructs, law based large scale information systems, temporal extension of Hohfeld, semantic-conceptual model, legal DNA.

1   Introduction

Most governmental institutions, including public administrations, are aware of the fact that the services they provide to citizens and companies, are primarily defined in laws, decrees and other regulations, collectively here referred to as the law. However if you look at the way they bring about these services and design the (e-)forms and (web) IT-services this clear connection between these services and some legal source defining them seems to be completely missing in nearly all cases. This lack of transparent connection between the legal sources and IT-systems will lead to increased complexity and high maintenance costs and decreased adaptivity when changes in policy or circumstances require it.

Dealing with change is something public administrations normally can handle very well as they are used to ever changing regulations and keeping their systems aligned

M. Janssen et al. (Eds.): EGOV 2014, LNCS 8653, pp. 133–146, 2014.

with their environments. However the way most administrations handle this can be characterized as an art rather than following a rational engineering approach. This is surprising given the interest of the process and amount of effort and money involved in it. What we observed in the more than 30 years working experience in business information systems, is that different stakeholders within the public administrations try to grasp the consequences of the regulatory or environmental changes for those issues they feel responsible for and then start to redesign the processes, (parts of) IT-systems, (e-)forms etc., without worrying too much that the partial solutions will together create the required, i.e. compliant, solution. As a result of this existing practice administrations can not guarantee the legitimacy of their acting, have difficulties explaining their (legal) decisions, deliver not always the services expected by their stakeholders, and are less adaptive and cost-effective as they could be.

In one of our previous publications (Van Engers & Nijssen 2014a) we have described part of our modeling approach, more specifically an analysis of legal relations, an analysis that is based upon the original work of Wesley Newcomb Hohfeld (see Hohfeld 2010, originally published 1913). We have extended the four basic relational categories with temporal relations and explicit events (legal actions) that allow us to analyze and describe regulations and situations subjected to regulations using a state-transactional view fitting the life-cycle of these legal relations and enabling for a service-oriented perspective combining the requirements from regulatory sources and the life events of the cases at hand.

Before introducing the Hohfeldian basic categories and explaining our extensions, let us explain some of the considerations we had when we started our quest for a semantic-conceptual modeling method for laws and regulations that would be the basis of an engineering approach for large-scale information systems in (public) administrations.

One of these considerations was that policymakers and legal drafters tend to limit their creativity by (re)using existing policies and regulations as examples. Mechanisms such as good drafting principles (in many countries the drafters are bound by these principles, in the Netherlands for example by the "Aanwijzingen voor de Regelgeving" in English "Directives for the Legal drafter") further limit the number of constructions the policymakers and drafters will produce when creating new regulations or change existing ones.

The operational units that are responsible for organizing the processes that make the regulations work also restrict themselves by basing the new functionalities that are implied by the new regulations on ones that are already known. This allows the administrations to keep close to existing or at least familiar processes with the assumption of a decrease in failure risks. In our many years of working in practice however we have not seen this reuse of abstract building blocks explicitly addressed, while we were more and more convinced this would allow us to build better information systems. These systems of course would primarily have to be correct implementations of the requirements that are given by laws and regulations.

2   Public Administrations and (Public) Service Design

From public administrations we expect that their activities and information systems supporting them, i.e. the administration's services, are derived from law. Not implementing services that would be required to fulfill legal obligations or allow citizens to execute their rights would disrupt our legal systems while offering services that are not connected to the law would rightfully be considered a waste of public money at least. In practice however, as far as we know, no method was used to systematically analyze sources of law and derive the required services in such way that the connection would be clear to all stakeholders. In 2012 in the Netherlands some public administrations together with universities and innovative companies of prime interest for e-government started to cooperate on these matters. The authors of this paper are member of that cooperation. We named this group the 'Blue Chamber' referring to the color of the walls of the room in which the first concrete ideas have taken shape. The authors of this focus on the fundamental research work in this groups' co-creative effort and report in this paper part of what they have accomplished.

As stated before our approach is partly based upon work of Hohfeld, who developed his legal relations in the early twentieth century. One could wonder why it takes so long to develop a method that would guarantee the correct implementation of law. Perhaps the most recent crisis in the Netherlands is a blessing in disguise forcing public administration to do more with less. The people representing the public administrations stressed that the conditions under which the government must perform its duties are constantly changing due to changes in legislation. The effects of these changes are to be implemented in services to citizens and businesses quickly and effectively. Citizens and businesses may expect reliable and expedient rendering of services. Obviously these services should provide answers to their questions, or offer a solution to their specific needs.

In recent decades, public administration has changed under the influence of digitisation. These changes affect the processes of implementing public services. Both the large-scale processes for handling cases of large groups of citizens, and processes for the treatment of individual cases in complex situations are affected. Examples can be found in the area of benefit provision, granting of subsidies, licensing and taxation. Central government, provincial governments and municipalities strive, as much as possible, to process applications for licenses, benefits and the provision of other public services electronically.

Successive governments have been working on a response to this development. Among other things, this has resulted in a government-wide vision[1] of the provision of services to citizens and businesses. This vision is based on customer-driven public services in which there is a central focus on the requests of citizens and businesses. The implementing bodies are expected to design their processes and services in such a way that they can meet the needs and perspectives of their customers. In other words, efficacy is central. A prime challenge will be to offer the desired effective processing of customer requests in an affordable and efficient manner.

---

[1] Established Government-Wide Vision of Services (Vastgestelde Overheidsbrede Visie op Dienstverlening) kst-26643-182 – Official Publications (in Dutch).

The effective and efficient handling of customer requests requires cooperation between different organisations. This helps diminish the meaning of the boundaries between layers of government and government organisations.

In order to play their part for and on behalf of citizens, it is necessary for the government organisations to design their processes and services in such a way that they can respond to changing conditions, changing stakeholder demands and changes in cooperation with other organisations.

In recent years, it has been the tendency for implementing bodies to refrain from concealing the rules in layers of IT systems, but to opt instead for an approach in which these rules are defined in such a way in IT systems that they can be more easily implemented and maintained. In legislation, the trend is to model information, rules and processes in an integrated fashion. This translation of legislation into integrated knowledge and process models is used as a specification for processes and IT systems. 'Rule-based or knowledge-based working', 'rule management', 'Knowledge as a Service' (KaaS) and 'agile implementation of legislation' are names that are used to describe this approach.

The approach aims to provide greater flexibility and agility in the implementation of new laws and/or regulations.

What is still lacking however is a uniform and coherent method to analyze and interpret sources of law that would achieve integrated information, rules and process models with which the desired flexibility and agility in the provision of information can be realized. Such an approach is therefore a prerequisite for the realization of a customer-oriented service and for securing collaboration between organizations (interoperability). The observations below from daily implementation practice illustrate the lack of a 'clear and coherent method of analysis for the interpretation of legislation by implementing bodies':

- Translating legislation into customer-driven service and product requirements for the implementation of processes and applications is usually quite time-consuming.
- The (contents of) services and processes are not sufficiently traceable to the legislation.
- Up till now, the translation of legislation into service and product requirements has often proved to be a process difficult to control. The procedure is not clear and is in part implied and depends on the individual 'translator'. Analysis usually takes place from this translator's own discipline (legal, implementation, information science or IT). The required expertise is scarce.
- Adequate support which allows for intelligent searching of the corpus of legislation is currently lacking and there is only limited support for adequately managing the results in conjunction.

It is our aim to help to solve these issues by developing the required method.

In that effort it was clear from day one that we had to clarify the meaning of the legal sources, i.e. the effects that it could potentially have for each of the addressees, first. A semantic-conceptual model of the legal source could create this required clarity. When developing our method we were primarily asking ourselves which are the kind of constructs that are required in the semantic-conceptual model such that the intent of the law can be maximally explicitly represented in a scalable semantic-conceptual model?

Regulations, for example a law, describe primarily the rights and duties of the parties with respect to certain matter. Rights and duties are terms that upon semantic-conceptual analysis can be usefully subcategorized. About a century ago Hohfeld described a solid framework for this subcategorization. His description however was – understandably at that time (1913) – reasonably informal and also it lacked some elements that would allow us to formally express the meaning of regulatory sources in such a way that it would fit our current needs.

In the next sections we will describe the formal semantic-conceptual model of that framework as a base to add requirements that have originated in more recent years.

3   The Original Hohfeldian Relations

Wesley Newcomb Hohfeld produced a landmark paper in the early years of the 20th century, clarifying the most important concept in the legal world: the legal relation (Hohfeld used both the terms legal as well as jural relation). One of Hohfeld's main ideas is that all legal relations consist of a set of atomic or elementary legal relations between two parties with respect to a certain matter, and each legal relation has only the following four possible pairs:

i.   One party has a **right** (claim) and another party has a **duty**,
ii.   One party has a **privilege** and another party has a **noright**,
iii.   One party has a **power** and another party has a **liability**, and
iv.   One party has an **immunity** and another party has a **disability**.

In Van Engers & Nijssen (2014a) we have paraphrased Corbin (see Corbin 1991 & 1921) and have posed the following about these four party-paired legal relations:

Suppose we have two parties, person A and person B.

Right and Duty. When person A currently has a right and person B has at the same time a duty with respect to matter M, person A is aware that the following holds: what must person B do for me (person A) with respect to matter M; person B is aware that for him the following holds: what must I (person B) do for person A with respect to matter M?

Privilege and Noright. When person A currently has a privilege and person B has at the same time a noright with respect to matter M, person A is aware that the following holds: what may I do with respect to M, without having regard for any other including person B; the noright party, in this case person B is aware that for him the following holds: what may person A do with respect to M, unrestrained by me (person B)?

Power and Liability. When person A currently has a power and person B has at the same time a liability with respect to matter M, person A is aware that the following holds: what new legal relation may I create between person B or between person B and another party, or me, with respect to M; the liability party, in this case person B is aware that for him the following holds: what new legal relation may person A create for me and another party with respect to M, without having any regard for my position?

Immunity and Disability. When person A currently has an immunity and person B has at the same time a disability with respect to matter M, person A is aware that the following holds: with respect to matter M person A is not subject to the power of person B to alter the legal relation of person A with respect to matter M (paraphrasing Corbin 1919, page 8). The disability party, in this case person B is aware that for him the following holds: person B cannot change the existing legal relation of person A with respect to matter M.

In Van Engers and Nijssen 2014 we have pointed at one of the major issues with Hohfeld's original work; it lacks a temporal perspective which is needed to understand how acts are related to the creation and termination of legal relations (typically created via a power-liability). Such perspective is essential for connecting the legal consequences to the acts performed, a perspective we need to when we want to build supporting IT systems. These IT systems after all will have to handle complex social situations and consequently we need to understand the sequences of actions that we have to be able support, by creating services for each of them. The power for every alien to receive asylum, for example, can be expressed as a power-liability relation, requiring a service to submit these requests and a service to inform the alien about the result of processing that request. In our method we therefore have include a temporal perspective, which allows us to understand the consequences of the creation and termination of Hohfeldian relations.

4   A Service Oriented Design Perspective on Hohfeld

In the previous section we have already pointed at one of the shortcomings of Hohfeldian analysis, i.e. the lack of an explicit temporal perspective. Another weakness is its mere focus on the institutional reality layer leaving the connection to brute reality underexposed. Figure 1 shows the connection between these layers.

Legal reasoning is part of the Institutional Reality layer. This Institutional Reality layer maps legal facts, using legal rules, to other legal facts. In other words it describes legal facts and legal (derivation) rules. Furthermore it describes legal metarules, such as rules that determine the applicability of other legal rules. The legal facts in the Institutional Reality layer have to be connected to the brute reality. Brute reality consists of the physical and informational or administrative brute reality. The brute facts represented as some data object can be 'qualified' or 'count as' some legal fact. Therefore (institutional) meaning is assigned to the brute facts through their qualification. It must be noted that in most court cases it is the qualification of brute facts that are disputed rather than the epistemic reasoning (i.e. drawing conclusions from legal facts and the applied legal rules). Intuitively one would think that each brute fact could be classified into one of two classes: legally relevant and legally irrelevant. However it is slightly more complex than this. One brute fact may be irrelevant from a certain perspective, such as the price of a car is irrelevant from the perspective of the traffic code, but might be relevant for some other perspective, like tax law. The specification of a semantic-conceptual model can help in detecting consequences of possible qualifications of disputed facts.

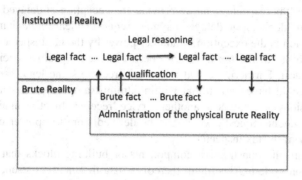

Fig. 1. Institutional Reality and Brute Reality. Legal reasoning with Institutional Reality maps legal facts to other legal facts. These legal facts are connected to the administration of brute reality (i.e. data representation of the physical world) by a process called qualification. This qualification gives (institutional) meaning to the brute facts, it defines what brute facts 'counts as' what legal facts.

The policy-makers and legislation drafters that create the regulatory sources, i.e. sources of law, expect that all relevant stakeholders are able to understand the meaning of the institutions described in those sources. This is because the stakeholders are supposed to understand the institutional consequences of their behavior (acts) given some qualification.

Acts performed in brute reality may have legal effects depending on their qualification. Some are qualified as the creation of a liability or the execution of a power thus creating legal relations in the institutional layer; others are qualified as failing to meet a duty and might result in a legal fact that provides the motive for someone to act upon it in brute reality. It must be noted that also not acting in some cases may have legal consequences (negligence).

Hohfeld's legal relations are always relations between two actor-roles, the buyer and seller, the taxpayer and tax inspector etc. From an organizational or information systems perspective this provides us with a nice demarcation of the internal and the external world. So we could for example describe all relations in the institutional reality in scope from the perspective of one actor-role, e.g. our minister, the tax inspector etc.. Since it are the execution of powers or the imposition of a duty that make others to act (consequence of the power-liability relation), the power-liability relations or the right-duty relations can force us to deliver a service, while allowing for the execution of a power obviously also can be seen as a service.

Combining this perspective selection, taking the position of one of the addressed actor-roles, with the power-liability focus provides us a service-oriented perspective on the legal domain at hand. Let us illustrate this with an example. Let's assume that a taxpayer has the power to request for a delayed payment given some conditions and that the tax inspector has the corresponding liability, and the associated duty when the power is executed, to handle the request. The consequent services the tax administration (assuming that the tax administration is the organization that implements the institutional concept 'tax inspector') has to provide are 'reception of delayed payment request' and 'provide decision on delayed payment request'. Please note that the production of the decision is the execution of another power by the tax inspector. It must be stressed that liability of the tax inspector doesn't include a positive decision, i.e. granting of the request. Furthermore, but this would require some legal background knowledge if we would have known that within administrative law one can usually object against decisions, we may need another service 'receive objection against decision on delayed payment request', which can be derived from the power of the requestor and liability of the tax inspector.

These services are the constructive components or building blocks that together form our information systems. The input thereof is data that may represent acts and brute facts allowing us to interpret this data and use it for (automated) legal reasoning. The legal consequences can in return be presented as output data of the system. Obviously we might want to present the reasoning (perhaps in reasoning steps) and the intermediary or derived legal facts as well.

5   Hohfeld in a Semantic-Conceptual Model

At the time Hohfeld published his landmark paper in 1913 little attention was paid to formal models. At that time there were no large information systems supporting government services. And at that time there was much less experience with diagrammatic representation of knowledge compared with today. If we recall that the first attempt of the now well-known periodic table started in 1789 and the current form was designed in 1923, then it is about time that we start to develop a "periodic table" for legal relations. Hohfeld laid a solid foundation in 1913. How should such a "jural periodic table" look like? We do not pretend we have the final answer but we believe a modest start is described hereafter.

What is a semantic-conceptual model? It is a formal model that:

1. Defines the scope of the subject. This is represented by explicitly defining the fact types aka kind of facts and by consequence the fact instances that are considered within scope;
2. Defines the associated derivation rules, if applicable. Derivation rules map fact sets to other fact sets, and can be interpreted as possible and permitted transitions of fact sets; derivation rules are performed by software;
3. Defines all the associated integrity rules. Integrity rules specify which fact sets within scope and transitions to new sets as a consequence of adding to and/or deleting facts from the fact base as well as mappings between fact sets, i.e. transitions,

are considered to be correct expressions; in more casual terms, the integrity rules specify the required quality of the fact sets and transitions. The integrity rules constitute what is usually referred to as the theoretical framework; integrity rules are checked by software;

4. Defines the associated behavioural rules, if applicable and the associated actor-roles; behavioral rules are performed by legal entities;
5. Defines the associated set of events (either jural actions by actors or time-induced events) and
6. Describes the definitions of the terms in natural language.

Please note that 1. through 5. constitute a formal semantic-conceptual model. The item under 6. is an informal component.

The question may be asked: Why do we need the informal component associated with 1. through 5.? To answer that question we need to go through the procedure how to model a law. The source of a semantic-conceptual model is the law and associated decrees, or treaties and regulations. The process that is used to produce a formal semantic-conceptual model for the law is a human process. A lot of essential model elements are implicit in a law. When humans are aware of the patterns containing implicit components as well as the explicit components, duly educated experts can produce a formal semantic-conceptual model. However for humans to do this job, including validation of the model, the definitions of the terms are an absolute prerequisite. Without these definitions there is hardly any chance that the model can be validated. Hence the list of terms and their definition is an indispensable part of the entire analysis and validation process, used to specify a semantic-conceptual model of a law and associated regulations.

A reasoner does, at first sight, not need the list of definitions. The reasoner can produce the results solely from the formal semantic-conceptual model and the fact base. However when a reasoner wants to communicate in a human friendly way, we recommend to make systematic use of this list. Hence there is a useful function for the list of definitions when the entire process is considered.

How is the scope of Hohfeld defined?

The first fact type is:

FT1: <Party-Right-Side> in the role of <Kind-Of-Right> has a legal relation with <Party-Duty-Side> in the role of <Kind-Of-Duty> with respect to <Matter>.

In Fig. 2 we see that within the scope of Hohfeld there are facts that conform to the fact type called "Legal relation". The fact type "Legal relation" consists of 5 variables. An example of a fact (instance) could be: A in the role of Claim has a legal relation with B in the role of Duty with respect to M. In practice there are millions of these fact instances that are within scope. The semantic-conceptual model declares such fact instances within scope of Hohfeld by the declaration of the fact type "Legal relation".

With this declaration we can express every Hohfeld legal relation. We want to remark that we recommend to explicitly model Matter as this is a domain specific set of facts.

In the CogNIAM protocol to develop a semantic-conceptual model, there is a rule that specifies that the modeler needs to have at least one functional integrity rule for every fact type. It is recommended to add this type of integrity rule with priority 1.

Integrity rule IR1: The combination of Party-Right-Side, Kind-Of-Right, Party-Duty-Side and Matter is unique.

An alternative formulation could be: The combination Party-Right-Side, Kind-Of-Right, Party-Duty-Side and Matter determines Kind-Of-Duty.

A fact instance of fact type FT1 is an instance of what Hohfeld called a legal relation. At the time of Hohfeld (1913) this was considered sufficient.

In these days (2014) where the government offers services based on laws and regulations, and a very typical characteristic of such laws and regulations is that they are almost constantly changing, we need more extended facts.

FT2: <Party-Right-Side> in the role of <Kind-Of-Right> has a legal relation with <Party-Duty-Side> in the role of <Kind-Of-Duty> with respect to <Matter>.This legal relation was established on <Date-Time-Established>, it starts to become effective on <Date-Time-Effectiveness-Start> and it has terminated respectively is supposed to end its effectiveness on <Date-Time-Effectiveness-Ended>.

But there are several integrity rules in the extended Hohfeld version needed in these days.

We first and for all have to cater for the "time travel" aspect. This means that we have to extend integrity rule IR1 as follows:

Integrity rule IR2: The combination of Party-Right-Side, Kind-Of-Right, Party-Duty-Side>, Matter and Date-Time-Validity-Start is unique.

There are precisely 4 kinds of rights in the Hohfeld approach. Hence we need a fact type and an integrity rule to express that formally. The fact type is:

TF3: Within the collection of kinds of rights there exist the <Kind-Of-Right>.

As we have limited space in this paper we will not include the complete diagrammatic representation of every fact type and integrity rule mentioned below.

Integrity rule IR4: Permitted values for Kind-Of-Right are {claim, privilege, power, immunity}. In a more casual language, Hohfeld recognizes the following kinds of rights: claim, privilege, power and immunity.

If we apply dimension analysis to the kinds of rights we come to the conclusion that we are dealing with two different subtypes:

ST1: Kind-Of-Right-State is a subtype of Kind-Of-Right

Integrity rule IR6: Kind-Of-Right-State permitted values are Claim and Privilege.

ST2: Kind-Of-Right-Dynamic is a subtype of Kind-Of-Right

Integrity rule IR8: Kind-Of-Right-Dynamic permitted values are Power and Immunity.

There are precisely 4 kinds of duties in the Hohfeld approach. Hence we need a fact type and an integrity rule to express that formally. The fact type is:

TF4: Within the collection of kinds of duties there exist the <Kind-Of-Duty>.

Integrity rule IR10 Permitted values for Kind-Of-Duty are {duty, noright, liability, disability}.

If we apply dimension analysis we come to the conclusion that we are dealing with two different subtypes of Kind-Of-Duty:

ST3: Kind-Of-Duty-State is a subtype of Kind-Of-Duty.

Integrity rule IR12: Kind-Of-Duty-State permitted values Duty and Noright.

ST4: Kind-Of-Duty-Dynamic is a subtype of Kind-Of-Duty.

Integrity rule IR14: Kind-Of-Duty-Dynamic permitted values Liability and Disability.

However Hohfeld has made it clear that he only considers the following pairs to be applicable:

FT5: <Kind-Of-Right> and <Kind-of-Duty> is a permitted kind of legal relation.

An alternative formulation could be: The combination <Kind-Of-Right>, <Kind-Of-Duty> is permitted.

Integrity rule IR16: In FT5 the following combinations are permitted {<Claim, Duty>, <Privilege-Noright>, <Power, Liability>, <Immunity, Disability.}

Integrity rule IR18: The combination of <Kind-Of-Right> and <Kind-Of-Duty> in FT2 is a subset of the combination of <Kind-Of-Right>, <Kind-Of-Duty> in FT5.

With the above declarations we see in the diagram at page ... that every legal relation has to have a couple that is permitted.

The Hohfeld model is fairly rich in casually defined integrity rules. To illustrate some of these we decided to confine ourselves to powers and immunities. We derive specialised fact types from the Hohfeld legal relation fact type to make the illustration more clear. In the fact type Power legal relation we have a fact type with three variables, derived from the fact type Legal relation. See Fig. 2. We can now formally model all the rules that Hohfeld formulated informally. The exclusion integrity rule exc4001 specifies that a given party on the right side and a given party on the duty side with respect to a given matter can only have one of power or immunity, never both.

We furthermore offer the opportunity to have fact instances that formally deny the existence of a power (called 'No power legal relation' in Fig. 2) or an immunity as persons find it sometimes useful to be able to express themselves that way.

The following set of terms will be defined, paraphrasing Corbin:

1. Legal relation. A legal relation is a relationship between two parties, one party in a certain kind of right and the other party in a certain kind of duty with respect to a specific matter.
2. Claim. A claim party has the right to ask the question: what must the duty holder do for me with respect to a specific matter?
3. Duty. A duty party has the obligation to ask himself the question: what must I do for the claim holder in this legal relation?
4. Privilege. The privilege holder may ask herself: what may I do, without regard for the noright party?
5. Noright. The noright holder may ask himself: what may the privilege holder do to me in this matter, without any regard for me?
6. Power. The power holder (party A) in a legal relation can ask herself: what new legal relations can I create between party D (the liability holder in the legal relation) and myself of another party?
7. Liability. The liability holder may ask herself: what new legal relations can the power holder create between me and himself and or others?
8. Immunity. The immunity holder may ask herself: which of my existing legal relations is safe from alteration by the disability holder?
9. Disability. The disability holder may ask himself: which of the legal relations of the immunity holder is impossible for me to extinguish?

The main parts of the semantic-conceptual model of Hohfeld in a diagrammatic representation:

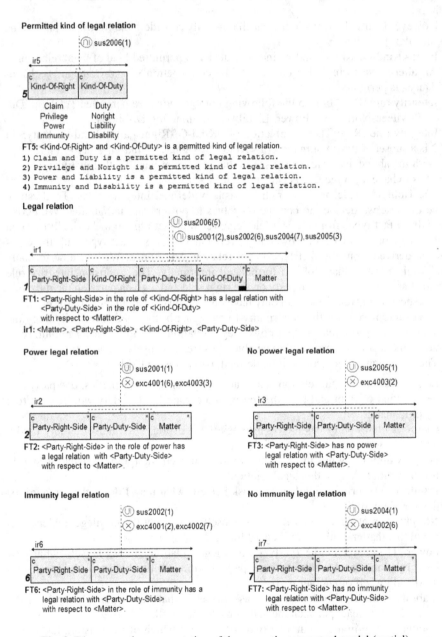

Fig. 2. Diagrammatic representation of the semantic-conceptual model (partial)

6   Conclusions

Working in the field of building large scale information systems for organizations that have to base their (IT-) services on rules that they take from sources of law, we have set ourselves, in co-creation with the members of the Blue Chamber, the goal to develop a systematic, repeatable approach that would allow these organizations improve their efficiency when designing and implementing such systems and keeping them aligned with changes in those sources of law.

We based our work upon the work of Hohfeld, but we have extended his initial categorical model of legal relations with temporal aspects allowing us to connect to events, and framed this extended Hohfeldian model in a formal semantic-conceptual model. Our conceptualization, as we have showed, has the advantage of clarity for it can be used to analyse complex legal rules and provides us with a mechanism that can 'calculate the meaning' of situations, by calculating the legal effects thereof. Consequently, we hope our approach is in tradition with what the great philosopher Gottlieb Wilhelm von Leibniz was dreaming of when he suggested 'calculemus', let's calculate, in his *'The Art of Discovery'* written in 1685!

In this paper we have presented the formal conceptual model including integrity rules that can be used as a basis for computing legal consequences, given some input situation and allows us to analyze and explain the legal interpretation of complex situations as well as complex rules.

The conceptualization presented here however also has some limitations. In this paper we have focused on an important part of what we have to model: institutional reality. Connecting the institutional reality to brute reality, particularly through qualification of brute facts into legal facts, is only briefly mentioned in this paper, a next paper will be needed to also describe how we see to cover this issue. Similarly, we have not addressed an equally important issue, representing brute reality by maintaining an administrative reality. This topic is specifically interesting for accountancy, business administration etc. When drafting regulations one would have to take this aspect into consideration, for without a proper administrative basis (i.e. brute facts) that can be qualified as legal facts one would have to make lots of effort to make the legal system work.

Despite the work that is still left for us to do, we are convinced that we came closer to our ideal, where drafters of laws and systems designers of services would work together to make life easier for all. By reusing building blocks in sources of law in abstract legal institutional constructions, expressed in legal relations and legal facts and their instantiations for specific regulations, and by standardization of descriptions of reality. Not only would this lead to better and more adaptive information systems in public administration, but also would it help citizens to better execute their rights and fulfill their obligations as well. Last but not least it would enable them to participate in the political debate, being better informed about the political consequences knowing the effects of regulations rather than groping in the dark.

References

1. Boer, A.: Legal Theory, Sources of Law, & the Semantic Web. Frontiers in Artificial Intelligence and Applications 195. IOS Press, Amsterdam (2009)
2. Boer, A., van Engers, T.: Knowledge acquisition from sources of law in public administration. In: Cimiano, P., Pinto, H.S. (eds.) EKAW 2010. LNCS, vol. 6317, pp. 44–58. Springer, Heidelberg (2010)
3. Boer, A.W.F., Van Engers, T.M.: Legal Knowledge and Agility in Public Administration. Intelligent Systems in Accounting, Finance and Management 20(2), 67–88 (2013)
4. Corbin, A.: Legal Analysis and Terminology, Yale Law School (1919)
5. Corbin, A.: Jural Relations and Their Classification, Yale Law School (1921)
6. Crosby, A.W.: The Measure of Reality: Quantification and Western Society, 1250-1600, p. 245. Cambridge University Press (1997)
7. Van Engers, T.M.: Knowledge Management, The Role of Mental Models in Business Systems Design (2001)
8. Van Engers, T.M., Nijssen, S.: Bridging Social Reality with Rules. Paper presented at IRIS (Internationales Rechts Informatik Symposion), Salzburg, Austria, to be published in Jusletter-IT (2014a)
9. Van Engers, T.M., Nijssen, S.: From Legislation towards Service Provision An Approach to Agile Implementation of Legislation. Paper Accepted for Presentation at EGOVIS 2014 in Munchen, September 1-5, and to be included in the proceedings (2014b)
10. Griethuysen, J.J. (ed.): Concepts and Terminology for the Conceptual Schema and the Information Base. ISO TC97/SC5/WG3, International Standards Organization, Central Secretariat, Geneva, Switzerland (1987) (originally published in 1982)
11. Hohfeld, W.N.: Fundamental Legal Conceptions as Applied in Judicial Reasoning (2010), Cook, W.W. (ed.), ISBN-13: 978-1-58477-162-3
12. Nijssen, G.M.: A Framework for Discussion in ISO/TC97/SC5/WG3, 78.09/01 (1978)
13. Nijssen, G.: A Framework for Advanced Mass Storage Applications. In: Conference Medinfo, Tokyo, pp. 1–21 (1980)
14. Nijssen, S., Valera, S.: An Architecture Ecosystem for the Whole Systems Perspective, Including System Dynamics, Based on Logic & Set Theory and Controlled Natural Languages. Working paper for the OMG Architecture Ecosystem SIG (2012)
15. Nyquist, C.: Teaching Wesley Hohfeld's Theory of Legal relations. Journal of Legal Education 52(1,2) (March/June 2002)

Modelling Process Intensive Scenarios for the Smart City

Riccardo Cognini, Flavio Corradini, Andrea Polini, and Barbara Re

Computer Science Division, School of Science and Technologies
University of Camerino, 62032 – Camerino (MC), Italy
{riccardo.cognini,flavio.corradini,andrea.polini,barbara.re}@unicam.it

Abstract. Smart city can be considered as a process-intensive environment that needs to be as flexible as possible to support a continuously evolving scenario. In this paper we present an approach to support flexibility of Business Processes regulating the behaviour of ICT systems deployed within a smart city. The approach permits to deal with large collections of process variants thanks to the integration of Business Process notations and Feature Model descriptions. The approach is applied to a smart mobility scenario with a specific focus on bike sharing systems.

1 Introduction

The smart city foresees the efficient integration and usage of resources and services in order to improve quality of life [1]. Smart city is a complex eco-system where enabling infrastructure supports application scenario such as mobility, energy, health, etc. In such a context each application scenario can be implemented starting from resources and services that are strictly related to city characterization (i.e. number of inhabitants and weather forecast). It also means that the same system can be implemented in different ways according to specific needs (i.e. the bus transportation system can be integrated or not with rail transport solutions). In such a context citizens and companies expect that Public Administrations provide added value services to be used in many different scenarios. The supporting IT infrastructure and related organizational aspects have to be conceived to be flexible in order to be aligned, with laws, the overall smart city policies, and objectives. These aspects are submitted to continuous changes in order to make the smart city idea more and more effective.

In response to such dynamic scenarios each smart city can implement different variants of the same Business Process (BP) to support a large set of interactive services. As a result BP variability becomes an important characteristic of any smart city initiative, in particular when IT systems are considered, and they need to be kept aligned with emerging requirements. In such line of research this paper intends to illustrate how a complex system, typical of a smart city scenario, can be modelled and represented taking into account possible variability points. In particular variability is represented thanks to a novel modelling approach that integrates BP notations and techniques used within the software product

M. Janssen et al. (Eds.): EGOV 2014, LNCS 8653, pp. 147–158, 2014.

line community. The proposed approach has been validated according to a real scenario such as the Bike Sharing System (BSS).

The paper is organized as follows. Section 2 presents some background material, and then Section 3 gives an overview of smart city services characteristics exemplified on the BSS. Section 4 describes the proposed approach and then Section 5 introduces more details on the application to BSS. Finally, Section 6 presents relevant related works, while Section 7 draws some conclusion and opportunities for future work.

2   Background

2.1   Business Process Management and Business Process Modeling

Business Process Management (BPM) "includes concepts, methods, and techniques to support the design, administration, configuration, enactment, and analysis of Business Processes" [2]. "A BP is a collection of related and structured activities undertaken by one or more organizations in order to pursue some particular goal" [3] with or without an electronic/digital support. In the smart city, BPs have to consider operations across services and organisations. Process model provides a horizontal view of the business focusing on connections, handovers and the responsibility for what happens between organisations. Starting from such integration and confirming the role of technology, it is important to take the point of view from the perspective of those who will use the service or of those will participate to its provisioning. Notations and tools supporting the BP abstraction can support smart city public-private services structure, their input and output, the interdependencies among different elements.

The accuracy of the BP modeling phase is critical for the success of an organization in particular in scenarios in which it is necessary to adapt to changing requirements. In order to design a BP different classes of languages have been investigated and defined.

Fig. 1. BPMN 2.0 Core Elements

In our work we refer to BPMN 2.0, an Object Management Group standard [4]. It is the most used language by domain experts due to its intuitive graphical notation. We have mainly used process diagrams, focusing on the point of view of system users. The following BPMN 2.0 elements (Fig. 1) are the core elements of the language and those we will use on the approach.

- **Events**, which are used to represent something that can happen. An Event can be a *Start Event*, representing the point in which the BP starts, while an *End Event* is raised when the BP terminates. Events are drawn as circles.
- **Activities**, which are used to represent a generic work to perform within a BP. An Activity can be atomic - *Task* - or not - *Sub-Process*. Activities are drawn as rectangles with rounded corners.
- **Gateways**, which are used to manage the flow of BP both for parallel activities and choices. Different types of gateways are available, the most used are reported in the following. A *Parallel Gateway* has to wait all its input flows to start and then all the output paths are started in parallel; it can behave as a fork respects to output paths or as a merge respects to input paths. An *Exclusive Gateway* gives the possibility to describe choices both in input and output, it is activated each time the gateway is reached and, when executed, it activates exactly one output path. An *Inclusive Gateway* gives the possibility to select among multiple output paths each time they are reached, it can behave also as inclusive merge. Gateways are drawn as diamonds.
- **Data Objects**, which permit to model documents, data, and other artifact used and updated during the BP, in most of the cases activity take data objects in input and give them back in output. Data objects can also be characterized by a state. A Data Object is represented by a portrait-oriented rectangle that has its upper-right corner folded over. States are represented using text within squared brackets located under the object name.

In order to model variability we combined the BPMN 2.0 standard with an approach based on features modeling, that is illustrated in the following section.

2.2   Software Product Line and Feature Modeling

Feature Model (FM) is a modeling approach emerged in the context of Software Product Lines (SPL) in order to support the development of a variety of products from a common platform. The approach aims at lowering both production costs and time in the development of individual products sharing an overall reference model, while allowing them to differ with respect to specific features in order to serve, e.g., different markets [5]. FMs are suitable to represent a family of software products, nevertheless in the last years they have been used also to represent commonality and variability in *Business Information Systems*, introducing the concept of BP family.

In a basic FM a tree representation is used to express relationships among features. Features constraints can be: *mandatory* when characteristics have to be available in each product (Fig. 2-A), *optional* when characteristics can be available or not in each product (Fig. 2-B), and *alternative* when characteristics cannot be present together in the same product (Fig. 2-D) [6].

Basic FM models are too restrictive to represent all the relationships between features which are useful to characterize a family of products [7]. As a result several FM extensions are currently available (e.g. to define feature cardinality).

Adopting richer notations it is possible to include: *OR features* used to express that at least one feature in a set must be included in a product (Fig. 2-C), *include relationship* used to express that a feature selection implies the selection of another feature, this can be a mono or two-way relationship (Fig. 2-E), and *exclude relationship* used to express that a feature selection implies to discard another one that is in another part of the tree (Fig. 2-F). As it is shown in the next sections we adopted a enricher FM notation to model BPs variability.

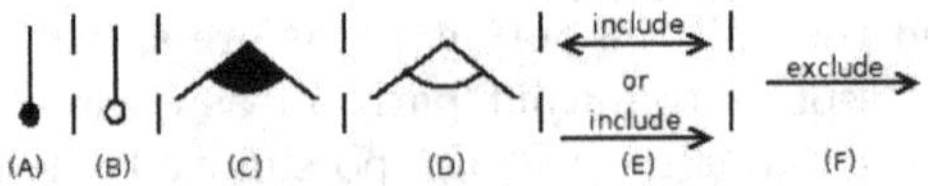

Fig. 2. Feature Models Constrains

3 Bike Sharing Systems: A Smart City Scenario

BSS has been chosen as application scenario of our work since it can be easily understood, and at the same time it is sufficiently complex to show the potentiality and needs of process based flexibility. Nonetheless it represents an interesting smart city system where a BSS is typically integrated with other "city functionalities". Within a smart city one of the main objective is to promote the dynamic combination of public service functionalities. New public services are created through pooling and sharing of resources, data and most importantly BP. This results in the need of managing flexibility starting from relevant and common characteristics of a BP.

Around the world the number of cities that have deployed, or plan to deploy, a BSS is continuously raising. Even though at a first glance BSSs could appear rather fixed, they present many variability points. The Oliver O'Brien portal[1] reports, at the time of writing, 104 cities around the world deploying a similar BSS for a total of 9.895 docking stations (i.e. points in the city where bikes can be taken and are generally returned). Nevertheless the characteristics of the listed cities are quite heterogeneous. As it can be imagined, completely different cities will employ variants of a BSS, where variability can relate both to structural characteristics, and to the modality used to provide the functionality to the users. Therefore even though all BSS look similar to each other, in reality the BSS are implemented in many different ways mainly in relation to the requirements of the smart city in which they are deployed. For instance, in case the city is mainly a touristic destination, it is important that the authentication mechanisms are simple and quick, since tourists will not like to waste their time in complex registration procedures. On the other hand, in case the city is not a major touristic destination registration mechanisms can be integrated with a general identity mechanisms, so that the identity card of the citizen can be used to access

---

[1] http://bikes.oobrien.com/global.php

to the many services made available by the city. Obviously in some case more than one authentication mechanism is necessary.

A BSS typically embeds many different BPs. In particular a BSS will include BP families to support the rental and usage of a bike (called *Bike Travel*), the technical maintenance of bikes (called *Bike Maintenance*), the monitoring of the bikes position (called *All Bike Now*), the user registration (called *User Registration*), the user un-registration (called *User Un-Registration*), and finally to support the users while they are using the bike (called *User Assistance Request*). Each different set include BPs that can be implemented according to many different variants depending for instance on the physical device that are included in the concrete system. The following basic architectural requirements/variants can be identified and than used in term of modelling.

Req1. Most BSSs provide users registration mechanisms to access the service. BSS registration can be done on the fly, using a docking station located near the bike and credit card payment method, or via dedicated form resulting in the delivery of pre-paid smart card (generally called bike card).

Req2. All BSSs provide a way to unlock bikes from the bike station, take the bike and travel. Existing BSSs implement two different locking mechanisms: (i) bikes can be unlocked using a dedicated device (i.e. smart card or credit card) and (ii) bikes can be unlocked automatically calling a number or asking via Short Message Service for the unlocked code.

Req3. Some BSSs provide tracking mechanisms to know the position of the bikes in the city, this can be done via Global Positioning System (GPS) or Radio Frequency IDentification (RFID) technologies; no BSS support both.

Req4. Some BBSs provide rewarding mechanisms that contribute to facilitate the distribution of bikes in different docking station.

Req5. All the BSSs are maintained thanks to specific agreements with supporting staff to repair bikes when they are at docking station.

Req6. Few BSSs are maintained thanks to specific agreements with supporting staff to repair bikes in the city during users travel.

Req7. Some BSSs provide to BSS staff the service "all bike now". It shows the position of all the bikes in the city, eventually in a map.

4   Variability Modeling Approach

FM Extension. In order to model variability of BPs for the smart city scenario we propose an extended version of FM, named business process Feature Model (bpFM), and then a set of mapping rules from bpFM to BPMN 2.0 fragments, permitting the derivation of a BP skeleton, according to a specific feature selection (configuration) from which a detailed BP can be successively defined. In bpFM features are BP activities and feature constraints express if an activity must or can be inserted in a BP variant, and if it must or can be included within an execution path. It is also possible to add information concerning the input and output data object related to an activity (feature in the model). In bpFM we include the following constraints.

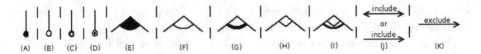

Fig. 3. bpFM Constraints

- *Mandatory Activity* means that the activity must be inserted in each BP model variant and it has to be included in each execution path (Fig. 3-A).
- *Optional Activity* means that the activity can be inserted (or not) in each BP model variant and it could be included (or not) in each execution path (Fig. 3-B).
- *Domain Activity* means that the activity must be inserted in each BP model variant but it could be included (or not) in each execution path (Fig. 3-C).
- *Special Case Activity* means that the activity can be inserted (or not) in each BP model variant, when it is inserted it has to be included in each execution path (Fig. 3-D).
- *Inclusive Multi Activities* means that at least one of the activities must be inserted in each BP model variant, and at least one of them have to be included in each execution path (Fig. 3-E).
- *One Optional Activity* means that exactly one of the activities has to be inserted in each BP model variant, and it could be included (or not) in each execution path (Fig. 3-F).
- *One Selection Activity* means that exactly one of the activities has to be inserted in each BP model variant, and it has to be included in each execution path (Fig. 3-G).
- *XOR Activities* means that all the activities must be inserted in each BP model variant, and exactly one of them has to be included in each execution path (Fig. 3-H).
- *XOR Selection Activities* means that at least one of the activities has to be inserted in each BP model variant, and exactly one of them has to be included in each execution path (Fig. 3-I).

To express input and output data object related to activities, bpFM use the BPMN 2.0 graphical representation including the possibility to associate states to data objects. Incoming and outgoing arrows are used to represent the input and output of the data object from activities. Furthermore our modelling approach supports the guidelines defined in [8] where a semantic for data object is provided. When two different data objects are input or output of the same activity, this means that both are needed or generated to process the activity. A data object cannot be in two different states at the same time. If the same object is linked to the same activity with two different states, it means that the activity execution needs the data object in one of the available states.

Mapping Rules from bpFM to BPMN 2.0. According to the feature constraints defined above we have defined a set of mapping rules that permit to automatically derive a BP fragments once a set of features is selected for configuration. For the sake of space we report the textual description of the mapping rules. In Fig. 4 we report the mapping for the case of *Inclusive Multi-Activities* and *XOR Selection Activities*.

- *Mandatory Activity* is always selected and it is mapped as an activity included in the execution path.
- *Optional Activity* if selected it is mapped as a combination of an activity and a gateway condition, so that two execution paths are possible, one including the activity and the other one not. When it is not selected it results with no mapping.
- *Domain Activity* is mapped as a combination of an activity and an exclusive gateway condition, so that two execution paths are supported one including the activity and the other one not.
- *Special Case Activity* is mapped as an activity but differently from the Mandatory Activity could not be selected, in this case no mapping is given.
- *Inclusive Multi Activities* are mapped as combination of an activities and an inclusive gateway condition, so that multiple paths are supported considering selection. In case only one activity is selected it is mapped as an activity (Fig. 4-A).
- *One Optional Activity* is mapped as an activity and an exclusive gateway condition, so that two paths are supported, one including the activity and the other one not.
- *One Selection Activity* is mapped as an activity.
- *XOR Activities* are mapped as a combination of the activities and an exclusive gateway condition, so that alternative paths are supported.
- *XOR Selection Activities* are mapped as activities and an exclusive gateway condition, so that alternative paths are supported; in case only one activity is selected it is mapped as an activity (Fig. 4-B).

The mapping we have defined is also influenced by the presence of data objects. Activities will keep the data object relation considering the state if available also in the generated fragments (Fig. 5).

Using the Approach. To model a BP from bpFM the designers follow three main steps. The first step foresees the features selection in the bpFM model to be included in the BP variant. At this stage the designer chooses the features representing the activity she considers necessary·to reach the objectives pursued by a BP family. Selected activities, and their relationships, result in a configuration (activities in grey in the bpFM figures) this is the input for the second step where BP fragments are automatically generated thanks to the mapping rules we defined. In particular, for each configuration BP fragments are generated. Fragments can also be already partially ordered depending from the fact that data object dependencies are present in the derived fragments. The final step concerns the modelling of BP variants. At this stage the designer will add control flow among the generated BP fragments. It is worth mentioning that the definition of different control flows, result in different BP variants starting from the same set of generated fragments.

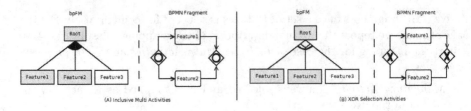

Fig. 4. Examples of Mapping Rules

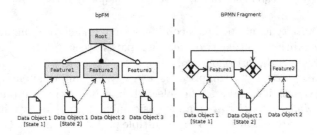

Fig. 5. Mapping Data Object

5   Modeling Bike Sharing System Supported Variants

According to the application of the proposed approach to the BSS many different BPs families can be defined. Each BP can be implemented differently taking into account the city characteristics. For each BP family we have defined a bpFM model and then according to the configurations we derived BP fragments and related BP variants.

- **Bike Travel** - This is the BP family in which a user (citizen or tourist) registers and accesses a BSS to pick up a bike from a bike station, then she uses the bike to go around the city, and at the end she will return the bike to the same or different bike stations.
- **Bike Maintenance** - This is the BP family in which a bike repairer (staff assigned to the maintenance of the BSS as a whole) checks the components of the bike in order to find damages. In case are damages she has to repair the bike.
- **All Bike Now** - This is the BP family that allow the BSS administrator to retrieve real time positions of the bikes.
- **User Registration** - This is the BP family in which a user (citizen or tourist) registers himself to the BSS in order to use a bike (this BP is optional because registration mechanisms are not always needed).
- **User Un-Registration** - This is the BP family in which a user (citizen or tourist) aims to unregister himself from the BSS (this BP is optional because registration mechanisms are not always needed).
- **User Assistance Request** - This is the BP family in which a user (citizen or tourist) asks for assistance in case the bike breaks during the travel.

For the sake of space we provide here some details about the application of the approach just to the Bike Travel BP family. Fig. 6 reports the bpFM model derived in cooperation with domain experts for the Bike Travel BP family (boxes in grey are those selected in a specific configuration, see below). The users registration functionality is included in the bpFM model using the feature called *Registration*. This is specified as an *Optional Activity*, to mean that the registration is considered optional in the Bike Travel BP since the activity can be inserted (or not) in one BP model variant. The consequence is that the user registration can be available or not in different instances of the BSS, so that in some systems registration has to be completed before taking a bike, whereas in other instances the user does not need to register. The activity (feature) could also be included within an execution path, in particular, if users are not already registered, the activity has to be performed, otherwise it can be skipped. Moreover, when registration is an available feature, it can be done in two different ways represented by the *Credit Card Registration* and *Bike Card Registration* features. This features are linked to the *Registration* feature via a *XOR Selection Activities* constraint. Therefore, if registration is chosen in a configuration, at least one of this two features has to be available, nonetheless users can choose only one mechanism to register to the system. The model is then completed with information concerning the other activities foreseen by the Bike Travel family to represent the system access, the usage of the bike, the bike tracking and the rewarding functionality.

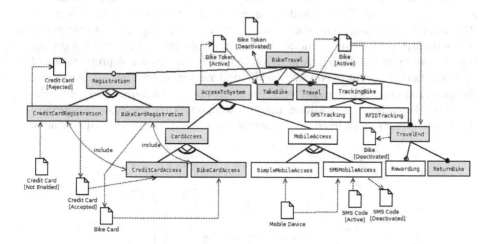

Fig. 6. Features selection in the BSS bike travel bpFM

In addition to the modelling of the activities and their relations it is also possible to include in the bpFM model information about data and their usage. In the Bike Travel BP family the following data have been modelled.

- *Credit Card* is related to user registration and system access. States are: *Not Enabled* when registration has not been done, *Accepted* when registration has been successfully done, and *Rejected* when registration has failed.
- *Bike Card* is related to the registration and it is used to access the BSS.
- *Mobile Device* is used to access the BSS.
- *SMS Code* is used together with the mobile device to access the BSS. States are: *Active* before the access has been performed and *Deactivated* as soon as the system is accessed.
- *Bike Token* is used to take the Bike. States are: *Active* before the bike unlock and *Deactivated* as soon as the bike is taken.
- *Bike* is the representation of the bike in the BSS. States are: *Active* after the bike unlock, and in this case we can use the *Bike* related data to know its position, and *Deactivated* as soon as the bike is returned.

Starting from Bike Travel bpFM model we can generate a large set of bike traveling BPs. For instance, in case the designer includes activities to register and to access the system, BPs can be based on Credit Card and/or Smart Card. This configuration results in the selection of the features as represented in the bpFM model of Fig. 6. Such selection are in gray in the figure. Using the defined mapping rules, considering the given configuration, a set of BP fragments are generated. The designer can then derive a fully defined BP variants, for instance (i.e. the one shown in Fig. 7). Similar activities have been carried out to derive models for the other BP families so to fully define the Bike Sharing System and its possible variants. The modelling experience resulted to be useful to express BPs variability in real cases studies such as the BSSs. The main advantage is that each BP family can be modelled starting from the bpFM model reducing the complexity of the modelling activity. Moreover, the explicit representation of variability points permits to improve the understanding scenario. In particular the proposed approach permits to BP managers to have a global view of all the possible BP variants. In addition the approach supports the representation of those data objects considered an important aspect to define needed BP variants.

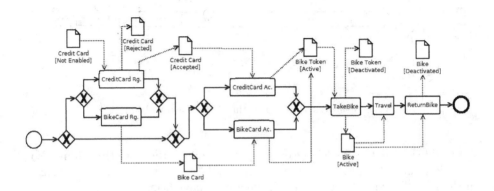

Fig. 7. A Bike Travel BP variant

Finally, the variant, automatically derived from BP fragments, permits to introduce a further level of customizability which is particularly useful in order to better fit to different smart city scenarios.

6   Related Works

BP flexibility is a hot topic that has been broadly considered during the last years [9] [10]. Considering a smart city context, the most interesting contribution has been given in defining multi perspective BP models variability focusing on BP, and representing separately people and things [11].

With reference to a more static scenario, when an administration has to modernise internal organization structures mainly address organizational changes and we realize that BPM starts to be a suitable tool in order to support innovation strategies. Several initiatives can be reported in such direction in Germany, in Switzerland and in Italy. Worth to be mentioned are the eCH framework[2], where a standardization for public service based on BP concepts has been given, and the PRODE project[3] where a reference framework for documents dematerialization involved in service delivery was given. Unfortunately, such contributions aim to create model reference for public sector without considering a way to change BP according to changing legislation, customer's needs and environment changes. Other contributions aim to face such needs from different point of views and applying different techniques [12] [13].

Finally, one of the most closed approach to model variability in administration is the configurable BP mode presented in [14]. The authors recognize that many BP in administration are mainly driven by legislation, but they also address some level of freedom regarding BP implementation in different municipalities considering different level of IT system implementation or size. For each BP the authors identified variations among municipalities and integrated them into a single, configurable process model, which can be also executed.

7   Conclusions and Future Work

Variability is an aspect that needs to be more and more taken into account when defining systems in changing and evolving context. This is certainly the case for systems to be deployed within a smart city ecosystem. This paper presented an approach to model variability of BP permitting to define in a single model many different variants of the same BP. The defined model can be successively instantiated into a concrete process taking into account the specific characteristics of the running context. Adopting the approach it is possible to reduce the complexity of managing many different variants of a BP and to share experiences between different smart city initiatives. We plan to extend our modeling effort to other systems and to study the relations and influences among different systems

---

[2] http://www.ech.ch/

[3] http://www.progettoprode.it/

available within the same smart city. At the same time we plan to augment the modeling notation with non functional aspects in order to permit their usage in planning the needed effort to deploy a system in a smart city context. Finally, we intend to investigate the adoption of the notation to drive run-time adaptation, in particular exploring the use of fragment in knowledge BP where a clear BP control flow is not given a priori.

Acknowledgements. This research has been partially founded by EU project LearnPAd GA: 619583 and by the Project MIUR PRIN CINA - 2010LHT4KM.

References

1. Chourabi, H., Nam, T., Walker, S., Gil-Garcia, J., Mellouli, S., Nahon, K., Pardo, T., Scholl, H.J.: Understanding smart cities: An integrative framework. In: 45th HICSS, pp. 2289–2297 (2012)
2. Weske, M.: Business process management concepts, languages, architectures, 1st edn. Springer (2007)
3. Lindsay, A., Downs, D., Lunn, K.: Business process – attempts to find a definition. Information and Software Technology 45(15), 1015–1019 (2003)
4. OMG, Business Process Model And Notation, BPMN 2.0.
5. Pohl, K., Böckle, G., Van Linden, F.D.: Software product line engineering, vol. 10. Springer (2005)
6. Kang, K.C., Cohen, S.G., Hess, J.A., Novak, W.E., Peterson, A.S.: Feature-oriented domain analysis (foda) feasibility study. Technical report, DTIC Document (1990)
7. Capilla, R., Bosch, J., Kang, K.C.: Systems and Software Variability Management. Springer (2013)
8. Awad, A., Decker, G., Lohmann, N.: Diagnosing and repairing data anomalies in process models. In: Rinderle-Ma, S., Sadiq, S., Leymann, F. (eds.) BPM 2009. LNBIP, vol. 43, pp. 5–16. Springer, Heidelberg (2010)
9. Valença, G., Alves, C., Alves, V., Niu, N.: A systematic mapping study on business process variability. International Journal of Computer Science & Information Technology 5(1) (2013)
10. Cognini, R., Corradini, F., Gnesi, S., Polini, A., Re, B.: Research challenges in Business Process Adaptability.. In: SATTA@SAC (2014)
11. Murguzur, A., De Carlos, X., Trujillo, S., Sagardui, G.: On the support of multi-perspective process models variability for smart environments. In: MODELSWARD (2014)
12. Schminck, A., Eid-Sabbagh, R.H., Weske, M.: Egovernment process knowledge ontology - business process knowledge interdependencies in the public administration. In: Horbach, M. (ed.) GI-Jahrestagung. LNI, vol. 220, pp. 722–735. GI,
13. Gong, Y., Janssen, M., Overbeek, S., Zuurmond, A.: Enabling flexible processes by eca orchestration architecture. In: Proceedings of the 3rd International Conference on Theory and Practice of Electronic Governance. ICEGOV 2009, pp. 19–26. ACM, New York (2009)
14. Gottschalk, F., Wagemakers, T.A.C., Jansen-Vullers, M.H., van der Aalst, W.M.P., La Rosa, M.: Configurable process models: Experiences from a municipality case study. In: van Eck, P., Gordijn, J., Wieringa, R. (eds.) CAiSE 2009. LNCS, vol. 5565, pp. 486–500. Springer, Heidelberg (2009)

Shared Services: Maverick or Originator?

Paolo Depaoli[1], Maddalena Sorrentino[2], and Marco De Marco[3]

[1] CeRSI-LUISS "Guido Carli" University, Rome, Italy
pdepaoli@luiss.it
[2] Università degli Studi di Milano, Milan, Italy
maddalena.sorrentino@unimi.it
[3] Università "Guglielmo Marconi", Rome, Italy
m.demarco@unimarconi.it

Abstract. The local governments of the OECD countries have attempted a number of sourcing practices over the past decades, including corporatization and collaborative arrangements. Sharing services is one of the latest options to emerge to cast a new actor, the shared service organization (SSO), in a lead role. To deliver services to the client councils these special-purpose vehicles adopt an alternative model that has prompted Information and Communication Technology (ICT) providers to evolve into this new species of enterprise, and to discard models based on publicly funded collaboration arrangements or the usual ICT outsourcing practices. This case study analyses the route taken by an Italian public company that reengineered its approach into that of an SSO to become a reference point for its customers and their ICT strategies. The article's general reflection on the changes under way supports the continuity of the basic organizational logics that inform the practices of public SSOs.

Keywords: Shared service, Sourcing arrangements, ICT, Public enterprises, Organization studies.

1 Introduction

The dramatic changes set to impact the Information and Communication Technology (ICT) sourcing strategies of councils equate to major challenges, despite the fact that the public managers now have access to a broader range of tools and more creative options [1, 2]. The shared service option is an emerging strategy originally developed in the corporate sector in the late 1980s [3]. A plethora of academic literature on ICT sourcing (e.g., [4, 5, 6, 7]) has demonstrated that, first, in-house sourcing, shared services and outsourcing form a continuum; second, rather than a ready-made dichotomy (i.e., outsourcing vs. shared services), the solutions are mixed and multiple; and, third, the viable sourcing choices are larger in scope and complexity.

"Shared services" is an umbrella term [8, 9] that signifies the concentration of one or more processes spread across one or more organizations or across more divisions of the same organization. A shared service organization (SSO) can aggregate activities, functions, systems and personnel in one single hub of competences from which it

M. Janssen et al. (Eds.): EGOV 2014, LNCS 8653, pp. 159–170, 2014.

manages these activities as core business processes. Large corporations use the SS option chiefly to achieve efficiency gains through the ongoing improvement of processes [3, 10]. In the public sector, precise government mandates and independent choice are the two factors driving central and local administrations [10, 11, 12] to progressively adopt SS arrangements. The US government's decision to close 800 of the country's 2000-plus data centres by 2015 is one example [13:18].

A variety of functions can be shared but the SS option is of special interest to Information Systems (IS). First, because information technology service sourcing has become the most common type of technology service that organizations seek from inter-organizational relationships [14:261] and, second, because many (if not all) other public services are dependent upon IS for their delivery [15].

This qualitative research investigates the supply-side of the SS option. Specifically, it seeks to respond to the research question *"What truly makes the SSO an originator?"* from the SSO perspective. Two important, interrelated issues underline how the SS option is not a given in central and local government, despite first impressions. The first is the tightly integrated nature [16] of IS processes with internal processes that requires the user council to make a significant organizational effort. The second is the brand loyalty issue whereby the councils tend to stick with their core IS providers. Despite the many countries predominated by tiny municipalities, little SS research has explored the coming together of these crucial issues. This is the knowledge gap the contribution starts to bridge, laying the groundwork for a future research agenda.

Using a case study approach, the paper maps the experience of a public-owned enterprise founded in 2004 to deliver ICT services to a group of small councils in Italy. Three years later the company, which started life as a typical Public-Private Partnership (PPP) to provide local governments with ICT outsourcing and facility management services, switched to an 'SSO' approach in order to manage a number of ICT-related functions for these public-sector clients.

The paper draws on extant literature and some empirical observations to argue that the public enterprise model, whereby a single supplier provides municipal clients with a full range of standardized ICT services, clashes with the strong relationships forged between the small municipalities and their software vendors, a situation that renders the model impracticable. But the case study shows how this can be successfully turned around when a public SSO is willing to adapt to the "multi-sourcing" strategies of its client councils, i.e., by offering a combination of ICT and business services sourced from multiple providers [17].

This contribution enriches the SS research in two ways: i) it reconstructs the journey of a public SS provider that surpassed the problems of the commonly accepted sector business model; and ii) proposes a general reflection on the underlying organizational logics that inform actual practices.

The paper first discusses the literature on the SS option in the public sector before providing a quick contextual guide to the Italian ICT market as a preamble to the case study. A description of the research design and the case itself is followed by an analysis of the empirical evidences with relative commentary. The insights gleaned are translated into practical suggestions of use to senior management and implications for research.

2   Related Work

Most IS literature approaches the shared services issue by asking classic questions such as "what", "why", "who" and "how" but leave many theoretical aspects unexplored (see the extensive review made by [18]). Indeed, only a very small number of cases use general organization theories such as Resource-based View, Dynamic Capabilities, IT Governance Theory, Resource Dependence Theory, Real Options Theory, and Transaction Cost Economics [ibidem: 1020], and then almost always from the perspective of the *recipients*, i.e., the decision makers of the user organizations responsible for exploring such arrangements.

Research on SS in local government ranks shared services arrangements as highly promising solutions for the councils' operational efficiency. Interestingly, and regardless of the observers' stances, the current debate (e.g., see [19, 20, 21] assigns a key role to the 'cost-cutting promise' and the potential to access expertise not held in-house [19:87, 9, 22] in the decisions to redesign internal functions via newly emerging 'market' relationships [23]. But the SS has other general advantages, from the elimination of effort duplication to the potential for greater organizational resilience and the creation of new capabilities [24:33, 18]. For example, Walsh and colleagues [3:202] argue that SS arrangements ideally facilitate a process of continuous innovation and improvement in the quality and cost-effectiveness of services. Research has also helped to shed light on the critical success factors of SS arrangements [15].

As Dollery and Akimov [11] observe, most studies tend to adopt a pro-local shared service arrangements stance with no evidence to the contrary. Nevertheless, Tomkinson [24:34-37] is one of the few authors to have analyzed both the general and the specific disadvantages of sharing arrangements in local government. General disadvantages include the implied relinquishing of control over resources, policies and practices between partner councils; obtaining the negotiation commitment of the potential sharers prior to the effective delivery of the service; and the complexity of managing potential staff displacements. Another recurrent theme is the risks related to the organizational change required of the user organizations [25].

The main SS business models have been classified by the research efforts that adopt a more conceptual approach [3,12, 26]. Joha and Janssen's work [12], for instance, not only identifies three typical SS configurations (i.e., centralized, federated, and decentralized) in a public sector context, but links each one to four discriminating dimensions (and respective variables): governance structure, strategic rationale, nature of the services, and customer orientation. The governance structure dimension addresses the question of how the service delivery is organized; the strategic rationale dimension addresses why the SS was set up in the first place; the nature of the services dimension provides answers to the type of services actually delivered; and the customer-orientation dimension refers to the SS users. This generalization enables us to depict a 'more granular and subtle' reality of the shared services and to use a multidimensional approach to investigate its articulated nature.

Ulbrich and Borman [25] have made a valuable contribution to understanding public SS. These authors, in observing that the appropriate level of standardization might vary between organizations based on their specifics needs, question the rational process standardization commonly indicated as a major lever used by an SSO to achieve synergies and high levels of services quality. Hence, an unbalancing of process standardization could cause shared service centres to transition into less effectively functioning modes.

This contingent view of process standardization breaks with the mainstream conceptualization of SS for at least two reasons. First, it contradicts the perspective that has favoured almost exclusively the attainment of high levels of process optimization, being the key goal in order to improve shared services. As the authors put it "process standardization might be counterproductive and negatively impact on a shared service centre's ability to reach its original goals" (ibidem: 2). Second, Ulbrich and Borman's reasoning includes the temporal dimension that is often neglected in the SS debate. In particular, when process standardization becomes unbalanced four natural trajectories (namely: centralized SS, outsourced SS, collaborative SS, and decentralized SS) occur. The reverse trajectories indicate an SSO's "freedom of action to not transition toward one of the four adapted service delivery modes" (ibidem: 3). Ulbrich and Borman suggest some managerial strategies to prevent SSO decline and to counterbalance the negative effects of transiting from one trajectory to another.

What can we learn from this brief literature overview? All the contributions cited see shared services as a dynamic field that deserves considerable attention to develop a better understanding of the factors at work and, thus, to enhance the possibility – for both the service takers and the service providers – of achieving successful outcomes. And, while researchers agree upon the fact that economic reasons prevail behind the SS option, the effort to address the *new* aspects of SS is sill embryonic: the SSO 'as an organizational entity in its own right' [18:34] is underexplored. Our objective here is to take an initial step forward to redress that asymmetry. To better orient the reader, Section 3 contextually frames the topics discussed.

3   Italian Councils and the Demand and Supply of ICT Services

Italy has 8100 local councils, all similar in organizational structure, services range, legal status and reporting requirements. The Italian municipalities have all implemented basic computerization, albeit with considerable differences in how they choose to manage their information technology and information systems.

Clearly, the fact that the smaller councils have few financial and professional resources to allocate to technological innovation means that ICT is only a blip on their organizational radar. Further, as observed by, among others, Italy's Ancitel (the national association for coordinating the ICT policies of the municipalities) the intense action of penetration by the demand-specific ICT companies has led to the current situation of the smaller councils. In fact, having colonized this market, these companies are now the de facto guiders of the small councils' innovation policies (for instance, in the field of e-government) and, as such, are determined to safeguard their role and usefulness as the more or less exclusive partner of each council [27].

The suppliers' digital administration know-how and in-depth knowledge of the municipal administrative processes outstrips that of even the large system integrators hired by the central government to help develop e-government. The influence this enables them to exert over the small councils comes from the contractual status they enjoy and the hegemony of "those who know best" what is good for the user [27:90].

4   Research Design, Data Collection, Data Analysis

That "good descriptions of what happens or what has happened on the ground" are necessary to effective theory-building and theory-testing [28] and the fact that the literature on SSO as an organizational entity in its own right is not yet fully consolidated [18] led the authors to choose the exploratory study approach. Indeed, a full picture of current and emerging public SSO trends is a solid foundation on which to chart a course of deeper exploration.

Research setting. Lombardy is a primary source of evidence for our analysis with its high fragmentation (out of a total of 1546, 1091 municipalities have 5000 or fewer residents) and approximately 500 inter-municipal arrangements in the most disparate sectors [29, 30]. The paper illustrates the case of Consorzio.IT ('CIT'), a public-owned SSO that supplies ICT services and support to 47 mostly small Lombard councils. After starting life as a typical PPP, CIT is now 100% controlled by SCRP, a multi-utility founded in 1963 by 47 municipalities and the Province of Cremona to manage waste disposal and water treatment.

CIT was selected for its good data access and the possibility to map the longitudinal history and evolutionary pattern of an enterprise that reengineered its approach after ditching the typical in-house business model initially adopted.

The authors conducted the field research from June 2012 to July 2013. Primary data collection was based on semi-structured, 40 to 60-minute interviews with CIT staff that addressed four main areas: activity, organization, environmental context, operations. The interviews were held with two top managers, the CEO, the commercial director, a second-level help desk line employee, and were transcribed by two researchers. Follow-up phone interviews with CIT were conducted in July 2013. Six mayors of user councils attending a public meeting also agreed to be interviewed. The three authors then discussed the information gathered.

5   The Case Study

CIT was founded exclusively to service small councils (5000 or fewer residents) when Italy's central government implemented several measures and allocated Euro 15 million to fund the inclusion of the small councils in the national e-government agenda. However, that sum, being far too low to fund all of Italy's small local governments, sparked uncertainty on the effective use of the resources.

This led the government to issue a new services provision measure that introduced the 'local area services centre' (in Italian, Centro servizi territoriali or 'CST'). Applicable to solely neighbouring councils, the CST was devised mainly for the phase prior to public engagement. Some Regions, including Lombardy, opened special lines to fund ICT infrastructure, hardware and software, and ICT aggregation [29].

Although two private ICT firms took minority stakes in CIT, their interest in growing the user base made CIT's full-outsourcing goal unattainable. With regional government funding CIT purchased the hardware needed to set up a CST data centre and a low-cost connectivity wireless network for the councils. However, this was not enough and, two years later, not one municipality had retired their information system and migrated to CIT. This forced CIT to reposition the business. The company's General Manager had a corporate TLC background and recruited a new Commercial Director; both managers had a marketing-oriented approach. The new commercial director decided to pay personal calls on the officers and councillors of the adjacent councils in order to *"understand their biggest problems."* (Commercial Director, CIT).

This revealed that *"80% of the cases were requests for operational help that often had nothing to do with connectivity or the performance of the software applications installed at the councils."* And by *"Speaking with the respective mayors"* the company learned of the *"need, voiced frequently, to implement widespread training. This issue had never been raised before so CIT started to organize base courses for the council staff. The next step was to convince the councils to use us as outsourcers for those technical activities that offered no particular advantages kept in-house. We followed that up with an offer of brand new services to complete and integrate the application portfolio"* (Commercial Director, CIT).

The ICT suppliers chosen and used by the councils were an additional challenge. Also here CIT had to work to mainly earn their trust. *"At first they saw us as a threat to their business. We had to convince them that our position was non-partisan and that our policy was never to pressure customers into anything. Today, the ICT suppliers see us as allies in certain respects because we're their sole spokesperson.... Some of them have even noticed an increase in revenues since they started to work with us."* (Commercial Director, CIT).

Following Joha and Janssen's work [12:33-34], the CIT business model can be divided into four interrelated dimensions: (1) governance structure; (2) strategic rationale behind the SSC; (3) nature of the services; and (4) customer orientation.

Governance Structure. CIT is a limited company with share capital of Euro 100,000, incorporated in Italy and based in Crema (a city of 33,000 inhabitants located in the Region of Lombardy). CIT is wholly owned by the public utility group SCRP SpA and therefore is the indirect expression of the multi-utility council partners of the Crema area. CIT and SCRP have the same CEO and the offices and technological resources of CIT are housed at the parent company's head office. CIT has six employees assigned to the following functions: Commercial (1), 1st-level help desk (2), 2nd-level help desk (2), Cartographic services (1).

The company uses the support of a Customer Relationship Management (CRM) system to perform and govern its assistance activities. In particular, a first-level call centre provides telephonic and online assistance and the company monitors the perceived quality of services with a customer satisfaction questionnaire.

CIT's CEO explained why, despite 2012 revenues of Euro 1.2 million, CIT reported only modest earnings in the past five financial years: *"Our goal is simply to achieve a fair balance between two needs: keeping a good managerial balance and minimizing the costs for the client councils."*

Strategic Rationale. The robust funding of the central and regional governments is what gave CIT its start-up momentum. Key arguments in favour of data centre consolidation according to the CST model were underpinned by the idea to optimize the core ICT standard services and thus achieve economies of scale and effectiveness. However, this clashed with the strategic rationale of the private partners to grow the business by giving preferred access to a captive client base. As a result, the private-sector minority shareholders exited the share capital, providing the catalyst that transformed CIT into an SSO.

CIT soon realized that the municipalities most pressing need was operational support for the users of the core information system (none of the IS providers delivered an adequate level of operational assistance). This led the company to reengineer its structure around this service and launch the help desk, which soon found its niche as a critical resource for the functioning of the client councils. All CIT's later decisions were guided by this same rationale of identifying potential needs and finding solutions (unbundling the ICT activities) that best meet the client's specific needs. Over time, these sourcing-related decisions map the sourcing path of an organization [31].

CIT's responses to the quintessential challenges posed in the diverse stages of the public service ICT value chain included: definition of innovation policies, research and identification of the technological solution, acquisition of the technological solution and implementation of the solution and service governance.

Nature of the Services. While CIT offers a standard range of services in terms of target client type, the variety and individual sourcing choices are differentiated. CIT's mix of services falls under two headings: i) assistance, and ii) ICT services. The former consists of the online help desk, legislative/regulatory assistance, software applications assistance. The second consists of the centralization of software applications, connectivity, e-mail management, website design, hosting and maintenance, software application programme development, back-up and disaster recovery, management of video-surveillance systems, software asset management.

The current services portfolio is the fruit of additional developments since 2007. Meanwhile, the ICT demand of the individual councils has become modular and articulated, creating a market in which several suppliers (including CIT) provide a range of solutions and services. Moreover, CIT runs online assistance for the partner councils in the event of regional and central government connectivity problems.

Customer Orientation. The multi-sourcing logic favoured by CIT, for example, its servers run the information systems of four different software providers, give the client councils complete freedom of choice when it comes to evaluating which of CIT's services best match their needs and requirements.

CIT's business-like approach means that it performs evaluations at client request to help this latter decide whether to "make it in-house" or 'buy it on the market'. For instance, in addition to its centrally hosted environment, CIT owns a virtual infrastructure (some 20 machines) located at the data centre of a Cremona public telecommunication services company. CIT is the epicentre of a system of relations, both external, i.e., from and to the user councils, and internal, i.e., from and to the sub-contractors. CIT is like a well-oiled hinge that joins the councils' demand for technological innovation to the potential capabilities of the market players, while the use of third parties enables CIT to keep both organizational structure and fixed costs lean.

6   Discussion

CIT is an example of supra-corporate model [24], i.e., a special-purpose vehicle that delivers services on behalf of all its partners. CIT is a small-sized enterprise that can claim all three of the publicness criteria of ownership, funding, and control [32]. While the primarily public dimension of CIT, especially its ownership, is very clear, the other two aspects are hazier. Several factors – all usually associated with the private company logic – point to CIT's *hybrid* nature: i) it is an established main player in a competitive market of peers; ii) it self-finances its operations (from services income), and iii) it pursues ongoing innovation in its offer by keeping track of the needs of its customers. However, given the physical proximity of parent company and subsidiary and that the SSO has the same top management as the group parent company, the potential influence of this mix of roles on CIT's choices and task environment relations cannot be ruled out.

The company's present guise is the result of a number of management decisions made basically to rectify past weaknesses. The most interesting aspect, which clashes somewhat with the conceptualization of Ulbrich and Borman [22], is that CIT embarks on not one but several trajectories in tandem, according to the level of process consolidation required by each client council.

The CIT case confirms that an SSO is not simple to implement. Small councils are usually risk-adverse and full outsourcing initiatives are loaded with unknown factors, above all related to organizational and cultural change, so it is highly probable that the initial proposal to retire the existing IS has been delegitimized, albeit in a creeping way, by the administrative staff of the councils in question. It is also likely that the incumbent suppliers felt threatened by the newcomer and did not just remain on the sidelines of these dynamics of resistance.

The relevance of the dimensions identified by Joha and Janssen [12] is that they shed light on how CIT articulated its business model. The brand new strategy devised by CIT to counter the councils' resistance was based on the fact that even the smallest had made the transition to basic computerization. This led CIT to design and offer a range of services around the IS already in place to address specific needs never tackled before. In other words, by adding technical and organizational capabilities to the ICT resources used by the councils, CIT identified a new market niche and became a point of reference for the local ICT offer. This strategy spurred the councils to take up the SS option. The mayors interviewed emphasized the relationship of trust forged with CIT, the flexibility of the offer and, above all, that it took into account that certain local councils might have already assigned internal competencies and resources to manage their ICT operations.

The service portfolio of this SSO is different to that of the usual consolidation ventures, such as a CST, which are driven by the needs of the service providers that want to sign up all their clients to the same platform and solutions or a catalogue of standard options. CIT inverted that trend by starting to listen to the users' actual needs, using these premises to craft a shared services offer 'customized for individual customer sets' [21]. In short, CIT 'retains the individuality of councils' [24:33]. This is a sharp break with the software provider's typically product-driven approach, which rarely seeks to grow the client's technological culture. This mediator role seems to strike a much-needed balance between standardization and customization, as suggested by Joha and Janssen [9]. On the other hand, the interviews did not enable us to evaluate the extent to which the company is aware of the potential risks of unbalanced process standardization [22]) as a result of giving complete freedom of choice to the client councils.

CIT's in-depth knowledge of the client's processes is a crucial resource in organizational terms and is its first factor of success. On the one side, the knowledge can be used strategically to improve CIT's understanding of its client councils' technological demand and, thus, to fuel competitive growth and reinforce its market position. On the other, the know-how can be used to empower the service content for existing and potential clients.

The overall recognition earned by CIT makes it a key player in a very important game, that of the implementation of the inter-municipal collaborations recently mandated by the Italian government. CIT actively supports the efforts of the councils by leveraging its tertiary nature both with the ICT suppliers and the individual ICT options offered: *"Getting both clients and suppliers around the same table means we can analyze the pros and cons of the solutions together and thus lay the foundations for shared choices"* (Commercial Director, CIT).

The second important success factor is that the knowledge acquired by CIT has placed it in a position to create client dependency and, therefore, to 'control' them. Nevertheless, the relationship of trust forged between client and supplier smoothes the way to technical solutions that minimize the "perceived costs of switching from the status quo", especially in terms of the psychological commitment [27:27]. The fact that the SSO is able to provide customized services and to use its knowledge and experience to anticipate the needs of the client puts other market options in the pale, making these suppliers and their products appear less attractive as CIT replacements.

Summing up, we could respond to the research question *"What truly makes the SSO an originator?"* by pointing to the mainstream literature's concentration on the exterior aspects of the SSO arrangements or the features of the SSO offering. However, these cannot be called tangible signs of change in organizational logics. Nor has the empirical case given any precise indications of change in the logic that guides the design of the organizational form, meant as the configuration of right and obligations of action, decision, control and ownership, and the coordination mechanisms [34:294].

Rather, what the empirical case does indicate is a 'subtle yet important process of incorporation of the clients within the boundaries of the company' [35] not in legal-formal terms but in the management of qualifying elements that connote the client-supplier relationship. Thanks to this knowledge, the SSO moves its influence toward the outside and consolidates itself in the technological environment on which the council's activities are wholly dependent [36]. In other words, it seeks to augment its 'exercisable control' [35] over external service receivers.

7   Conclusions and Implications

That the SSO does not cross the boundaries of the dominant organizational logic in favour of design solutions capable of augmenting the company's level of exercisable control over its own task environment is the central thesis of this article. The analysis suggests that Consorzio.IT is a *pocket-sized* SSO, the product of an evolutionary trajectory where nothing can be taken for granted. CIT has succeeded in staking its place in the market and is an apparent case of *virtuous localism*.

However, the business model adopted up to now cannot be replicated across the board should CIT decide to pursue growth-by-expansion strategies, such as extending its market to non-SCRP member councils in the local area, which is anyway prohibited by Italian public tender law and the recent measures issued in conjunction with the government's spending review, and while CIT could tap into new outlet markets by undertaking a corporate restructuring project that, let's say, leverages SCRP SpA's holdings in other local utilities, this would indubitably affect the group parent company's strategic agenda and confirm the SSO's role as a tool of local governance.

The paper contributes to *research* because it extends the reasons beyond economic self-interest to other meaningful aspects of the ICT sourcing options, such as the role and preferences of the relevant actors. In addition, it reflects on the key role of ICT services in the processes of regulation, i.e., the coordination and control processes; and on the centrality of the public SSO in the system of multiple local relations.

In terms of the implications for *practice*, the study enables us to formulate some useful lines of intervention for SSO senior management. In particular, the sustainability of public enterprises that deliver services according to the SS model to the small councils in particular is contingent on: (a) creating value from technological investments, management systems and managerial resources already in place; (b) minimizing organizational switching costs; (c) aligning with the multi-sourcing strategies of the clients; and (d) defining an affordable price policy that matches the services effectively delivered and not the logic of a captive market.

For obvious reasons, the findings of this study (based on one case alone) are not enough to demonstrate the theory proposed. Nevertheless, the authors believe that certain aspects can be transposed to some broader contexts, e.g., over a wider spectrum of organizational settings, also comparatively. A deeper analysis of the above findings and those of other international case studies that address local government SSOs prospects a promising research path (the authors thank the anonymous reviewer for this suggestion) that could form the basis for decision makers to reflect on a 'vendor' perspective. A further, perhaps more ambitious avenue for future research would be to formulate a theoretical framework for the public SSO to give us a more focused lens on this type of service provider. For instance, and purely for indicative reasons, drawing on organization studies theories that focus on analyzing the processes of action and decision could be a fruitful contribution.

References

1. IRPA: Il capitalismo municipale. Roma: IRPA Istituto per la ricerca nella pubblica amministrazione (2012)
2. Warner, M., Hebdon, R.: Local Government Restructuring: Privatization and Its Alternatives. Journal of Policy Analysis and Management 20(2), 315–336 (2001)
3. Walsh, P., McGregor-Lowndes, M., Newton, C.J.: Shared Services: Lessons from the Public and Private Sectors for the Nonprofit Sector. Australian Journal of Public Administration 67(2), 200–212 (2008)
4. Willcocks, L.P., Lacity, M.C.: Global sourcing of business and IT services. Palgrave Macmillan. New York (2006)
5. Lacity, M.C., Khan, S.A., Willcocks, L.P.: A review of the IT outsourcing literature: Insights for practice. Journal of Strategic Information Systems 18(3), 130–146 (2009)
6. Lacity, M.C., Khan, S., Yan, A., Willcocks, L.P.: A review of the IT outsourcing empirical literature and future research directions. Journal of Information Technology 25(4), 395–433 (2010)
7. Schwarz, A., Jayatilaka, B., Hirschheim, R., Goles, T.: A Conjoint Approach to Understanding IT Application Services Outsourcing. Journal of the Association for Information Systems 10(10), 748–781 (2009)
8. Local Government Association: Shared Services,
   `http://www.local.gov.uk/web/guest/productivity/-/`
   `journal_content/56/10171/3510759/ARTICLE-TEMPLATE`
   (retr. from May 11, 2013)
9. Joha, A., Janssen, M.: Factors influencing the shaping of shared services business models: Balancing customization and standardization. Strategic Outsourcing: An International Journal 7(1), 47–65 (2014)
10. Accenture: Driving High Performance in Government: Maximizing the Value of Public-Sector Shared Services The Government Executive Series (2005)
11. Dollery, B.E., Akimov, A.: Are shared services a panacea for Australian local government? A critical note on Australian and international empirical evidence. International Review of Public Administration 12(2), 89–102 (2008)
12. Joha, A., Janssen, M.: Types of shared services business models in public administration. In: 12th Annual International DGO Research Conference, pp. 26–35. ACM, College Park (2011)
13. Ghia, A.: Capturing value through IT consolidation and shared services. McKinsey on Government (Autumn), 18–23 (2011)
14. Hui, P.P., Fonstad, N.O., Beath, C.M.: Technology service inter-organizational relationships. An agenda for information technology service sourcing research. In: Cropper, S., Ebers, M., Huxham, C., Smith Ring, P. (eds.) The Oxford Handbook of Inter-Organizational Relations, pp. 256–280. Oxford University Press, Oxford (2008)
15. Borman, M., Janssen, M.: Critical Success Factors for Shared Services: Results from Two Case Studies. Paper presented at the 45th HICSS, Maui, Hawaii, USA (2012)
16. McIvor, R., McCracken, M., McHugh, M.: Creating outsourced shared services arrangements: Lessons from the public sector. European Management Journal 29(6), 448–461 (2011)
17. Levina, N., Su, N.: Global Multisourcing Strategy: The Emergence of a Supplier Portfolio in Services Offshoring. Decision Sciences 39(3), 541–570 (2008)

18. Fielt, E., Bandara, W., Suraya, M., Gable, G.: Exploring Shared Services from an IS Perspective: A Literature Review and Research Agenda. Communications of the Association for Information Systems 34, 1001–1040 (2014)
19. Alford, J., O'Flynn, J.: Rethinking Public Service Delivery. Palgrave Macmillan, Basingstoke (2012)
20. Pollitt, C., Bouckaert, G.: Public Management Reform. In: A Comparative Analysis: New Public Management, Governance, and the Neo-Weberian State, 3rd edn., Oxford University Press, Oxford (2011)
21. Sako, M.: Outsourcing versus shared services. Communications of the ACM 53(7), 27–29 (2010)
22. Scannell, M., Bannister, F.: Shared Services in Irish Local Government. In: Scholl, H.J., Janssen, M., Wimmer, M.A., Moe, C.E., Flak, L.S. (eds.) EGOV 2012. LNCS, vol. 7443, pp. 114–125. Springer, Heidelberg (2012)
23. Ulbrich, F., Borman, M.: Preventing the gradual decline of shared service centers. Paper presented at the AMCIS 2012, Seattle, Washington, August 9-12 (2012)
24. Bovaird, T.: Developing new forms of partnership with the 'market' in the procurement of public services. Public Administration 84(1), 81–102 (2006)
25. Tomkinson, R.: Shared services in local government: improving service delivery. Gower, Aldershot (2007)
26. Huxham, C., Vangen, S.: Doing Things Collaboratively: Realizing the Advantage or Succumbing to Inertia? Organizational Dynamics 33(2), 190–201 (2004)
27. Niehaves, B., Krause, A.: Shared service strategies in local government – a multiple case study exploration. Transforming Government: People, Process and Policy 4(3), 266–279 (2010)
28. Ancitel: Le ICT nei comuni italiani. Ancitel, Roma (2010)
29. IReR: Lo stato delle forme associative tra enti locali in Lombardia. Milano: Consiglio Regionale della Lombardia (2009)
30. Sorrentino, M., Simonetta, M.: Assessing local partnerships: an organisational perspective. Transforming Government: People, Process and Policy 5(3), 207–224 (2011)
31. Mola, L., Carugati, A.: Escaping 'localisms' in IT sourcing: tracing changes in institutional logics in an Italian firm. European Journal of Information Systems (21), 388–403 (2010)
32. Andrews, R., Boyne, G.A., Walker, R.M.: Dimensions of Publicness and Organizational Performance: A Review of the Evidence. Journal of Public Administration Research and Theory 21(suppl. 3), i301–i319 (2011)
33. Polites, G.L., Karahanna, E.: Shakled to the Status Quo: The Inhibiting effects of incumbent system Habit. Switching Costs, and Inertia on New System Acceptance, MIS Quarterly 36(1), 21–42 (2012)
34. Grandori, A.: Organizzazione e comportamento economico. il Mulino, Bologna (1999)
35. Masino, G.: Le imprese oltre il fordismo. Carocci, Roma (2005)
36. Zardini, A., Rossignoli, C., Mola, L., De Marco, M.: Developing Municipal e-Government in Italy: The City of Alfa Case. Exploring Services Science, pp. 124–137. Springer International Publishing (2014)

Assessing Policy Making for ICT Innovation: A Decision Support Research Agenda

Ciara Fitzgerald and Frédéric Adam

Business Information Systems, University College Cork, Ireland
cfitzgerald@ucc.ie,
FAdam@afis.ucc.ie

Abstract. Our study explores European telecare policy and considers the different types of uncertainties for policy makers when addressing ICT innovation. We specifically examine 14 European countries in our study using document analysis, expert interviews and workshops. The findings reveal nuances in how policy makers are reacting to the uncertainty of telecare technologies as a representative of ICT innovation. Our contribution lies in exploring decision support as per Alter's contention that to improve the quality of decision making we most focus on broadly defined avenues for decision support rather than exclusively Decicion Support Systems [1]. Following Earl and Hopwood (1980), we analyse the case of European telecare policy and outline implications to strengthen policy making for ICT innovation [2]. Our study is pertinent to policy makers as we argue that they will increasingly be challenged to consider 'responsible innovation' in their policy making efforts.

Keywords: Decision Support, ICT Innovation, Policy Making, Responsible Innovation, Telecare Technologies.

Track: Particular domains of study in e-government and e-governance such as emergency and disaster response management, policy making, law enforcement, compliance and criminal justice.

1 Introduction

We are living in an innovation age challenged with increasing complexity of decisions in all aspects of society. Such ICT innovations, advancing at an unprecedented rate, demand a sophisticated policy response to assess the impact of the rapid technological advances on society. We are keen to investigate the different types of uncertainty facing policy makers in the context of ICT innovation. This study provides a wide-ranging analysis of European policy relating to telecare and telemedicine. The purpose of our study is to explore policy measures related to telecare and home-based telemedicine in the European countries/regions represented by a consortium of 14 European countries. This case is of interest as European countries are challenged with an ageing population. Between 2000 and 2050, the proportion of the world's population over 60 years will double from about 11 % to

M. Janssen et al. (Eds.): EGOV 2014, LNCS 8653, pp. 171–180, 2014.

22 %. The absolute number of people aged 60 years and over is expected to increase from 605 million to 2 billion over the same period. The world will have more people who live to see their 80s or 90s than ever before. The number of people aged 80 years or older will have almost quadrupled to 395 million between 2000 and 2050. Indeed the probability of needing care increases with age. Less than 1 % of those younger than 65 years need long-term care, while 30 % of the women aged 80 years or over use long-term care services, on average across the OECD [3]. Recent innovative developments in technology have produced ICT devices supporting elderly people. Information and communication technology (ICT)-based care technologies include real-time audio and visual contacts between patients and caregivers; embedded technologies such as smart homes, clothes and furniture to monitor patients inside and even outside their homes; electronic tagging of dementia patients and more biotechnological innovations, such as implants and devices for chronic disease monitoring. These technologies cover a wide range of innovations, from those already functioning to those that are prospective and theoretical. They provide health care and enable elderly people to maintain their autonomy and allow them to live independently for a longer period of time. These technologies are subsumed under the term telecare. However as well as the positive benefits, theorists are speculating on the social and legal risks of telecare, specifically regarding the issue of technology failure and the onus of responsibility, be it users or the providers of the technology [4]. It is worth noting the intention of this paper is not to determine the ethics of telecare. Rather, this paper supports the call by Yanga and Zhiyong Lan (2010) for the need for further study to facilitate our understanding of efficient policy making for ICT innovation [5]. Given telecare technologies is a ripe area of innovation which will have positive and potentially challenging societal implications, our research objective is to explore the different types of uncertainties for policy makers addressing ICT innovation.

We situate this study against the backdrop of 'responsible innovation', a growing scholarly appreciation that the advancements in ICT should be situated within a societal context focused on the future consciousness of societal well-being. Responsible Innovation is recognised to be a dynamic concept enacted at multiple levels and is forecasted to feature on the political agenda in the coming years [6]. The term Responsible Innovation is defined as 'taking care of the future through collective stewardship of science and innovation in the present' [6 pp 3]. Our study contributes to this paradigm as it explores policy makers' response to telecare innovation and explores to what extent policy is considering the opportunities and challenges of telecare within the context of the aging society wellbeing. Within this agenda of 'Responsible Innovation', our paper will outline how decision support can facilitate better technology assessment processes, which are needed to manage innovations in ICT. The rest of the paper is organised as follows. The next section presents the literature review focusing on ICT policy making and decision support. Following this, we outline the methodology, then the findings, followed by a discussion of the findings before concluding with outlining implications for policy makers.

2   Literature Review

2.1   ICT Policy Making

ICT policy making is a much studied area for scholars, as countries grapple with new innovative technologies and question their impact. Governments are challenged to scientifically assess societal, ethical, legal and economic aspects of technology. However, Delvenne et al (2011) argues uncertainty is no longer contained within modern structures of policy making. Specifically, they argue the current challenge for policy makers is to accommodate the uncertainty and dynamics of patterns to offer the decision- making process "a context-determined and temporally limited orientation for action that makes learning through experience possible" [7:p. 18]. Furthermore, no discussion on such complex decision making is meaningful without a discussion of the lmitations which apply to Human Decision making, as described by Simon under the term of bounded rationality [8]. Scholars argue under conditions of bounded-rationality, decision makers seemingly "do what they can" or in some cases, "make-do". To further complicate matters, when contemplating boundaries in ICT policy decision making, traditional boundaries are not imposed, but constructed, bargained, negotiated and appropriated by stakeholders [7]. We speculate such boundary-less domains can result in ambiguity of decision making within a fluid environment. Policy makers need urgently to respond to demands of citizens to engage more pro-actively with politics in policy decisions that heavily concern particular stakeholder groups and citizens [10]. We question if policy makers as decision makers in such fluid environments are indeed 'muddling through' as per Lindblom (1959) [9]. If so, we propose a decision support lens can make a potentially powerful contribution and will provide recommendations of real pragmatic value for policy makers. Our study will address the need for more clearly defined and systematic theoretical and empirical studies to facilitate our understanding of efficient policy decisions [5].

2.2   Decision Support

Following Alter, one should explore how decision support can be provided when considering the feasibility of DSS. Alter (1992, 2004) has repeatedly pointed out that the development of DSS was secondary to the objective of improving the quality of decision making, calling for a focus on decision support rather than decision support systems [11,1]. To provide decision support, one should concentrate on developing an overall system of decision making which is based on evidence and supported by expert advice. The use of DSS in a political context can be problematic as studies found that the inherent rationality of the DSS was in conflict with how participants usually make decisions as well as with the political process [15]. We are keen to further explore the feasibility of DSS in a policy making context for ICT innovation. We argue decision making for ICT innovation policy making addresses a number of categories of uncertainty [2]. Specifically policy making for ICT innovation considers the following:

- Uncertainty about the mechanics of technologies - the what question
- Uncertainty about their impact - the who and how questions
- Uncertainty about societal preferences - the why questions

Earl and Hopwood (1980) have theorised on the nature of uncertainty and, leveraging Thompson and Tuden (1959), they have distinguished uncertainty about the cause and effect relationship versus uncertainty which relates to the preferences of the stakeholders [2, 12]. Silver (1991) also proposes a reflection on the difference between guidance underpinned by information and guidance aimed at prescribing choices, which he respectively labels *informative* decisional guidance and *suggestive* decisional guidance [13]. In general, DSS applications must rely on the existence of clear modelling and reasoning to underpin the optimisation algorithms that are being applied. The key issue is therefore whether societal decisions in the area of ICT lend themselves to the development of what Earl and Hopwood (1980) term *answer machines* and what happens when the level of uncertainty and ambiguity involved means that the provision of the answer machine can potentially compromise the ability of policy makers to make the right choices. Earl and Hopwood (1980) have warned against trying to hide the true complexity of societal problems (focusing on developing DSS), rather than embracing it (focusing on improving the quality of decisions). Where assumptions are made about the future, or where consensus has not yet arisen in an organisation or society, decision support should not provide artificially complete ready-made answers and should, instead, promote judgement and dialogue amongst stakeholders. Although the concept of decisional guidance may appear intangible, Earl and Hopwood's (1980) recommendations provide tangible avenues for analysing decisional guidance in terms of its fit with the problems facing policy makers [2]. We propose therefore that certain societal problems with a given technology can lead to suggestive guidance, whereas others cannot and should not, given the state of development of policy-makers' understanding or the absence of a clear societal consensus. This has clear implications for the type of dialogue which must take place in society in relation to different types of innovations. This paper explores policy making in the area of telecare technology as an example of ICT innovation and considers how DSS can support policy making, be it as suggestive guidance or otherwise.

3   Methodology

The methodology utilized in this study is an in-depth case study approach. The case-study method has been widely recommended for study areas that are not yet well understood and lack formal theories [14]. It is particularly relevant for our study as there are very few studies on the actual use of DSS in a political context [15]. It has also gained particular popularity in the public policy literature because of 'the depth and richness' the result can provide for enlightened public policies [16]. Since ICT innovation and decision support is a comparatively new and underexplored policy issue, a case study approach can provide rich context-dependent knowledge to assist policy-making. The fourteen countries in the European case study were Austria, Belgium, Bulgaria, The Czech Republic, Denmark, Germany, Hungary, Ireland, Lithuania, Norway, The Netherlands, Portugal, Spain and Switzerland. The selection of countries signifies the participating partners in a FP7 funded project called PACITA[1]. The categories used to capture consistent data on each country, were as follows; Definitions, National Demographic Trends, National policies, Policy Enablers, Policy Enactors, Actor Involvement Incentives, Service Providers, Technologies in use, and a Risk Analysis. The choice of categories for inclusion were grounded in relation to its practical purposes as per recommended for studies analyzing and comparing ICT for Aging Society policies [17].

Specifically, we explored the definitions used in policy documents in the 14 European countries in the study. Then, we assessed demographic conditions. Next we examined specific national policies. Following this, we investigated the key actors involved. We categorized them as policy enablers and policy enactors. On consultation with national experts, there appears to be many risks but these are not recognised in policy discussions thus far. Extensive desk research was conducted for each country. To complement this, policy experts were contacted for additional information that was not easily accessible via secondary sources. The richness of information differed from each country; however this is not problematic as it reflects their differing levels of policy sophistication in the area of telecare. Therefore there are some apparent nuances in the approaches but this adds to the complexity of the findings. For the purpose of this study, relevant legal and policy documents, government publications and scholarly literature were examined, documenting developments up until September 2013. Documentary search and analysis were complemented by a series of semi-structured in-depth interviews. Finally we held a workshop with key experts to validate our results, which led to further relevant analysis as outlined in the following section.

4   Case Study

The primary function of telecare technology is to address the challenge of an ageing population. The societal challenges which emerged from our analysis are an increase in life expectancy, an increase in dementia and other age related illnesses, rising cost of care and increased demand for independent living solutions. Emerging technological advances in telecare and telemedicine pose new challenges for policy makers particularly with regard to uncertainty over cause and effect of the innovative technology. The findings provide a basis for commentary and serve to promote awareness of the policy status in telecare in Europe, as represented by the European countries in our study. We present the findings as per the categories of uncertainty, presented in the literature review. Specifically, we discuss uncertainty about the mechanics of technology, uncertainty about their impact and uncertainty about societal preferences.

---

[1] http://www.pacitaproject.eu/

4.1   Uncertainty about the Mechanics of Technologies – The What Question

Our findings reveal common interpretations of telecare and telemedicine are used in national documents. However they are used interchangeably in many contexts. There are a number of interrelated concepts such as Ambient Assisted Living, eHealth, Assistive Technology, ICT in Health, Welfare Technology and Telehealth. This level of uncertainty is not conducive to effective policy making. There needs to be a definitive understand of what telecare technology is. Furthermore, there are differing levels of sophistication regarding telecare. Firstly, there is difference in timeline. For example 1993 was the earliest policy initiative in Austria whereby a tax funded long term care system which is independent from income was introduced. Since then, all countries in our study have documents referencing telecare, or equivalent but to varying levels of comprehensiveness. For example, the policies are at various levels of a continuum concerning frameworks for security and strategies for encouraging adoption. For example some countries are proactive in seeking opportunities for encouraging the development of telecare, whilst others are reactive and seek only to fulfil the minimum requirements of regulation. The following are areas of uncertainty about the mechanics of technologies which arose from our analysis.

- What is telecare technology?
- What are the best policies to encourage the development of telecare?
- What are the regulatory requirements?

4.2   Uncertainty about Their Impact – The Who and How Questions

Our findings reveal evidence of fragmented, uncoordinated decision making and implementation in the telecare domain with no central responsibility for policy making in all countries of in our study.   In the category of Policy Enablers, our findings highlighted a surge in the number of government departments getting involved in the telecare domain. Due to the various groups involved we can deem telecare policy to be a complex policy making subject. To add to the complexity, there is also an additional dimension of regional versus national policy, for example in the case of Belgium. We argue there is no single group taking responsibility for the formulation of telecare policy and this can be deemed a weakness. In the category of Policy Enactors, our findings reveal there is a mix of non profit, voluntary, and non-governmental agencies involved. Their roles are varied and include raising awareness, and dissemination of research. Similarly, we argue there is a sense of unaligned discourse in the implementation of policies relating to telecare. When researching telecare service providers, we found private firms to be dominant. There are both service and product offerings. There are a growing number of startups in this field and it is particularly common area found among spinouts from universities. A particularly interesting case is the Hagen Committee in Norway. This is a national program for municipal innovation in care where 1% of care services budget allocated to Innovation in the form of a Private public partnership. However, other countries have yet to formalize initiatives to encourage innovation between private and public institutions. This is an area which could be further explored. The following are areas of uncertainty about the impact which arose from our analysis.

> - Who should be responsible for the formulation of telecare policy?
> - Who should be responsible for the implementation of telecare policy?
> - How will public- private partnerships encourage advancement of telecare technology?

4.3   Uncertainty about Societal Preferences – The Why Questions

Surprisingly, the societal preferences of telecare were largely absent in national telecare policy documentation. At the workshop with experts we were engaged in an interesting discussion on the risks associated with telecare. Here, a multitude of types of risks were identified including Privacy Risk, Social Risk, Technology Risk, Legal Risk and Financial Risks. The most common privacy risks were concerned with legal rights and ethical considerations not being fully addressed. The social risk of isolation was considered and the question of forced or voluntary participation was raised. The technology risk of how to secure data storage and transmission of sensitive health data were identified. Also the polarized dilemma of technology driven innovation versus user need innovation was questioned and the ramifications of this debate for policy making. Also legal risks were articulated; specifically the medical responsibility was questioned in the technology versus practitioner onus of responsibility debate in the time of malpractice. The legal risk of the lack of legislation and regulation in this space was also recognised. Finally the financial risk was discussed as to the question of who is responsible for the costs of the telecare technology. The following are areas of uncertainty about the societal preferences which arose from our analysis.

> - Why are telecare risks not being discussed at policy level?

5   Implications of Research

As evident from our multiple country study, decision making regarding telecare policy is a fragmented, challenged process, with differing levels of sophistication. Our interest lies in decision support as a provision to holistic policy making in telecare to address the grand challenge of ageing. We argue policy makers, when challenged with policy making in ICT innovation are suffering from a crisis of legitimacy as evident from the different types of uncertainty. As articulated by Kovisto et al 2009, innovation processes have shifted from 'the positivist and rationalist technology-focused approaches towards the recognition of broader concerns that encompass the entire innovation system, including its economic, social and economic perspectives' [18: p1164].

As there are nuances among countries in their policy efforts, we argue decision support can frame the uncertainty over preferences and reduce uncertainty over cause and effect. Carter and Bélanger (2005) argue government agencies must understand the factors that influence citizen adoption of innovation [19]. Their findings indicate that perceived ease of use, compatibility and trustworthiness are significant predictors of citizens' intention to adopt technology. Similarly, other studies highlight trust as the key success factor in technology acceptance of multi criteria decision support systems in the case of high impact decisions [20]. We advance this argument and argue decision support can help promote judgment and dialogue with citizens thus providing rich material.   In support of our argument, Rose and Grant (2010) argue that involvement from all stakeholders, including citizens of various ICT means and capabilities is a requisite for successful implementation [21].

We propose a research agenda to explore further decision support mechanisms to support ICT policy making for an Aging Society. We propose a number of implications are to be considered as evident from the findings of our case study of European telecare policy. As shown in our case study, none of the 14 countries have a dedicated policy for telecare. Whilst all recognize their national demographic trends demand a telecare response, there are a wide variety of responses in how the countries in our study are engaging with telecare. A decision support response can frame the uncertainty and present suggestive decisional guidance as per Earl and Hopwood (1980) recommendation, thus instilling trust and legitimacy in the policy making process [2]. Our findings recognize the challenge of applying a DSS to a decision in complicated and contested matters such as the use of technology in the aging society yet we support a DSS offering of suggestive guidance with the following two caveats. Firstly, policy- makers need to understand the clear societal consensus [2], and secondly, where assumptions are made about the future, or where consensus has not yet arisen in an organisation or society, decision support should not provide artificially complete ready-made answers and should, instead, promote judgement and dialogue amongst stakeholders [2].

Furthermore, decision support can increase integrity and honesty in policy decisions, two vital components to the success of transformation of policy making in technology. Public sector values are the foundation from which the idea of genuine transformation ultimately derives [22]. The second implication of a decision support framework will promote a sense of action thus ensuring a sense of positivity about ICT policy decision making. The final implication will translate a respect for the citizen. Decision support for policy making in ICT innovation will support moving beyond a utilitarian and unidirectional approach to technology, thus foster engagement through institutionalization of citizen engagement and debate on contentious issues in ICT through increased transparency in the outcomes of decisions [23].

6   Concluding Comments

The paper will be of interest to IS scholars, policy makers, and society in general as we explore decision support to enhance ICT policy making. Specifically, our study provides a picture of the uncertainty in policy making relating to ICT innovation, and lends itself to further study of how decision support can frame uncertainty. We have considered 14 countries and their policy approaches to telecare. We suggest that contemplating decision support will frame uncertainty and deliver a number of implications, including legitimacy of policy, infer a sense of action and deliver a respect for the citizen. Our framework supports the feasibility and desirability of shaping and steering decision support in ICT innovation policy making.

References

[1] Alter, S.: A work system view of DSS in its 4th decade. Decision Support Systems 38(3), 319–327 (2004)

[2] Earl, M.J., Hopwood, A.G.: From management information to information management. In: Lucas, Land, Lincoln, Supper (eds.) The Information Systems Environment. IFIP, pp. 133–143. North-Holland (1980)

[3] OECD, Live Longer, Work Longer. OECD. Paris (2011)

[4] Percival, Hanson: Big brother or brave new world? Telecare and its implications for older people's independence and social inclusion. Critical Social Policy 26(4), 888–909 (2006)

[5] Yanga, L., Zhiyong Lan, G.: Internet's impact on expert–citizen interactions in public policymaking—A meta analysis. Government Information Quarterly 27(4), 431–441 (2010)

[6] Stilgoe, J., Owen, R., Macnaghten, P.: Developing a framework for responsible innovation. Research Policy (2013)

[7] Delvenne, P., Fallon, C., Brunet, S.: Parliamentary technology assessment institutions as indications of reflexive modernization. Technology in Society 33(1–2), 36–43 (2011)

[8] March, J., Simon, H.: Organisations. J. Wiley, New York (1958)

[9] Lindblom, C.: The science of 'muddling through'. Public Administration Review, 779–788 (1959)

[10] Wimmer, M., Scherer, S., Moss, S., Bicking, M.: Method and Tools to Support Stakeholder Engagement in Policy Development: The OCOPOMO Project. International Journal of Electronic Government Research 8(3), 98 (2012)

[11] Alter, S.: Why persist with DSS when the real issue is improving decision making? In: Jelassi (ed.) Decision Support Systems: Experiences and Expectations. North Holland (1992)

[12] Thompson, J.D., Tuden, A.: Strategies, structures, and processes of organizational decision. Bobbs-Merrill (1967)

[13] Silver, M.S.: Decisional guidance for computer-based decision support. MIS Quarterly 15(1), 105–122 (1991)

[14] Yin, R.K.: Case study research: Design and methods, vol. 5. Sage (2009)

[15] Andersson, A., Gronlund, A., Astrom, J.: You can't make this a science- Analysing decision support systems in political contexts. Government Information Quarterly 29(4), 543–552 (2012)

[16] Silverman, D.: Doing qualitative research: A practical handbook. SAGE Publications Limited (2013)

[17] Ishmatova, D., Thi Thanh Hai, N.: Towards a framework for analysing and comparing ICT policies for Aging Society Policies: A First Approximation. In: ICEGOV 2013, Seoul, Republic of Korea, October 22-25 (2013)

[18] Koivisto, R., Wessberg, N., Eerola, T., Kivisaari, S., Myllyoja, J., Halonen, M.: Integrating future-oriented technology analysis and risk assessment methodologies. Technological Forecasting and Social Change 76, 1163–1176 (2009)

[19] Carter, L., Bélanger, F.: The utilization of E-Government services: Citizen trust, innovation and acceptance factors. Information Systems Journal 15(1), 5–25 (2005)

[20] Maida, M., Maier, K., Obwegeser, N., Stix, V.: Success of multi criteria decision support systems: The relevance of Trust. In: 46th Hawaii International Conference on System Systems, pp. 1530–1605 (2013)

[21] Rose, Grant: Critical Issues pertaining to the planning& implementation of e-government initiatives. Government Information Quarterly 27(1), 26–33 (2010)

[22] Bannister, F., Connolly, R.: ICT, public values and transformative government: A framework and programme for research. Government Information Quarterly (2014) (forthcoming)

[23] Evans, A.M., Campos, A.: Open Government Initiatives: Challenges of Citizen Participation. Journal of Policy Analysis and Management 32, 172–185 (2013)

Open Government Data: Facilitating and Motivating Factors for Coping with Potential Barriers in the Brazilian Context

Claudio Sonaglio Albano[1] and Nicolau Reinhard[2]

[1] Unipampa, Federal University of Pampa, Bagé, Brazil
claudio.albano@unipampa.edu.br
[2] School of Economics, Business and Accounting, Business Department,
University of Sao Paulo, Brazil
reinhard@usp.br

Abstract. The use of Open Government Data (OGD) involves multiple activities developed by networks of users with different capacities and goals, along a value chain. These users, and also government agents supplying OGD recognize benefits, motivations, barriers, facilitating and inhibiting factors in the process. This paper surveyed the perceptions of Brazilian OGD users and government agents, in order to provide information for the improvement of OGD supply and use.

Keywords: open government data, benefits and barriers, facilitating and motivating factors.

1   Introduction and Research Question

According to the [21], open government data (OGD) is the publication and dissemination of public sector information on the Internet, shared in a logically understandable format, to allow its reuse in machine-readable form.

The potential advantages arising from the participation in OGD initiatives, have to be seen in conjunction with the difficulties for the realization of these benefits. According to [17], it should not be expected that simply by opening their data, governments will be able to generate the expected benefits for administrations and society.

The success of OGD initiatives requires an extensive interaction between governments and society [5, 7, 18]. According to these authors, governments are not able to follow technology changes with the desired agility, due to excessive bureaucracy and regulations. The private sector or non-profit organizations manage to be more competent to deliver information to citizens and enable them to better use the public information available.

The challenges in the implementation of OGD projects are due to the multiple interactions among players, information flows, technologies and the interests involved in these initiatives, resulting in a dynamic process of interactions between

M. Janssen et al. (Eds.): EGOV 2014, LNCS 8653, pp. 181–193, 2014.

governments and society, building networks between the organizations. According to [9, 10], this understanding is not yet fully available in guides, tools, techniques and theories to deal with open government data, motivating the present study's research question: Can a greater understanding of users' network and the motivating and facilitating factors to cope with the potential barriers and inhibiting factors, seeking potential benefits and advantages, help public administrators to achieve better results with their OGD projects?

The survey was conducted with Brazilian users and government suppliers of OGD and is aimed at providing a contribution to public administrators by enabling a greater understanding of the factors that may support their OGD projects. It must be noted that Brazil, despite the enacted legislation mandating OGD at all levels of government, is still at an early stage of OGD supply and use.

2   Literature Review

2.1   Potential Benefits and Advantages

According to [13] the their first stage of ODG maturity, the goal of governments initiatives is to allow transparency and control of government actions. Society is then able to create products and services, useful both for society and governments, with the possibility of generating new economic activities, among other social benefits and advantages.

[12] classifies these possible benefits into three major groups: political and social, economic, and technical and operational. Political and social benefits are related to issues involving transparency, democracy, promotion of citizenship, among others. Promoting a greater stimulus to innovation, the ability to generate new products and services, the integration between government and society, among others, are associated with economic benefits. The possibility for governments and society to work in cooperation to improve processes, through the use of knowledge (and collective capabilities) is related to potential operational and technical benefits and advantages.

According to [20] some countries have progressed beyond the mere access to data, where the Open Datahas shown that it not only produces significant changes in the public sector, but it generates synergies in innovation and entrepreneurship. In the Brazilian context, authors [4], argue as key benefits that can be achieved through OGD projects: greater promotion of citizenship, ability to develop new products and services from governments to society, greater efficiency for governments, among others.

2.2   Potential Barriers and Inhibiting Factors

There are, however, challenges, barriers and inhibiting factors to OGD initiatives. [6] suggests as challenges: technical problems in information processing, information collected in different ways and for different purposes, work overload to make this information available, heterogeneity of users and their inability to work with the information, among others. Other factors that may be regarded as potential barriers and inhibiting factors involve the "understanding" of the data by society (discussed in the topic – quality and usability of the content available, in addition to structural and technological issues of public organizations [19, 23].

[12] classifies the potential barriers and inhibiting factors into six major groups, which are as follows:institutional, complexity of the tasks, use and participation, legislation, quality of information and techniques.Institutional factors are associated with cultural and structural issues of public entities.Likewise, Government's internal problems, but related to technical issues, are associated with the complexity of the task.

The uneven motivation of society to participate in OGD initiatives, as well as their capacity to use these data are related to the factor use and participation. There are also legal issues on which information may be made available, as well as their use. The quality of information is related not only to the quality of the information available, but also to the relevance of the information to its users, and finally, technical issues are related to the information technology tools that support the provision of information.

[4] in their respective studies developed in the Brazilian context, identify as major barriers and inhibiting factors in the context of OGD projects: the low capacity of society to access and use the information; this fact generates lack of interest and low interaction.Technical issues, involving the quality and format of the information available, and finally, aspects related to legislation.

2.3   Facilitating and Motivating Factors – Interorganizational Networks

Networking is essential for an organization to be able to integrate the new requirements in a scenario marked by the importance of technology, information and knowledge. An OGD project is established by government, but it may involve several entities of a single government or several governments, such as websites that accept data from other governments. Analysing the relationships between organizations is a complex task, especially in environments of heterogeneous relationships (that is, involving public and private organizations).

The complexity is further enhancedwhen each participant organization has diverse interests and bonds and is able to simultaneously participate in several networks. It is important to identify which factors sustain the relationships established in interorganizational networks. In this sense basically, two main aspects are seen as able to sustain these relationships, the motivating aspects and the facilitating aspects. According to [16] the motivating aspects refer to needs of organizations to participate in networks to achieve commercial advantages, legal advantages, or advantages from other sources. Other motivating aspects include: the power that an organization has over the others; the possible gains when cooperating with third parties; obtaining legitimacy and stability through the established partnerships.

For [3, 8, 22], the facilitating factors are related to the governance that can be sought on networking, the search for reliability (especially in unstable environments), and establishing a greater reputation, are examples of facilitating factors. Obtaining advantages through the exchange of information, as well as the investments made by an organization (through training, tools, etc.) can help organizations to establish relationships in complex environments. Concepts of the Gift Economy, like reputation, reciprocity, communities, etc., can be recognized in the motivations of OGD users and should be considered by governments to promote OGD [1, 14].

3   Open Government Data in Brazil

In 2011, Brazil became a member of the Open Government Partnership (OGP), making a commitment to encourage and promote public policies of transparency and publish data in open format. As a result of this commitment, on November 18, 2011, the Law No. 12527 was enacted, which entered into force on May 16, 2012, regulating the constitutional right for citizens to have access to government data at all levels. Special situations had already been regulated by laws and decrees between 2009 and 2010. The effective implementation of these regulations, however, is still a challenge, specially at the municipal level, as demonstrated by the nationwide survey on Electronic Government 2010 [2]. Government initiatives include the 2012 conference for open data, organized by the Office of the Comptroller General (CGU), who is also responsible for monitoring the compliance with the law.

4   Reference Model

The paper's research questions are: a) identify the benefits expected by users and government from the use of open government data (OGD), and its barriers and inhibiting factors; b) identify the network of players (individuals and organizations), their roles and motivations in the use of OGD. [12] provided the concepts for the OGD benefits and barriers. The resulting categories for analysis are displayed in Table 1.

Table 1. Categories defined for data analysis

Category	Category characteristics
Benefits and advantages Source: [12] Topic – 2.1	Items:political, social, economic and operational or technical.
Barriers and inhibiting factors.Source: [12] Topic – 2.2	Items:Institutional, complexities of the task, use and participation, legislation, quality of information and techniques.
Facilitating and motivating factors.Source: Interorganizational Networks Topic – 2.3	OGD activities.References or citations to the activities and their goals.

[11] provided the conceptualization of primary and support activities for the open data value chain, with Organizational Network Theory providing the rationality of members participation in the network [16] and the reference network model is displayed in Figure 1.

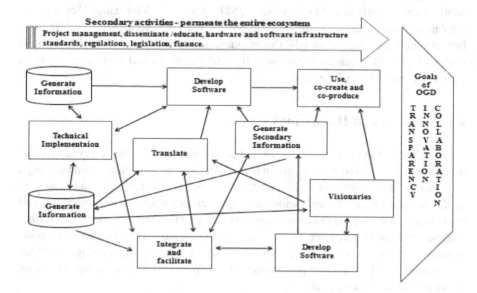

Fig. 1. Reference Network Model: Authors of work

5   Methodological Procedures

The research used an interpretative approach, based on qualitiative data from surveys of a convenience sample. Data collection was performed in two stages. First, we conducted semi-structured interviews, consisting of questions regarding the respondents OGD activities, expected benefits, facilitators and motivators, barriers and inhibiting factors, with a sample consisting of authors' contacts from events related to the subject, internet directories and search in websites for open government data projects, resulting in: seven government representatives (employees of government entities/agencies with open data projects); five developers (professionals working with software based on open data); two professors from public universities; one investigative journalist and three representatives of civil society organizations, totaling 18 respondents.

These respondents indicated the sample for the second data collection (open interviews): a journalist; one member of each: a state government; a municipal government (also a journalist); a non-governmental organization with mainly technical activity; a private for-profit organization that develops tools for the provision of open data; two non-governmental and non-profit organizations that operate by integrating other organizations; a federal government agency; a private for-profit company that operates in healthcare with open data, and alsotwo scholars and a software developer (who develops applications based on open data).

The research also included documentary:Brazilian legislation on the provision of public data, in particular, the Law No. 12527 (Access to Information Act – AIA), regulations and decrees of the federal government that formalized the National Infrastructure for Open Data (INDA), minutes and action plans of INDA. Content analysis was used to analyse the transcriptions of interviews and documents, using an a priori categorization of concepts.

6   Results and Discussions

First, we present the potential benefits and advantages that can be achieved in OGD initiatives, as perceived by the respondents (members of governments and society), followed by the barriers and inhibiting factors. The benefits and advantages, as well as the barriers and inhibiting factors are separated according to the interviews and documents, following the opinions of members of governments and society, as further analyses will make reference to these two groups separately. The survey's results indicate that the respondents views correspond to the very initial stage of Open Government of [13]. Their expectations of OGD provided by public administration are limited to the first stage of [13].

Our research aimed at a) verifying the possibility of a network of non-governmental agents   also realizing the functionalities of stages 2 and 3 [13], depending on the public agents providing the data in a form that allows those agents to select integrate and recombine the data according to their specific needs; and b) Identifying required infrastructure (legal, technical, etc.) to support these network activities.

Engaging users in these activities would, of course, not preclude public agents from also performing these activities. Non-government agents, however, could be more motivated to do it, since they would perceive more directly the value of the activity, therefore increasing the sustainability of the value chain.

As an example of government action, one local government agency in our sample provides the users with private working spaces, where they can store their queries and data sets. This space, however, in order to benefit from the network, would have to allow also importing and combining data from external sources, providing also analysis and display tools and allow sharing and collaboration among different users.

This would be particularly important for the use of statistical, georeferenced and text data that may require specialized resources for analysis and manipulation, differing from the use of individual transaction data. This is also a response to the "Specific Assets" facilitating factor, the most cited. (INDA as a framework was heavily cited).

6.1   Benefits and Advantages, Barriers and Inhibiting Factors

This section firstly presents the results and analyses of the benefits and advantages found for governments. Political and social factors are mentioned as major benefits. Among these factors, transparency and processes that generate greater integration and reliability between government and society stand out. The second group of potential benefits and advantages refers to operational and technical aspects, which include the optimization of internal processes and the greater possibility to use data through the collaboration of various stakeholders, even among several governments. Possible benefits and economic advantages received little emphasis, but respondents stated that they may be achieved through a greater collaboration and incentive to innovation.

For society, political and social factors are also mentioned as possible benefits and advantages, including issues related to greater transparency and citizenship. Operational and technical factors are mentioned, including the possibility of offering new products and services to society and to generate greater integration between society and government. New functionalities with greater provision of information allow the development of new capabilities, especially through the networked collaboration between different segments of society, with a reference to the use of collective knowledge as a source of benefits. For government, benefits and economic advantages are mentioned with lower frequency.

The major inhibiting factors and barriers for governments are related to technical factors, especially the format and quality of information made available. Institutional factors, such as structural and political issues are the second group of factors mentioned as potential barriers. Legislation comes shortly after, indicating the lack of clarity about privacy as the most mentioned factor. Finally, mentioned as possible barriers within governments are issues related to the low interest of civil servants to cooperate with these initiatives.

Members of society, similarly to government members, understand the same technical issues as the biggest barriers, mainly, the format and quality of information. However, the lack of interest in the use of the information provided is mentioned as the second biggest barrier among the members of society. Issues related to legislation are mentioned as the third group of barriers, once again the clarity about which information can be made available is mentioned with emphasis.

6.2   Facilitating and Motivating Factors

The first group of respondents mentioned as facilitating and motivating factorsthe network of other players (or organizations).In the interviews of the second round of interviews, the researchers aimed a identifying the activities of each user category. Table 2 displays the answers grouped according to the occupations or backgrounds of the respondents.

Table 2. Facilitating and Motivating Factors (I)

Players and organizations	Activities developed	Goals
Journalists	Disseminate information among their peers and society in general, train other colleagues (teaching courses) and supervise the compliance with the LAI, in addition to supporting non-governmental entities (with technological activity) that operate with the subject.Encourage the publication of open data and "evangelize" society on OGD.	Generate a greater demand for OGD
Public Servants	Collect data among the various entities of their agency for publication.There are basically two data sources:dataconsidered of interest by internal governmetmembers or that have been demanded by society.They work along with governmental organizations formally to regulate the OGD operations of other organizations.Performtechnical activities to enable the publication of these data.	Make data available
Software developers	Work in software development through projects and events called Hackatons.At these events participants develop short projects.This action can be casual, highly driven by the occurrence of these events.	Develop applications based on OGD

Table 2a. Facilitating and Motivating Factors (II)

Players and organizations	Activities developed	Goals
Scholars	Their activities are motivated by their interest in some specific area (health, budget, etc.), and they seek to have these data used by society.	Promote greater interest in the subject.
Non-governmental organizations (for-profit) with technical expertise.	Develop technical tools to facilitate (support) the supply of data in an open format.	Offer products and technical tools.
Non-governmental organizations (non-profit) without technical expertise.	Organize the OGD content to be published, supportorganizations in their search for financial and technical resources for OGD activities.	Promote the participation of civil society and government entities on the subject.
Nongovernmental organizations (for-profit) without technical expertise.	Acts as intermediary between government and society, helping citizens to find and access specific government services	Add products and services to their portfolio of solutions.
State organization with technical expertise	Offer access to raw data and elaborated information. Provide metadata, tools for query, analysis and presentation of data. Can act in partnership with other organizations.	Produce and disseminate socioeconomic and demographic statistics and analyzes

Table 2a. (*continued*)

International organization operating in Internet on the subject	Has strong international presence in the definition of rules and standards for the Internet, having also worked heavily in the Brazilian ecosystem of open data and OGD. Is active in Brazil in the standardizing activities, promotion and advocacy of OGD, producing publications and events.	OGD Promotion and advocacy, contribute to normatization
Non-governmental organizations (for-profit) with technical expertise.	Develop technical tools to facilitate (support) the supply of data in an open format.	Offer products and technical tools.
Non-governmental organizations (for-profit) with technical expertise.	Develop technical tools to facilitate (support) the supply of data in an open format.	Offer products and technical tools.

6.3 Facilitating and Motivating Factors for Coping with Potential Barriers and Inhibiting Factors

In Table 3, the barriers are confronted with the respective facilitating and motivating factors, which can support the reduction or even the elimination of these barriers.

Table 4 shows how the facilitating and motivating factors confronting the barriers can provide better conditions for the benefits and advantages to be effectively achieved.

Table 3. Barriers, facilitating and motivating factors

Barrier	Who faces it?	Facilitating and motivating factors.
Technical factors	Government	Civil servants, whose job is to develop activities that
Technical factors	Society	can technically facilitate the access to information; Software developers demand enhanced quality information for their applications Nongovernmental organizations (for-profit) with technical expertise, developinghigh quality applications (platforms) International organization promoting the dissemination of ODG use and standards.
Institutional factors	Governments	Journalists, scholars and the international organization working with OGD. They can pressuregovernmentfor increased effort, agility, quality in informationprovision.
Legislation	Governments	Journalists, as watchdogs of government compliance
Legislation	Society	with legislation and promoting society's interest in OGD. Scholars, civil servants contribute to improvement and solution of problems with the legislation.
Use and participation	Governments	Journalists, scholars, non-governmental organizations (non-profit), international organization working on the
Use and participation	Society	dissemination and increasing society' awareness and interest in OGD.

Table 4. Benefits X facilitating and motivating factors

Benefit	Who seeks it?	Facilitating and motivating factors.
Political and social Transparency, integration and reliability	Government	Journalists, scholars and non-profit non-governmental organizations, promoting the subject tosociety.Mayhelp in the use of data by improving the interaction between government and society.
Political and social Transparency and greater exercise of citizenship	Society	Scholars, by conducting research (and studies) in specified areas also contribute to the achievement of these advantages.
Operational and technicalOptimization of internal processes and increased use of data	Government	Public servants, by promoting greater use of the data, with higher quality, provide greater collaboration between governments.
Operational and technicalSupply of new products and services.	Society	Software developers and organizations that develop tools for the provision of data, by creating the technical conditions for these activities.Journalists, scholars and nongovernmental non-profit organizations without technical expertise, by suggesting possible niches or opportunities for the development of new products and services.
Economic Greater collaboration	Government	Public servants, by disseminating the subject internally, are able to allow greater collaboration, and possibly the development of our products and services to governments.
Economic use of collective knowledge	Society	All players (and organizations) by integrating their activities and objectives.

Based on tables 3 and 4, it is possible to see how the players and organizations, mentioned as facilitating and motivating factors, through their activities, may face the aforementioned barriers and how they can contribute to the benefits (also mentioned by the respondents) to be achieved.

There are some players, such as journalists and scholars, who clearly have activities aimed at fostering greater activities from this context, because they seek to monitor the information available and verify their usefulness and importance to society. These activities contribute to the dissemination of the subject, and it could generate a greater interest from society on the subject, so that society can then require higher quality from governments when undertaking these initiatives, mitigating some barriers and enabling some benefits.

Other players, such as developers, public servants, organizations of society perform activities with technical bias. Barriers related to technical issues were the most cited by the respondents (between governments and society), so the presence of these players is important as they can require from the governments the provision of information with higher quality or develop products that support this activity.

Finally, organizations of society, non-profit and with no technical purposes, may indicate to the players (with technical expertise), being supported by journalists and scholars, possible niches of operation based on OGD.This activity may impact the context, causing a greater interest in the use of this information.

7   Final Considerations

One result of the study is the confirmation by the Brazilian study of previous studies [12] regarding the benefits and advantages expected from OGD initiatives. Respondents perceive OGD as important to promote greater government efficiency and develop citizenship. Barriers are related to technical aspects (quality and format of information), legal issues and the still reduced interest of society in the subject.

A contribution of our paper is the recognition by the players of the importance of the network of users to facilitate and motivate OGD use. Concepts from Interorganizational Network Theory are helpful in systematizing these perceptions, but also, onn its more prescriptive side to guide government agents in its participation and support of these networks.

The main contribution of this study, especially for the Brazilian context, is to identify the facilitating and motivating factors, as a way to cope with the potential barriers.Players and organizations identifiedother players and organizations as possible facilitating and motivating factors, enabling a greater and better participation of everyone.

The results of the study may help governments to develop OGD initiatives with greater effectiveness, since by being awareofthe factors that can help coping with the barriers and inhibiting factors, they will beable to formulate strategies to integrate them into their initiatives, aiming atachieving greater and better results. Among these strategies, the integration of these facilitating and motivating factors in their initiatives should surely be included, thus providing better conditions for the development of their activities and consequently that all participants of these initiatives are able to achieve better results.

To Future Research, the OGD user network should, by its nature, be very dynamic and global. Our survey did not consider the business use of OGD, that should involve different networks, value chains and user motivations, therefore requiring a possibly different research approach. The importance of this research is increased by the economic potential of OGD use by companies [15].

References

1. Benkler, Y.: The Wealth of Networks (2006),
   http://www.benkler.org/Benkler_Wealth_Of_Networks.pdf
2. CGI. Brazilian Internet Steering Committee, Survey on the use of Information and Communication Technologies in Brazil ICT Electronic Government 2010 (2011)
3. Cox, A.: The art of the possible: relationship management in power regimes and supply chain. International Journal of Supply Chain Management 9(5), 346–356 (2004)
4. Craveiro, G., Santana, M., Albuquerque, J.P.: Assessing Open Government Budgetary Data in Brazil. In: ICDS 2013, The Seventh International Conference on Digital Society (2013)
5. Davies, T.G., Bawa, Z.A.: The Promises and Perils of Open Government Data (OGD). Special Issue: Community Informatics and Open Government Data 8(2) (2012), Disponível em: http://ci-journal.net/index.php/ciej/issue/view/41 (access ins May 2012)

6. Dawes, S.S., Helbig, N.: Information strategies for open government: Challenges and prospects for deriving public value from government transparency. In: Wimmer, M.A., Chappelet, J.-L., Janssen, M., Scholl, H.J. (eds.) EGOV 2010. LNCS, vol. 6228, pp. 50–60. Springer, Heidelberg (2010)
7. Espinoza, J.F., Recinos, I.P., Morales, M.P.: Datos Abiertos: oportunidades y desafíos para Centroamérica con base en una cadena de valor. In: Conferencia Regional de Datos Abiertos para América Latina y el Caribe - 2013 – Montevideo, Uruguay (2013)
8. Grandori, A.: An organizational assessment of interfirm coordination modes. Organization Studies 18(6), 897–925 (1997)
9. Helbig, N., Cresswell, A.M., Burke, B.G., Pardo, T.A., Reyes-Luna, L.: Modeling the Informational Relationships between Government and Society. In: Open Government Consultative Workshop, June 26-27. CTG, Albany (2012)
10. Helbig, N., Cresswell, A.M., Burke, B.G., Reyes-Luna, L.: The Dynamics of Opening Government Data (2013), http://www.ctg.albany.edu/publications/reports/opendata/opendata.pdf (acessojaneiro 2013)
11. Hughes, J.: Why Open Data is necessary but not sufficient to make a difference (2011), http://www.slideshare.net/janet-hughes/how-to-make-the-flowers-bloom
12. Janssen, M., Charalabidis, Y., Zuiderwijk, A.: Benefits, Adoption Barriers and Myths of Open Dataand Open Government. Information Systems Management 29, 258–268 (2012)
13. Kalampokis, E., Tambouris, E., Tarabanis, K.: A classification scheme for open government data: towards linking decentralised data. 266 Int. J. Web Engineering and Technology 6(3) (2011)
14. Lathrop, D., Ruma, L.: Open Government: Collaboration, Transparency, and Participation in Practice, 1st edn. O'Reilly Media (2010)
15. McKinsey, Open data: Unlocking innovation and performance with liquid information (2013), http://www.mckinsey.com/insights/business_technology/open_data_unlocking_innovation_and_performance_with_liquid_information (access in November 2013)
16. Oliver, C.: Determinants of interorganizational relationships: integration and future directions. Academy of Management Review 15, 241–265 (1990)
17. Prince, A., Jolías, L., Brys, C.: Análisis de La cadena de valor del ecosistema de Datos Abiertos de La Ciudad de Buenos Aires. In: Conferencia Regional de Datos Abiertos para América Latina y el Caribe - junio de 2013 – Montevideo, Uruguay (2013), http://www.princeconsulting.biz/pdf/7.pdf (accessed August 2013)
18. Robinson, D., Zeller, W., Yu, D.: Government data and the invisible hand. Yale Journal of Law and Technology 11, 160 (2009)
19. Sayogo, D.G., Pardo, T.: Exploring the Motive for Data Publication in Open Data Initiative: Linking Intention to Action. In: 45th Hawaii International Conference on System Sciences (2012), http://www.ctg.albany.edu/publications/journals/hicss_2012_datasharing (acesso em dezembro 2012)
20. Solar, M., Concha, G., Meijueiro, L.: A Model to Assess Open Government Data in Public Agencies. In: Scholl, H.J., Janssen, M., Wimmer, M.A., Moe, C.E., Flak, L.S. (eds.) EGOV 2012. LNCS, vol. 7443, pp. 210–221. Springer, Heidelberg (2012)
21. W3C. The Open data Handbook, http://opendatamanual.org (2009) (accessed September 2011)

22. Williamson, O.E.: The Economics of Governance. The American Economic Review 95(2), 1–18 (2005)
23. Zuiderwijk, A., Janssen, M., Choenni, S., Meijer, R., Alibaks, R.S.: Socio-technical Impediments of Open Data. Journal of e-Government 10(2), 156–172 (2012), http://www.ejeg.com; ISSN 1479-439X 156 ©Academic Publishing International Ltd Zuiderwijk

Analyzing Stakeholders in Complex E-Government Projects: Towards a Stakeholder Interaction Model

Vanessa Greger, Dian Balta, Petra Wolf, and Helmut Krcmar

Fortiss – An-Institut der TU München, Munich, Germany
{vanessa.greger,dian.balta,petra.wolf,
helmut.krcmar}@fortiss.org

Abstract. To complete e-government projects successfully, various stakeholders with different interests need to be taken into account. So far, stakeholder models in the e-government context focus on individual stakeholder perspectives. They do not show or analyze interactions between stakeholders in detail. However, taking stakeholders' interactions into account is important, since stakeholders influence each other - which can result in a change of their perspectives. Hence, our contribution illustrates how a stakeholder interaction model helps identifying different stakeholder perspectives. Therefore, we reviewed literature on existing stakeholder models. Besides, we conducted a stakeholder analysis in an e-government project in Germany and elicited stakeholders, assigned them to corresponding categories and modeled a stakeholder interaction model. Finally, we compared the findings of the literature review with the developed model. This contribution enlarges the theoretical foundations of the e-government research field. The stakeholder interaction model can be used by practitioners to identify stakeholders and their interactions.

Keywords: stakeholder analysis, stakeholder interaction model, e-government project, public sector, public administration.

1   Introduction

Many electronic government (e-government) projects are not completed successfully or not at all [1, 2]. One reason for this is the fact that the project's success is compromised by issues evolving during the collaboration between e-government project partners. These issues are mostly based on the involvement of a large number of different stakeholders. Examples thereof include decision-makers of different federal or local public administrations or intermediaries (e.g. software companies or consultants). In particular, these stakeholders often have different, conflicting interests and priorities depending on their perspective on the project and the project phase [3, 4]. This hinders the consideration of all their requirements. Hence, a detailed and structured stakeholder management is a prerequisite for implementing e-government projects successfully [5]. Therefore, all stakeholders need to be identified

M. Janssen et al. (Eds.): EGOV 2014, LNCS 8653, pp. 194–205, 2014.

and their concerns, interests and requirements regarding the e-government solution need to be analyzed and prioritized using stakeholder analysis techniques [6, 7].

Addressing those issues in our paper, we follow the widespread definition of Freeman et al. and define a stakeholder as "any group or individual who can affect or is affected by the achievement of a corporation's purpose" [8]. Besides identifying the stakeholders and their needs, interactions between them need to be considered, as stakeholders can significantly influence each other through their interactions. This can result in a change of the stakeholder's perspective on the e-government project. For example, stakeholders having a strong lobby can influence the project management. In consequence, the project staff needs to consider specific requirements of these particular stakeholders. This is the case even if other previously planned requirements cannot be taken into account any longer. In summary, we understand interactions as communication between stakeholders in order to exchange resources, like information or funds [9, 10].

So far, existing stakeholder models only consider the perspective of individual stakeholders without showing interactions between them in detail. However, in order to understand changes in the stakeholders' perspective, it is necessary to consider and analyze interactions between them. Until now, there is a lack of research on who the stakeholders in complex e-government projects are and how they interact with each other. In our paper, we present findings of a literature review on already existing stakeholder models. Furthermore, we perform a stakeholder analysis on the example of the pre-filed tax filing system in Germany[1]. This e-government project is conducted by one German public administration designing an e-government solution to be used by other public administrations. We aim at identifying and categorizing the stakeholders of this particular e-government project as well as modeling stakeholder interactions. This is the first step to design and conduct e-government projects as closely to all stakeholders' benefits as possible. Finally, our contribution compares the derived stakeholder interaction model with the stakeholder models found in literature. For this purpose, our research is guided by the following questions:

- What does a stakeholder interaction model in e-government projects look like?
- Taking into account the stakeholder models identified in literature, to what extent does the stakeholder interaction model enrich the existing body of knowledge?

The remainder of this paper is structured as follows: First, the research methodology is explained. Second, the findings of the literature review are presented. Third, we illustrate and explain the derived stakeholder interaction model. Afterwards, our findings are discussed and compared. Finally, a conclusion is made and further research is outlined.

---

[1] We are grateful for the support provided by ISPRAT e.V. in terms of funding our research project at the Chair for Information Systems (TU München). We further thank all project participants and interviewees, especially the project staff for their most helpful input and feedback during the project.

2   Research Methodology

A literature review according to Webster and Watson [11] was performed in order to identify already existing stakeholder models. Using the keywords "stakeholder" and "e-government", we searched databases, e-government specific conferences and journals. Our initial search yielded 66,846 results, including duplicates. In a first step, we screened titles upon relevance to our research goals. In case a title was considered relevant, we screened the corresponding abstract as well. Hence, we were able to identify 48 papers as input for the third step of a comprehensive paper review including the full text content. These papers were read and categorized using the following categories:

(i)   *no stakeholder enumeration or classification,*
(ii)   *only stakeholder enumeration* and
(iii)   *stakeholder model.*

Papers classified into the first category are not relevant for our further analysis. These papers are either not e-government specific or refer to the importance of stakeholders without a further enumeration or classification. Hence, 26 papers are seen as relevant, as they contain a stakeholder enumeration or a stakeholder model. Analyzing them in more detail, we found that 18 out of the 26 papers contain a stakeholder enumeration and only eight papers describe a stakeholder model. These papers were analyzed in more depth in regard to their categorization, interaction and scope. In order to guarantee reliability and validity, the papers were classified by two researchers.

Moreover, we conducted a stakeholder analysis on the example of an e-government project within a German state administration. This project aims at upgrading the German tax filing system ELSTER by the possibility of automatically loading tax relevant information into the system. In order to identify and categorize the stakeholders of this project, we conducted a semi-structured interview with three members of the project management team of the e-government solution. Further, we participated in a workshop, where information about the e-government solution was communicated to so-called ELSTER deputies. We also searched through official websites for information about this e-government solution. On the basis of this information, we identified and categorized the stakeholders and, consequently, derived a stakeholder interaction model. Afterwards, this model was examined and approved by the project leader. Finally, we compared the developed stakeholder interaction model with the stakeholder models found in literature.

3   Findings

3.1   Literature Review

The papers were analyzed using the mutually exclusive categories *stakeholder enumeration* and *stakeholder model*. 18 out of the 26 relevant papers were grouped into the first category. This category contains, for example, project-related papers, e.g. [12-14], listing rather specific stakeholders. Other exemplary papers in this category demonstrate stakeholders by using a graphical representation [4, 15, 16]. Since these approaches contain only enumerations of stakeholders without defining further categories, we did not include those models into our further analysis. Reviewing the literature, we identified exemplary stakeholders like citizens, enterprises, officers, local government agencies, local government staff, media, steering committees or politicians (e.g. [12, 15, 17-19]). We also found research work based on case studies similar to the one we focus on, e.g. Tan, Pan and Lin (2005) analyze stakeholders of e-government projects on the example of the electronic tax filing system in Singapore. They present government, tax officials, taxpayers, employees and the Inland Revenue Authority of Singapore (IRAS) as stakeholders of an electronic tax filing system [20]. However, they do not illustrate a further categorization of these stakeholders or interactions. Furthermore, three papers comprise a stakeholder model whose classification is based on the rating of the stakeholders [21-23]. As our focus is on the identification and categorization and not on the rating, we also excluded these papers from our analysis.

In a second step, the eight remaining papers presenting a stakeholders' categorization were analyzed by using three attributes (Table 1). The attribute *categorization* explains the composition of entities in each model in more detail. As we aim at designing a stakeholder model which also considers the interrelationships between stakeholders, we added the attribute *interaction* in order to take note of the awareness of interactions between categories. The attribute *scope* informs if there is a relation to a particular project (project specific) or not (generic). The findings of this analysis are shown in Table 1.

The stakeholder models are characterized by varying numbers of categories, ranging from two to seven categories. Besides, five out of eight models relate to a specific project. Additionally, five models show interactions between categories. In the following, we will describe the stakeholder models in more detail.

Flak and Rose [28] focus on a governance and management perspective regarding stakeholders in the e-government domain. Their findings are rather generic. The authors clearly state that their model shows no interaction between the categories. They point out initial priorities in future research in order to cover the existing research gap. In a further study, Flak, Sein and Saebo [24] identify two main categories, link stakeholders to these categories and show interaction types between them. However, their categories are still rather generic. De [25] also identifies two categories - a demand side and a supply side. He allocates the project-related stakeholders to these two categories, based on the direction of their interactions. We found that the categories of Flak, Sein and Saebo [24] are similar to those of De [25], as the category *government* can be seen as the *supply side* and the *citizens* present the *demand side*.

Johannessen, Flak and Saebo [29] focus on e-government stakeholders at a municipal level. The interactions are analyzed in regard to the communication needs between the resulting categories. We noticed that their categories extend those of Flak, Sein and Saebo [24] by a political category. Beside this, the *citizen* category of Flak, Sein and Saebo [24] is divided into *business* and *organizations / citizens* [29].

Table 1. Analysis of stakeholder models

Author	Categorization	Interaction	Scope
[24]	2 categories: *government, citizens*	yes	generic
[25]	2 categories: *demand side, supply side*	yes	specific
[26]	3 categories: *government* (divided into *decision maker, management* and *service provider*), *citizen* (divided into *user* and *engaged user*), *business* (*consultant / vendor*)	yes	specific
[27]	4 categories: *data controllers, data subjects, data providers, secondary stakeholders*	no	specific
[28]	4 categories: *internal stakeholders, other governmental agency stakeholders, citizens, organizational stakeholders*	no	generic
[29]	5 categories: *political, government administration, civil society* (divided into *business* and *organizations / citizens*)	yes	specific
[30]	5 categories: *inspection zone, limitation zone, collaboration zone, orientation zone, legitimacy zone*	no	specific
[31]	7 categories: *drivers, constructors, owners, sources, recipients, third parties, operators*	yes	generic

The model by Fedorowicz, Gogan and Culnan [27] is designed for the tax domain. It aims at addressing privacy concerns and its categories are related to the procedures conducted in this special privacy case. Further, this model does not show any interaction.

A stakeholders' influence analysis on managers at a municipal level was conducted by Gomes and Gomes [30]. They conclude that the type of influence is more important than the number of stakeholders. The authors elicited eleven stakeholders and categorized them according to the kind of influence they carry out on decisions.

Based on this categorization in regard to the influence, they found five categories. We noticed that the authors focus on decision-making by a single institution, driven by bidirectional interaction with each category of stakeholders. However, they give no information regarding the interactions between individual stakeholders or between categories.

A generic, but rather comprehensive view on stakeholders in the e-government field is provided by Heeks [31]. His model emphasizes the inclusion of interactions in detail, i.e. between different stakeholder groups. However, this model contains only categories without naming stakeholders in detail. Further, interactions are only shown between one particular stakeholder category (*operators*) and all other categories. This approach is similar to the model proposed by Axelsson and Lindgren [26]. They analyze stakeholders in the context of e-services by building categories with more specific subcategories. Furthermore, they describe interactions between stakeholders and one particular organization. Still, they do not show the various interactions that take place between the stakeholders.

In summary, we found some stakeholder models which are used to identify, structure and analyze stakeholders. The categories in these models have different levels of detail depending on the context in which they are designed. Besides, some stakeholder models show interactions. However, these interactions are not analyzed in detail or are only shown for one category in the stakeholder model. Finally, we noticed that almost all categories can be allocated to a supply side and demand side. Some models partly align the categories to the lifecycle of e-government projects [25, 31]. This can help to identify all stakeholders of each phase of the lifecycle and to derive the requirements, interests and concerns of the stakeholders depending on the particular project phase.

3.2   Case Study

Before presenting our findings of the case study, we will briefly give some background information: In Germany, tax filing is situated on the federal state level. The federal states are cooperating in developing and running the electronic tax filing system ELSTER. Hence, a large number of different decision-makers is involved. These decision-makers are both internal, i.e. within public administrations, and external (e.g. consultants). Further, they are located on different levels, e.g. federal, state or regional level. The exemplary project (called pre-filed tax system) aims at upgrading ELSTER by the possibility to provide tax data to citizens and to load this data automatically into the system. The project is characterized by a hierarchy with several levels and decision-processes within the project team and between different federal states. Besides, there are many intermediaries (e.g. software companies or consultants) who have influence on the project's success. Moreover, the e-government solution has heterogeneous target groups, as every citizen aged over 18 years should be able to use it. This e-government solution can be accessed by citizens on a voluntary basis since January 2014.

Figure 1 shows the stakeholder interaction model identified by conducting a stakeholder analysis. During the literature review, we noticed that the categories of many existing models can be divided into a demand side and a supply side. We applied this classification as a basis for the stakeholder interaction model and extended it in detail by adding further categories. Besides, we allocated the categories to phases of the lifecycle of an e-government project, starting with the assignment (*strategic project owner*), over the design and implementation (*operating project owners* and partly *supporters*) to the usage and application (partly *supporters*, *external users* and *internal users*).

The derived stakeholder interaction model comprises five categories: *Strategic project owners* are stakeholders who decide to conduct a project and commission it. *Operating project owners* implement the project. *Supporters* help *operating project owners* by implementing and operating the e-government solution. Further, they also help the *external users* solving problems occurring during the usage of the e-government solution. Besides this positive influence, supporters can also have negative influences. For example, on the one hand software producers can promote the deployment and usage of the solution by integrating the provided functions into their product. On the other hand, they can evaluate this function as useless and hence, they will criticize or even hinder the project. The fourth category contains the already mentioned *external users* who use the e-government solution and may benefit from it. They do not belong to the public administration – contrary to the *internal users*. *Internal users* are stakeholders who interact with *external users* and receive the output of the e-government solution's usage. Each stakeholder, identified during the stakeholder analysis, is assigned to exactly one stakeholder category.

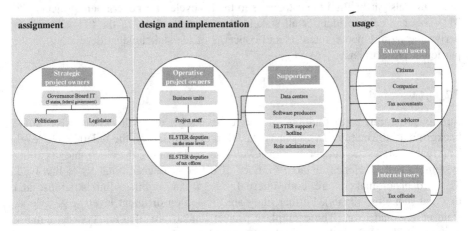

Fig. 1. A stakeholder interaction model for the German pre-filed tax system

In a first step, we derived the following interactions between the five categories:

- *strategic project owners* and *operative project owners*,
- *operative project owners* and *internal users*,
- *operative project owners* and *supporters*,
- *supporters* and *external users*,
- *supporters* and *internal users* as well as
- *internal users* and *external users*.

We noticed the absence of interactions between strategic project owners and internal or external users. Besides, operative project owners do not directly interact with external users. Hence, neither strategic project owners nor operative project owners have knowledge about the external users' requirements regarding the developed system. This can result in an assignment for implementing an e-government solution which does not meet the external users' needs or which is not applicable in the internal users' daily work. Further, our interviewees did not mention the media as a stakeholder. However, in our opinion, the media can have a significant influence on the success of an e-government project due to their (positive or negative) reports.

In a second step, we analyzed the interactions between the stakeholders in more detail. The connecting lines in the stakeholder interaction model (Figure 1) represent various interactions between stakeholders:

- The *governance board IT* interacts with the *project staff* by commissioning them to develop the e-government solution and providing them with funds for the project.
- The *project staff* communicates with the *ELSTER deputies on a state level* in order to inform them about the e-government solution. Further, the *project staff* interacts with *business units* in order to exchange information about legal or functional requirements.
- *ELSTER deputies on a state level* communicate with the *project staff* and the *governance board IT* by exchanging information about requirements derived from the practical usage of the developed system. Moreover, they inform *ELSTER deputies of local tax offices* about what the developed system looks like and how it can be used. Hence, the exchanged element is the know-how about the e-government solution. *ELSTER deputies of local tax offices* need to interact with *tax officials* in order to help them to answer requests of *citizens*. In this case, know-how about the system is the exchanged element in the interaction between *tax officials* and *ELSTER deputies of local tax offices*.
- *Tax officials* communicate *external users'* requirements regarding usage and system to *ELSTER deputies*. Besides, *tax officials* interact with the *role administrator* by exchanging information about which *external users* need further authorizations for using the system.
- In case of problems concerning the pre-filed tax system, all *internal* and *external users* can contact the *ELSTER support* or *ELSTER hotline*. In this interaction, the exchanged element is information about current problems and know-how about the system.
- Employees in *data centers* and the *project staff* interact by exchanging technical requirements.
- *Software producers* communicate with the *project staff* in order to propose technical requirements, so that they can integrate the pre-filed tax filling function into their software product.

In sum, we noticed that various elements are exchanged during a huge number of interactions. Identified elements are for example know-how about the e-government solution or special technical or functional requirements.

4   Discussion

In the following, we will discuss the existing stakeholder models and the derived stakeholder interaction model regarding the categorization, the assignment of categories and interactions.

On the one hand, the categories of the existing models are specific, as they are based on a project context [27, 30]. Hence, they cannot be transferred to another e-government context in a meaningful manner. On the other hand, the existing stakeholder models are rather generic [24, 25, 28]. We noticed that the categories derived from our case study can be incorporated in some of the generic models (e.g. [24-26, 29]). For example, the categories *strategic project owners*, *operative project owners*, partly *supporters* and *internal users* represent the government side presented in the model of Flak et al. [24], whereas *external users* are the citizens in their model. We point out that using more specific categories is helpful for identifying and analyzing stakeholders. However, the categories need to be specific in such a way so that they can be transferred to different e-government projects. Consequently, a balance between too generic and too specific categories is necessary. We assume that the categories of the developed stakeholder interaction model consider this trade-off. Even if stakeholders vary depending on the project domain, the five categories are still applicable. Thus, the presented stakeholder interaction model can be transferred to other e-government projects.

Analyzing the existing models, we noticed a lack of approaches, in which categories are assigned to phases of the lifecycle of an e-government project. Only two models [25, 31] consider partly different project phases. However, all e-government projects pass through similar phases [32]. Hence, we argue that it is useful to assign the defined categories to these phases. This guarantees the independence of the categories from the project domain and that the categories can be applied to all e-government projects. Further, this assignment facilitates the analysis of (potential) stakeholders, since all stakeholders can be identified considering the lifecycle of an e-government project. Considering this, we designed our categories according to processes related to the e-government solution from the beginning on, over the implementation to the use and application (Figure 1).

Most of the existing stakeholder models represent punctual interactions between categories. Two of them have only two stakeholder categories [24, 25]. This limited number of categories complicates a more detailed analysis of interactions between stakeholders. One model lays a special focus on communication needs, which present a specific set of interactions between categories [29]. Thus, we interpret this focus as a limitation, since interactions are not only limited to communication needs.

Heeks [31] as well as Axelsson and Lindgren [26] consider the interactions of one stakeholder category with all other categories. However, further interactions are not taken into account and exchanged elements are not described. In sum, except of these two models [26, 31], none of the models discusses interactions between the stakeholders' categories in detail. On the contrary, we found that it is important to analyze interactions between all stakeholders. We highlight the importance as follows: Interactions need to be identified and analyzed, as stakeholders can significantly influence each other through communication and interactions. This can result in a change of the stakeholder's perspective on the e-government project. A stakeholder interaction model can help considering interactions between all stakeholders' categories as well as the stakeholders themselves. Thus, we enlarged the existing models by representing interactions on a stakeholder (e.g. between role administrator and finance officer) and category level.

5   Conclusion and Further Research

Our paper illustrates a stakeholder interaction model and analyzes to what extent this model can enrich the body of knowledge in regard to already existing stakeholder models. Thus, our aim is to contribute to the creation of a theoretical foundation of the e-government research field. Consequently, our paper gives a comprehensive overview over stakeholders of complex e-government projects as opposed to the narrow scope of stakeholder models so far. We identified five general categories in which stakeholders can be classified, namely *strategic project owner, operative project owner, supporters, external users* and *internal users* and allocated them to the lifecycle of e-government projects. The presented stakeholder interaction model shows various interactions which take place in this particular project. Hence, it sheds light on the interrelationships and the exchanged elements. We noticed that almost no stakeholder model identified during the literature review shows detailed interactions between stakeholders. Hence, we conclude that our stakeholder interaction model can extend the existing stakeholder models by illustrating various interactions. Finally, our contribution helps e-government practitioners to identify and categorize stakeholders and to understand stakeholders' interactions by designing an interaction model for their e-government project.

In terms of future research, a more extensive, empirical evaluation of the stakeholder interaction model is proposed in order to extend the model and to explore further implications towards stakeholder analysis. We aim at contributing to this goal by conducting semi-structured interviews with members of all stakeholders groups in our particular project. Hence, we focus on the identification of interaction directions by analyzing the kind of interactions in more detail. Moreover, we will elicit and further analyze concerns, interests and requirements of different stakeholder groups. Finally, we will derive guidelines for practitioners on how they can use the stakeholder interaction model in order to identify, classify and estimate the influence of their stakeholders on the project's success.

References

1. Savoldelli, A., Codagnone, C., Misuraca, G.: Explaining the eGovernment Paradox: An Analysis of Two Decades of Evidence from Scientific Literature and Practice on Barriers to eGovernment. In: ICEGOV 2012, Albany, NY, USA (2012)
2. Mertens, P.: Schwierigkeiten mit IT-Projekten der Öffentlichen Verwaltung: Neuere Entwicklungen. Informatik Spektrum 35(6), 433–446 (2012)
3. Brown, M.M.: Technology diffusion and the 'knowledge barrier': the dilemma of stakeholder participation. Public Performance & Management Review 26(4), 345–359 (2003)
4. Flak, L.S., Nordheim, S.: Stakeholders, Contradictors and Salience: An Empirical Study of a Norwegian G2G effort. In: 2006 39th Hawaii International Conference on System Sciences (2006)
5. Mainardes, E., Alves, H., Raposo, M.: A model for stakeholder classification and stakeholder relationships. Management Decision 50(10), 1861–1879 (2012)
6. Bryson, J.M.: What to do when stakeholders matter: Stakeholder identification and analysis techniques. Public Management Review 6(1), 21–53 (2004)
7. Bryson, J.M., Patton, M.Q.: Analyzing and Engaging Stakeholders. In: Wholey, J., Hatry, H.P., Newcomer, K.E. (eds.) Handbook of Practical Program Evaluation, pp. 30–54. Jossey-Bass, San Francisco (2010)
8. Freeman, R.E., Harrison, J.S., Wicks, A., Parmar, B.L., de Colle, S.: Stakeholder Theory: The state of the art. Cambridge University Press, Cambridge (2010)
9. Levine, S., White, P.E.: Exchange as a Conceptual Framework for the Study of Interorganizational Relationships. Administrative Science Quarterly 5(4), 583–601 (1961)
10. Sharp, H., Finkelstein, A., Galal, G.: Stakeholder Identification in the Requirements Engineering Process. In: 10th International Workshop on Database & Expert Systems Applications. IEEE (1999)
11. Webster, J., Watson, R.T.: Analyzing the Past to Prepare for the Future: Writing a Literature Review. MIS Quarterly 26(2), 13–23 (2002)
12. Neuroni, A.C., Fraefel, M., Riedl, R.: Inter-organizational Cooperation in Swiss eGovernment. In: Janssen, M., Scholl, H.J., Wimmer, M.A., Tan, Y.-h. (eds.) EGOV 2011. LNCS, vol. 6846, pp. 259–272. Springer, Heidelberg (2011)
13. Gega, E., Elmazi, I.: E-Government and Public E-Services in Albania: Trends and Challenges. International Journal of Management Cases 14(2), 34–41 (2012)
14. Gnan, L., Hinna, A., Monteduro, F., Scarozza, D.: Corporate governance and management practices: stakeholder involvement, quality and sustainability tools adoption. Journal of Management & Governance 17(4), 907–937 (2013)
15. Chigona, W., Roode, D., Nabeel, N., Pinnock, B.: Investigating the impact of stakeholder management on the implementation of a public access project: The case of Smart Cape. South Africain Journal of Business Management 41(2), 39–49 (2010)
16. Flak, L.S., Nordheim, S., Munkvold, B.E.: Analyzing Stakeholder Diversity in G2G Efforts: Combining Descriptive Stakeholder Theory and Dialectic Process Theory. e-Service Journal 6(2), 3–23 (2008)
17. Berner, M.M., Amos, J.M., Morse, R.S.: What constitutes effective citizen participation in local government? Views from city stakeholders. Public Administration Quarterly 35(1), 128–163 (2011)
18. Hardy, C.A., Williams, S.P.: Assembling E-Government Research Designs: A Transdisciplinary View and Interactive Approach. Public Administration Review 71(3), 405–413 (2011)

19. Wolf, P., Krcmar, H.: E-Government: Bürger, Politiker und Unternehmen als Anspruchsgruppen. In: Roters, G., Turecek, O., Klinger, W. (eds.) Digitale Spaltung, pp. 21–24. Vistas Verlag, Berlin (2003)

20. Tan, C.-W., Pan, S.L., Lim, E.T.K.: Managing Stakeholder Interests in e-Government Implementation: Lessons Learned from a Singapore e-Government Project. Journal of Global Information Management 13(1), 31–53 (2005)

21. Zhang, J., Dawes, S.S., Sarkis, J.: Exploring stakeholders' expectations of the benfits and barriers of e-government knowledge sharing. The Journal of Enterprise Information Management 18(5), 548–567 (2005)

22. Scholl, H.J.: Applying Stakeholder Theory to E-Government: Benefits and Limits. In: 1st IFIP Conference on E-Commerce, E-Business, and E-Government 2001, Zurich (2001)

23. Yang, K., Callahan, K.: Citizen Involvement Efforts and Bureaucratic Responsiveness: Participatory Values, Stakeholder Pressure, and Administrative Practicality. Public Administration Review 67(2), 249–264 (2007)

24. Flak, L.S., Sein, M.K., Sæbø, Ø.: Towards a Cumulative Tradition in E-Government Research: Going Beyond the Gs and Cs. In: Wimmer, M.A., Scholl, J., Grönlund, Å. (eds.) EGOV. LNCS, vol. 4656, pp. 13–22. Springer, Heidelberg (2007)

25. De, R.: E-Government Systems in Developing Countries: Stakeholders and Conflict. In: Wimmer, M.A., Traunmüller, R., Grönlund, Å., Andersen, K.V. (eds.) EGOV 2005. LNCS, vol. 3591, pp. 26–37. Springer, Heidelberg (2005)

26. Axelsson, K., Lindgren, I.: Public e-services for agency efficiency and citizen benefit: findings from a stakeholder centered analysis. Government Information Quarterly 30(1), 10–22 (2013)

27. Fedorowicz, J., Gogan, J.L., Culnan, M.J.: Barriers to Interorganizational Information Sharing in e-Government: A Stakeholder Analysis. The Information Society 26(5), 315–329 (2010)

28. Flak, L.S., Rose, J.: Stakeholder Governance: Adapting Stakeholder Theory to E-Government. In: Communications of the Association for Information Systems, vol. 16, pp. 642–664 (2005)

29. Johannessen, M.R., Flak, L.S., Sæbø, Ø.: Choosing the Right Medium for Municipal eParticipation Based on Stakeholder Expectations. In: Tambouris, E., Macintosh, A., Sæbø, Ø. (eds.) ePart 2012. LNCS, vol. 7444, pp. 25–36. Springer, Heidelberg (2012)

30. Gomes, R., Gomes, L.O.M.: Depicting the arena in which Brazilian local government authorities make decisions: What is the role of stakeholders? International Journal of Public Sector Management 22(2), 76–90 (2009)

31. Heeks, R.: Benchmarking e-government: Improving the national and international measurement, evaluation and comparison of e-government. In: Irani, Z., Love, P. (eds.) Evaluating Information Systems. Butterworth-Heinemann, Oxford (2008)

32. Wieczorrek, H.W., Mertens, P.: Management von IT-Projekten: Von der Planung zur Realisierung, 3rd edn. Springer, Heidelberg (2008)

LAN House* Implementation and Sustainability in Brazil: An Actor-Network Theory Perspective

Carla Danielle Monteiro Soares and Luiz Antonio Joia

Brazilian School of Public and Business Administration at Getulio Vargas Foundation,
Rio de Janeiro, Brazil
carladanielle@hotmail.com
luiz.joia@fgv.br

Abstract. LAN Houses have featured as key locations for thousands of Brazilians who otherwise have no access to the Internet. Thus, the scope of this study is to investigate the implementation and sustainability trajectory of a LAN House from an Actor-Network Theory perspective. In order to achieve this, single case study methodology was adopted to address the implementation and sustainability of a LAN House in Jardim Catarina, city of São Gonçalo in the State of Rio de Janeiro, Brazil. The result of this investigation supports the importance of government programs and actions as key actors to implement and sustain these endeavors. Lastly, it becomes clear that a LAN House is not actually a digital inclusion agent, despite its relevance to regions with lower rates of income, since the owner performs the role of "digital broker," whereby most of LAN House users are denied full digital inclusion.

Keywords: LAN House, Actor-Network Theory, Digital Inclusion, Digital Exclusion, Brazil.

1 Introduction

In recent years, Brazil has expended considerable efforts to provide its citizens with access to information, digital technology and other benefits generated by Information and Communication Technologies (ICT), with the objective of enhancing the social and economic development of the country [1]. In partnership with the private sector, this movement has relied on initiatives such as tax deductions to reduce the cost of computers, investments in Internet cafes, the deployment of ICT laboratories in public schools, among other measures instituted through public policies and by NGOs [1].

It is also a fact that access to digital information and technology has grown and is on the increase in Brazil, especially in underprivileged areas, by means of the deployment of LAN Houses, according to data from the Brazilian Internet Steering Committee [2]. Moreover, 49% of the Brazilian population had some form of Internet access in 2012 and of these 49%, 19% gained access via LAN Houses [3].

---

* In Brazil, LAN House is the expression assigned to a Paid Internet Access Center.

M. Janssen et al. (Eds.): EGOV 2014, LNCS 8653, pp. 206–217, 2014.
© IFIP International Federation for Information Processing 2014

Despite the recent decline in the number of users accessing the Internet via LAN Houses, this type of establishment is still the second largest provider of public access to ICTs in the country, after the main provider, namely home access. Moreover, there are around 100,000 LAN Houses in the country, with 87% of users belonging to lower income classes, i.e. people who would not have access to the World Wide Web if it were not for the existence of this type of commercial institution [3-4].

Notwithstanding their apparent importance, there are few studies on the success of LAN Houses in Brazil, in terms of their implementation and sustainability in the national context. Thus, the research question of this work is: "How have the implementation and sustainability trajectories of LAN Houses been in Brazil, from an Actor-Network Theory (ANT) perspective?"

2   Theoretical References

2.1   LAN Houses

LAN Houses first appeared in South Korea in 1996 as an entertainment option. They were net gaming houses using LAN (Local Area Network) technology, which included an in-series linkup of computers to exchange information.

In Brazil, the first LAN House opened in São Paulo in 1998, using the same business format proposed by the LAN Houses in Korea. However, the format experienced changes over the years, as the gaming entertainment house lost ground to access to information via the Internet for work, study, relationships and the practice of online and network gaming.

There are around 100,000 LAN Houses in Brazil, generating about 250,000 direct jobs [5]. However, of these estimated 100,000 establishments, only five thousand of them are formally registered [5]. According to the Brazilian Internet Steering Committee (CGI.br), over 85% of LAN Houses have not been formally registered because the legislation does not recognize the activity [6]. Nonetheless, LAN Houses are the main point of access to the Internet for lower income classes. Approximately 80% of Brazilians of these classes access the Internet through paid access centers. These paid centers cater to 47% of the population, who pay between US$0.50 and US$1.00 per hour for Internet access use. In this portion of the population, about 80% of users frequent centers as they do not have a computer at home [6].

The concentration of these paid access centers occurs not only in the outskirts of large cities – in underprivileged communities – but also in inland cities far from the major urban centers [6]. They are usually simple but adequate facilities to provide the intended service. Besides access to the Internet, the LAN Houses offer other additional services, including games, communication apps (Skype, MSN, etc.), electronic/digital copying and printing, computer courses, etc. They also provide electronic commerce via the Internet and the purchase of products through the supply of credit from the owner of the establishment [6].

2.2   Actor-Network Theory

The Actor-Network Theory – also called the sociology of translation – has been a popular approach in the Information Systems (IS) literature, due to its conceptualization of technology as one of the 'actors' in any Actor-Network analysis [7]. Thus, this approach has been used by several IS researchers to study the complex repertoire of actions associated with the implementation of technologies [8-10].

Technologies are heterogeneous artifacts that embody trade-offs and compromises [11]. In particular, technologies can embody social, political, psychological, economic and professional commitments, skills, prejudices, possibilities and constraints, being continuously shaped and reshaped by the interplay of a range of heterogeneous forces within the networks [11-12].

In particular, the Actor-Network Theory, or ANT, does not acknowledge differences between people on the one hand and objects on the other [13]. For instance, for ANT objects might authorize, allow, afford, encourage, permit, influence, block, prohibit and so on [14]. In effect, this approach portrays society as a socio-technical web where technical objects participate in building heterogeneous networks that bring together both human and non-human actors of all types [15].

In addition to this, ANT is highly appropriate when actors negotiate interests and try to gain influence in complex IS implementations [10, 16]. Therefore, many researchers believe that ANT has much to offer to IS research [9, 17-18], as ANT seems suitable for examining contradictory group formation processes associated with actor-networks related to IS implementation. For instance, ANT was used to examine the implementation of Geographical Information Systems in India [8] and the assessment of digital inclusion in a Brazilian municipality [19], to name only a few applications of ANT in IS research.

The dynamics associated with the formation of an actor-network accrues primarily from the process called translation. Translation means offering new interpretations of interests and channeling people in different directions [12-13]. The results of such translations are a slow movement from one place to another [14]. Hence, translation is the strategy by which the actor-network renders itself indispensable in the network building process. Thus, translation is the mechanism by which actors recruit other actors and ensure their faithful allegiance [18]. The strategies used in translation will depend on the circumstances, including negotiation, persuasion, seduction, simple bargaining, and even coercion [16]. Finally, it is worth mentioning that it is impossible to revert to a point at which a certain translation once was [13]. In other words, one cannot reverse a translation, which leads to the concept of irreversibility [14].

In order to illustrate the concept of translation clearly, an approach that distinguishes four interrelated moments of translation was proposed, namely: problematization, interessement, enrolment and mobilization [13]. These four moments are neither linear nor broadly inseparable [15].

The first moment, namely problematization, is the process by which actors position their project as indispensable to others. Interessement, in turn, involves a group of actions by which an entity attempts to impose and stabilize the identity of the other actors. In the enrolment phase, a black box effect is created, which involves enrolling and controlling other actors. Indeed, interessement achieves enrolment if it is successful in creating alliances, while mobilization represents the successful alignment of actors [13].

Other concepts related to the formation of actor-networks include both the obligatory passage point (OPP) and inscriptions. OPP refers to a situation that must occur for all the actors to achieve their interests when a change in a network is introduced [13]. Inscription, in turn, refers to the way technical artifacts embody patterns of use [20].

Lastly, it can be argued that ANT does not seek to uncover causes and effects in an endeavor so much as unveil the dynamic processes of collective actions reflected in the life cycle of an actor-network, which is the aspect to be further analyzed in this work [21].

Based on what has been presented about Actor-Network Theory, one can perceive that this approach is applicable in Information Systems research. This being the case, the aforementioned concepts associated with ANT might be useful for understanding LAN House implementation and sustainability processes in Brazil.

3   Research Method

This work adopts the case study method in conjunction with ANT to analyze the implementation and sustainability of a LAN House in a Brazilian municipality. As mentioned above, ANT is an approach for analysis of longitudinal and complex scenarios. Therefore, it was decided to analyze the case trajectory, involving many actors, such as entrepreneurs, frequenters, technical artifacts, local infrastructures, public policies, who interacted with the LAN House.

Case study methodology has been used in a positivist perspective in Information Systems research since the 1980s [22], becoming an important method for research in this knowledge field in the past 30 years [23]. However, this investigation is closer to a critical interpretative perspective [24-27], as ANT was the theoretical background for this work.

Critical interpretative case studies need to follow criteria to assess their quality and soundness. Four criteria are singled out for evaluating critical interpretative research regarding its ontological and epistemological assumptions, namely authenticity, plausibility, criticality, and reflexivity [25]. Thus, this investigation followed these criteria in order to ensure the quality of data collection and analysis.

This work sought to support its authenticity by using multiple sources of evidence collected throughout the year 2012. These included informal interviews with the LAN House owner and frequenters, as well as participant and direct observations undertaken in meetings and activities related to the operation of the LAN House. It also included a broad collection of documents related to the enterprise under analysis.

The plausibility of the work was accomplished via data analysis supported by the adopted literature review and comparison with results found in previous studies. Thus, a case that took place in a LAN House similar to the majority of same in Brazil was analyzed. Yet, as interpretative research, this work did not pursue an objective truth that could be generalized. It sought instead to understand how actor interactions influenced the implementation and sustainability of the LAN House.

Besides, this research sought to be critical when it unveiled the controversies associated with the implementation and sustainability of a LAN House. In the case under analysis, these controversies arose from diverse interests between the LAN House owner and the frequenters, as well as inscriptions in technical artifacts. Thus, this investigation tried to depict reality, leading readers to reflection.

Lastly, reflexivity is associated with the personal bias of the researchers. Therefore, the authors disclosed their role in this investigation. One of the authors worked actively in the data collection, interacting with the owner and frequenters of the LAN House under analysis. Furthermore, the other author, who was not involved in the data survey, sought to remove eventual biases perceived in the description of the case.

4   Case Description

4.1   The Jardim Catarina Suburb

This research was conducted in the Jardim Catarina suburb, located in the city of São Gonçalo in the Metropolitan Region of the State of Rio de Janeiro. The city of São Gonçalo has the second largest population of the State of Rio de Janeiro (999,728 inhabitants) [28]. Moreover, the Jardim Catarina suburb has a total area of approximately seven square kilometers, with 176 streets and avenues, and about 23,000 households with approximately 73,000 inhabitants [29].

The economically active resident population in this neighborhood consists of a small percentage of the middle class and a majority of low-income earners, underemployed and self-employed. About 11.5% of the heads of households are in the 20 to 30-year-old bracket, having no education, and 70% of these have a maximum of three years of schooling, which highlights the precariousness of the educational status of its residents [30].

The monthly income of the heads of households in Jardim Catarina is on average US$970.00. However, radical differences are found in the older areas of the suburb, constrained in environmental and social terms. The households in these areas have an average monthly income of US$540.00, well below the average for the suburb [31].

Thus, based on information about the Jardim Catarina suburb – its demographic and social aspects, its size and characteristics of an outlying suburb, in addition to the dearth of studies on this suburb – this setting was considered a relevant choice for carrying out this research.

4.2   Fox Video Rental Store and LAN House

Fox Video Rental Store and LAN House, hereinafter called Fox, located on one of the main streets of Jardim Catarina suburb, started operating in 2003 as a video rental store. In 2007, it became a LAN House with good customer turnover throughout the day (about 30 people). However, the most intense number of people in the establishment begins after 5 p.m. when young people return from school or work and go to the LAN House. On weekends, movement increases after 2 p.m. The majority of users are young people from 14 to 20 years old, seeking a place to meet friends, play games, access the social network and listen to music. Some students also go to the LAN House to do their homework, some of which is done by the owner of the establishment himself. Nevertheless, the LAN House also has patrons of other age groups, such as adults between the ages of 30 and 55 and children aged 10 to 14. The group aged over 30 usually goes to the LAN House in search of other services such as consulting e-government websites, printing of bank payment slips, preparing curriculum vitaes and checking e-mail, rarely accessing the Internet themselves.

Some users say they go to Fox because they have no Internet access at home, but contend that even if they did they would still continue to frequent the location because it is a nice place to meet up with friends.

According to the owner, in the early days of Fox, between 2006 and 2007, the store was always full with all the computer workstations busy. The turnover of the business was basically distributed as follows: 80% from hours of Internet access and the remainder derived from other services such as CD copying, faxing, and printing. Currently (circa 2013), Fox has an average of 100 active clients and Internet access no longer contributes so much to the turnover of the store, accounting for a mere 20% of total sales.

5   LAN House Implementation and Sustainability Trajectories

By using the owner of the LAN House as a point of reference, it was possible to identify the actors involved in the trajectory of the implementation of the paid access center. It was also possible to understand the applications and two relevant translation processes that occurred during the formation of the network of actors, namely the setting up of the LAN House and the sustainability of same via introduction of electronic government services.

The setting up of the LAN House is considered a moment of relevant translation as it marks the implementation of the paid access center, i.e. how this network was formed with its associations and interactions. The second moment of translation, namely the sustainability of the LAN House via introduction of e-government services is also relevant as it ensured the continued existence of the paid access center, offering new service options, both for the community and for the owner, who assumed a new role as will be seen below, namely that of digital broker.

5.1   The First Translation Process: Implementing the LAN House

The first four moments of this translation process are detailed below, namely problematization, interessement, enrolment and mobilization.

Problematization
The problematization phase occurs from the moment the owner decides to open the paid access center as a solution to compensate for the loss of revenue of the video rental store. Therefore, this actor – the owner – identifies and defines the role of other actors required for the formation of this heterogeneous network. The elements that are

identified as relevant actors are the technical artifacts (equipment and software), local infrastructure and the young patrons of the rental store, in addition to the owner.

Interessement

With the actors identified in the problematization stage, the LAN House was set up as a circumscribed network in an environment focused on technical artifacts and with the commitment of the lead actor, the owner, having all the actors aligned to his purpose. To achieve this, the owner took some steps to become indispensable and stabilize the roles of the other actors in the formation of the network.

The technical artifacts were purchased and installed with the help of a computer technician, who temporarily allied with the interests of the principal actor to instruct him how to install the software. However, this human actor did not join the network, distancing himself before its materialization.

With respect to the young patrons, the owner encouraged them to acquaint themselves with the LAN House. Once he had attracted the interested parties, the owner consolidated the alignment of their interests to evaluate the participation of (human and non-human) actors necessary for the setting up of the LAN House, in a heterogeneous network, focused on an obligatory point of passage, namely the establishment of the new undertaking.

Enrolment

After the interessement stage comes the enrolment phase, in which the main actor, i.e. the owner of the LAN House, effectively defines the roles. At this point, this actor establishes and coordinates the roles of all actors who will represent his interests in the network of stable alliances, namely:

- Performance of the chosen computers and installed software.
- Layout of the physical space of the store divided between the video rental area and the LAN House.
- Performance of the broadband provider.
- The role of the young people who frequented the rental store, not only as patrons of the paid access center, but also as its promoters to the local community.

Mobilization

The translation is completed with the mobilization in which the main actor, after garnering the widespread acceptance and involvement of his interests, mobilizes all stakeholders and can therefore speak on behalf of a group of heterogeneous actors with sundry interests in a single network mobilized by them [13].

In this context, the entities involved have acquiesced to unforeseen mobility, in which the initially dispersed actors were regrouped in a given time and place. This occurred when the owner became the representative of all concerned – users of his video rental store and part of the neighborhood – with the material and technical artifacts converging to create a network of access to ICT.

Once all the elements involved in the trajectory of the implementation of the LAN House were aligned in accordance with their prescribed roles, these agreements should be incorporated in a material medium, which, according to the Actor-Network

Theory is defined as inscription. Thus, by means of various inscriptions that occurred during the trajectory of the implementation of the LAN House, the creation of the paid access center was achieved.

However, when analyzing the implementation of the first LAN House translation process, the existence of another actor is detected. In the perspective of ANT, this actor, namely the "Computers for All" program of the Federal Government is a key player, though not mentioned by the LAN House owner. This actor was included in the network by an event independent of its intentions, since it was the result of the action of another actor, such that the owner benefited from the reduction in prices of computers to create the LAN House. Thus, the Federal Government played an important role in reducing the cost of computers, facilitating their acquisition, not only by people with low purchasing power but also by the owner of the LAN House, who benefited from the reduced price and the financing terms offered by retail stores.

Another fact worthy of note from the perspective of the Actor-Network Theory is the degree of irreversibility that this network has acquired as the inscriptions were established. The bonds formed between the (human and non-human) elements over the course of the implementation of the LAN House established a significant degree of convergence and coordination of the network. Accordingly, the number of elements incorporated into the new establishment – adaptation of space, installation of equipment, increased demand among young people for Internet access, and increase in the profitability of the business – prevented the disruption of this relationship. Thus, thinking of dismantling the LAN House and returning it to its original state, i.e. only a video rental store, consequently becomes unviable, which strengthens the state of irreversibility of the first translation process of this network.

5.2 The Second Translation Process: Sustaining the LAN House via Electronic Government Services

The second translation process occurred after the establishment and operation of the LAN House, with the introduction of a new actor in the network: e-Government services.

This artifact appears as an important actor for the LAN House leading to a transformation and shift in interests, artifacts, people and enrolments [13], appropriated by the lead actor in order to achieve his own goals.

To understand the importance of the role of this new actor and its interactions with other elements associated with the network, the four moments of this second translation process were analyzed, also describing this new actor.

Problematization

With the increase in the number of computers and access to the Internet in the underprivileged communities, the number of hours of Internet access in the LAN House is on the decline. The owner detects a reduction in revenue. In the meantime, the search for electronic public services that the state promotes for citizens begins to emerge. Thus, a relevant actor is identified: e-Government services.

With the goal of providing public services to the population via the Internet, the Federal Government developed actions of the e-government program, prioritizing the use of ICT to democratize access to information. However, actions related to e-government services have not reached those lacking access to ICTs, namely the underprivileged population who need to have access to the provision of public services by electronic means. Thus, e-government, even unintentionally, becomes a relevant actor to the LAN House, which, through its owner, shall provide such services to the community in which it operates.

Thus, according to the owner of the LAN House, there appears a new user profile: adults, over the age of 24 to 26, who do not have access to a connected computer and/or printer, and who have the LAN House as a point of reference for the services offered by government agencies through access to ICTs. From the perspective of ANT, this new actor joins the network, proposing and demanding new enrolment and interactions between the human and non-human elements, such as availability of a quality printer and knowledge on the part of the main actor about the use of online services offered by the government and his own services.

Interessement
The owner of the LAN House promotes the possibility of access to e-government services for this new user profile. Thus, he aligns his interests with those of the people who wish to take advantage of this type of service.

Enrolment
Users of e-government services frequent the property while the owner assumes a new role, serving as an intermediary to assist their access to these e-government services.

Mobilization
The translation is completed with the continuity of the LAN House in the community. Therefore, once again, the LAN House becomes an obligatory point of passage for these actors, who need to go to the LAN House to access online public services. The main actor (the owner) thus offers this type of service in the LAN House, always with a view to increase his billing.

Therefore, with the actors mobilized around the interests of the principal actor, the inscription of e-government services occurs, with the owner buying a new printer and registering for credit protection service, entering into an agreement with the neighboring real estate broker to offer digital services, conducting enquiries, printing dockets, among other digital services.

In addition to this, the users of the LAN House come to consider it as a digital convenience center with the owner providing online services in addition to e-government services. These include copying digital media, checking e-mail, doing homework and online research, developing curriculum on the Internet, among others. The owner, therefore, assumes the role of digital broker with the responsibility of sending, preparing and registering documents online, hampering most LAN House users from achieving full digital inclusion.

As demonstrated in the two previous cases of translation, there is no pre-defined, structured and established social order in the ANT approach, but actors associating and disassociating in a permanent dynamic of relationships. For this reason, new negotiation processes and inscriptions are made and new networks are formed.

6   Final Remarks

This research presented two relevant translation processes as well as the four associated moments in which the actors had different levels of interest and alignment. From the analysis of these translations, it was seen that although the LAN House does not promote effective digital inclusion, it is important to highlight the relevance of this type of establishment in low-income areas, which consequently have restricted access to computers and the Internet such as the Jardim Catarina suburb in São Gonçalo.

In this sense, it should be stressed that the power to democratize access to the Internet exercised by thousands of LAN Houses spread around the country gives them a social function, as in addition to access to ICT, they promote the access of the underprivileged to a range of important community services hitherto inaccessible to them. This scenario demonstrates the extent to which the paid access centers serve the environment in which they operate, either by facilitating access to the World Wide Web or as online service providers. In this way, they respond to the dynamics of ICTs via the expansion of computer use by individuals and the dissemination of public services via the Internet offered by the State to its citizens.

In this context, it can be claimed that the LAN House currently plays a new role, namely that of a digital convenience agent. Consequently, the owner also has a new attribute, i.e. that of digital dispatcher, promoting and exercising the role of processing, expediting and sending documents of its users by digital means. This fact hampers LAN House users from pursuing effective digital inclusion, especially those who resort to it with a view to the use of the available e-government services, as there is a person who can do that on behalf of them, as was set forth before. These findings indicate the need to redesign or re-evaluate public policies, so that LAN House users can feel fully digitally included, eliminating the owner's role as digital dispatcher.

Finally, to understand the importance of this subject not only for Academia but also for the Government – through public policies aimed at reducing the number of digitally excluded people in the country – new research is required, as also supported by other researchers [32-33]. This includes case studies in LAN Houses located in other outlying suburbs from the perspective of ANT, to verify the possible existence of other actors in the constitution of the network, as well as analyze the availability of online e-government public services and the extent to which they can influence the sustainability of LAN House business. In addition, more research should be conducted into the role of the LAN House owner as a digital broker, identifying to what extent old practices are merely presented in a new guise.

References

1. Gomez, R., Camacho, K.: Who uses ICT at Public Access Centers? In: Second Annual ICIS Conference, SIG GlobDev Workshop, Phoenix, Arizona (December 14, 2009)
2. CETIC.BR: Pesquisa sobre o Uso das Tecnologias da Informação e da Comunicação no Brasil: TIC Domicílios e TIC Empresas 2008. São Paulo: Comitê Gestor da Internet no Brasil (2009)
3. CETIC.BR: Pesquisa sobre o Uso das Tecnologias da Informação e da Comunicação no Brasil: TIC Domicílios 2012. São Paulo: Comitê Gestor da Internet no Brasil (2012)
4. Neri, M.: Mapa Da Inclusão Digital. Rio de Janeiro: FGV-CPS, http://www.cps.fgv.br/cps/bd/mid2012/MID_sumario.pdf
5. ISUU: Anuário - A Rede de Inclusão Digital 2012/(2013), http://issuu.com/mandacarudesign/docs/anuario_arede_2012_issuu
6. CGI.BR: Pesquisa sobre o uso das tecnologias da informação e da comunicação no Brasil: TIC LANHOUSES 2010. São Paulo, Comitê Gestor da Internet no Brasil, http://op.ceptro.br/cgi-bin/cetic/tic-lanhouse-2010.pdf
7. Walsham, G., Sahay, S.: Research on information systems in developing countries: Current landscape and future prospects. Information Technology for Development 12(1), 7–24 (2006)
8. Walsham, G., Sahay, S.: GIS for district-level administration in India: problems and opportunities. MIS Quarterly 17(3), 39–65 (1999)
9. Monteiro, E.: Actor-network theory and information infrastructure. In: Ciborra, C. (ed.) From control to drift. The Dynamics of Corporate Information Infrastructure, pp. 71–83. Oxford Univ. Press (2000)
10. Stanforth, C.: Using actor-network theory to analyze e-government implementation in developing countries. Information Technologies & International Development 3(3), 35–60 (2006)
11. Bijker, W.E., Law, J.: Shaping Technology/Building Society: studies in socio-technical change. MIT Press (1992)
12. Latour, B.: Science in action: How to follow scientists and engineers through society. Harvard University Press (1987)
13. Callon, M.: Some elements of a sociology of translation domestication of the scallops and the fishermen of St. Brieux Bay. In: LAW, J. (ed.) Power, Action and Belief. A new Sociology of Knowledge?. Routledge & Kegan Paul, London (1986)
14. Latour, B.: Reassembling the social: an introduction to actor-network theory. Oxford University Press, Oxford (2005)
15. Law, J.: Notes on the Theory of the Actor Network: Ordering, Strategy and Heterogeneity. Centre for Science Studies. Lancaster University, http://www.lancs.ac.uk/fass/sociology/papers/law-notes-on-ant.pdf
16. Nhampossa, J.L.: Re-thinking technology transfer as technology translation: A case study of health information systems in Mozambique. Doctoral Dissertation University of Oslo Norway (2005)
17. Macome, E.: On implementation of an information system in the Mozambican context: The EDM case viewed through ANT lenses. Information Technology for Development 14(2), 154–170 (2008)
18. Elbanna, A.R.: The Theoretical and Analytical Inclusion of Actor Network Theory and its Implication on ICT Research. Actor-network Theory and Technology Innovation: Advancements and New Concepts, p. 130 (2011)

19. Teles, A., Joia, L.A.: Infoinclusão em Piraí Digital: Evidências Empíricas a partir da Teoria Ator-Rede. Journal of Information Systems and Technology Management 9(2), 369–390 (2012)
20. Rhodes, J.: Using Actor-Network Theory to Trace an ICT (Telecenter) Implementation Trajectory in an African Women's Micro-Enterprise Development Organization. Information Technologies & International Development 5(3), 1–20 (2009)
21. Heeks, R., Seo-Zindy, R.: ICTs and Social Movements under Authoritarian Regimes: An Actor-Network Perspective. In: UK Academy for Information Systems Conference Proceedings (2013)
22. Benbasat, I., Goldstein, D., Mead, M.: The Case Research Strategy in Studies of Information Systems. MIS Quarterly 11, 369–386 (1987)
23. Paré, G.: Investigating Information Systems with Positivist Case Study Research Communications of the AIS. 13(18), 233–264 (2004)
24. Mitev, N.: Postmodernism and Criticality in Information Systems Research. What Critical Management Studies Can Contribute Social Science Computer Review 24, 310–325 (2006)
25. Pozzebon, M.: Conducting and Evaluating Critical Interpretive Research: examining criteria as a key component in building a research tradition. In: Kaplan, B., et al. (eds.) Information Systems Research: Relevant Theory and Informed Practice, pp. 275–292. Kluwer Academic Publishers, London (2004)
26. Walsham, G.: Interpretive case studies in IS research: nature and method. European Journal of Information Systems 4(2), 74–81 (1995)
27. Tsang, E.W.G.: Case Studies and Generalization in Information Systems Research: A critical realist perspective. Journal mof Strategic Information Systems 23(2), 174–186 (2014)
28. IBGE: Pesquisa Nacional por Amostra de Domicílios (PNAD/2010), http://www.ibge.gov.br/home/download/estatistica.shtm
29. Prefeitura Municipal de São Gonçalo, http://www.saogoncalo.rj.gov.br
30. SEBRAE: Diagnóstico socioeconômico do Bairro do Jardim Catarina. Rio de Janeiro: Sebrae; DATA/UFF (2000)
31. Dominguez, M.T.: Jardim Catarina: Memória e Movimentos Cotidianos numa Periferia Fluminense, http://www.encontro2012.historiaoral.org.br/resources/anais/3/1340288900_arquivo_jardimcatarina_memoriaemovimentos cotidianosnumaperiferiafluminense_final.pdf
32. Kumar, R.: e-Choupals: A Study on the Financial Sustainability of Village Internet Centres in Rural Madhya Pradesh. Information Technologies and International Development 2(1), 29 (2004)
33. Sey, A., Fellows, M.: Literature Review on the Impact of Public Access to Information and Communication Technologies. CIS, University of Washington, http://library.globalimpactstudy.org/sites/default/files/docs/CIS-WorkingPaperNo6.pdf

Bridging the Digital Divide at the Regional Level? The Effect of Regional and National Policies on Broadband Access in Europe's Regions

Pau Palop García[1], Basanta Thapa[2], and Björn Niehaves[2]

[1] Humboldt Universität zu Berlin, Berlin, Germany
pagarcip@hu-berlin.de
[2] Hertie School of Governance, Berlin, Germany
{thapa,niehaves}@hertie-school.org

Abstract. Reducing the digital divide is one of the main policy objectives of the "Europe 2020 Strategy" (2010) and the "Riga Declaration" (2006). To this end, the EU transfers structural funds for broadband expansion to regional governments rather than to the national level which is typically seen as the decisive actor in broadband expansion. To explore the relevance of the regions in widening broadband access, we analyze the influence of economic, demographic and institutional factors on broadband expansion at the regional and national level. In order to account for the interplay between both levels of government, we employ a multi-level regression model. We find that regional level variables are able to explain part of broadband access improvement. Significant variables are ERDF expenditure dedicated to broadband expansion, the status of regional broadband diffusion in 2008 and the national degree of inter-platform competition. The paper concludes that, although there is evidence of the role of the regions in the European policy process, the national level still performs an important gatekeeper function and that national ICT strategies are needed to successfully close the geographical digital divide in the EU.

Keywords: Broadband, Digital Divide, e-exclusion, regions, ERDF.

1   Introduction

Closing the digital divide between regions is a major objective of the European Union (EU). Information and communication technology (ICT) have hugely gained in importance on the EU agenda since the Bangemann Report in the early 1990s [1], and the Riga declaration in 2006. Nowadays, ICT is seen as a key driver of economic competitiveness by the European Commission, EU member states and policy analysts alike [1], but also as a potential new source of spatial inequalities among European regions. To bridge this digital divide, the EU has introduced the Digital Agenda setting ambitious ICT goals to be accomplished by 2020, especially in the area of broadband coverage [2]. To this end, the European Commission channels financial support through the European Structural Funds to the European regions, thus effectively

M. Janssen et al. (Eds.): EGOV 2014, LNCS 8653, pp. 218–229, 2014.
© IFIP International Federation for Information Processing 2014

bypassing the national level of the member states and empowering the regions [3]. However, it remains unclear whether regions are the appropriate level for policy measures on broadband expansion. Typically, national agencies are in charge of the design and implementation of broadband expansion strategies as well as the regulation of the broadband market [4]. Thus, the provision of EU funds for this objective to the regions may unnecessarily turn broadband expansion into a complex multi-level governance issue without improving policy impact. While the role of the regions in policy formulation and implementation has been the subject of a whole body of literature on multi-level governance [5, 6], the regions' role in broadband expansion has not been examined yet.

In order to address this research gap, the main objective of this study is to examine to what extend the European subnational level is able to explain the differences in the expansion of broadband – and therefore in closing the digital divide – in the EU. In other words, we analyze whether regional governments' policies on broadband expansion have produced observable results in bridging the digital divide in the EU. Findings in this regard are of direct relevance to the way the EU's Digital Agenda is implemented.

The remaining paper is structured as follows: First, we review related work on broadband diffusion to identify determining factors for broadband expansion on the regional as well as the national level. Then, we develop a multi-level regression model. This analysis is applied to the broadband improvement of 114 EU (2008-2012). Finally, we discuss our results and their implications for theory and policy.

2   Related Work

2.1   Broadband Diffusion

Since the mid-2000s, scholars from different disciplines (mainly economics, information systems, computer and political science) have tried to explain why some countries have expanded their broadband networks faster than others. The existing explanatory models propose a diverse set of factors: For instance, economic studies focus on market characteristics such as competition or prices [7, 8] while policy-oriented studies highlighted the impact of regulatory policy and governance structures on broadband diffusion [9]. In this section, we review the discussed drivers of broadband expansion in three categories: economic, demographic and institutional factors.

2.1.1   Economic Factors
Most of the literature on broadband expansion has been focused on economic factors. Questions such as how the level of market competition is related to the improvement of broadband access or what the effect of overall economic performance on broadband expansion is have been addressed by different scholars in the past two decades. Although efforts to find out the effect of economic variables on broadband expansion have been made before, the conclusions of these studies vary. For example, Bouckaert et al. (2010) studied broadband penetration in 20 OECD countries focusing on

competition as the main explanatory variable[1]. The authors observed a significant positive effect of inter-platform competition and a significant negative effect of service-based intra-platform competition on broadband diffusion. Additional variables, such as time trend, Gross Domestic Product (GDP), volume of personal computers, population density, and price proved significant in the model [7].

In a comparative study on fixed and mobile broadband networks, Lee et al. (2011) also distinguished between the above-mentioned three types of competition, finding that unbundled local loop (ULL), income, population density, education and price were significant factors affecting broadband diffusion [8].

Comparing broadband adoption among US states, Aron and Burstein (2003) concluded that inter-platform competition is the key variable to explain broadband diffusion [10]. Similarly, Grosso (2006) found that income, competition and unbundling were significant drivers for broadband diffusion in his study of 30 OECD countries [11].In a study of 100 countries, Garcia-Murillo (2005) focused only on the impact of unbundling on broadband deployment. She found that unbundling an incumbent's infrastructure was only significant in middle-income countries. In addition, her study showed that GDP, population and competition had a positive effect on broadband diffusion [12]. In 159 countries Lee and Brown (2008) also found that platform competition, ULL, broadband speed, ICT use[2] and content[3] contribute significantly to the adoption of broadband technologies [13].Examining broadband diffusion in five Latin American countries, Ngwenyama and Morawczynski (2009) observed a significant positive effect of GDP on broadband diffusion, as well as a negative impact of prices. In terms of education-related variables it emerged that only the number of universities in a country had a positive significant effect [14].

In one of the hitherto most holistic models of broadband diffusion, Cava-Ferreruela and Alabau-Munoz (2006) found competition, the cost of deploying, infrastructure, economic indicators and demographic indicators to be significant [15].Cadman and Dineen (2006) hypothesized that less concentrated broadband markets, led to higher broadband penetration. They found that the Herfindahl-Hirschman Index (HHI),[4] a market concentration measurement, could explain 82 percent of the variation in broadband penetration in 21 EU countries [16].In a recent study, Yates and colleagues (2013) tested if national policy initiatives, regulatory measures and governance practices have an impact on mobile broadband diffusion. Using data from 121 member countries of the OECD and regression analysis, the authors concluded that only the level of competition, the aggregate income of the country and the ICT basket prices had a significant impact on mobile broadband diffusion [9].

Based on this review, we include economic indicators in our model. First, the level of market competition, measured by the Herfindahl-Hirschman Index for inter and intra-platform competition. Second, we include GDP and unemployment as indicators of economic performance.

---

[1] They distinguished between three types of competition. Inter-platform competition and intra-platform competition (divided between facility-based and service-based).

[2] Personal computer penetration per 100 inhabitants.

[3] Internet hosts per 100 inhabitants.

[4] Share of the market and the shares of other platforms used in the country for broadband.

2.1.2 Demographic Factors

Different demographic factors have also proven relevant to broadband diffusion. Tertiary education, for example, is found to be an important factor in broadband expansion [14]. On the other hand, in their comparison of 30 OECD countries, Bauer et al. (2005) found that not only economic variables were significant to explain broadband diffusion, but also the level of urbanization (operationalized as population density) [17]. Accordingly, we introduce population density and the aggregated level of education as demographic factors into our model.

2.1.3 Institutional Factors

In recent years, institutional factors have received increasing attention in studies on broadband diffusion. For example, Gulati et al. (2011) controlling for economic, political, social and educational factors, found that countries with better governance and higher investment in ICT experience faster broadband diffusion [18].

Turk et al. (2008) studied factors and strategies that foster the adoption of broadband networks in the EU, identifying e-service usage and the ICT sector environment as significant indicators. Their study also concluded that penetration and diffusion of broadband are not the outcome of a single factor, but of an 'interplay' between different factors [19] (p. 948). Thus, we incorporate institutional variables both at the regional and national level in our model.

3   Research Design

3.1   Research Question and Hypothesis

Following our research objective and the theoretical discussion above, our study challenges the established idea that the national level is the most relevant level of government in broadband expansion. Therefore, our research question reads:

RQ: Is the regional level relevant in bridging the digital divide in the EU?

ICT strategies, especially concretely broadband expansion policies, are usually implemented at the national level. Central governments are typically responsible for regulating market competition, orchestrating comprehensive infrastructure plans, or devising e-government strategies and digital inclusion policies. However, to examine the EU's policy of channeling ICT infrastructure funds to the regional level, we assume that the regions play a significant role in broadband expansion. More precisely, we argue that policies at the regional level of government impact the pace of broadband expansion in that territory. Therefore, the main hypothesis of this paper reads:

H1: Regions that actively follow a broadband expansion strategy are closing the digital divide faster than regions without a broadband expansion strategy.

When we refer to the "regional level", we mean not only the regional characteristics (economic, demographic or institutional), but especially to policies or strategies developed at the subnational level by regional institutions. In this paper, we argue that the EU regional level has two main paths to influence broadband expansion. First, by developing an ICT strategy that includes broadband expansion goals. And second, by using the ERDF to foster broadband. Based on this two influence paths, we break down the main hypothesis in two sub-hypotheses:

H1.1. Regions that developed a specific regional ICT policy that included broadband expansion are closing the digital divide faster than regions without a specific regional ICT policy.

H1.2. The more ERDF funding a region allocates to broadband expansion, the greater the improvement of broadband access.

If decisions taken by governments at a regional level – such as the amount of ERDF dedicated to broadband expansion or the development of a specific ICT strategy – are able to explain a large part of the variance of broadband expansion, this hypothesis would be confirmed. This means that the relevance of the subnational level in closing the digital divide would be proven. In contrast, if the effect of the regional level disappears when controlling for national characteristics, the hypothesis would be falsified.

3.2   Intervening Variables

3.2.1   Dependent Variable

The dependent variable, broadband expansion, is operationalized as the improvement in the percentage of households that have broadband access in a particular region between 2008 and 2012[5]. This variable is obtained by dividing the percentage of households that had broadband access in 2012 by the percentage of households that had broadband access in 2008[6]. Therefore, the notation of the dependent variable is:

$$\text{IMPROVE} = \frac{\text{Broadband Access 2012}}{\text{Broadband Access 2008}} \tag{1}$$

3.2.2   Independent Variables

Regional-Level Variables

In our model, the economic factors included at the regional level are regional Gross Domestic Product at market prices per capita and regional unemployment rate, both

---

[5] We choose this period of time to cover the 2007-2013 European Regional Development Fund Framework. Therefore, 2008 is selected as the baseline and 2012 as the most recent available data within this ERDF framework.

[6] Broadband access is defined as the "percentage of households that are connectable to an exchange that has been converted to support xDSL-technology, to a cable network upgraded for Internet traffic, or to other broadband technologies" [20]. Raw data was obtained from the regional database provided by Eurostat.

extensively used in previous research on broadband diffusion. As a demographic factor, population density is included as a proxy for a region's level of urbanization [13]. Regarding institutional variables, the model includes a measurement of regional authority (Regional Authority Index, RAI) proposed by Hooghe, Marks and Schakel [21, 22]. It is well established in the literature that the role of the regions depends to an important extent on the member states, in this sense, Hooghe (1996) demonstrated the "[...] considerable variation in the degrees of multi-level governance through partnership across Member States, in large part shape by the pre-existing territorial distribution of power. Thus, where a strong national government was determined to retain control over the domestic impact of structural policy, it retained considerable powers to do so" [21] (p.207).

In addition, two variables related to the ESF are included. First, ICT expenditure per capita allocated by the regions during the ESF framework 2007-2013[7] (R.EXPEN). This variable is calculated on the basis of data from the Operational Programmes (OPs) presented by the regions and approved by the European Commission for the funding period 2007-2013. In their OPs, the regions and member states had to classify the expenditure in 74 given categories proposed by the Commission. One of these categories (category 10) is related to Internet and broadband expenditure. For the regions that assign funding to category 10, the total amount of resources dedicated is registered and then divided by the total regional population.

The second variable is a binary variable that registers if a region designed a specific ICT policy during the 2007-2013 period (R.ICTPOL). The information for this variable was obtained from the Regional Innovation Monitor database of the European Commission and our own internet-based search (top 20 results of Google search for "ICT policy OR Information Communication Technology OR Innovation Policy AND *Name of the Region*" in the respective regional/national language)[8].

The Regional Broadband Access Score of 2008 (R.BROAD2008) is included as a control variable. It is assumed that the diffusion stage in which a given region is at in 2008 would determine broadband access improvement[9].

---

[7] Council Regulation (EC) No. 1083/2006 of 11 July 2006 establishes that all Member States that joined the EU before 2004 had to ensure that the 60 per cent of expenditure for the Convergence objective and the 75 per cent of expenditure for the regional competitiveness and employment objective matched the Lisbon Agenda strategic priorities (Art. 9).

[8] Regions with languages that could not be covered by the author were coded "-1". The variable was developed between 20/06/2013 – 4/08/2013. The countries included in the analysis are: Austria, Germany, Denmark, Spain, Portugal, Italy, Netherlands, Belgium, Finland, Sweden, Ireland and the United Kingdom.

[9] For example, it is expected that regions with a 90 percent broadband access rate in 2008, and therefore at the last stage of the diffusion curve, would have improved less than regions at an earlier stage of diffusion (such as regions with a broadband access rate of 40 percent in 2008, for instance).

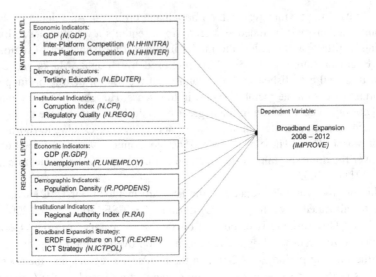

Fig. 1. Research Model (own elaboration)

National-Level Variables

The national-level variables roughly follow the same pattern as at the regional level. Therefore, national GDP per capita (N.GDP) as well as the national unemployment rate (N.UNEMPLOY) are included in the model. The share of students in tertiary education (N.EDUTER) has also been included as a proxy to capture the level of education in a given country [8], [22]. In this paper, in accordance with Distaso et al. (2006), the standard Herfindhal Index (HHI) is used to measure intra-platform competition (N.HHINTRA). Based on the platform market shares, the Standard Herfindhal Index for inter-platform competition (N.HHINTER) is included in order to operationalize the level of competition between different technological platforms that offer broadband[10].

Finally, in line with the work of Yates et al. (2013), two institutional-related variables are included. First, the Corruption Perceptions Index 2012 (N.CORRUPTION), provided by Transparency International. Second, the Regulatory Quality Index 2012 (N.REGULATION), proposed by the Worldwide Governance Indicators, that provides information about citizens' perception of the ability of government to devise and implement regulations that permit and promote private sector development [23].

3.3   Research Model

While previous research on broadband diffusion focused on the national level, EU funding for broadband expansion is channeled to the regional level. Our model

---

[10] Data for HHI_{intra} and HHI_{inter} is provided by Distaso et al. (2006). HHI_{intra} provides a relative measure of concentration within the DSL technology, HHI_{inter} is a more general measure of the absolute concentration of the broadband market (Distaso et al., 2008, p.9).

therefore explores whether broadband expansion could be determined by the regional rather than the national level (see Figure 1).

4   Methodology

4.1   Method Selection

This paper uses multi-level regression analysis to answer the research question and test the hypothesis stated in the previous chapter. This type of regression analysis allows for the estimation of the effect of variables measured at different levels (in this case, regional and national) and also makes it possible to test if the regions behave homogeneously within the national territory [24, 25, 26]. Multi-level regression assumes that the data is hierarchically organized, with a dependent variable measured at the lowest level and explanatory variables existing on all levels [27] (p.11). In our model, we assume that regions are embedded within the national level.

4.2   Dataset

The dataset used in this study is composed of 25 variables, distributed between the dependent variable (IMPROVE) and two groups of independent variables, one with the variables measured at the European regional level (as the DV) and one group measured at the national level. The dataset includes information on 114 regions (Level NUTS 2) in 12 countries of the EU 15: Austria, Germany, Denmark, Spain, Portugal, Italy, Netherlands, Belgium, Finland, Sweden, Ireland and United Kingdom. Thus, the dataset includes information about the 42.2 percent of the Level NUTS 2 regions of the European Union, 42.8 percent of the 28 European countries and 80 percent of the EU 15 countries[11].

4.3   Data Analysis

The final regression has been developed step-by-step, comparing different nested models and analyzing the effects of introducing or deleting variables, interactions or limitations. The lower level of the multi-level regression, level 1, corresponds to the European regions. The dependent variable, broadband access improvement (R.IMPROVE) and important independent variables, such as regional Gross Domestic Product (R.GDP), regional unemployment rate (R.UNEMPLOY), regional authority index (R.RAI), regional ICT Policy (R.ICTPOL) and regional ICT expenditure (R.EXPEN) are measured at this level.

Level 2 corresponds to the national level. At this level, independent variables such as national Gross Domestic Product (N.GDP), national Corruption Perception Index

---

[11] The regions of France and Greece have not been included due to a lack of information which is necessary to calculate the dependent variable. Luxembourg has been omitted because it only consists of one region. Data was obtained from Eurostat and, in the case of regional ICT policies, through our own research.

(N.CPI), national regulatory quality (N.REGQ), national HHI intra-platform (N.HHINTRA) and national HHI inter-platform competition (N.HHINTER) are measured.

The variable R.ICTPOL is permitted to vary randomly across groups and it also introduces cross-level interactions: It is possible that some level 2 variables interfere in level 1. In the case of this paper, the interactions are introduced for the economic indicators. It is hypothesized that the slope between regional GDP and IMPROVE and between regional unemployment and IMPROVE within groups varies as a function of a level-2 variable, namely national GDP. This model tests whether average national GDP in a country is able to explain group by group variation in the relationship between, on the one hand regional GDP and IMPROVE and, on the other hand, regional unemployment (R.UNEMPLOY) and IMPROVE. The notation of this model is:

$$IMPROVE_{ij} = \beta_{0j} + \beta_1(R.UNEMPLOY) + \beta_2(R.POPDENS) + \beta_3(R.RAI) + \beta_4(R.ICTPOL) + \beta_5(R.EXPEN) + \beta_6(R.GDP) + r_{ij}$$

$$\beta_{0j} = \gamma_{00} + \gamma_{01}(N.GDP) + \gamma_{02}(N.REGQ) + \gamma_{03}(N.CPI) + \gamma_{04}(N.EDUTER) + \gamma_{05}(N.HHINTRA) + \gamma_{06}(N.HHINTER) + u_{0j}$$

$$\beta_{1j} = \gamma_{10}$$
$$\beta_{1i} = \gamma_{40} + \gamma_{11}(N.GDP)$$

The first row of the equation indicates that regional broadband improvement is the result of the groups' intercept and a component that reflects the regional scores on the independent variables included. The second line states that each groups' intercept is a function of a common intercept (y_{00}) plus a component that reflects the linear effect of average group variables and a random between-group error [31] (p.56). The third line indicates that the variable R.ICTPOL varies randomly between groups[12].

5   Results

The model (see Table 1) is able to account for the 90.0 percent of the total variance of IMPROVE (Adjusted R^2 Wald= 0.903). The significant variables are R.BROAD2008, with a negative relationship with IMPROVE (β= -0.022, p=0.00, Table 1, row 2), inter-platform competition (N.HHINTER), also positively related to IMPROVE (β = 0.54, p= 0.02; Table 1, row 12) and R.EXPEN (β = 0.003, p=0.09; Table 1, row 5). No cross-level interaction results are significant. Following Hox's (1994) recommendation, the R.UNEMPLOY and N.GDP are maintained in the model, although they are not significant (p. 27).

---

[12] Statistical analyses were carried out using R Studio version 0.97.551. Multi-level regressions were calculated using Linear and Nonlinear Mixed Effects Models (nlme) R package (v.3.1-108) developed by Pinheiro et al. (2013). Descriptives were calculated using the Procedures for Psychological, Psychometric, and Personality Research (pysch) R package (v.1.3.2) developed by Revelle (2013). To test the goodness-of-fit of the multi-level models, the goodness-of-fit-measures for linear mixed models with one-level-grouping (lmmfit) package developed by Maj (2011) was used (v. 1.0) [28, 29, 30].

Table 1. Multi-level regression analysis final model (N=114)

	Value	Std.Error	DF	t-value	p-value
(Intercept)	1.9570	0.2831	95	6.91	0.0000
R.BROAD2008	-0.0223	0.0016	95	-14.26	0.0000
R.POPDENS	-0.0000	0.0000	95	-0.11	0.9125
R.RAI	-0.0015	0.0030	95	-0.49	0.6244
R.EXPEN	0.0030	0.0017	95	1.74	0.0854
R.ICTPOL	0.0060	0.0234	95	-0.26	0.7978
N.GDP	-0.0004	0.0019	5	-0.20	0.8465
N.CPI	0.0036	0.0049	5	0.72	0.4985
N.REGQ	0.2467	0.1730	5	1.43	0.2133
N.EDUTER	0.0000	0.0000	5	1.63	0.1630
N.HHINTRA	-0.2958	0.3810	5	-0.78	0.4726
N.HHINTER	0.5379	0.1671	5	3.22	0.0235
R.UNEMPLOY:NGDP	-0.0000	0.0000	95	-1.49	0.1407
N.GDP:R.GDP	0.0000	0.0000	95	0.82	0.4154

6   Discussion

6.1   Findings

Evidence of the regional level's relevance for the improvement of broadband access in the EU was found. The final multi-level regression model includes one significant regional variable related to the concrete regional ICT strategy: the expenditure of structural funding on broadband access. Unexpectedly, the fact that a given region developed a specific ICT policy during the period 2008-2012 is not relevant for the improvement of broadband access. Thus, the hypothesis of this paper is partially proven: the findings show that the regional broadband access scores for 2008 are significant for understanding the expansion of broadband across European regions between 2008 and 2012 (β= -0.022, p=0.00, Table 1, row 2). The higher the broadband access in a given region in 2008, the lower the expansion in the analyzed period. Also, the amount of ERDF expenditure spent on broadband expansion (R.EXPEN) is significant, i.e. more ERDF expenditure on broadband expenditure means stronger improvement of broadband access between 2008 and 2012 ($\beta = 0.003$, p=0.09; Table 1, row 5). The remaining regional variables do not prove significant. With regard to national characteristics, only inter-platform competition (N.HHINTER), is significant to explain broadband expansion ($\beta = 0.54$, p= 0.02; Table 1, row 12). This means that the higher the competition, the higher the improvement on broadband access.

6.2   Implications for Theory

During the past twenty years, the literature on broadband diffusion has found significant variables that could explain different broadband expansion patterns across countries. This paper makes three main contributions to the current state of broadband diffusion. First, it shifts the unit of analysis to the regions. Although broadband access improvement is usually a centralized policy with national agencies in charge of implementation, this paper proves that regions, at least in the European context, are relevant actors. Second, the findings of this paper confirm that the degree of competition within the market is a key factor for explaining broadband diffusion [4], [7], [11],

[13], [16]. The final model reveals that the regions in countries with higher scores on the inter-platform competition score, improved more during the period between 2008 and 2012. Third, this paper also demonstrates that the previous degree of broadband is highly significant for explaining broadband diffusion during the period 2008-2012.

6.3   Policy Implications

This paper provides evidence of the role that the regions play in the implementation of ICT policies and the potentially decisive role that they can have to bring forward the information society all over the European Union. Since regional ERDF expenditure turned out to be significant for broadband expansion, the current role of EU regions in the ERDF process should be reviewed. Regions, as the jurisdictions in charge of implementation of the ERDF, should participate more actively in the designing phase of the ERDF.

6.4   Limitations

As a pioneering effort to assess the role of regions in broadband expansion, this paper is not without limitations. First, our variable on the existence of a regional ICT strategy should be handled cautiously. As it is based on manual Internet searches, it likely to be incomplete. Second, our sample of EU regions is selective. Including Eastern countries could provide additional insights.

References

1. Dabinett, G.: EU mainstreaming of the information society in regional development policy. Reg. Stud. 35, 168–173 (2001)
2. European-Commission, Digital Agenda for Europe 2010-2020. URL Httpec Eur. Euinformationsocietyindexen Htm Httpec Eur. Euinformationsocietydigital-Agendaindexen Htm (2010)
3. Euroactiv: Commission claws back up to €200 million broadband funding in budget breakthrough. Euroactiv. (2013)
4. Distaso, W., Lupi, P., Manenti, F.M.: Platform competition and broadband uptake: Theory and empirical evidence from the European Union. Inf. Econ. Policy 18, 87–106 (2006)
5. Bauer, M., Börzel, T.: Regions and the European Union. Handb. Multi-Level Gov. (2010)
6. Le Galès, P., Lequesne, C.: Regions in Europe: The Paradox of Power. Routledge (1998)
7. Bouckaert, J., Van Dijk, T., Verboven, F.: Access regulation, competition, and broadband penetration: An international study. Telecommun. Policy 34, 661–671 (2010)
8. Lee, S., Marcu, M., Lee, S.: An empirical analysis of fixed and mobile broadband diffusion. Inf. Econ. Policy 23, 227–233 (2011)
9. Yates, D.J., Gulati, G.J.J., Weiss, J.W.: Understanding the Impact of Policy, Regulation and Governance on Mobile Broadband Diffusion. In: 46th Hawaii Int. Conf. on. Syst. Sci. HICSS 2013, pp. 2852–2861. IEEE (2013)
10. Aron, D., Burnstein, D.: Broadband adoption in the United States: An empirical analysis. SSRN Work. Pap. (2003)

11. Grosso, M.: Determinants of broadband penetration in OECD nations. Aust. Commun. Policy Res. Forum (2006)
12. Garcia-Murillo, M.: International broadband deployment: The impact of unbundling. Commun. Strateg (2005)
13. Lee, S., Brown, J.S.: Examining broadband adoption factors: an empirical analysis between countries. Info 10, 25–39 (2008)
14. Ngwenyama, O., Morawczynski, O.: Factors affecting ICT expansion in emerging economies: An analysis of ICT infrastructure expansion in five Latin American countries. Inf. Technol. Dev. 15, 237–258 (2009)
15. Cava-Ferreruela, I., Alabau-Munoz, A.: Broadband policy assessment: A cross-national empirical analysis. Telecommun. Policy 30, 445–463 (2006)
16. Cadman, R., Dineen, C.: Broadband Markets in the EU: the importance of dynamic competition to market growth. Strategy Policy Consult Netw Ltd (2006)
17. Bauer, J.M., Kim, J.H., Wildman, S.S.: Effects of national policy on the diffusion of broadband in OECD countries. UFL-LBS Workshop Future Broadband Wired Wirel. Gainsville Fla. (2005)
18. Gulati, G., Yates, D.: The Impact of Governance Indicators and Policy Variables on Broadband Diffusion in the Developed and Developing Worlds. SSRN Work. Pap (2010)
19. Turk, T., Jerman Blažič, B., Trkman, P.: Factors and sustainable strategies fostering the adoption of broadband communications in an enlarged European Union. Technol Forecast Soc Change 75, 933–951 (2008)
20. Eurostat: Eurostat regional yearbook 2010. Publications Office of the European Union-Luxembourg (2010)
21. Hooghe, L., Marks, G.: Europe with the regions: channels of regional representation in the European Union. Publius J. Fed. 26, 73–92 (1996)
22. Flamm, K., Chaudhuri, A.: An analysis of the determinants of broadband access. Telecommun Policy 31, 312–326 (2007)
23. Kaufmann, D., Kraay, A., Mastruzzi, M.: Governance matters VIII: aggregate and individual governance indicators. World Bank Policy Res. Work. Pap, pp. 1996–2008 (2009)
24. Bryk, A., Raudenbusch, S.: Hierarchical linear models: Applications and data management methods. Newbury Park Sage Publ Delgado JI Lopez-Fernandez Luna JD 1993 Influ Dr Gend Satisf Users Med Care 31, 795–800 (1992)
25. Bosker, R., Snijders, T.: Multilevel analysis: An introduction to basic and advanced multilevel modeling. SAGE Publications (1999)
26. Brown, R.D., Hauenstein, N.M.: Interrater agreement reconsidered: An alternative to the rwg indices. Organ Res Methods 8, 165–184 (2005)
27. Hox: Applied Multilevel Analysis. TT-Publikaties (1994)
28. Pinheiro, J., Bates, D., DebRoy, S., Sarkar, D.: Linear and nonlinear mixed effects models. R Package Version 3, 57 (2007)
29. Revelle, W.: Psych: Procedures for psychological, psychometric, and personality research. R Package Version 1019 (2011)
30. Maj, A.: Lmmfit: Goodness-of-Fit-Measures for Linear Mixed Models with One-Level-Grouping. R Package Version 1 (2011)
31. Bliese, P.: Multilevel Modeling in R (2.2)-A Brief Introduction to R, the multilevel package and the nlme package (2013)

Designing a Second Generation of Open Data Platforms: Integrating Open Data and Social Media

Charalampos Alexopoulos[1], Anneke Zuiderwijk[2], Yannis Charapabidis[1], Euripidis Loukis[1], and Marijn Janssen[2]

[1] Univertity of the Aegean, Dept. Information and Communication Systems Engineering, Samos, Greece
{alexop,yannisx,eloukis}@aegean.gr
[2] Delft University of Technology, Faculty of Technology, Policy and Management, Delft, The Netherlands
{a.m.g.zuiderwijk-vaneijk,M.F.W.H.A.Janssen}@tudelft.nl

Abstract. Two important trends in government that are emerging in the recent years have been on one hand the exploitation of the Web 2.0 social media, supporting a more extensive interaction and collaboration with citizens, and on the other hand the opening of government data to the citizens through the Internet, in order to be used for scientific, commercial and political purposes. However, there has been limited attempt of integrating them. Using a design science approach a second generation of open government data (OGD) platforms has been developed, which offer to the users both the 'classical' first generation functionalities, and also a comprehensive set of additional novel Web 2.0 features. The latter aim to provide support to the users in order to generate value from ODG. They enable users to become 'prosumers', both producing and consuming data. These novel capabilities for performing various types of processing, information and knowledge exchange, and collaboration were found to be useful and valuable by users in a first evaluation.

Keywords: open government data, open data, open government, public sector information, e-infrastructures, e-government, Web 2.0, social media, prosumers.

1   Introduction

In the recent years two important technological trends in government have been on the one hand the exploitation of the social media for supporting a more extensive interaction and collaboration with and between persons, and on the other hand the opening of government data to the public, in order to be used for scientific, commercial and political purposes. Both these concepts are associated with the 'open government' concept, which has transparency, public participation, and collaboration as its main components [6]: opening government data is strongly associated with the first one, while social media use is strongly associated with the second and the third.

M. Janssen et al. (Eds.): EGOV 2014, LNCS 8653, pp. 230–241, 2014.

Social media have started being used as a tool for increasing citizens' participation in their decision and policy making processes, collecting opinions, knowledge and ideas from citizens, and promoting government transparency and accountability [1-5]. Government - much later than the private sector - attempts to take advantage for the above purposes of the unprecedented capabilities that the new Web 2.0 paradigm provides to simple non-professional users for developing, distributing, accessing, rating and commenting on various types of digital content, and also for the creation of on-line communities. At the same time there is a renewed interest to exploit 'public sector information', by making it available to the citizens and other government agencies (different from its initial creator) through the Internet, in order to be re-used for the generation of both social and economic value [6-12]. Government is one of the largest creators and collectors of data in many different domains. These data might be used for many other purposes, quite different from the ones of their initial creation/collection, e.g. for various scientific, commercial and political purposes.

So far there has been limited attempt to integrate these two developments. As will be explained in more detail in section 2.2, the existing open government data (OGD) platforms provide to their users mainly functionalities for searching and downloading datasets, but limited functionalities for stimulating and facilitating the generation of value from them. This is quite negative taking into account the big investments made by numerous governments for the development and operation of OGD platforms. Literature (e.g. [12-13]) has pointed out that simply opening and publicizing government data will not automatically lead to the generation of social and economic value, and that appropriate stimulation actions have to be taken for this purpose. Therefore it is of critical important to conduct research in order to develop mechanisms for the stimulation and facilitation of value generation from these OGD investments. The underlying premise of our research is that the incorporation of social Web 2.0 functionality in OGD platforms can stimulate value creation by providing networking, interaction and collaboration support among their users. In addition this allows for the consumption and production of content ('pro-sumption') at the same time.

In particular, our paper follows a design science approach in order to develop a second generation of OGD platforms, which offer to the users both the 'classical' first generation functionality, and a comprehensive set of additional novell Web 2.0 oriented functionality aiming to stimulate and facilitate value generation from OGD. This can be very important for the increase of the social and economic value generated from the big investments in OGD platforms. The functionality of such a Web 2.0 OGD platform is described and evaluated using both quantitative and qualitative techniques.

The paper is organized in six sections. In the following section thebackground is presented. Then in section 3 the methodology adopted for the development of this Web 2.0 OGD platform is presented, followed by a description of its functionality in section 4. The results of the first evaluation are outlined in section 5, while in the final section 6 conclusions are drawn and future research directions are proposed.

2   Background

2.1   Web 2.0 Social Media Use

Web 2.0 constitutes a quite different Internet paradigm from its predecessor Web 1.0. It promotes the generation of content of various types by simple and non-expert users, the development of relationships and online communities among them, and the extensive interaction, collaboration and sharing of content and information [14]. A big number of social media platforms have been developed adhering to these characteristics. According to [15] the main capabilities of Web 2.0 social media are:

i) User-generated social content: social media enable users to submit content which other users can access, rate and comment.
ii) Social networking: users of social media join together in online communities, which allow them to see profile information about the people to whom they are connected, and to share information and have extensive interaction with them.
iii) Collaboration: users engage in conversations, co-creation of content, collaborative problem solving, and collective action.

The above capabilities were initially exploited by private sector firms and later started being adopted and utilized by government agencies. Social media can offer government agencies significant opportunities for: i) increasing citizens' participation and engagement in public policy making, by providing to more groups a voice in discussions of policy development, implementation and evaluation; ii) public services co-production, by enabling government agencies and the public to develop and design jointly government services; iii) crowdsourcing solutions and innovations, by exploiting public knowledge and talent in order to develop innovative solutions to the increasingly complex societal problems; iv) promoting transparency-accountability, and in this way reducing corruption, by enabling governments to open up large quantities of activity and spending related data, and at the same time enabling citizens to collectively take part in monitoring the activities of government; v) increasing information and knowledge exchange among government agencies [1-5, 16-20].

2.2   Opening Government Data

In the last decade there has been an increase in activities and investments towards opening up of public sector information to the public, in order to be used for scientific, commercial and political purposes [6-12, 21-23]. This information can be valuable for scientific research in many different domains (e.g. in the social, political, economic, administrative and management sciences), and can contribute critically to the development of the 'e-Science' paradigm [9-10]. Furthermore, it can be used by citizens and journalists for gaining better and deeper understanding of and insight into the activities and spending of government agencies. This should result in evidence-based, mature and effective political processes. Also, OGD can have a positive impact on innovation and economic growth, as they enable the development of new applications, products and services.

Four types of OGD value generation mechanisms are identified in [24-25]: i) efficiency mechanisms (public sector organizations through OGD generate economic value by increasing internal efficiency and effectiveness), ii) transparency mechanisms (public sector organizations generate social value by offering increased transparency into government actions, which reduces 'information 'asymmetry' between government officials and citizens, and therefore misuse of public power for private benefits and corruption), iii) innovation mechanisms (private sector firms generate economic value through the creation of new products and services), iv) participation mechanisms (private sector firms generate social value through participating and collaborating with government).

Many OGD platforms, often in the form of portals, have been developed and operated by government agencies. The existing first generation of OGD digital infrastructures offers mainly basic functionalities for searching and downloading data by the users of these data, and for uploading data by their providers. The majority of these portals offer simple free-text search and theme-browsing functions for the discovery of datasets. Only some portals have recently taken advantage of Semantic Web by providing semantically enriched discovery services, such as performing SPARQL queries. Most OGD platforms limit their data provision services to a simple download functionality, and only a few of them provide functionality to view datasets on a map or various types of charts.

Furthermore, there are no functionalities for processing the datasets in order to improve them, adapt them to specialized needs, or link them to other datasets (public or private), and then for uploading-publishing new versions of them, or for uploading users' own datasets. Furthermore, the 'Linked Data' paradigm is adopted only by some recently developed initiatives, whereas traditional and longstanding public data sources are reluctant to adopt Linked Data andSemantic Web technologies. Also, only a few OGD platforms collect the needs of users for additional datasets in a formal and systematic manner. The majority have only general-purpose feedback web forms for collecting comments and suggestions from users, which typically concern the technical aspects of the platform rather the actual datasets provided. Only some portals include datasets' rating and commenting. Another important weakness are the limited-functionalityfor networking, interaction and collaboration among users, in order to generate value from the provided datasets.

In general this first generation of OGD platforms follows mainly the Web 1.0 paradigm, aiming mainly to make OGD available, but do not offer to users functionality supporting the generation of value from them. There is a clear distinction between content producers (public administrations) and content users (research communities, businesses and citizens), and limited interaction and collaboration among them. Our research makes a contribution towards filling the above gaps and overcoming the above weaknesses, through the design of a second generation of OGD platforms, which combine and integrate opening data on one hand, with exploiting the main characteristics of the social media on the other hand, in order to stimulate and facilitate value generation from the OGD.

3   Design Methodology

A design science approach was adopted, since "design [...] is concerned with how things ought to be, with devising artefacts to attain goals" [26]. In particular, the Design Science Research Methodology (DSRM) of Peffers et al. [27] was used, consisting of the following six steps:

1. Problem identification and motivation. The problem identified was that little support for creating value of OGD by users is provided, whereas Web 2.0 social media tools can be used for this.

2. Define objectives of a solution. Various sources were used to define the particular objectives of a solution to the above problem, including six semi-structured interviews, a questionnaire and four workshops. The interviews were conducted with open data experts between December 2011 and January 2012. The questionnaire was conducted between April 2012 and September 2012. Both the interviews and the questionnaire provided information about the state of the art of using open public sector data in general, and problems that are experienced in this regard. The questionnaire also asked for activities related to open data use that people would like to conduct, how important and useful they found them. In total 111 people completed the questionnaire. Furthermore, four workshops were conducted at international events to gather information about requirements for a second generation OGD platform. The workshops aimed at engaging various open data users from different countries, so that different types of requirements can be identified. The workshops were conducted between May 2012 and September 2012 and involved 65 participants.

3. Artefact design and development. The previous step of the DSRM led to the design of the Web 2.0 OGD platform, which is described in the following section 4.

4. Artefact demonstration. A first prototype of it was developed and was publicly demonstrated. The platform was presented to open data users at several events (e.g. conference workshops and presentations), and also via Twitter, LinkedIn, Facebook and newsletters.

5. Evaluation. Within an 18-month period, the first prototype of the artefact was evaluated by six groups of students from twoUniversities in the Netherlands and one University in Greece. Since the evaluation concerns a prototype, we were not able to evaluate the whole design of the Web 2.0 OGD platform described in section 4. Evaluations took place in October 2012 (n=21 and n=33), May 2013 (n=15), September2013 (n=19), October 2013 (n=20) and November 2013 (n=30). Most participating students had followed lectures on open data and were familiar with the topic. All evaluations consisted of an online questionnaire, a usability test and a qualitative discussion. In each of the evaluation sessions, the participants were asked to conduct a number of tasks that represented open data use on a Web 2.0 OGD portal. We refer to the whole of these tasks as a usage scenario. More features were added after each iteration of the platform development, based on the evaluation results. The findings of each evaluation were used to further specify the requirements for this new generation of Web 2.0 platforms and to further improve it.

6. <u>Communication of the artefact</u>. The artefact was communicated to potential open data users by giving presentations at conferences, organizing workshops, writing publications, sending newsletters to many open data users and using social media.

4   Platform Functionality

The functionality provided by this advanced OGD platform we developed based on the design methodology presented in the previous section 4, to the two main stakeholders, the open data users and providers, is shown in Table 1. We focus on its novel Web 2.0 features. It includes a wide set of capabilities for data processing, enhanced data modeling (flat, contextual and detailed metadata), commenting existing datasets and expressing needs for new datasets, datasets quality rating, users groups formation and extensive communication and collaboration within them, data linking, publication/ upload of new versions of existing datasets and advanced data visualization.

Table 1. Novel Web 2.0 Functionalities

	Functionality	Stake-holder	Description
1	Data Processing	Provider/User	(a) data enrichment - i.e. adding new elements - fields, (b) metadata enrichment - i.e. fill in missing fields, (c) data cleansing - e.g. detecting and correcting ubiquities in a dataset, matching text names to database IDs (keys) etc., (d) converting datasets other formats, (e) submitting various types of items - e.g. visualisations, publications - related to a dataset and (f) datasets combination and mash-ups.
2	Data Enhanced Modeling	Provider/User	description of flat, contextual and detailed metadata of any metadata/vocabulary model.
3	Feedback and Collaboration	Provider/User	(a) communicate our own thoughts and ideas on the datasets to the other users and the providers of them through comments that we can enter on them, (b) read interesting thoughts and ideas of other users on the datasets through comments entered on them, (c) express our own needs for additional datasets that would be interesting and useful to us, (d) get informed about the needs of other users for additional datasets and (e) get informed about datasets extensions and revisions.
4	Data Quality Rating	User	(a) communicate to the other users and the providers the level of quality of the datasets we perceive, (b) get informed on the level of quality of the datasets perceived by other users through their ratings.

Table 1. (*continued*)

5	Grouping and Interaction	Provid-er/User	(a) searching for and finding other users-providers having similar interests with us, in order to have information and knowledge exchange and cooperation with them, (b) forming groups with other users-providers having similar interests with us in order to have information and knowledge exchange and cooperation with them, (c) maintaining datasets/working on datasets within one group, (d) communicating with other users/providers through messages in order to exchange information and knowledge, (e) getting immediately updated about the upload of new versions and enrichments of datasets maintained/worked on within the group, or new relevant items (e.g. publications, visualizations, etc.).
6	Data Linking	Provid-er/User	(a) Data and metadata linking toother ontologies in the Linked Open Data Cloud, (b) Capabilities of querying data and metadata through Sparql Endpoints.
7	DataVersions Publica-tion/upload	Provid-er/User	Support for publication/upload of new versions of the existing datasets, and connection with previous ones and initial datasets.
8	Data Visualiza-tion	User	Advanced datasets' visualization capabilities (maps, charts, plots and other)

5   Evaluation

We proceeded next to the evaluation of this advanced second generation OGD platform. The evaluation covered both its classical and novel features, but in this paper we report on the latter, as they are our main focus.

The quantitative part of the evaluation included the design of a questionnaire,which was distributed to users of the OGD platform (who implemented some usage scenarios of it, acting both as data users and providers). All these questions have the form of positive statements, and the users were asked to enter the extent of their agreement or disagreement with these statement by answering the question: "To which extend do you agree with the following statements?". A five point Likert scale was used to measure agreement or disagreement with (i.e. positive or negative response to) such a statement (1=Strongly Disagree, 2= Disagree, 3=Neutral, 4=Agree, 5=Strongly Agree). Table 2 lists the questions, and the corresponding average rating results. All of them are between 3 (neutral) and 4 (agreement to the positive statement), which indicates a positive attitude of the users towards this novel functionality. The highest ratings are for the feedback and collaboration capabilities allowing the exchange of comments on existing datasets and needs for new datasets. Given that a prototype was used in this evaluation, and a complete platform can perform even better, these results give a clear indication that users value these web 2.0 social web features.

Table 2. Questions and results concerning Web 2.0 features

Functionalities	Average Ratings
Data Processing	**3,34**
The platform provides good capabilities for data enrichment (i.e. adding new elements - fields).	3,43
The platform provides good capabilities for metadata enrichment (i.e. fill in missing fields).	3,42
The platform provides good capabilities for data cleansing (e.g. detecting and correcting ubiquities in a dataset, matching text names to database IDs (keys) etc.).	3,41
The platform provides good capabilities for converting datasets to another format.	3,39
The platform provides good capabilities for linking datasets (including linking RDF files to LOD cloud).	3,40
The platform provides good capabilities for submitting various types of items (e.g. visualisations, publications) related to a dataset.	3,43
The platform provides good capabilities for datasets combination/ Mash-ups.	3,42
Feedback and Collaboration	**3,61**
The platform enables me to read interesting thoughts and ideas of other users on the datasets through the comments they enter on them.	3,64
The platform enables me to communicate my own thoughts and ideas on the datasets to the other users and the providers of them through comments I enter.	3,62
The platform enables me to express my needs for additional datasets that would be interesting and useful to me.	3,62
The platform enables me to get informed about the needs of other users for additional datasets.	3,61
The platform enables me to read interesting thoughts and ideas of the users on the datasets and the extensions I have uploaded by reading the comments they entered on them.	3,59
The platform enables me to get informed on the level of quality of the datasets and the extensions I have uploaded that is perceived by the users of them by reading their ratings.	3,59
The platform enables me to get informed about the needs of the users of the datasets and the extensions I have uploaded for additional ones.	3,58
Data Quality Rating	**3,53**
The platform enables me to get informed on the level of quality of the datasets perceived by other users through their ratings	3,53

Table 2. (*continued*)

The platform enables me to communicate to the other users and the providers the level of quality of the datasets that I perceive	3,52
Grouping and Interaction	**3,47**
The platform enables searching for and finding other users having similar interests with me in order to have information and knowledge exchange and cooperation	3,48
The platform enables forming groups with other users having similar interests with me in order to have information and knowledge exchange and cooperation	3,47
The platform enables maintaining datasets/working on datasets within one group	3,47
The platform enables communicating with other users through messages in order to exchange information and knowledge	3,46
The platform enables getting immediately updated about the upload of new versions and enrichments of datasets maintained/worked on within the group, or new relevant items (e.g. publications, visualizations, etc.)	3,45

From the qualitative discussions that were organized in each of the evaluation sessions it became clear that the novel Web 2.0 features of the OGD platform were evaluated positively by the participants. For instance, one of the participants of the third evaluation session said that the prototype was quite valuable because it "stimulates exchange of information and improvement of datasets". In the same evaluation session it was also pointed out that it is "easy to add comments" and that "the rating system for datasets is useful". A participant in the next evaluation session said that "the quality rating system is nice" and another participant stated: "I like the idea that you can make a request for a dataset. If you cannot find it yourself, the community will help you". In the fifth and sixth evaluation sessions the participants were also very positive about the data request feature. It was mentioned that "nice that you can see whether a request has been satisfied" and "I like the idea that the community will help you find a dataset making only a request for it". Despite that there were several difficulties with the use of this prototype (e.g. difficulties with visualizations of dataset and the response times), the participants stated that overall it was easy to use.

The participants of the discussions also stated that there were various areas for improvement of the prototype. One important area concerns the limited amount of users at that time, so more users are necessary to create a network effects. It was commented "the platform is only useful when you have many users", and "very little feedback provided up until now". One participant described that there is some uncertainty about whether the extended or added datasets by users (and not by government agencies) are correct and reliable. Another participant stated that a useful additional feature for addressing this issue could be to enable users to rate other users, and users to obtain credits when they conduct 'positive' activities, such as uploading interesting datasets. This can lead to the development of a users' reputation mechanism.

Furthermore, the participants stated that the prototype could be improved by: a) improving search capabilities of the list of people registered on the OGD platform,

b) enhancing group creation capabilities, c) enabling sending private message to another user, d) having a better Wiki-like layout, e) making the rating system more clearly visible and f) by showing the number of replies on a data request on top of the page. All the above comments and suggestions of the users were taken into account for the development of a new version of the platform.

6   Conclusions

Government agencies are increasingly interested in opening their data, in order to be used for scientific, political or commercial purposes (i.e. development of new value added services/applications). This has led to big investments for the development and operation of a first generation of OGD platforms. These platforms offer mainly capabilities for searching and downloading datasets, but limited capabilities for stimulating and facilitating the generation of value from them. Using a design science approach a second generation of Web 2.0 OGD platforms has been developed, offering to the users both the 'classical' first generation capabilities, and also a comprehensive set of additional Web 2.0 social media oriented capabilities. A first evaluation of this new concept shows that users appreciate these novel social Web 2.0 oriented features, and find them useful and valuable. So we have some first evidence that the proposed integration of these two major technological trends observed in government in the recent years, social media and data opening, can be succesful and beneficial.

Our research has interesting implications for research and practice. It opens up a new stream of research towards the enhancement of the classical OGD platform with novell features supporting data 'pro-sumption' and also interaction and collaboration with other users and government agencies, which can benefit from the extensive research that has been conducted in the computer supported collaborative work and communities' of practice domains. Furthermore, OGD practice should move from the simple provision of data to the support and facilitation of their exploitation and value generation from them, using both technological and organizational instruments. Further research is required in this direction, including the development of more advanced versions of this OGD platform, and its further evaluation by different groups of 'more professional' users (than the students who have participated in these first evaluations), such as researchers, journalists, politicians, value added services and application developers.

Acknowledgements. The research presented in this paper has been conducted as part of the ENGAGE FP7 Infrastructure Project (its full title is 'An Infrastructure for Open, Linked Governmental Data Provision Towards Research Communities and Citizens' – see http://www.engage-project.eu/wp/).

References

1. Bertot, J.C., Jaeger, P.T., Grimes, J.M.: Promoting transparency and accountability through ICTs, social media, and collaborative e-government. Transforming Government: People, Process and Policy 6(1), 78–91 (2012)

2. Bonsón, E., Torres, L., Royo, S., Flores, F.: Local e-government 2.0: Social media and corporate transparency in municipalities. Government Information Quarterly 29, 123–132 (2012)
3. Chun, S.A., Luna Reyes, L.F.: Editorial - Social media in government. Government Information Quarterly 29, 441–445 (2012)
4. Margo, M.J.: A Review of Social Media Use in E-Government. Administrative Sciences, Administrative Sciences 2(2), 148–161 (2012)
5. Criado, J.I., Sandoval-Almazan, R., Gil-Garcia, J.R.: Government innovation through social media. Government Information Quarterly 30, 319–326 (2013)
6. McDermott, P.: Building open government. Government Information Quarterly 27(4), 401–413 (2010)
7. Janssen, K.: The influence of the PSI directive on open government data: An overview of recent developments. Government Information Quarterly 28, 446–456 (2011)
8. Kundra, V.: Digital Fuel of the 21st Century: Innovation through Open Data and the Network Effect. Joan Shorenstein Center on the Press, Politics and Public Policy, Harvard (2012)
9. Commission of the European Communities: Communication fromthe Commissionto the European Parliament. In: The Council and the European Economic and Social Committee on Scientific Information in the Digital Age: Access, Dissemination and Preservation. COM. 56 Final, Brussels (2007)
10. Commission of the European Communities: Communication from the Commission to the European Parliament. In: The Council, the European Economic and Social Committee and the Committee of the Regions – ICT Infrastructures for e-Science. COM, 108 Final, Brussels (2009)
11. Luna-Reyes, L.F., Bertot, J.C., Mellouli, S.: Editorial - Open Government, Open Data and Digital Government. Government Information Quarterly 31, 4–5 (2014)
12. Zuiderwijk, A., Janssen, M.: Open data policies, their implementation and impact: A framework for comparison. Government Information Quarterly 31, 17–29 (2014)
13. Janssen, M., Charalabidis, Y., Zuiderwijk, A.: Benefits, adoption barriers and myths of Open Data and Open Government. Information Systems Management 29(4), 258–268 (2012)
14. O'Reilly, T.: What is Web 2.0: Design patterns and business models for the next generation of software. Communications and Strategies 1, 17–37 (2007)
15. Davis, T., Mintz, M.: Design features for the social web: The Arcquitecture of Deme. In: Proceedings of 8th International Workshop on Web-Oriented Software Technologies - IWWOST (2009)
16. Bovaird, T.: Beyond engagement and participation: User and community coproduction of public services. Public Administration Review 67(5), 846–860 (2007)
17. Torres, L.H.: Citizen sourcing in the public interest. Knowledge Management for Development Journal 3(1), 134–145 (2007)
18. Lukensmeyer, C.J., Torres, L.H.: Citizensourcing: Citizen participation in a networked nation. In: Yang, K., Bergrud, E. (eds.) Civic engagement in a network society, pp. 207–233. Information Age Publishing, Charlotte (2008)
19. Bertot, J.C., Jaeger, P.T., Grimes, J.M.: Promoting transparency and accountability through ICTs, social media, and collaborative e-government. Transforming Government: People, Process and Policy 6(1), 78–91 (2012)
20. Linders, D.: From e-government to we-government: Defining a typology for citizen coproduction in the age of social media. Government Information Quarterly 29, 446–454 (2012)

21. Dekkers, M., Polman, F., De Velde, R., De Vries, M.: MEPSIR – Measuring European Public Sector Information Resources: Final report of study on exploitation of public sector information – benchmarking of EU framework Conditions. Report for the European Commission, Brussels (2006)
22. European Union: Directive 2003/98/EC of the European Parliament and of the Council of 17 November 2003 on the re-use of public sector information. Official Journal of the European Union, Luxembourg (2003)
23. Commission of the European Communities: Communication from the Commission to the European Parliament. In: The Council, the European Economic and Social Committee and the Committee of the Regions – Open Data: An Engine for Innovation, Growth and Transparent Governance. COM, 882 Final, Brussels (2011)
24. Jetzek, T., Avital, M., Bjorn-Andersen, N.: The Value of Open Government Data: A Strategic Analysis Framework. In: Proceedings of SIG eGovernment pre-ICIS Workshop, Orlando, USA (2012)
25. Jetzek, T., Avital, M., Bjorn-Andersen, N.: The Generative Mechanismsof Open Government Data. In: Proceedings of of the 21st European Conference on Information Systems (ECIS), Utrecht, The Netherlands (2013)
26. Simon, H.A.: The Sciences of the Artificial, 3rd edn. MIT Press, MA (1996)
27. Peffers, K., Tunanen, T., Rothenberger, M.A., Chatterjee, S.: A Design Science Research Methodology for Information Systems Research. Journal of Management Information Systems 24, 45–77 (2008)

Categorization of Brazilian Internet Users and Its Impacts on the Use of Electronic Government Services

Marcelo Henrique De Araujo and Nicolau Reinhard

School of Economics, Business and Accounting, Business Department
University of Sao Paulo, Av. Prof. Luciano Gualberto, 908 05508-900, Sao Paulo, Brazil
{marcelo.haraujo,reinhard}@usp.br

Abstract. This paper explores the micro-data from the ICT Households Survey in order to categorize the Brazilian Internet users according to the diversity of activities undertaken by these users on-line and assess the propensity of these Internet user groups to use e-gov services. The Amartya Sen's Capability Approach was adopted as theoretical framework for its consideration of people's freedom to decide on their use of the available resources and their competencies for these decisions, leading to the use of e-government services. This paper uses a positivistic approach a descriptive and exploratory analysis of secondary data (micro-data) from the 2007, 2009 and 2011 editions of the ICT Household survey.

Keywords: Capability Approach, Electronic Government Services, Internet use patterns.

1 Introduction

In Brazil, e-government (e-gov) initiatives have become popular among the citizens due to the diversity of electronic services available to the population, such as electronic voting system, filing an income tax return report, scheduling medical appointments, enrollment of students in public schools, among others [1,2]. However, the success of these initiatives (e-gov) depends on the access and predisposition to use the ICT resources in the interaction between the government and the civil society.

Public policies for digital inclusion in the country encourage both the individual access (through tax reduction on computer equipment, promoting the purchase of computers and access to the Internet) and the collective access, which includes the offer and availability of Internet access in public access centers (for example, Public Telecenters and Cybercafés)[3, 4, 5].

Through its Center of Studies on Information and Communication Technologies (CETIC.br), the Brazilian Internet Steering Committee (CGI.br) conducts surveys in order to generate statistics about the use of Information and Communication Technologies (ICTs). For the purposes of this paper, the data used were taken from their ICT Household Survey, a survey conducted annually and whose data enable the generation of indicators about the availability and use of the Internet by the Brazilian population.

M. Janssen et al. (Eds.): EGOV 2014, LNCS 8653, pp. 242–252, 2014.
© IFIP International Federation for Information Processing 2014

This research is based on the following objectives: (i) Categorize the Internet users based on their Internet use (for example, personal communications, entertainment, business applications, etc.) and (ii) Explore the relationships of their predisposition to use the e-gov services with the abovementioned categories. The analysis is based on the ICT Household Survey micro-data for the years 2007, 2009 and 2011. The Capability Approach [6] was adopted as a theoretical framework, for its consideration of people's freedom to decide on their use of the available resources and their competencies for these decisions, leading to the use of e-government services.

Although the theme had already been explored by [7], the contribution of this paper is the characterization of the different groups of Internet users based on their usage of the Internet - and assessing the propensity to use the e-gov in each one of these groups.

The paper is structured as follows: Section 2 discusses the theoretical principles that guide this research. In Section 3, the reference model and the adopted methodological strategy are presented. Section 4 discusses the main results and findings of this research. Section 5 presents final remarks.

2   Literature Review

2.1   The Capability Approach

The Capability approach [6] was developed in order to offer an objective basis for interpersonal perceptions of welfare [8,9] thus overcoming limitations of the utilitarian approach, in which this type of comparison - essential for the welfare economy - would not be possible.

According to the Capability Approach [6], simply providing a commodity or resource does not directly imply a direct increase in the welfare of a community, due to the multiple manners this resource can be used (capability) and the results obtained by the effective use of this commodity (functioning). Therefore, the assessment of a resource (commodity) and its use depend on a set of cultural, social and knowledge factors, named conversion factors. Thus, from the access conditions to a certain commodity and the referred conversion factors, individuals recognize a set of resources, which will be assessed based on the possibility of access and perception of use. Consequently, reducing this initial set to its capability [6] [10], that is, a smaller set of resources that they will take into consideration to make their choices of use. Based on these capabilities, the individuals decide how they will use these resources in order to achieve their functioning, that is, the result of the effective use of these resources, which, in a last analysis, will lead to their utility, for example, exercise of rights, welfare [10].

2.2   ICT Household Survey

The ICT Household survey, performed annually since 2005 by the Brazilian Internet Steering Committee (CGI.br), aims at mapping the availability of ICT resources by the Brazilian population [11] (ICT Household Survey 2012).

The survey uses methodological standards developed by the OECD (Organization for Economic Co-operation and Development), Eurostat and by the Observatory for the Information Society in Latin America and the Caribbean (OSILAC), and Economic Commission for Latin America and the Caribbean (ECLAC), thus allowing international comparisons. The sampling plan is based on the national Census and Household Sample Survey.

3   Research Methodology and Reference Model

The paper's reference model, presented in Figure 1, is based on the Capability Approach [6].

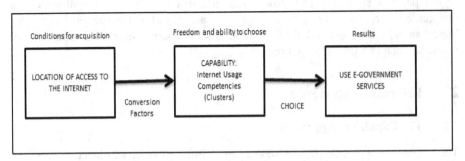

Fig. 1. Reference Model: Capability Approach (Source: adapted from [7], [9])

The objective of this model is to demonstrate the factors influencing the individuals' decisions to use electronic government services. The model consists of three main constructs: (i) conditions to obtain (or access) the resource; (ii) freedom and ability to choose (capabilities); (iii) results (functioning).

The survey's answer to the question "the most common or favorite access location to the internet" was used to operationalize the first construct. As a proxy to users' capabilities, the study constructs factors based on the survey's questions regarding the frequent usage of other Internet services: communication, leisure and entertainment activities, information search and on-line services. This study improves on previous analyses performed by [7], where capabilities were represented directly by the usage of e-mail, e-finance, e-commerce services. The last construct synthesizes the target phenomenon of this research, that is, the use of e-government services. For that end, this concept was operationalized through a binary primitive, indicating whether the Internet users made use of electronic government services in the last 12 months.

This study aims also to categorize Internet users, in order to understand the factors that drive or restrict the use of e-gov services. Differently from other models that are based on users' beliefs and attitudes (for example, perception of utility and facility), this paper is based on observed user behavior (actual usage of Internet services) and explores the mediation chain showed by the Internet users' choices and actions, attributes that are directly measured by the ICT Household Survey.

This research uses a positivistic approach a descriptive and exploratory analysis of secondary data (micro-data) from the 2007, 2009 and 2011 editions of the ICT Household Survey, Table 1 presents the survey's variables used in the paper.

Table 1. Variables

Variables for this study	ICT Survey questions and Categories
Social Class	AB (combined), C, and DE (combined);
Internet Access Location	Most common access location (Home, Work, At someone else's home, Telecenter, Cybercafe, Other place).
Use of Electronic Government Services	Yes/No
Internet Use for Communication	Several
Internet Use for Information Search and On-line Services	Several
Internet Use for Leisure and Entertainment	Several
Internet Use for Financial Services	Several
Internet Use for Education and Training	Several

The first variable presented in Table 1 is a construct derived from respondents' demographic attributes; due to the small sizes of classes A and D, the data were combined in three groups: Class AB (upper class); Class C (middle class); Class DE (lower class).

The variable "Use of Electronic Government Services" is a dichotomous measure that maps the Internet users that used any of the e-gov services in the last 12 months.

The other (binary) variables represent the different Internet uses, represented by a set of binary metric that explores several activities connected to communication (e.g. e-mail, instant messages, participation in networking websites), information search and on-line services (e.g. search for health information), leisure and entertainment (e.g. on-line games, virtual reality environments), financial services (consult and transactions via internet banking), and education and training activities (e.g. school activities, on-line courses, etc.).

Statistical analysis was performed through multivariate statistical techniques (Binary Factor Analysis, Logistic Regression and Clusters Analysis), using SPSS and Stata tools.

Binary Factor Analysis and the Cluster Analysis were used for the construction of user categories.

Due to the great amount of activities explored in each one of the Internet use patterns, the Binary Factor Analysis technique was applied in order to reduce the problem dimension. Cluster Analysis, using the factorial scores of the latent factors was then applied to identify homogenous Internet user groups regarding the multiple activities performed on the Internet. These clusters were used as proxies for the capabilities of the reference model (Figure 1).

Binary logistic regression technique was used to assess the relationship of the clusters with the users' preferred Internet access locations and also to establish the relationship of the clusters with the use of e-gov services.

Binary logistic regression is a technique that aims at studying the relation between the independent, metric and non-metric variables, and a binary dependent variable [12]. In order to perform the logistic regression, a stepwise procedure was used (with 95% of confidence level). Since the study is not focused on creating predictive models, it was decided to analyze only the odds ratio measures of the statistically significant independent variables.

4   Analysis and Discussion of Results

In accordance with the objectives of this study, the Internet users were categorized based on their uses of the Internet. The ICT Household Survey lists a number of categories of Internet uses: (i) communication (for example, e-mail, networking websites); (ii) information search and on-line services; (iii) leisure and entertainment (for example, on-line games, virtual reality); (iv) financial services (consult and transact via internet banking); (v) education and training activities (for example, on-line courses).

Due to the great number of variables in each one of these categories, Binary Factor Analysis statistical technique [13] was used in order to reduce these variables to a smaller number of latent factors. This analysis was applied to each one of the five abovementioned categories, for each year of the survey (2007, 2009 and 2011) Eigenvalues equal to or higher than 1 were used a criterion for factors retention. Furthermore, where necessary, a Varimax orthogonal rotation was applied, yielding one single significant factor for each category (except for the leisure and entertainment activities category with two factors). The analysis resulted in the following single factors: (a) communication; (b) information search and on-line services; (c) financial services; and (d) education and training.

For the leisure and entertainment activities, the first latent factor gathered all the variables related to the activities with high degree of interaction and collaboration among Internet users, such as participating in virtual reality environments, on-line games, etc. The second factor represented the non-interactive activities (for example, listening to on-line radios, reading news and magazines, etc.). Therefore, the first factor was called "interactive and collaborative activities," and the second one was called "non-interactive activities."

The standardized factor scores derived from the factor analysis were then used as input for the cluster analysis. In order to define the number of clusters, hierarchical clustering was initially applied, defining the "between groups", and the "squared Euclidean distance" as clustering and distance method, respectively. The results suggested the formation of three clusters. Then, the non-hierarchical clustering was applied through k-means algorithm, in order to create the three clusters, whose final positioning is showed in tables 2, 3 and 4.

Table 2. Final Cluster Centers (2007)

	Cluster		
	1	2	3
Communication	0.10	-1.08	0.48
Information Search and On-line Services	-0.28	-0.98	0.68
Interactive and Collaborative Activities (Leisure and Entertainment)	0.82	-0.92	-0.06
Non-interactive Activities (Leisure and Entertainment)	-0.59	-0.82	0.79
Financial Services	-0.07	-0.65	0.37
Training and Education	-0.16	-0.89	0.55

Table 2, shows the differences in profiles of the three user groups: cluster 2 has a negative value for all different Internet use patterns, indicating that this cluster gathers Internet users that make very little use of the analyzed Internet uses. Therefore, these Internet users are characterized as sporadic users. On the other hand, the data on cluster 3 present positive sign for almost all Internet use activities (except for leisure and entertainment interactive and collaborative activities), indicating that this group has a more Advanced profile when compared to the previous cluster. And, finally, cluster 1 has an intermediate profile (regarding the Internet use patterns) compared to the abovementioned clusters, with a higher leisure and entertainment component.

Table 3. Final Cluster Centers (2009)

	Cluster		
	1	2	3
Communication	-0.47	0.80	0.31
Information Search and On-line Services	-0.69	0.96	0.56
Interactive and Collaborative Activities (Leisure and Entertainment)	0.09	0.55	-0.44
Non-interactive Activities (Leisure and Entertainment)	-0.70	0.61	0.77
Financial Services	-0.32	1.72	-0.36
Training and Education	-0.55	0.83	0.42

The analysis of the 2009 data (Table 3) and 2011 (Table 4) shows a cluster formation similar to 2007 (only with clusters in different order).

The Cluster Analysis for each of the three years resulted in a set of three clusters with similar composition between the years. The observation of the factor loadings led the authors to name them as "Advanced use", "Intermediate use" and "Sporadic use".

Table 4. Final Cluster Centers (2011)

	Cluster		
	1	2	3
Communication	1.03	-0.57	0.31
Information Search and On-line Services	0.80	-0.69	0.70
Interactive and Collaborative Activities (Leisure and Entertainment)	1.22	-0.08	-0.78
Non-interactive Activities (Leisure and Entertainment)	0.33	-0.62	0.92
Financial Services	0.14	-0.44	0.70
Training and Education	0.74	-0.57	0.52

Table 5. Electronic government use by Internet user clusters (percentage)

	Advanced use			Intermediate use			Sporadic use		
	2007	2009	2011	2007	2009	2011	2007	2009	2011
Use of e-gov	56.4	93.7	82.7	83.7	80.3	89.4	88.8	54.3	50.7
Non-use of e-gov	43.6	6.3	17.3	16.3	19.7	10.6	11.2	45.7	49.3

Table 5 shows the percentage distribution of the e-gov services users in each one of the proposed Internet user clusters. The analysis of the table 5 data shows that the e-gov services are widely used by the Internet users with the Advanced and intermediate use profile. On the other hand, in the Internet user group of sporadic use, the use of e-gov services has decreased. Therefore, the Table 5 data shows that the proportion of Internet use the e-gov services is much higher among those with higher proficiency in the Internet use (Advanced and intermediate users groups).

Table 6. Internet Access Location by Internet user clusters (percentage)

	Advanced use			Intermediate use			Sporadic use		
	2007	2009	2011	2007	2009	2011	2007	2009	2011
Home	25.5	56.3	75.6	39.0	52.4	67.8	43.8	35.9	54.9
Work	13.6	28.6	10.6	25.1	18.7	22.8	25.8	12.3	13.3
School	4.0	0.6	1.0	3.3	3.1	0.9	2.7	2.7	1.3
Someone else's home	12.7	5.4	3.6	7.8	6.7	2.2	6.2	12.5	9.3
Telecenter	1.6	0.0	0.4	1.2	0.7	0.1	1.1	1.3	0.5
Cybercafé	40.9	8.8	7.2	22.9	18.1	4.9	20.2	34.5	18.5
Other Location	1.7	0.2	1.5	0.7	0.4	1.2	0.2	0.8	2.2

The Table 6 data shows the Internet access location distribution for each group. The data clearly show an increase of the Internet use preferably at home in all groups. However, the Internet use at home is much higher for the advanced use group (75.6% in 2011) and intermediate group (67.8% in 2011) than the sporadic use group (54.9% in 2011). Table 6 also shows that Cybercafés are, in percentage terms, the second most important access location for this (underprivileged) last group.

Table 7. Internet Access Location by Internet user clusters (percentage)

	Advanced use			Intermediate use			Sporadic use		
	2007	2009	2011	2007	2009	2011	2007	2009	2011
Class AB	29.5	64.0	52.5	45.6	45.7	64.3	53.0	32.0	36.4
Class C	54.8	33.5	44.0	47.4	47.7	33.5	38.0	56.1	54.2
Class DE	15.8	2.5	3.5	7.0	6.5	2.2	9.0	11.8	9.4

Table 7 presents the Internet user groups in relation to the socioeconomic status of their members, showing that the three groups are composed mainly of class AB members (upper class) and class C (middle class). The proportion of Internet users in class DE (lower class), although small in all clusters, is greater in the Internet user group of sporadic use.

4.1   Use of Electronic Government Services

The paper's objective was to assess the survey' s respondents decision to use e-government services, based on their preferred Internet access location, mediated by their patterns of Internet usage patterns (use groups).

For this purpose binary logistic regression was used, yielding the odds ratios, that measure how much, maintaining the other conditions constant, each one of the explanatory variables increases the chance of occurrence (or probability) of the studied phenomenon (e-government usage). Tables 8, 9 and 10 show the odds ratio values (of statistically significant attributes at 95% of reliability) of different Internet access locations according to the probability of the individual belonging to each one of the analyzed Internet groups.

Table 8. Contribution of the Internet access location to the Advanced Internet user group

	C			DE		
	2007	2009	2011	2007	2009	2011
At Home and Work	0.43	3.34	2.24	0.28		
At someone else's home						
Cybercafé						
Telecenter						

Table 9. Contribution of the Internet access location to the intermediate Internet user group

	C			DE		
	2007	2009	2011	2007	2009	2011
At Home and Work	1.55		2.25			5.50
At someone else's home		0.51				
Cybercafé		0.48				
Telecenter		0.24				

Table 10. Contribution of the Internet access location to the sporadic Internet user group

	C			DE		
	2007	2009	2011	2007	2009	2011
At Home and Work	2.11	0.33	0.36	2.70	0.43	0.35
At someone else's home						
Cybercafé						
Telecenter			4.71			

The data in Tables 8, 9 and 10 show that the preferred Internet use at home or at work (individual access) has a positive impact on the chance of belonging to the Internet user group of Advanced and intermediate use. On the other hand, Table 10 showed that Internet use at home or at work implies the reduction in the probability of belonging to the Internet sporadic use group. Therefore, it demonstrates that the individual access (home or work) encourages the development of capabilities.

Table 11. Contribution of different Internet user groups to the decision of using e-gov services (odds ratio)

	C			DE		
Groups (Clusters)	2007	2009	2011	2007	2009	2011
Advanced Use	0.17	6.80	2.93	0.31	7.15	4.23
Intermediate Use	3.71	2.50	4.60	3.20	3.37	10.93
Sporadic Use	4	0.24	0.19		0.23	0.12

The data in Table 11 shows that belonging to the proposed Internet user groups (capability measure) positively impacts the use of electronic government services. Odds ratio values were much higher among the members of the intermediate and advanced use groups, respectively. The propensity to use the e-gov services was shown to be greater among the users of the intermediate use group, compared to the advanced Internet users. An analysis of the data in Tables 3 and 4 emphasizes that the main difference between these two groups is the use intensity of interactive and collaborative activities of leisure and entertainment (for example, on-line games, virtual environment). Therefore, such competence could benefit the use of e-gov services in the intermediate Internet user group. On the other hand, the data showed odds ratio lower than 1 for Internet users of sporadic use, indicating that belonging to this group implies the reduction in the potential use of e-gov services. In other words, the data emphasizes that the lower competence Internet users tend not to use e-gov services.

5   Conclusions

The objective of this research was to categorize the Brazilian Internet users according to the diversity of activities undertaken by these users on-line and assess the propensity of these Internet user groups to use e-gov services. The results of this research showed the formation of three different groups of Internet users, called (i) Advanced use, (ii) Intermediate use, and (iii) Sporadic use. The first group gathers the Internet users with most competence in Internet use, that is, those who make use of all or almost all analyzed Internet use patterns. The second group consists of Internet users that perform a lower number of activities on the Internet, but that are characterized by the most extensive use of interactive and collaborative activities of leisure and entertainment, such as participating in virtual reality environments and on-line games. Finally, the last group comprises the Internet users with a more mundane (sporadic) use of the Internet, limiting themselves to the performance of few activities on the Internet (when compared to the previous groups).

Regarding the propensity to use e-gov services, the results showed that the Internet users belonging to the advanced and intermediate use groups were more likely to use the e-gov services. On the other hand, the Internet users of the sporadic use group were less likely to use the e-gov services. These results strengthen the notion that the development of Internet use competence has a positive impact on the propensity to use e-gov services. The results also demonstrated that the Internet user group of intermediate use presented a higher tendency to use e-gov services than the Internet user group of advanced use. Such tendency is possibly related to the extensive use of interactive and collaborative activities of leisure and entertainment performed by this user.

In summary, the paper showed the users' preferences for internet access location and the capabilities that favor their use of e-government services.

These findings indicate the appropriateness of enacted public policies that have addressed internet access problems through varied initiatives: at the regulatory and fiscal levels, connectivity rates, especially mobile have dropped significantly due to increased competition among service providers (the creation of a state-owned nationwide broadband network, mandatory users' free mobility between providers), reduction on taxes on entry-level computers, tablets and communication services. There are large direct public investments in connectivity to schools, free wi-fi access in public spaces, with satellite connection being provided to remote rural areas (Amazon Region). Schools with increased connectivity are then able to promote computer literacy. More affordable access to devices and internet connection contributed to the widespread use of communication services, especially social network services, on mobiles (mostly smartphones but also tablets). As a response, e-gov services are increasingly being offered to social class D and E citizens for mobile devices.

References

1. Avgerou, C., Ganzaroli, A., Poulymenakou, A., Reinhard, N.: Interpreting the trustworthiness of government mediated by Information and Communication Technology: Lessons from electronic voting in Brazil. Information Technology for Development 15, 133–148 (2009)

2. Reinhard, N., Moya, R.W.: The Adoption of Electronic Filing For Individual Income Tax Returns In Brazilian. In: International Conference on E-Business (ICEB), Proceedings of ICEB 2012, Beijing (2002)
3. Lemos, R., Martini, P.: LAN Houses: A new wave of Digital Inclusion in Brazil. Information Technologies & International Development 6, 31–35 (2010)
4. Mori, C.K., Assumpção, R.O.: Brazilian Digital Inclusion Public Policy: achievements and challenges. The Journal of Community Informatics 3(3), 1–6 (2007)
5. Madon, S., Reinhard, N., Roode, D., Walsham, G.: Digital inclusion projects in developing countries: Processes of institutionalization. Information Technology for Development 15, 319–340 (2009)
6. Sen, A.K.: Development as freedom. Oxford University Press, Oxford (1999)
7. Araujo, M.H., Reinhard, N.: Factors Influencing the Use of Electronic Government Services in Brazil. In: Joint Proceedings of Ongoing Research of IFIP EGOV 2013 and IFIP ePart, IFIP EGOV 2013, pp. 140–149. Koblenz (2013)
8. Prendergast, R.: The concept of freedom and its relation to economic development – a critical appreciation of the work of Amartya Sen. Cambridge Journal of Economics 29(6), 1145–1170 (2005)
9. Robeyns, I.: The Capability Approach: a theoretical survey. Journal of Human Development 6(1), 93–117 (2002)
10. Reinhard, N.: The Challenges of Universal Access: Models and Management – an invitation research. In: CGI. Survey the Use of Information and Communication Technologies in Brazil 2005-2009, pp. 189–198. CGI, São Paulo (2010)
11. CGI. Survey on the use of Information and Communication Technologies in Brazil: ICT Households and Enterprises 2012. Brazilian Internet Steering Committee, Sao Paulo (2013)
12. Hair, J.F., Black, W.C., Babin, J.B., Anderson, R.E., Tatham, R.L.: Multivariate Data Analysis. Pearson Prentice Hall, New Jersey (2006)
13. Bartholomew, D., Steele, F., Moustaki, I., Galbraith, J.: The Analysis and Interpretation of Multivariate Data for Social Scientists. Chapman and Hall/CRC Press, London (2002)

A Decision Model for Data Sharing

Silja M. Eckartz, Wout J. Hofman, and Anne Fleur Van Veenstra

Dutch National Institute of Applied Science, Technical Science Department,
P.O. Box 5050, 2600 GB Delft, The Netherlands
{silja.eckartz,wout.hofman,anne_fleur.vanveenstra}@tno.nl

Abstract. Data-driven innovation has great potential for the development of innovative services that not only have economic value, but that help to address societal challenges. Many of these challenges can only be addressed by data sharing of public and privately owned data. These public-private data sharing collaborations require data governance rules. Data governance can address many barriers, for example by deploying a decision model to guide choices regarding data sharing resulting in interventions supported by a data sharing platform. Based on a literature review of data governance and three use cases for data sharing in the logistics sector, we have developed a data sharing decision model from the perspective of a data provider. The decision model addresses technical as well as ownership, privacy, and economical barriers to sharing publicly and privately owned data and subsequently proposes interventions to address these barriers. We found that the decision model is useful for identifying and addressing data sharing barriers as it is applicable to amongst others privacy and commercial sensitive data.

Keywords: Data Governance, Data-Driven Innovation, Public Service Innovation, Open Data, Decision Model.

1   Introduction

Data is often proclaimed to be the new oil – or the new gold – for innovation and economic growth [1]. 'Open' and 'big data' raise high expectations [2]. Open data is the provisioning of data by government organizations for free in a re-useable format [3]. Most literature takes a so-called push approach in which the data availability will contribute to public – and private sector – innovation [4]. A law such as the Freedom Of Information act in the United States, and expectations of economic growth and innovation [1] are drivers for open data. Open data aims for organizations to become more transparent and thereby accountable to citizens [5], to realize economic activity [6] or to increase organizational efficiency and effectiveness by better decisions [7]. Big data is the processing of large, (un)structured and real-time data sets for a wide variety of purposes, including the objectives of open data. Both developments are expected to not only create new economic activity, but also to contribute in addressing societal issues and challenges, such as a decrease of CO_2 emissions, or a decrease of the costs incurred for health services or social welfare. Jetzek et.al [8]

M. Janssen et al. (Eds.): EGOV 2014, LNCS 8653, pp. 253–264, 2014.
© IFIP International Federation for Information Processing 2014

have constructed and validated a model for value generation by open government data, where they have defined value from an economical and social perspective. According this model, open data has only a marginal impact on innovation.

Societal challenges can no longer be addressed by public organizations alone, they are often based on a combination of public and privately owned data. However, data sharing by private organizations may pose other challenges as those posed to public organizations [4] since private organizations have their competitive position to consider. Organizations often find the process of opening data cumbersome and many challenges and barriers occur [9]. To support the value creation with data, this paper develops, based on literature and practice, an approach to identify barriers to data sharing from the perspective of the public and the private sector, and proposes interventions to overcome these challenges and barriers.

Based on a literature review of data governance and open data, we first identify barriers to data sharing. These barriers are subsequently validated and potential interventions to overcome these barriers are identified by looking at three use cases from the logistics sector, using an interpretivist methodology [10]. Interpretivist research is "aimed at producing an understanding of the context of the information system, and the process whereby the information system influences and is influenced by the context" [11]. The use cases are investigated using on desk research and interviews with stakeholders.

In the next section, barriers to data sharing are identified from literature. Subsequently, we present three use cases of data sharing in the logistics sector that are used to validate the barriers and identify the barriers found in literature. Based on the literature and on these use cases, we present a decision model for data sharing. Subsequently, we discuss the model and present conclusions and recommendations for further research.

2   Literature Review

This section identifies and analyzes potential barriers to data sharing from literature on data governance and open data.

The management of data is of raising importance for many organizations given the growing supply of structured as well as unstructured data [12]. Data governance is an emerging discipline and comprises parts of IT governance [13]. Weill and Ross [14] distinguish IT governance and IT management where governance refers to the decisions that must be made to ensure effective management and use of IT and to whom these decisions are makes, and management involves the actual decision making and implementation. According to Thomas [15], "data needs to be governed as it has neither will nor intent of its own. Tools and people shape the data and tell it where to go. Therefore, data governance is the governance of people and technology." Data governance covers aspects such as data quality, data management, metadata management, access rights, decision rights, accountability, and data policies. [16] Data governance literature shows that barriers to data sharing differ when considering open data, which is a form of data sharing by public organizations with private organizations, and data sharing in between private organizations.

Literature on open data often takes a so-called push approach in which the data availability will contribute to public – and private sector – innovation [4]. From a data governance perspective, the most dominant open data barriers are found to focus on data quality. Data quality is specified in more detail by Batini et al. [17]. Domain-specific metadata describing the data origin, the data production date, data provenance, and for which applications the data can be used is of crucial importance. Data quality aspects that should be considered with respect to the entire data set are: accessibility, data format, semantics, conciseness, completeness, believability and reputation [18]. Data quality aspects that should be considered with respect to data elements are: validity, completeness, consistency, uniqueness, timeliness, accuracy and preciseness [19]. Other technical barriers to re-using open data are the publishing of data in a format that is not machine readable, the lack of an Application Programming Interface (API), difficulties to processing data sets, the lack of a linking or combining functionality, and difficulties in configuring data transformation [7,13,14].

Other authors take a broader perspective on open data. For example, Jetzek et al. [8] constructed and validated a model for value generation by open government data, where they have defined value from an economic and social perspective. Besides technical barriers, Zuiderwijk et al. [4], Janssen et al. [20], and Barry et al. [21] analyze potential barriers to publishing open data according to various perspectives: political, social, economic, institutional, operational, and legal. Political barriers include a lack of support, a lack of attention and a lack of knowledge about open data. Among the social barriers are a lack of interaction with users, difficulty to measure impact, cultural differences and risks and liability with respect to providing low data quality. The lack of business models is a main economic barrier to open data. Institutional barriers include a lack of standards, a lack of an open data policy, an inability to handle user requirements and a lack of guidelines. Data fragmentation, a lack of services, a lack of metadata, changing or a lack of clear semantics, and a lack of information on data quality are among the operational barriers. And the legal barriers include licensing, policy differences, lack of (detailed) policy.

In settings where data is shared with or between private organizations, most barriers to data sharing are related to privacy or to competition regarding economically sensitive data. While many authors mention privacy issues, not all of them explicitly elaborate on specific privacy problems [22]. Bizer et al. [23] elaborate the perspective of the user of data and especially the privacy issues related to combining several data sources. As long as data from several sources is viewed separately it might not involve any privacy issues but as soon as one data source is combined with another privacy threats might arise. In all settings it is important to have clear defined decision rights [14]. These are often defined by general IT governance and ownership structures. We further see that there is limited tool support and competing licenses for data sets.

Based on literature on data governance and open data we identify five main categories of barriers to data sharing: technical, data quality, ownership, privacy and economic. We consider barriers like political, institutional, and lack of or missing business models identified in open data literature as drivers to data sharing, which are a prerequisite for analyzing data sets. Our overall model addresses these conditions, but they will not be part of the proposed decision model. Technical barriers include barriers related to re-use and precision and recall of data and/or their source [24], which can be improved by metadata as an intervention. Data quality is addressed by aspects related to individual data as well as to datasets.. Data ownership regards the question of who is allowed to use and determine re-use of data and who has decision rights. Data privacy is not mentioned as a barrier in open data literature; we can only assume that it is addressed in specifying data policies, but it is mentioned in literature on data governance. Economic barriers include interventions like billing and invoicing of data usage and address liability, which also relates to data quality. Barriers in open data literature rank liability as a social risk, but one could also consider liability from a commercial perspective among businesses.

3 Logistics Use Cases

This section presents three use cases in the logistics sector to validate the identified barriers as well as identifying interventions for overcoming these barriers. Logistics is considered as an application area for data sharing, since it is a fairly complex environment with many Small and Medium sized Enterprises (SMEs) and a limited number of globally operating large enterprises. Each of these enterprises is autonomous, but has to adhere to international trade agreements that also address data sharing like the Rotterdam Rules [25] that specify a clear separation of concern between transport of cargo and activities like declarations and warehousing with commercial information. Furthermore, it is generally expected that data sharing can improve decision making [7] and contribute to efficiency and effectiveness of logistics [26]. In this particular dynamic environment, the use cases considered cover i) infrastructure data provided by Rijkswaterstaat, ii) data sharing between two container terminals that serve as hubs in logistics networks and have to process large amounts of data obeying the aforementioned Rotterdam Rules, and iii) the prediction of turnaround times at one container terminal in the Rotterdam port that has to be able to load and discharge vessels and at the same time the arrival and departure of containers by road. These environments are all data intensive environments with real time data requirements. The first use case about Rijkswaterstaat is based upon a detailed web-analysis done by two researchers independently. Input for use cases two and three has been collected during two in-depth interviews with stakeholders from the terminals. Given the complex and data intensive nature of the three use cases we believe that the most important barriers have been identified and argue that these use cases are sufficient for a first validation of our decision model. In-depth case studies are needed to strengthen our validation and further develop and validate Step 4 of the decision model.

3.1 Use Case 1: Infrastructure and Its Usage

Rijkswaterstaat (RWS) is a Dutch governmental organization that is part of the Department of Infrastructure and Environment (I&M), RWS is responsible for the design, construction, management and maintenance of the main infrastructure facilities, such as highways, water systems and waterways (www.rijkswaterstaat.nl/en/about_us/). The organization is publishing a number of data sets as open data, such as data sets of normal and current water heights and a map containing the location of objects for roads and waterways like lighting objects, painting on the surface of roads, traffic signs, locks, and bridges. The data is not only published on a map at the RWS website, but also available via the Dutch national open data portal. The map in which all this data is available is compatible with international standards of the Open Geospatial Consortium (OGC) for the exchange of geographical data.

As the organization is a public organization, they feel the obligation to publish its data. However, not all RWS data is available as open data. Roughly, the data held by the organization can be divided into static data specifying the infrastructure, which is updated yearly or a few times a year, and real-time data like traffic congestions and waiting times at locks and bridges. While most static data is published, not all real-time data sets are made available as open data. One reason is that some notifications are published as push messages (events) rather than raw data because of their urgency. It supports so-called data driven actions [27] required to improve decision making in situational awareness [7]. Also, some of the data is duplicated. Furthermore, the organization protects some data sets that contain personal data. One example is the real-time location of barges. Often, the barge operators live on their barges and therefore a barge is considered as a 'house' in terms of privacy laws. To protect the privacy of the barge operators, these data are only published anonymized.

3.2   Use Case 2: Sharing Data between Two Container Terminals

Lots of logistics operations occur between container terminals in the Netherlands, one for instance in the Rotterdam port and another functioning as inland port. However, little information is shared between these terminals. This use case examines the potential of information sharing for two terminals to improve their planning, be able to use the capacity of barges better and increase transshipment volumes at terminals. Shared data includes bookings, timetables, available capacity, and vessel or barge movements.

The analyzed data set includes privacy and potentially commercial sensitive information. While the location of inland barges is currently published as open data, the destination of these barges is not published. This information can be privacy sensitive as some inland shippers live on their vessels (see the previous use case). Thus, an intervention to filter out privacy sensitive information needs to be in place. Next to privacy issues, another challenge is commercial sensitivity. Sharing data on barge capacities could decreases transport prices leading to lower profits for barge operators. Sharing booking data could unveil commercial relations between logistic partners, which is considered sensitive from a competitive perspective. Intervention mechanisms are required in filtering commercial sensitive data and new business models are necessary for sharing capacity data. Thus, it is a challenge to find an economic model for sharing data between two terminals. Two options can be considered: i) a terminal sells its data to its partners and ii) the terminals make bilateral agreements about mutual data exchange. Such agreements should also include service level agreements (SLAs) about data quality and technical formats. The terminals should further specify who is liable for the data.

3.3   Use Case 3: Prediction of Turn around Times at Terminals Based on Open Data

Time and place (location) are important aspects of logistics. Waiting times decrease the profit of carriers, since transport capacity cannot be utilized during waiting. In this respect, there is a carrier demand for predictable turn around times at drop off or pickup locations like terminals. Currently, these locations are still a 'black box' which operation is determined by its internal processes and the large number of trucks arriving and departing at its location. In the case of a terminal in the Rotterdam port, this often results in a queue at its gate. Carriers could respond to the demand for more information about turnaround times at a terminal, by collecting and sharing information about the location, the average speed the destination and activities at that destination of their trucks. This information could help to determine turn around times at different locations in order to help i) carriers to improve their planning and ii) terminals to better manage container drop off and pickup. Information could be collected using the estimated time of arrival determined by the route planner systems used in most trucks. Other information could be provided by on board units used by truck drivers to report their activities.

Sharing this information involves i) privacy issues (information about location and destination could disclose commercial relations of a carrier), ii) economic investments and collaboration structure to set up a data sharing platform (a business model needs to be thought of, e.g. subscription) and iii) technical aspects like data formats and semantics, as currently no standard format is used to describe the location of a truck.

4   A Decision Model for Data Sharing

This section introduces a decision model for organizations to decide if they want to open their data, based on the literature review and the use cases. Firstly, the overall decision model is presented and secondly, individual aspects are described with potential interventions.

4.1   The Decision Model

We found both data governance and open data literature to address a decision structure, albeit in a different way. Decision rights in data governance literature address the decision structure and decision processes [14], while open data literature addresses data policies from different perspectives, e.g. political on international (for instance European Union perspective) and national level, and institutional, based on a decision structure that is taken for granted. Based on the insights gained from the literature review and use cases we structure the barriers to data sharing into a decision model (figure 1). It is structured into four steps: identification of the goal of data sharing (Step 1), identification of incentives for individual stakeholders (Step 2), identification of barriers, also referred to as constraints, to data sharing (Step 3) and the definition of the process to publish data (Step 4). Examples of goals (step 1) are for instance accountability to citizens and improved decisions (section 1). A business case and business model are examples of incentives for individual organizations (step 2). Our proposed decision model addresses detailed analysis of individual data sets (step 3), within the context of goals and incentives. This third step supports data analysis by five categories identified in literature: ownership, privacy, economic, data quality, and technical. Each of these categories contains detailed questions to support decisions regarding data sharing. The process to open date (Step 4) consists of a step-by-step guidelines covering technical aspects, such as data conversion, metadata requirements and URI strategies as well as organizational aspects around governance. A detailed description of this step is out of the scope of this paper.

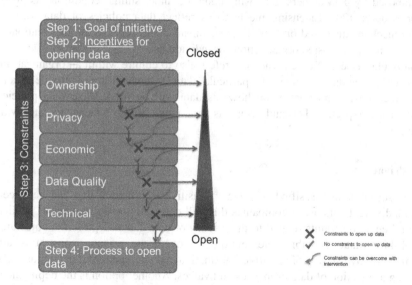

Fig. 1. Decision model for opening up data

The decision model works as follows. If a certain constraint to data sharing is present in a given situation, the next step is to analyze if the constraint can be overcome by an intervention. For example, when a privacy constraint occurs, anonymization by filtering or aggregation by combining a data set into a single record, are potential interventions. Interventions are usually of a technical nature, but also include organizational mechanisms. When no suitable intervention can be identified the data set cannot be shared. Hence the arrow shown on the right-hand side of figure 1. The next sections describe the five categories for analysis in more detail and introduce, where possible, interventions. The decision model should be applied both on a data set level as well as on individual data properties and even data values of a data set (see for instance [28]). It should be noted that the decision model that is presented in this section, often serves as an example rather than a definite set of issues that needs to be addressed. While the categories remain more or less the same, for every use case new issues can be added to the categories.

4.2 Ownership

Only the owner of the data can make a decision about whether to publish data or not. If more than one organization owns data, all involved organizations need to agree on opening up the data. If one or more of the data owners are negative about opening up the data one possible intervention would be to start a process that informs all skeptical data owners about the advantages of open data. Improving trust is another important intervention needed at this point in the process. Involvement and support from higher management is essential for improving trust and for establishing a culture that is positive about open data. Licensing could be an intervention describing particular rules imposed by data owners. Licensing could be under similar conditions as given for open source [29]. Licensing mechanisms reflect data policies of data owners. Security mechanisms based on identity mechanisms could serve as an intervention to share data only with trusted organizations or individuals.

A particular aspect of data ownership refers also to culture within an organization. In many cases, the data manager of a particular data set is unwilling to provide data to others, since he has no control on how his data will be used. Clear data policies (institutional perspective, [4]) and decisions structures [14] are a means to cater with these barriers.

4.3 Privacy

If a data set contains classified or privacy sensitive information that can be traced back to individual persons or companies this will constrain the data owner to publish the data. Legal constraints related to the privacy of data can also present a constraint to publishing data. Possible interventions to overcome privacy constraints are anonymization by filtering of sensitive information and aggregation of data, thus, only publishing a selection of data properties and values. Another option is the deployment of access control mechanisms combined with identity management that regulates data access. This intervention limits the openness of the data and is therefore especially applicable for company data with access restrictions and less for open data in general. In case interventions are not carried out successfully the data cannot be opened up.

4.4 Economic

Several elements related to the economic and business value aspects of a data set may hinder publication. Often data owners do not have a clear view on which data to publish as they are unaware of the potential of the different data sets. Since data is also considered to have a large economic value [1], data owners also expect to make profit with their data. It is difficult for individual data owners to assess the value of data sharing for collaboration (see the logistics cases). In the case that a data owner currently earns money by providing his data, this will constrain the publication of the data – at least openly. The data owner could consider sharing the data only among a few organizations, and assess if there are other ways to earn money with the data when it is published (even among a few organizations). This means that the data set may be opened up but is only available for a fee (Open data business model), which is one possible intervention. Monitoring, billing, and invoicing have to be supported as intervention mechanisms, potentially with different business models.

Economic sensitivity may constrain the data to be opened up. Economic sensitivity refers to the consequences for the business processes and even the business model of a company. Opening up commercial sensitive data, such as available transport capacity, may result in a decrease of the commercial rates offered by that company and thus its profitability. Yield management mechanisms need to be in place to ensure that companies do not experience negative financial consequences when opening up data but can benefit from improved insights in consumer behavior. Another constraint to open data may be that the actual costs of publishing the data might be too high for the data owner. Only if the business case for opening data is positive the data should actually be published. To address these economic constraints it could be considered, especially when multiple organizations collaborate in a network: i) to share the costs of opening up data, ii) to define a pricing structure for data set usage and iii) to set up a separate organization to govern and maintain the data and its usage. Each of these interventions requires monitoring functions of a data sharing platform.

4.5   Data Quality

A data provider is responsible for the quality of the data that is published. Poor data quality of a data set or a selection of data properties should prevent the data from being published. Data quality could also have impact on liability in case poor data leads to accidents, incidents or increased turn around times. A related issue is that data gathered in a specific context may not be useful in another context, even though the quality 'in itself' is good. If data quality is a constraint, one needs to dive into the data to analyze if the data quality can be improved on the constraining factors to still be able to open up the data. One example is to explore whether the data set can be extended with other data to improve completeness. If data quality is too low, or if the data is not applicable in any other situation, the data set should not be opened up. In any case metadata describing the data quality should be added [27], [14]. To allow for re-use of data by others, as much context information as possible about data should be provided. Furthermore, social interaction with the data should be supported: data is often most used and most easy to interpret when a community can be built around the data platform where the data is published. Data visualization can play an important role in this.

4.6   Technical

The technical format of a data set may be a constraint to open the data [30]. If the data is unstructured it may be difficult to convert it into a machine-readable format relevant to a data user. The size of the data set, the existence of a semantic model, and identifiers are other technical issues that need to be considered. For this group of issues, many interventions are possible. Examples include: offering the data in a structured format; reusing existing vocabularies and ontologies; publish the data according to existing data standards. Most technical interventions should be accompanied by an economic intervention.

5 Discussion

Based on barriers that organizations can apply on individual data sets, data properties, and data values, the decision model presented in the previous section provides a number of interventions. The decision model can be applied on individual data sets in the context of goals like economic growth or improved decisions (section 1) and incentives like a business case for an individual organization [4]. In the decision model, we have structured the issues in five categories that reflect a data owner's perspective, which encompasses the perspectives for open data [4]. As literature of open data considers only government data, the decision model for data sharing also considers decision structures [14], commercial sensitivity, and potential business models for data sharing amongst competitors derived from logistics use cases. The latter also refers to the institutional barrier of the inability to process data user demands, whereas in the private sector data is shared to the benefit of both a data provider and – user. Based on governance literature and the use cases, private and commercial sensitivity has been included in the decision model.

Different incentives may apply to individual organizations. On a high level, we found that a distinction can be made between legal and economic incentives. The legal incentives are centered around any regulatory measures that can be taken by the government to stimulate open data. Examples are compliance to safety or environmental regulations or compliance to directives regarding open data. The economic category includes incentives that lead to economic gains for the organizations that publish their data, such as efficiency gains, enlarging their customer base, or creating a competitive advantage. Reciprocity is another incentive as one organization is often more willing to publish data if this is matched by another organization opening their data. If neither economic nor legal incentives to publish data can be identified the process to open the data set is usually aborted as it is unlikely that a positive business case can be identified for data publication.

Analysis of data sets is not only to be done on the level of a data set, but particular data properties and data values need to be considered. It implies that data analysis requires a detailed knowledge of semantic models of a data set, including vocabularies. Analysis on a high level of detail is necessary as intervention mechanisms also have to deal with that level of detail, for instance by implementing access control at the level data properties and – values. Interventions that can be applied are for instance attribute based access control, but these require particular tool support for managing access control rules combined with identity management of partners. Although this complexity is not required in open (government) data, it will be required by the private sector and thus potentially impact public-private collaboration leading for instance to economic growth [1].

The decision model provides a number of intervention mechanisms. One intervention mechanism could potentially be used to address different barriers and an intervention mechanism can be viewed in the context of another mechanism. Security interventions can for instance be applied in the context of a data policy. An extensive mapping of interventions to barriers in different contexts needs more attention in future research.

6   Conclusion

This paper presents a decision model for sharing publicly or privately owned data based on both a literature review and three logistics use cases. The decision model contains details addressing individual barriers in each of the five categories identified. Since we have taken use cases for data sharing in the private sector, other barriers than the ones identified for open data are introduced in our decision model, e.g. commercial sensitivity. We have also introduced a number of interventions, whereas the implementation of these interventions in for instance a data sharing platform still needs to be elaborated. Our objective is to create Web based tools supporting the decision model, in which a data owner can select particular intervention mechanisms that are supported by, for instance, a data platform. Such tools need to cater with various details of data set analysis.

Data governance literature emphasizes the importance of a decision structure [14] for data sharing in the private sector, since goals and incentives need to be clear to all stakeholders. Goals can be formulated at a macro level, e.g. (inter)national or regional, and incentives need to be formulated at organizational level, e.g. by a clear business case or a data sharing strategy supported by management. These goals and incentives are drivers for analyzing data sets as formulated by our proposed decision model. Lack of a clear decision structure, an implicit decision structure, or lack of goals and incentives for individual organizations might be a barrier to the uptake of economic growth and innovation. Organizing data use for instance from a situational awareness perspective [7] could be the basis to stimulate data sharing.

A final finding is that organizations can apply the decision model, without making a distinction to whether the data will be publically available without any restrictions (open data), or whether data will be shared in a closed community. The model introduces interventions like restricted access based on authorization and access control rules. Thus, the model can be a basis for data driven innovation for open and big data in the context of goals and incentives.

References

[1] European Commission, Digital agenda: Turning government data into gold, European Commission, Brussels (2011)
[2] Manyika, J., et al.: Big data: the next frontier for innovatioin, competition, and productivity. McKinsey&Company (2011)
[3] Janssen, K.: The influence of the PSI directive on open government data: An overview of recent developments. Government Information Quarterly 28(4), 446–456 (2011)
[4] Jaeger, P., Bertot, J.: Transparancy and technological change: ensuring qeual and sustained public access to government information. Government Information Quarterly 27(4), 371–376 (2010)

[5] Harrison, T., Pardo, T., Cook, M.: Creating Open Government Ecosystems: a research and development agenda. Future Internet 4(4), 900–928 (2012)

[6] Endsley, M.R.: Toward a theory of situation awareness in dynamic systems. Human Factors: The Journal of the Human Factors and Ergonomics Society 37(1), 32–64 (1995)

[7] Zuiderwijk, A., Helbig, N., Gil-Garcia, J., Janssen, M.: Guest Editors' Introduction. Innovation through open data: a review of the state-of-the-art and an emerging research agenda. Journal of Theoretical and Applied Electronic Commerce Research 9(2) (2014)

[8] Jetzek, T., Avital, M., Bjørn-Andersen, N.: Generating Value from Open Government Data. In: The 34th International Conference on Information Systems, ICIS 2013 (2013)

[9] Janssen, M., Charalabidis, Y., Zuiderwijk, A.: Benefits, Adoption Barriers and Myths of Open data and Open government. Information Systems Management 29(4), 258–268 (2012)

[10] Klein, H., Myers, D.: A set of principles for conducting and evaluating interpretitive field studies in information systems. MIS Quarterly 23(1), 67–93 (1999)

[11] Walsham, G.: Doing interpretive research. European Journal on Information Systems 15(3), 320–330 (2006)

[12] Mingers, J.: Combining IS research methods: towards a pluralist methodology. Information System Research 12(3), 240–259 (2001)

[13] Janssen, M., Zuiderwijk, A.: Open data and transformational government. In: TGov Conference, London (2012)

[14] Barry, E., Bannister, F.: Barriers to open data release: a view from the top. In: 2013 EGPA Annuaul Conference, Edinburgh (2013)

[15] Weill, P., Ross, J.: IT Governance: how top performers manage IT decisions rights for superior results. Harvard Business School Press, Boston (2004)

[16] Weber, K., Otto, B., Osterle, H.: One size does not fit all - a contigency approach to data governance. Journal of Data and Information Quality (JDIQ) 1(1), 4 (2009)

[17] Batini, C., Scannapieco, M.: Data Quality: concepts. Springer, Heidelberg (2006)

[18] Knight, S., Burn, J.: Developing a framework for assessing information quality on the World Wide Web. Informing Science, 159–172 (2005)

[19] Nousak, P., Phelps, R.: A scorecard approach to improving data quality (January 1, 2002), http://www2.sas.com/proceedings/sugi27/p158-27.pdf (accessed March 14, 2014)

[20] McDonnell, Big Data Challenges and Opportunities (2011), http://spotfire.tibco.com/blog/?p=6793

[21] Bizer, C., et al.: Linked Data - The Story So Far (2011)

[22] Batini, C., Scannapieco, M.: Data quality: concepts, methodologies, and techniques. Springer, Heidelberg (2006)

[23] United Nations, Rotterdam Rules (2008), http://www.uncitral.org/pdf/english/texts/transport/rotterdam_rules (accessed 2012)

[24] Dalmolen, S., Cornelisse, E., Stoter, A., Hofman, W., Bastiaansen, H., Punter, M., Knoors, F.: Improving sustainability throuhg intelligent cargo and adaptive decision making. In: E-Freight 2012. Delft (2012)

[25] Esmeijer, J., Bakker, T., Munck, S.D.: Thriving and surviving in a data-driven society, TNO, Delft (2013)

[26] Hofman, W., Bastiaansen, H.: A global IT infrastructure improving container security by data completion. In: ECITL, Zaragoza, Spain (2013)

[27] Miller, P., Styles, R., Heath, T.: Open data commons, a license for open data. In: LODW 2008, Beijing (2008)

[28] Berners-Lee, T.: Linked Data - four rules (June 18, 2009), http://www.w3.org/DesignIssues/LinkedData

Policy, Process, People and Public Data

Ann-Sofie Hellberg

Örebro University, Informatics, Örebro, Sweden
ann-sofie.hellberg@oru.se

Abstract. The aim of this paper was to analyze an implementation of the public data agenda to address the lack of empirical research on the subject. The focus of the paper is on the interplay between policy, process and people. The approach was qualitative, interpretive research and data was gathered through interaction, interviews and observations over a period of 20 months. Findings showed that the policies are a bit opportunistic and that it is not clear what data that should be made available to attract citizens to take part in the agenda, raw data or processed data? Furthermore, the incentives for citizens to engage in the public data agenda were not obvious. I therefore wonder, do we believe too much in information? Are we being information determinists?

Keywords: Public Data, Open Government Data (OGD), Public Sector Information (PSI), E-government, T-government, Public Sector Reform.

1   Introduction

According to the Digital Agenda for Europe there are structural weaknesses in Europe's economy [1]. The primary goal today must therefore be to get Europe back on track and one way to do that is through making public data available for re-use. It has been estimated that by opening up public data overall savings could amount to €40 billion a year in the EU making public data a major asset [2]. However, public data is not just an economic asset, it is also expected to be a key driver in the promotion of transparency and accountability and the view is that opening up public data will foster the participation of citizens in political and social life. The expectations are huge, public data is seen as an unprecedented opportunity enabled by the use of new technologies that will "turn Europe's public data into a motor for innovation, growth and transparency" [2].

The public data agenda is persuasive. However, the history of government is replete with policy failures [3]. When it comes to new technology and new ideas, governments are not slow to catch on. Important to keep in mind is, nevertheless, that there is a huge difference between what is technologically possible and what is actually realistic if you look at the big picture. Technology changes faster than most everything else, for instance, the law, administrative power, culture, organizational structures, government structures, political arrangements, society and, last but not least, human behavior [3]. If we look at the faith in technology to contribute to public sector reform, this faith have existed for at least 50 years traced back to Leavitt and

M. Janssen et al. (Eds.): EGOV 2014, LNCS 8653, pp. 265–276, 2014.
© IFIP International Federation for Information Processing 2014

Whisler 1958 [4]. The big discussion about public sector reform that had to do with information and communication technologies (ICTs) was, however, initiated in the 1980s [5]. The goal of the reform was to decentralize the public sector as this was seen as a way to make it more flexible. It was also believed that ICTs could support this and use of ICTs became, consequently, intertwined with these objectives. The result was the rise of e-government, a generic term for research on the use of ICTs in the public sector [5].

The outcome of the reform was not the expected. Fragmentation increased as individual government agencies became accountable for their own activities and tasks. The result was, consequently, more organizational borders creating barriers to cooperation instead of making coordination easier [5]. Accordingly, the reform did not live up to the expectations. The wished for transformation is defined as "multi-level, multi-dimensional, and long-term organizational change, through the implementation of IT for reform purposes in order to achieve a situation that is qualitatively different than before" [5]. The promise of this transformation has been repeated over and over in the literature (for example, [6]) but there is no empirical evidence of it actually happening [3, 7-10]. To make it happen it has been considered important to see government and citizens as one decision-making entity, i.e. to get away from the view that government is a service provider and citizens are customers. Accordingly, citizens should take part in and guide the development [11].

The drive for transformation is the primary explanation to why initiatives such as the public data agenda are proposed. The active promotion of open government policies and open data was initiated around 2009 and has since then spread quickly [12]. Today, 63 countries are connected to the Open Government Partnership, an international platform for governments committed to become more open, accountable, and responsive to citizens [13]. The public data agenda is, consequently, fairly new and there is a lack of empirical research because of this. This knowledge gap has managerial and public policy implications [12]. One strategy proposed for working with the public data agenda is arranging open innovation competitions [2] and I study one such effort to address this lack. What I specifically direct attention to is the interplay between policy, process and people in this work. The public data agenda is expected to lead to transformation. For this to happen there is a need for a productive interaction between these three parts: policy to set the agenda and process to make data available and attract people to take part. Because policy without process and people is only visions, not reality, and process without people is only data made available. If data is not used there are no benefits. There is hence a need for understanding the interplay and the research question asked is consequently: "How do policy, process and people interact when implementing the public data agenda?"

2   The Three Interrelated Themes – Policy, Process, and People

In this section I address policy, process and people as three interrelated themes. With *policy* I refer to a statement of intent used to guide decisions to achieve desired goals. In this case the public data re-use vision, the expected benefits and identified challenges according to the report from the European Commission [2]. With *process* I refer to the actions performed to make public data available and the promotion of its re-use. With *people* I refer to the people involved in the described process and the re-users. Re-users could, for example, be citizens, businesses, media, etc. In this paper I focus on re-use by citizens because of the requirement that citizens should take part in and guide the development [11] and because citizens were the main target group in the studied case.

The aim of policies is to address particular problems. When new challenges arise changes are made to policies. Usually the changes are small and incremental but there can also be major changes when established systems are judged inadequate [14]. This is called policy change and is, according to many researchers, initiated by bottom-up approaches in some way [14-17]. Hajer [17] says that nowadays, policy making is as much a matter of citizens and enterprises acting as it is a matter of direct government intervention. Policy changes are, consequently, seldom controlled from the top; they are rather the result of informal actors (peoples) complex processes [15].

2.1   Policy

The drive for public sector reform is the primary explanation to why initiatives such as the public data agenda are proposed. According to the European Commission report *Open data - An engine for innovation, growth and transparent governance* there are many benefits of open public data re-use [2]. The major purpose of the EU 2020 strategy is to put Europe's economies onto a high and sustainable growth path. To this end, Europe will have to strengthen its innovative potential and use its resources in the best possible way. One of these resources is public data. Opening up public data will, according to the report, foster participation of citizens in political and social life. However, the existing regulatory tools and their implementation, the lack of awareness of administrations and businesses and the slow uptake of innovative technologies are holding back the development of a true market for the re-use of public data. What must be done is, therefore, to: "create the right framework conditions for the re-use of public sector information across the European Union, and to support the projects and infrastructures that can turn Europe's public data into a motor for innovation, growth and transparency". Since public data are produced at all levels of government, there is a need to act at all levels: local, regional, national, and EU level [2].

2.2   People

Today, more and more public data are made available [18-22] and there is a lot of talk about potential benefits. Expected benefits are, for instance, transparency, collaboration, participation, economic and social value [23] which will result from innovative service development [24]. This innovative service development should be performed by people seeing value in taking part in the agenda. However, according to existing research there is a need to entice people to participate. For instance, Lofi and Krestel [25] proposed combining information processing techniques with micro-blogging to increase transparency in political processes and to encourage internet users to participate. Furthermore, use of open data requires knowledge found in different communities, that is, across core stakeholder groups in the public data community [18]. The data needs to be interpreted and interpretation is always a function of a collective which makes it difficult for people to take part [18, 26]. Graves and Hendler [20] therefore claim that there is an important portion of the population who could benefit from the use of public data but are unable do so because they cannot perform the essential operations needed to collect, process, merge and make sense of the data. Public data can be powerful, plentiful, and relevant to citizens' concerns [24] but there is a need to extend knowledge on strategies to facilitate and attract businesses and citizens to participate, collaborate and re-use public data [27]. Jorge et al. [28] claim, for instance, that the way information is made available does not tend to promote citizens' independent analysis.

2.3   Process

Because of the difficulties of interpretation Cornford et al. [26] stated that the availability of public data solves nothing. Public data covers valuable information about our society [29], which has the potential to empower citizens and create a digital content industry if challenges are dealt with properly. One key challenge is, consequently, to make sense of the data [19, 20, 22, 26, 30]. Public data are frequently offered in heterogeneous formats missing clear semantics that clarify what the data describe [30]. To make it easier to understand the data, one proposed solution is visualization [19, 20].

Furthermore, another barrier to overcome is the challenge posed by public access to public data which is challenging due to the complexity of the public information ecosystem [29]. It is not stand alone information that is the focus of interest but information that is part of a whole in which different data sets needs to be linked and connected to other data sets and services. Many researchers are, thus, addressing the need for integration and linking [31-33]. Linking data is seen fruitful and good for promoting re-use and transparency [31].

Making public data available imposes new burdens on the public sector. Davis and Frank [34] reflect upon the circumstance that many datasets are constructed in the process of being opened. They are not pre-existing artifacts waiting to be transferred, which it can appear like when talking about public data. To convert from raw data to high quality linked data on a large scale requires resources that are not always available [35]. These new burdens are just additional burdens if making public data available does not lead to the desired benefits which are dependent on re-use. There is, hence, a need for understanding the whole process of making public data available, understandable, usable, and the consequences of doing so.

3   Research Approach

The research carried out was qualitative, interpretive research [36] in which the empirical material was gathered through interaction, interviews and observations. Kendall and Kendall [37] argues to work closely together with people in the field helps us understand a phenomenon in its context including its members (people), its interactions (processes), its purpose, how it manages to survive, and what good it does for society and individuals (which is related to policy goals). That is, a much needed holistic approach to information systems research. In order to understand human behavior we need to understand the social context where they occur [38]. The main data collection method for this paper was therefore observation through participation. I took part in the organization of an open innovation competition and also conducted interviews with the other organizers; the project leader and representatives from the municipality, County Administrative Board, and a local IT business. This made it possible to capture multiple perspectives. The participation consisted of 17 project events, the aim of which was initially to create the competition, thereafter to plan its implementation, and eventually to launch it. The interviews (n=7) were of narrative character [39] in which the interviewees were asked to narrate about their experiences of participating in the project and their work with promoting open public data. In average, the interviews lasted for about one hour each and they were recorded and transcribed. The participation material, in turn, were minutes from meetings, i.e. records of the happenings during the meeting and the decisions taken. The collection of empirical material started in April 2012 and lasted to December 2013, a period of 20 months.

After gathering of the empirical material, a "story" (see section 4) was developed from it, i.e. a description of the process taken place and the outcomes. The aim of the story was to capture and present the competition process in as much detail as possible. When developing the story different empirical materials were put together to capture the process. The step after the development of the story is to use it as a unit for analysis. This was done in the discussion part of this paper in which the story was reflected upon in relation to the policy documents and existing research. Regarding my interaction in the case, I was one of the initiators of the competition and I was actively involved in setting it up for the first time. However, once it was set up I stepped back and left the rest of the work to the other project members. So I did work in the domain in close collaboration as proposed by Kendall and Kendall [37] with more intense interaction during the first competition and less interaction during the second competition. During the second competition 2013, I was not involved in organizing the competition. However, I attended the Kick-off and Hackathon to observe and I took part in the jury work when the competition was completed to get insight into the outcome of it.

4   The Open Innovation Competition

The case studied is a local effort of making public data available and promoting its reuse. This case took place in Örebro, a Swedish municipality. Örebro has a population of approximately 140 000 citizens making it the 7th largest municipality in Sweden. Open public data is a relatively new phenomenon, but public access to government held information is not. In Sweden Freedom of Information laws have existed since 1766 to guarantee public access to government documents [41]. However, this municipality decided, recently, to include work with open data in their strategies on how to carry out the public work. The ambition is to create open data that is free and without limiting licenses to contribute to openness, transparency and easily accessible service. The belief is that this allows for the development of apps and external web solutions rooted in users' different needs [42].

The approach to promote re-use of public data was to arrange an open innovation competition. The initiative for the competition was taken in spring 2012 after an open data seminar held at the County Administrative Board. After the seminar I and a colleague arranged a meeting with a representative from the municipality who on a daily basis works with open data. Together, we decided to hold a competition to promote re-use of local public data. To create the competition a project group was needed. The next task was, thus, to find people interested in taking part. At the university I turned to the department working with external relations. This turned out fortunate as they, at the time, already was working with promoting open innovation. They became, consequently, very interested in the idea. Besides, also the County Administrative Board and a local IT business became involved. The competition was, consequently, a result of collaboration between the university, the municipality, the County Administrative Board and a local IT consultant business. We all had our own reasons for participating. My reason was to get input to my research, the representative from the municipality participated because the municipality had taken the strategic decision to work with open data, the County Administrative Board was involved because of their work with the Digital Agenda and the local IT business saw it as an opportunity to promote the own company and brand. The work was, however, voluntary. It was in line with regular work duties for most of us, but it was self-imposed.

The first competition was arranged in autumn 2012. The preparations for it consisted of 12 project meetings. Public data was provided by the university, by some of the municipalities in the county, and by the County Administrative Board. All municipalities (n=12) in the county were asked to contribute with open data. The task was to make five data sources available, sources considered relatively easy to publish. Four of the twelve municipalities succeeded with the task, one municipality published one data source, the others did not contribute. Regarding the selection of data we provided the contestants with maps, invoices, lists of schools, fishing waters, nursing homes, car and bicycle traffic flows, income support, grades in school, course evaluation data, visitor data to the largest municipality in the region and minutes from the city council for several of the municipalities in the region, etc.

To market the competition we used social media (Facebook, Twitter and LinkedIn) and a web page was set up. Besides, there was advertisement in the local newspaper as well as posters put up at the project members' work places and at the campus at the university. Also, e-mails were sent out through the Chamber of Commerce and Industry to all IT companies in the region. At the university we also talked to students, asked teachers to inform before class and we sent out information about the competition through the university's learning system. Also, a Kick-off and a Hackathon was arranged at the university.

In 2012 the competition was mainly promoted through social media, the web page, and advertising. The promotion was, thus, meant to reach out to a broad audience. With this we, however, did not succeed. At the Kick-off there were only a handful of people and none of the participants showed interest in the Hackathon. When the registration period expired we had few contestants which led to the decision to extend the registration period. This turned out to be counter-productive as it did not result in any new contestants, just the loss of some previously interested. The contestants could participate in two categories: a) by developing a completed service, or b) by sending in an idea to a service that could be developed in the future. In total, we received six contributions, four apps and two ideas. Some of these contributions were, however, the result of pressure, i.e. people was directly asked to contribute. In the project group we thought that the marketing that we had done would have been enough, but we were forced to learn the lesson that it is difficult to reach out with the public data agenda and that there is a need for even more marketing than the one we had done.

In autumn 2013 the competition was arranged again because the strategy was to make it an annual event. This year I was not involved in organizing the competition as I now wanted to be able to study the project without affecting the strategies. However, I attended the Kick-off and Hackathon to observe. I also took part in the jury work when the competition was already completed to get insights into the outcome of it. In 2013 the project group consisted of almost the same people as previous year. However, the representative from the County Administrative Board changed, and a representative from the Chamber of Commerce and Industry was added to the group. The strategy chosen, by project management, was to implement the competition so it could be coordinated with some other activities happening within the same period of time. The reason was that they wanted to make the competition visible to an existing audience, i.e. to boost from established events. The Hackathon, for instance, was this year held during the Global Entrepreneurship Week and the prize award ceremony was held at the national conference for the Digital Agenda.

When launching the competition 2013 there were some lessons learned and consequently also changes. One lesson was that the marketing needed to be more direct. One strategy chosen was therefore to turn to secondary schools in the region. The hope was that the pupils at secondary schools would be easier to reach out to if they could have the possibility to work with their contributions on school time. This was a hope by project management which they succeeded with; it was possible to make such an agreement with the teachers. The teachers thereby become intermediaries for the task as it now was their job to recruit pupils, i.e. contestants. This also meant a change in categories to compete in. In 2013 it was possible to compete in one of two categories; one for pupils and one for others. The idea class was, thus, removed. The reason was that it would be too many categories otherwise, and there was also a wish to get more services than in 2012.

Furthermore, more marketing was performed. For instance, there was an interview in the radio and presentation at two events arranged by the Chamber of Commerce and Industry etc. The outcome of the competition 2013 was a larger interest for the Kick-off. Nearly four times as many as 2012 attended the event (n=39) which indicates that the project management succeeded better this year with getting "the message" out. Two of the approached schools were present. Also the Hackathon attracted a larger audience. Present at the Hackathon were ten pupils from one of the schools and two teachers from the same school. The other school who attended the Kick-off was not present at the Hackathon because they did not manage to get the pupils interested. Furthermore, at the Hackathon were also people from several IT businesses, a representative from the Swedish transport agency, organizers of a local music festival, as well as project members. Also media attended both TV and radio. In total there were about 50 people present at the Hackathon who mingled with the contestants to see what they were doing. Of the people present, approximately a fifth was contestants, the others were people curious and with own motives. For instance, the organizers of the local music festival wanted to get hold of someone who could work with their webpage, a task they succeeded with. There was, hence, raised awareness about the competition this year but, sadly, there were not many more contestants. In the end, the outcome of the competition 2013 was four contributions, i.e. services. This can be compared to the six contributions 2012 (of which four were services, i.e. the same amount).

5   The Interplay Between Policy, Process and People

In 2012, when I started working with the competition I and the other project members thought, perhaps a bit naively, that people would be interested in taking part. My expectation was that there would be many contestants if we just organized the competition. This assumption turned, however, out to be problematic. To have the ability to take part there is first a need for knowledge on the subject. Not many have this, because in general people do not know what public data is. Secondly, there is a need for competence to understand and use the data. Existing research says that the way information is made available does not tend to make people committed [28], the data must be processed to attract people to take part [31, 33]. Some solutions proposed are, for instance, visualization [19, 20], linking and integration [31, 32], but the question is, who should do this? Should processing of the data be performed in the re-use process or is it a requirement for re-use?

Besides, taking part in re-use requires not only understanding the data, but also knowledge about public affairs and skills in service development etc. and the question is, is it realistic to have such demands on citizens? Not only should they be interested, they must also be skilled in many areas. Furthermore, another barrier is the lack of clear incentives. The incentives for developing services are to benefit from them somehow and these benefits come from people using the developed services. However, the public interest for the service that won the competition 2012 turned out to be small, only a handful of people have used it and the service that won 2013 could, unfortunately, not be fully developed to realize its true potential because of lack of data sources needed. This is a problem because if there is limited interest for the services there are no clear incentives for building them. The reason for the low interest is that the data is local and consequently the services and their audience too.

Our selection of data made available could, of course, be criticized but on municipal level public data is usually not that much more exiting. Existing research talk about linking different sources [31-33] and this could be a solution. But it is not clear who should do it. Hence, both the assumption of ability and willingness is problematic at local government level. Local data has limitations and this is one important aspect to bear in mind. In this case, re-use of public data did not come "automatically", in fact, it did not even come with the competition's prizes. In 2012 there was a cash prize of 20 000 SEK (approximately €2300), but since that did not motivate people this was changed in 2013. In 2013 the prize was instead to have the opportunity to create business connections. The prize was to take part in an agile project at an IT company, something that could potentially, in the future, lead to an employment. However, that did, apparently, not motivate enough either.

When policies (for example [2]) write about public data there seems to be an assumption of interest in re-use. In this case, it was not so. This is, according to the representative from the municipality, a problem because re-use is believed to be important to get others to cooperate:

> *"It's a chicken and egg situation. So you have to have some respect for it, it does not go in two weeks, it's a few years before getting this out, and before getting up re-use it is difficult to argue for open data internally in the organization."*

It is, consequently, not just an interplay, it is an "intermess" between policy, process and people in this agenda. It is not clear who should do what and where the borders of the process begin and end. Neither is it clear where the ideas and beliefs come from. Olsson [15] argues that policies are the result of informal actors' (peoples') complex processes. Consequently, on what grounds they are based is not obvious.

What is clear is, nevertheless, the expectation of transformation. This goal has, however, not been realized even though it has been a goal for many years now [4]. What is the difference now? Public data is expected to lead to increased transparency because of availability of information. The question then is, how much more available does it become if the interest for re-use is limited? Freedom of information laws have existed for long time [41] and made it possible to get hold of the information also previously if interested. So, if data is only published, does availability increase? Availability is dependent on some activity in which the data becomes easier to understand. To make something electronically available is not the same as making it understandable, comprehensible and usable. Availability is more than the act of publishing. Therefore, is it realistic to believe that making public data electronically available contributes to strengthening of the public sector? Maybe I say, but it comes down to what happens next and as previously said, this is difficult to predict.

6   Conclusions

The aim of this paper was to answer the question of: "How do policy, process and people interact when implementing the public data agenda?". The findings showed that:

- **Policies** seem to be a bit opportunistic. Transformation is an ambitious goal and according to the report from the European Commission resources must be used in the best possible way. The public data agenda is a good initiative but there seems to be an assumption that re-use will happen automatically. This case has, however, showed that this is not something that can be taken for granted.

- The borders of the **process** of making data accessible are blurry. It is not firmly established what data that should be made available to attract re-use, raw data or processed data. Accordingly, it is not clear where the process ends.

- A consequence of the above statement is that it is not clear who should do what. A belief is that citizens should re-use the data to make it understandable to others, but if they cannot understand the data themselves this is not realistic. Consequently, there is, probably, a limited group of **people** who can do this work and to make it further complicated, this case showed that their incentives for doing it are not obvious.

The findings in this paper address the research gap of empirical data on the public data agenda. The public data agenda is a good political end but as seen in this case, it can be questioned if it really is built on a realistic ground. According to the report from the European Commission there are societal challenges to solve and public data is presented as one solution. However, data is just ones and zeroes and I therefore wonder, do we believe too much in information? Many researchers have pointed out that there is a tendency for over-reliance in technology, i.e. technological determinism. Is this information determinism? Will we in the future, talk about this agenda as that? I have only studied one case and can therefore not answer such questions, but the case has shown that it is important to raise them. Accordingly, there is a need of more research.

References

1. European Commission, A Digital Agenda for Europe (2010),
   http://eur-lex.europa.eu/LexUriServ/LexUriServ.do?uri=com:
   2010:0245:fin:en:pdf
2. European Commission, Open data An engine for innovation, growth and transparent governance (2011),
   http://eur-lex.europa.eu/LexUriServ/LexUriServ.do?uri=
   COM:2011:0882:FIN:EN:PDF
3. Bannister, F., Connolly, R.: Forward to the past: Lessons for the future of e-government from the story so far. Information Polity 17(3), 211–226 (2012)
4. Leavitt, H., Whisler, T.L.: Management in the 1980s. Harvard Business Review 36, 41–48 (1958)
5. van Veenstra, A.F.E.: IT-induced Public sector Transformation. Boxpress (2012)
6. Irani, Z., Elliman, T., Jackson, P.: Electronic transformation of government in the UK: a research agenda. European Journal of Information Systems 16, 327–335 (2007)
7. Lips, M.: E-Government is dead: Long live Public Administration 2.0. Information Polity 17(3), 239–250 (2012)
8. Heeks, R., Bailur, S.: Analyzing e-government research: Perspectives, philosophies, theories, methods, and practice. Government Information Quarterly 24(2), 243–265 (2007)

9. Andersen, K.V., Henriksen, H.Z.: The first leg of e-government research: domains and application areas 1998-2003. International Journal of Electronic Government Research (IJEGR) 1(4), 26–44 (2005)

10. Grönlund, Å.: State of the art in e-Gov research: surveying conference publications. International Journal of Electronic Government Research 1(4), 1–25 (2005)

11. Heidelberger, C.A.: Citizens, Not Consumers. In: Weerakkody, V., Janssen, M., Dwivedi, Y. (eds.) Handbook of Research on ICT-Enabled Transformational Government: A Global Perspective (51-71). Information Science Reference, Hershey (2009)

12. Alanazi, J.M., Chatfield, A.T.: Sharing government-owned data with the public: A cross-country analysis of open data practice in the middle east. Paper presented at the 18th Americas Conference on Information Systems, AMCIS 2012, pp. 335–344 (2012)

13. Open Government Partnership, What is the Open Government Partnership (2014), http://www.opengovpartnership.org/

14. Mintrom, M., Norman, P.: Policy Entrepreneurship and Policy Change. Policy Studies Journal 37(4), 649–667 (2009)

15. Olsson, J.: The Power of the Inside Activist: Understanding Policy Change by Empowering the Advocacy Coalition Framework (ACF). Planning Theory and Practice 10(2), 167–187 (2009)

16. Sabatier, P.: Theories of the Policy Process. Westview Press, Boulder (2007)

17. Hajer, M.: Policy without polity? Policy analysis and the institutional void. Policy Sciences 36, 175–195 (2003)

18. Ojo, A., Janssen, M.: Aligning core stakeholders' perspectives and issues in the open government data community. In: Proceedings of the 14th Annual International Conference on Digital Government Research, pp. 293–294 (2013)

19. Artigas, F., Chun, S.: Visual analytics for open government data. In: Proceedings of the 14th Annual International Conference on Digital Government Research, pp. 298–299 (2013)

20. Graves, A., Hendler, J.: Visualization tools for open government data. In: Proceedings of the 14th Annual International Conference on Digital Government Research, pp. 136–145 (2013)

21. Wenzel, F., Köppl, D., Kießling, W.: Interactive toolbox for spatial-textual preference queries. In: Nascimento, M.A., Sellis, T., Cheng, R., Sander, J., Zheng, Y., Kriegel, H.-P., Renz, M., Sengstock, C. (eds.) SSTD 2013. LNCS, vol. 8098, pp. 462–466. Springer, Heidelberg (2013)

22. de Cesare, S., Foy, G., Partridge, C.: Re-engineering Data with 4D Ontologies and Graph Databases. In: Franch, X., Soffer, P. (eds.) CAiSE Workshops 2013. LNBIP, vol. 148, pp. 304–316. Springer, Heidelberg (2013)

23. Albano, C.S.: Open government data: a value chain model proposal. In: Proceedings of the 14th Annual International Conference on Digital Government Research, pp. 285–286 (2013)

24. Shadbolt, N., O'Hara, K.: Linked Data in Government. IEEE Internet Computing 17(4) (2013)

25. Lofi, C., Krestel, R.: iParticipate: Automatic tweet generation from local government data. In: Lee, S.-g., Peng, Z., Zhou, X., Moon, Y.-S., Unland, R., Yoo, J. (eds.) DASFAA 2012, Part II. LNCS, vol. 7239, pp. 295–298. Springer, Heidelberg (2012)

26. Cornford, J., Wilson, R., Baines, S., Richardson, R.: Local governance in the new information ecology: the challenge of building interpretative communities. Public Money & Management 33(3), 201–208 (2013)

27. Chan, C.M.: From Open Data to Open Innovation Strategies: Creating E-Services Using Open Government Data. In: 2013 46th Hawaii International Conference on System Sciences (HICSS), pp. 1890–1899 (2013)
28. Jorge, S., Sá, P.M., Lourenço, R.P.: Financial transparency in local administration's entities in portugal: Analysis of the information disclosed online. Revista Portuguesa De Estudos Regionais 31(1), 39–54 (2012)
29. Ding, L., Lebo, T., Erickson, J.S., DiFranzo, D., Williams, G.T., Li, X., Hendler, J.A.: TWC LOGD: A portal for linked open government data ecosystems. Web Semantics: Science, Services and Agents on the World Wide Web 9(3), 325–333 (2011)
30. Hoxha, J., Brahaj, A.: Open Government Data on the Web: A Semantic Approach. In: 2011 International Conference on Emerging Intelligent Data and Web Technologies (EIDWT), pp. 107–113 (2011)
31. Heise, A., Naumann, F.: Integrating open government data with Stratosphere for more transparency. Web Semantics: Science, Services and Agents on the World Wide Web 14, 45–56 (2012)
32. Kaschesky, M., Selmi, L.: Fusepool R5 linked data framework: concepts, methodologies, and tools for linked data. In: Proceedings of the 14th Annual International Conference on Digital Government Research, pp. 156–165 (2013)
33. Böhm, C., Freitag, M., Heise, A., Lehmann, C., Mascher, A., Naumann, F., Schmidt, M.: GovWILD: Integrating open government data for transparency. Paper presented at the WWW 2012 - Proceedings of the 21st Annual Conference on World Wide Web Companion, pp. 321–324 (2012)
34. Davies, T., Frank, M.: 'There's no such thing as raw data': exploring the socio-technical life of a government dataset. In: Proceedings of the 5th Annual ACM Web Science Conference, pp. 75–78 (2013)
35. Cyganiak, R., Maali, F., Peristeras, V.: Self-service linked government data with dcat and gridworks. In: Proceedings of the 6th International Conference on Semantic Systems, vol. (37) (2010)
36. Myers, M.D., Avison, D.: An introduction to qualitative research in information systems. Qualitative Research in Information Systems 4 (2002)
37. Kendall, J.E., Kendall, K.E.: Storytelling as a Qualitative Method for IS Research: Heralding the Heroic and Echoing the Mythic. Australasian Journal of Information Systems 17(2) (2012)
38. Moen, T.: Reflections on the narrative research approach. International Journal of Qualitative Methods 5(4) (2006)
39. Lindseth, A., Norberg, A.: A Phenomenological Hermeneutical Method for Researching Lived Experience. Scandinavic Journal of Caring Sciences 18, 145–153 (2004)
40. Creswell, J.W.: Qualitative inquiry & Research Design. Sage publications, Thousand Oaks (2007)
41. Government Offices of Sweden. Public Access to Information and Secrecy Act (2009), http://www.government.se/content/1/c6/13/13/97/aa5c1d4c.pdf
42. Örebro Municipalityyu78, Övergripande strategier och budget 2013 med plan för 2014-2015 (2012), http://www.orebro.se/download/18.245d51b813c84113b6e80002966/1392724512641/%C3%96vergripande+strategier+och+budget+2013+med+plan+f%C3%B6r+2014-2015.pdf

Is the Public Motivated to Engage in Open Data Innovation?

Gustaf Juell-Skielse[1], Anders Hjalmarsson[2], Paul Johannesson[1], and Daniel Rudmark[2]

[1] Department of Computer and Systems Sciences, Stockholm University
Stockholm, Sweden
{gjs,pajo}@dsv.su.se
[2] Viktoria Swedish ICT / University of Borås, Gothenburg, Sweden
{anders,daniel}@viktoria.se

Abstract. Governments aim to increase democracy by engaging the public in using open data to develop mobile apps and citizen services. They make information available (open data) and organize innovation contests to stimulate innovation with the goal to make new services available for the public to use. But will the public take on the challenge to both develop and provide services to each other? In this paper we use a case study from public transportation to investigate the motivation for individuals and teams to participate in innovation contests. The results show that the motivation for participating is primarily related to fun and enjoyment. We argue that in order to better meet the goals of open data innovation, governments need to follow through the full service innovation cycle and also care for making citizen coproduction in the execution and monitoring phases fun and enjoyable. Currently there is little chance for participants to make profit on a competitive market so governments need to provide other mechanisms to ensure service provisioning. For future research it is suggested to investigate how the later stages of open data innovation can be supported in order to meet the overall goals of open data innovation.

Keywords: Open data, citizen coproduction, innovation contest, motivation, e-service, mobile application.

1 Introduction

In their quest to strengthen democracy and to promote economic growth, governments strive to become more open, and since the 1980's the number of countries with freedom of information laws have increased more than fivefold [1]. Openness and transparency are viewed as fundamental to democratic participation as well as trust in government and prevention of corruption [2, 3].

In order to improve openness and transparency, governments are stimulating the provisioning and use of open data. For example, the European Commission has issued a directive on the re-use of public sector information [4]. In addition to strengthening democracy, open data is believed to be an untapped well of future prosperity [5]. Public administrations in Europe control large volumes of information collected by numerous public authorities and services. The outcome of the proper manipulation and

M. Janssen et al. (Eds.): EGOV 2014, LNCS 8653, pp. 277–288, 2014.
© IFIP International Federation for Information Processing 2014

management of this information is expected to enhance the EU economy with at least €40 billion each year [5].

But turning government information into value is not done overnight. First, data need to be made available and in formats easy to manipulate [37], and therefore public authorities are beginning to publish data[1] in open formats in conjunction with application protocol interfaces to support its manipulation by services. Second, services, such as mobile apps, that transform open data into value [6] need to be designed, executed and monitored according to the service lifecycle [7].

However, so far the competitive market has largely failed to generate revenues for the developers [8]. It is estimated that less than 0.01 % of all developers can expect a return on their investments by 2018, even for mobile services related to games and entertainment. Users have high expectations for what should be paid for, and today mobile services are rather used by companies to build brand recognition and product awareness than for making profit.

An alternative to the competitive market model is the collaborative production model where the public is engaged in service innovation [9, 10]. But while professionals in a competitive market are driven by financial incentives, the motivation for individuals to engage in collaborative production is most probably different. For example, earlier studies on software developers engaged in open source projects reveal that fun and enjoyment, alongside with user need and intellectual motivation, are the top drivers [11, 12].

To accelerate the development of new service ideas and prototypes, innovation contests, such as idea competitions and digital innovation contests, have become popular instruments [13, 14]. However, only a few of the service prototypes developed at innovation contests become viable digital services [15].

Although much has been written about citizen co-production in traditional areas such as neighborhood watches [16, 17], little is known about the motivation for citizens to engage in collaborative service development in a globally connected world [7]. Despite this lack of knowledge, governments are now embracing e-government visions on the assumption that the public will engage in such endeavors, se for example "A vision for public services" [18].

The question of interest in this paper is the motivation for the public to engage in innovation on open data. So far there is little scholarly work on why and how the public participate in collaborative production of digital services. We use a case study from public transportation to investigate the motivation for individuals and teams to participate in innovation contests. The result of the study is an increased understanding of the motivational factors triggering individuals to participate in collaborative production of digital public services. It also enhances the understanding on the requirements for how governments should organize the later stages of the service development cycle when relying on the public for its production.

The paper is organized in seven sections. Section two contains an extended background discussing key concepts followed by a case description in the third section. In

---

[1] See for example www.datacatalogues.org for publicly available data sources.

section four we describe the method and in section five the results are presented. Section six contains a discussion of the results and in section seven we conclude the paper and suggest areas for future research.

2   Innovation and Coproduction Using Open Data

Innovation has been described as a linear process of sequential events from research and idea generation to commercialization [19]. The linear process model has been challenged due to a lack of feedback loops [20]. The chain-linked innovation process model, presented by Kline [21], is a simultaneous model including elements such as research, invention, innovation, and production. Rothwell [22] argues that innovation also involves interaction both internally and with external parties such as customers and suppliers. This model has been furthered into open innovation [23], where organizations innovate with partners to share risks and rewards.

According to Linders [7], innovation of digital services can be described as a loop model including three phases: design, execution and monitoring. It is a simpler model than ITIL (Information Technology Infrastructure Library[2]), which has become the de facto standard for describing the digital service lifecycle [24]. ITIL is a linear model that consists of five sequential steps including strategy, design, transition, operation and continual improvement. The European Commission uses Linders' loop model in its vision for public services [18].

2.1   Coproduction of Digital Services

Through the emergence of the Internet and ubiquitous communications, coproduction may find new forms and increase dramatically [7]. Osimo et al. [9] call the coproduction of digital public services between citizens and public and private organizations *collaborative e-government* and defines it as "any public service that is electronically provided by government, citizens, NGOs, private companies and individual civil servants, in collaboration or not with government institutions, based on government or citizens-generated data" [9, p.14].

While studying third-party development, Linders [7] focuses on the relationship between citizens and governments in the coproduction of public services. He identifies three different types of coproduction: Citizen sourcing, Government as a platform and Do it yourself government. Citizen sourcing is where citizens produce for governments, government as a platform where governments produce for citizens, and do it yourself government where citizens produce for citizens. Linders [7] then classifies citizen co-production according to the three phases of the service innovation process, see Figure 1. However, he does not take into account other actors involved in coproduction, such as private companies and NGOs.

---

[2] ITIL is a registered trademark of the United Kingdom's Cabinet Office.

	Citizen sourcing (C2G)	Government as a platform (G2C)	Do it yourself government (C2C)
Design	Citizen consultation (e.g. eParticipation)	Informing and nudging (government using behaviour economics to design services that encourage the socially optimal option, e.g. through data mining)	Self-organisation (e.g. community portal)
Execution	Crowd-sourcing and co-delivery (trying to find a solution to a problem through the knowledge of the public or personalisation of services)	Ecosystem embedding (government agents becoming part of the community for example through openly sharing government knowledge, infrastructure and assets, e.g. government open sourcing)	Self-service (government expecting citizens to provide a public service themselves, whereby government may provide the facilitating framework, e.g. car-pooling is the 2nd largest commuter transportation system in the US)
Monitoring	Citizen reporting (e.g. FixMyStreet)	Open book government (proactive information dissemination, empowering citizens to hold their government to account, e.g. data.gov)	Self-monitoring (online citizen testimonials)

Fig. 1. Classification of citizen co-production. Based on [7, p. 449]

2.2   Understanding Third Party Developer Motivation

As third-party developers typically aren't paid up-front for their work [25] but instead pursue development in return for e.g. future potential income [26] or intrinsic rewards [27], it is important to understand the different motivations for this type of development [28].

Previous research has observed that such motivations can be surprisingly heterogeneous. As the importance of third-party software has skyrocketed in the last years, more entrepreneurially oriented developers are hoping to ship "blockbuster applications" [29]: by drawing on first-mover advantages (such as exploiting new technical affordances provided by device manufacturers and/or unoccupied niches in the service ecosystem) [29, 30], signaling partnership with market-leading firms [26] or accessing otherwise unattainable downstream capabilities through minor investments (e.g. by publishing applications in application marketplaces) [26, 29, 31] small and independent developers may reap substantial monetary rewards for their development work.

However, a large portion of third-party developer work is also undertaken without expected monetary compensation [27]. In third-party application development previous research have observed that e.g. learning a new technical platform [30, 31], improving existing services [32], the freedom of undertaking autonomous work [29, 30, 31] as well as the sheer enjoyment of programming [33, 27] as salient motivators for developers to freely engage in development of publically available services.

This wide array of motivation has implications for organizations governing open development efforts. E.g. Boudreau and Lakhani [28] argue that to attract actors with commercial interests, innovation is favored by market-like structures, where as more intrinsically motivated actors is best governed through communities. In sum, when organizations wants to tap into outside development capabilities, they need to 1) recognize the rich spectrum of motivations and 2) work to support these motives (whether it is financial turnover or catering for the disbursement of more "invisible wages" related to application development). One such way of tapping into these capabilities is to arrange digital innovations contests.

2.3 Digital Innovation Contests

Innovation literally means something new and original that breaks into a market or society. As such innovation is a process that always involves competition in some form. Over the years, a number of different types of contests have been discussed in order to control and organize innovation: idea competition [35], community based innovation [13, 36], online innovation contests [13], and digital innovation contests [14].

Piller and Walcher [35] state that the value with an idea competition is that the contest provides a mechanism by which users can transfer innovative ideas to firms and other organizations. Consequently, a core challenge of organizing an idea competition is to motivate users to provide innovative ideas, which the initiator of the contest then can transform to new services and products [35]. The concept of innovation contests is extended in Bullinger and Moeslein [13] when presenting the concept of online innovation contests, who distinguish ten key design elements when setting up idea competitions.

Füller et al [36] provide, through the concept of community based innovation, support for how to identify, access and interact with lead users in online communities in order to stimulate valuable input at different stages during the innovation process [36].

These concepts for controlling innovation does not take into account the possibilities that open data brings to an innovation process. "Open data is data that can be freely used, reused and redistributed by anyone – subject only, at most, to the requirement to attribute and share alike" [37]. This as they merely focus on idea generation for which open resources as data is not needed. Consequently, Bullinger and Moeslein [13] do not discuss the provision of open data as a design element when organizing innovation contests for that purpose.

Building on that lack of support, the concept of *digital innovation contest* was introduced in 2012. Digital innovation contest is defined as "an event in which third-party developers compete to design and implement the most firm and satisfying service prototype, for a specific purpose, based on open data" [14, p.2]. Events of this kind are based on the nature of an idea competition, however, they also stimulate and encourage third-party involvement in the making of the actual end result; not merely using end users to provide ideas and other input at different stages of the innovation process [35, 36]. Consequently, while idea generation is an important activity in a digital innovation contest, software design, implementation and testing as well as service operation and monitoring are also crucial activities that have to be performed [14].

3   Case Description

The case selected was the innovation contest Travelhack 2013 organized by SL, the public transportation organization of Stockholm, Samtrafiken, a service provider owned by transportation organizations in Sweden, and the research institute Viktoria Swedish ICT. The main objective for organizing the contest was to provide a platform for the best developers in Sweden to design and develop novel digital service prototypes that support travellers using public transportation, and by this increase the attractiveness of public transportation. The reasons for selecting the case was that the goals of the innovation contest resemble the overall goals of open government data, and that the organizers provided a catalogue of open traffic data[3] as well as promoted use of open data from other areas, for the participants to develop on[4]. The contest was held in the winter and spring of 2013 and spanned three months, divided into three phases: idea, preparation and final. Proposals on ideas were divided into three categories:

— Digital services that make public transportation trips more fun
— Digital services that make public transportation more efficient
— Digital services that make public transportation more accessible to everyone, especially passengers with cognitive disabilities.

A jury then evaluated the ideas based on four criteria: innovativeness, potential to make impact, technical feasibility, and usefulness. Out of a total of 58 proposals, 25 teams were invited to the final and 21 participated. The purpose of the final - which was organized as a 24-hour hackathon - was to have contestants finalize the prototypes, select winners, and promote the result to invited venture capital providers. During the final, the organizers and data providers supported the teams on-site together with business coaches to finalize their pitches to the expert jury.

The organizers had no intention to acquire any of the participant's services after the contest, and instead venture capital providers were invited to the final. However, no teams have so far managed to attract funding from the invited venture capitalists, however through other means of finance the development, one year after the contest, is ongoing in at least six of the teams.

4   Research Method

In this study the aim is to investigate the motivation for the public to engage in open data innovation. We selected a case study of public organizations arranging an innovation contest based on open data made available through an open data catalogue. The case corresponds well with the overall goals that governments have with open data, namely to 1) make government data available in open formats for services and mobile apps and 2) stimulate the development of services and mobile apps to create public

---

[3] Trafiklab.se.
[4] For example: Spotify, Oxify, Skype, Bing Maps, Windows 8, Windows Phone och Rebtel.

value. Hence we argue that the case is representative for service innovation on open government data, and the results and conclusions may be applicable to similar cases.

To collect data we developed a survey based on the motivation model developed by Bodreau and Lakhani [28]. We used a seven step Likert scale to measure the levels of motivation. A seven step Likert scale was chosen in favor of a five step Likert scale in order to receive better discrimination of the responses [38]

The survey was directed to the participants of Travelhack 2013. We received 39 responses from a total of 76 participants giving a response rate of a little more than 50 %, which is considered as satisfactory. To complement the survey, interviews with 20 of the 21 teams were conducted including questions about their intention to finalize their service and make it available to the public. The survey was conducted in conjunction with the final, and the team interviews were carried out during a period of 2-4 months after the final using telephone interviews and a prepared interview guide. These interviews were carried out with the team leaders who then represented the whole team.

5   Results

In total, 76 individuals organized in 21 teams participated in the final of Travelhack 2013. The final resulted in 21 service prototypes of which four were awarded prizes in different prize categories

5.1   Who Participated in the Contest?

The majority of participants, almost three fifths, were citizens with an interest in and ability to develop digital services. Two thirds of the citizens viewed themselves as being hackers while the remaining third of the citizens consisted of students, researchers, community teams and friends. Community teams are characterized by a shared interest in development. Almost a fifth of the participants were project teams representing companies and one fourth were start-up companies with the aim to generate business from the service. Start-ups represent a category of participants in between citizens and established companies. Start-ups are characterized by a shared intent among the team members to make business from the developed service and that the business is in its early stages of trading. The organizers of the contest had consciously aimed toward engaging participants from these categories in order to stimulate broad participants from different groups interested in building new services based on open data.

5.2   Motivation for Participating in the Contest

The motivation for individuals to participate in the innovation contest were primarily intrinsic where the top three triggers were fun and enjoyment, intellectual challenge and status and reputation, see Table 2. User need, an extrinsic type of motivation, scores fairly high while other extrinsic triggers related to money, reciprocity as well as signaling and career concerns score the lowest.

Table 1. Summary of results from the survey of motivational factors. Listed in order of popularity. Levels are measured in a Likert scale, where 7 is the highest score and 1 is the lowest.

Motivation	Avg.	Dev.	Type
Fun and Enjoyment	6,8	0,6	Intrinsic
Intellectual Challenge	6,3	1,2	Intrinsic
Status and Reputation	6,0	1,4	Intrinsic
User Need	5,8	1,6	Extrinsic
Professional and Personal Identity	5,5	1,8	Intrinsic
Autonomy	5,3	1,8	Intrinsic
Learning and Skills Development	4,9	2,0	Extrinsic
Money	4,9	1,8	Extrinsic
Reciprocity	4,7	1,9	Both
Signaling and Career Concerns	4,3	2,2	Extrinsic

Most of the motivational factors are self explanatory but professional and personal identity, reciprocity as well as signaling and career concerns might need some further explanation. Professional and personal identity refers to the intrinsic motivation of strengthening the view of the participant as a competent developer ("I *am* an iPhone developer"). Reciprocity denotes the sense of developing services for free but expect counter-services such as organizer recognition in return, and signaling and career concerns refers to participants' motivations to develop showcases for future employers or customers.

5.3   Following Up on Development Status

Four months after the final one third of the teams were still active developing their service, see Table 1. However, 83 % of the teams planned to develop their prototype into a working service. Out of these, 83 %, 60 % of the teams intended to finalize the service on their own while 40 % planned to do it in collaboration with others, either through direct collaboration or by selling the rights of the service to a third party.

Table 2. Development status and future plans for the teams participating in the final of Travelhack 13

Development status and plans	Percentage
Active development	33%
Plan to finalize the service	83%
- the team on its own	60%
- in collaboration with others	40%

6   Discussion

Given the results of this investigation, the main motivation for individuals to participate in development of public services is similar to the motivation for developers to participate in open source communities: fun and enjoyment alongside with intellectual challenge and status. Despite a significant number of participating teams from companies and start-ups, money scored low as motivational factor. One potential explanation for this can be that the teams were aware of the low chances of making profit on a market for public services. Although more than 80 % of the teams planned to finalize their service, only one third had actually 2-4 months after the contest continued the development. It is also possible that the organizers' decision not to acquire any of the services after the contest, and a lack of interest from venture capitalists, discouraged the teams continue developing. One exception is the winner of the innovation contest, *Resledaren*, who after the contest in a consortium consisting of the team in collaboration with the organizers won an application for innovation funding to push on the development of the service in to a market ready service. This visualizes a gap that must be bridged for teams in order to externally fund and continue the development. It also visualizes that additional competences (provided by the organizers) have to be engaged by a team in order to bridge the gap. In this case the organizers' experiences in writing proposals for funding were used to identify the available funding opportunity and create a bid that won the external funding.

Travelhack 13 is a good example of an innovation contest for open government data. The organizers have spent much effort in creating an attractive event and informing about it. However, the event only supported the first parts of the design phase of the service development life cycle. There was no support for the subsequent phases of finalizing the design, execution and monitoring from neither the organizers nor the venture capitalists. We argue that for collaborative production of public services to occur and for the public to engage in this production, public organizations need to establish mechanisms to support all phases of the service development life cycle. So far there are minimal chances for developers to make profit on open data services and mobile applications.

If governments are to engage the public in collaborative production, the motivation for individuals and different types of groups needs to be better understood and managed. In her seminal work on collective action, Ellinor Ostrom [17] points to a number of factors affecting how groups of individuals are prepared to manage a common good. E.g. clear rules and structures are required for how governments hand over responsibility to the public. Following the same strands of argument, we claim governments need to establish policies and mechanisms for the latter phases of the service development lifecycle. Arranging innovation contests is a good way of generating ideas and prototypes but it is not enough to tap the potential well of fortune that open data represents.

Innovation contests focus on developers. But maybe the successful collaborative production of public services needs to involve other actors and competences as well, actors that do not have the competence to develop services but to provide the services for the benefit of other citizens. Maybe there is a need to identify actors that have other motives than developers to engage in the execution and monitoring phases of the service development life cycle.

7   Conclusions and Future Research

The question at the center of this paper is the motivation for the public to engage in innovation on open data to strengthen democracy and enhance economy. We conclude that participants in innovation contests for open data primarily are motivated by fun and enjoyment and other intrinsic factors prior to the contest. Money and signaling and career concerns score low in our investigation as initial factors motivating the public to engage in open data contests. We also conclude that innovation contests like Travelhack 13 do not take into account the entire service lifecycle leaving participants on their own finalizing their digital services and finding ways to provide them to the public. Therefore, for future research we propose to increase the understanding of collaborative production of digital services and design and evaluate new mechanisms for supporting the later phases of digital service execution and monitoring.

References

1. Relly, J.E., Sabharwal, M.: Perceptions of transparency of government policymaking: A cross-national study. . Government Information Quarterly 26(1), 148–157 (2009)
2. Brito, J.: Hack, mash, & peer: Crowdsourcing government transparency. Columbia Science and Technology Law Review 9, 119–157 (2008)
3. Bertot, J.C., Jaeger, P.T., Grimes, J.M.: Using ICTs to create a culture of transparency: E-government and social media as openness and anti-corruption tools for societies. Government Information Quarterly 27(3), 264–271 (2010)
4. Janssen, K.: The influence of the PSI directive on open government data: An overview of recent developments. . Government Information Quarterly 28(4), 446–456 (2011)
5. European Commission, Open Data: An engine for innovation, growth and transparent governance. Communication 882, Brussels, Belgium (December 2011)
6. Jetzek, T., Avital, M., Bjørn-Andersen, N.: The Value of Open Government Data: A Strategic Analysis Framework. In: 2012 Pre-ICIS Workshop (2012)
7. Linders, D.: From e-government to we-government: Defining a typology for citizen co-production in the age of social media. . Government Information Quarterly 29(4), 446–454 (2012)
8. Dulaney, K.: Predicts 2014: Mobile and Wireless. Gartner Report (2013)
9. Osimo, D., Szkuta, K., Pizzicannella, R., Pujol, L., Zijstra, T., Mergel, I., Thomas, C., Wauters, P.: Study on collaborative production in e-government. SMART 2010-0075. European Commission (2012)
10. Boudreau, K.J., Lakhani, K.R.: How to manage outside innovation. Image (2012)
11. Lakhani, K.R., Wolf, R.G.: Why hackers do what they do: Understanding motivation and effort in free/open source software projects. Perspectives on free and open source software 1, 3–22 (2005)
12. Shah, S.K.: Motivation, governance, and the viability of hybrid forms in open source software development. Management Science 52(7), 1000–1014 (2006)
13. Bullinger, A.C., Moeslein, K.: Innovation Contests - Where are we? AMCIS 2010 Proceedings. Paper 28 (2010)
14. Hjalmarsson, A., Rudmark, D.: Designing digital innovation contests. In: Peffers, K., Rothenberger, M., Kuechler, B. (eds.) DESRIST 2012. LNCS, vol. 7286, pp. 9–27. Springer, Heidelberg (2012)

15. Hjalmarsson, A., Johannesson, P., Juell-Skielse, G., Rudmark, D.: Beyond innovation contests: A framework of barriers to open innovation of digital services (Forthcoming 2014)

16. Levine, C.H., Fisher, G.: Citizenship and service delivery: The promise of coproduction. Public Administration Review, 178–189 (1984)

17. Ostrom, E.: Governing the commons: The evolution of institutions for collective action. Cambridge University Press (1990)

18. European Commission, A vision for public services. Draft Version (June 13, 2013)

19. Booz, A., Hamilton: New products management for the 1980s. Booz, Allen and Hamilton Inc. (1982)

20. Kline, S.J., Rosenberg, N.: An overview of innovation. The Positive Sum Strategy: Harnessing Technology for Economic Growth 14, 640 (1986)

21. Kline, S.J.: Innovation is not a linear process. Research Management 28(4), 36–45 (1985)

22. Rothwell, R.: Successful industrial innovation: critical factors for the 1990s. R&D Management 22(3), 221–240 (1992)

23. Chesbrough, H.W.: Open innovation: The new imperative for creating and profiting from technology. Harvard Business Press (2003)

24. Hochstein, A., Zarnekow, R., Brenner, W.: ITIL as common practice reference model for IT service management: formal assessment and implications for practice. In: Proceedings of the IEEE International Conference on e-Technology, e-Commerce and e-Service, EEE 2005, pp. 704–710. IEEE (2005)

25. Ghazawneh, A., Henfridsson, O.: Balancing platform control and external contribution in third‑party development: the boundary resources model. Information Systems Journal 23(2) (2012)

26. Ceccagnoli, M., Forman, C., Huang, P., Wu, D.J.: Cocreation of Value in a Platform Ecosystem: The Case of Enterprise Software. MIS Quarterly 36(1), 263–290 (2012)

27. Boudreau, K.J., Jeppesen, L.B.: Unpaid Complementors and Platform Network Effects? Evidence from On-Line Multi-Player Games. SSRN eLibrary (2011),
http://ssrn.com/paper=1812084 (retrieved)

28. Boudreau, K.J., Lakhani, K.R.: How to manage outside innovation. MIT Sloan Management Review 50(4), 69–75 (2009)

29. Qiu, Y., Gopal, A., Hann, I.-H.: Synthesizing Professional and Market Logics: A Study of Independent iOS App Entrepreneurs. Presented at the ICIS (2011)

30. Bergvall-Kåreborn, B., Bjorn, M., Chincholle, D.: Motivational profiles of toolkit users – iPhone and Android developers. International Journal of Technology Marketing 6(1), 36–56 (2011)

31. Bergvall-Kåreborn, B., Howcroft, D.: Mobile Applications Development on Apple and Google Platforms. Communications of the Association for Information Systems 29(1), 30 (2011)

32. Rudmark, D., Arnestrand, E., Avital, M.: Crowdpushing: The Flipside of Crowdsourcing. In: Proceedings of the ECIS (2012)

33. Rudmark, D.: The Practices of Unpaid Third-Party Developers – Implications for API Design. In: Proceedings of the AMCIS (2013)

34. Rudmark, D.: The Practices of Unpaid Third-Party Developers – Implications for API Design. In: Proceedings of the AMCIS (2013),
http://aisel.aisnet.org/amcis2013/EndUserIS/
GeneralPresentations/3 (retrieved)

35. Piller, F.T., Walcher, D.: Toolkits for idea competitions: a novel method to integrate users in new product development. R&D Management 36, 307–318 (2006)

36. Füller, J., Bartl, M., Ernst, H., Mühlbacher, H.: Community based innovation: How to integrate members of virtual communities into new product development. Electronic Commerce Research 6(1), 57–73 (2006)
37. Open Knowledge Foundation. The Open Definition 28, 2014–2013 (March 28, 2014), http://www.opendefinition.org
38. Nunally, J.C., Bernstein, I.H.: Psychonometric theory. McGraw-Hill Publishers, New York (1994)

Dialectics and Contradictions in Public Procurement of Information Systems

Carl Erik Moe[1] and Maung Kyaw Sein[1,2]

[1] Department of Information Systems, University of Agder, Kristiansand, Norway
{Carl.E.Moe,Maung.K.Sein}@uia.no
[2] Luleå University of Technology, Luleå, Sweden

Abstract. Public procurement of Information Systems is a highly complex process. Not surprisingly, systems often fail to meet the needs for which they were procured. One of the main causes of this is the contradictions between goals of different stakeholders. Identifying and understanding these conflicts and contradictions are essential to develop strategies to improve the procurement process. In this paper, we present a case study where we examined the procurement process of a system carried out by a public entity in Norway. Using dialectic theory and stakeholder theory as interpreting lenses, we identified a number of conflicts and contradictions. Some of the contradictions resulted from conflicting and divergent goals of the various stakeholders across groups but also within groups, while others resulted from differing goals of policies and regulations.

Keywords: Public procurement of IS, Dialectics, Stakeholder theory.

1 Introduction

Procurement has become the most common way of acquiring information systems (IS), especially in the public sector. However, this is a highly complex process [1]. There are numerous instances of failed procurement projects (e.g. the GOLF-project in Norway). One of the main causes of this is conflicting goals. These goal conflicts may be due to incompatible political goals, such as ensuring open and fair competition versus preference for local vendors, or they can be due to conflict between short-term and long term goals of the projects. Such projects also involve a variety of stakeholder groups who have diverse and often conflicting interests which adds to the existing conflicts. To develop appropriate strategies to deal with conflicting goals we first need to identify them.

Two streams in the literature have examined these issues. One stream has examined the conflicts and contradictions that surface in IS projects in general [2-4] and in the public sector in particular [1, 5]. The theoretical premise of several of these studies has been dialectics [4, 6-8]. The other stream has focused on stakeholders and how differing interests lead to contradictions and often conflicts in IS projects in general [3, 9] and in eGovernment in particular [10-12]. While each

M. Janssen et al. (Eds.): EGOV 2014, LNCS 8653, pp. 289–300, 2014.

stream has produced valuable insights, they only address part of the problem: either the nature of the conflicts or the interests of the stakeholders. Only a few studies have used both perspectives to provide a more complete picture (e.g. [13]).

We propose that combining dialectical theory with stakeholder theory provides us with a sharper theoretical lens to understand the conflicts and contradictions that arise in a public IS project, especially in public procurement. A better understanding of this process can lead to better strategies to cope with challenges. To examine our proposition, we conducted a case study of the procurement of an EHR system (Electronic Health Record) in Norway and interpreted the data using concepts from dialectics and stakeholder theories. We unearthed a number of contradictions that underlay the procurement process and identified the role of various stakeholders in these contradictions.

The rest of the paper is organized as follows: In the next section, we discuss some of the conflicting goals in public procurement. We then briefly describe the two theoretical perspectives, namely, dialectics and stakeholder theories. Next, we describe our case and our data analysis, and then present our findings. We conclude the paper by discussing our findings in relation to existing literature and suggest areas for future research.

2   Conflicting Goals in Public Procurement

Public procurement is regulated in most countries and thus differs from private procurement. The European Union (EU) applies two public procurement directives with the underlying principles of transparency and non-discriminatory competition [14, 15]. All public procurements above a threshold value of 200 000 € (for 2014) should be announced as a call in EU's tender electronic database (TED). Some countries have additional national threshold levels; which requires calls to be announced in the national database.

A public entity may face a number of dilemmas or conflicting goals in a procurement process. Among these is the dilemma between the principle of equal opportunities for all competitors and preferences for a specific software vendor, or for local vendors. Many states in the US have criteria related to promoting the efforts of small businesses, women, and minorities when choosing contractors [16]. Dilemmas exist between creating requirements specifications up front or developing the system specification as an integral part of the procurement process [5]. The latter option allows for greater learning from the vendors. These dilemmas are further complicated when stakeholders have different and often conflicting interests. This challenge may be tougher in the public sector than in the private sector, as organizations that are subject to political controls are more likely to face multiple sources of authority that are potentially conflicting [17]. In public procurement, we can expect contradicting interests between vendors and procuring entities. While procurement managers and CIOs want a clear, complete and detailed picture of requirements, vendors find requirement specifications too detailed and extensive [18]. Vendors are often left with the task (and the power) of providing the answers as to whether their software meet the functionality requirements. This can create a challenge for the procuring entities. Moreover, different user groups may have different goals [9] which often leads to compromises on software functionality and application of power to overcome user resistence [3]. It is often extremely difficult for all stakeholders to agree on the objectives for a new system (Swanson 1988, in [19], p. 11). The sheer variety of stakeholders make public procurement of IS a highly complex process. Figure 1 depicts this complexity.

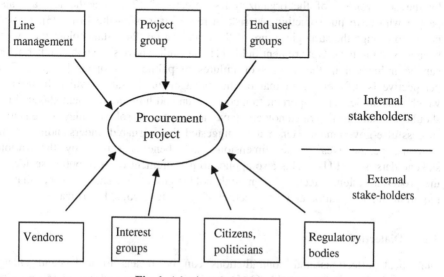

Fig. 1. A basic stakeholder model

It is a misconception that stakeholder theory advocates equal treatment of all stakeholders [20]. An organizational entity may have several conflicting goals or interest groups competing for priority [21]. Oppositions may be external to the organizational entity Vendors have their obvious interest of doing business, and this interest may not align with the internal stakeholders.   Interest groups, such as chambers of commerce may try to influence a municipality to procure from vendors in the region. Elected politicians may have a say as representatives for the citizens. Lastly regulatory bodies enforce regulations.

In practice a procurement project may have an even more complex stakeholder map than shown in figure 1. End user groups may not be homogeneous but may have different interests. Even members in the project group may have conflicting interests. Line management may have different interests, depending on the functional area they represent. Further, stakeholders' relative preferences may vary over time [4]. Public procurement can be a rather long process, hence a stakeholder group such as end users can´t be expected to sustain the same interest in a procurement all through a project.

3   Theoretical Premises

To understand the complexity of the public procurement process discussed above, we draw upon two theoretical premises, stakeholder theories and dialectics.

3.1   Stakeholder Theory

A stakeholder can be defined as "any group or individual who can affect or is affected by the achievement of the organization's objectives" [22]. Stakeholders are also people who have put something at risk in relationship with the firm [23], or with power to change the strategic future of the organization [24]. Stakeholder theory has been adopted in the e-Government field [11] and studies have shown that stakeholders can be influential in the success or failures of public IS projects [10, 25]. This perspective is different from that of the management literature which focuses on which stakeholders are important to a corporation and how these salient stakeholders should be managed.   Stakeholders have a significant role to play in ensuring successful e-government. Hence it is suggested that a shared understanding of the interests, perspectives, value dimensions, and benefits sought by the various stakeholders is vital [12]. This also applies to procurement of IS in public sector. As the procured system affects different stakeholder groups, we should expect that the requirement specification and the selection of the system would be critical.

3.2   Dialectics

Dialectical reflections and contradictions can be means to understand change processes in IS development [2, 6]. Contradictions can be understood as opposites (thesis and anti-thesis), but not necessarily conflicts. In dialectics theory, stability and change is explained by reference to the balance of power between the opposing entities [21]. The opposing entities may be between different commitments for one group, or between different stakeholder groups with contradicting goals (e.g. nurses involved in a project and other nurses not involved).

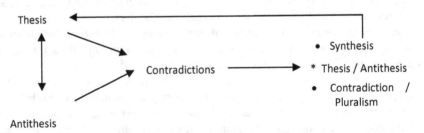

Fig. 2. Dialectical process lens (adapted from [21])

The dialectic process (Fig. 2) can result in three possible outcomes: (a) synthesis which is a negotiated compromise between the thesis and the anti-thesis (b) the thesis or the anti-thesis prevails, or (c) no resolution; the thesis and the anti-thesis remain in a state of pluralism or conflict. A synthesis may in turn lead to a contradicting antithesis which may set off another dialectical process.

Dialectical approach has been suggested for studying IS implementation which is conceived as a complex intertwined set of social and political interactions [19]. Dialectics has been applied to analyze learning [7] and misalignments in ERP implementation [8]. We therefore found dialectics useful in our study.

3.3   Summary

In this section, we put forward two theoretical premises that we argue can be relevant to understand the complex public procurement process. While stakeholder theory and dialectics has been previously applied in combination in analysis of e-government cooperation [13], and enterprise implementation [7, 8], to our knowledge it has not been used in examining public procurement. In our study we attempt to demonstrate how combining the two analytical lenses can provide a better understanding of public procurement of information systems. We describe the case next.

4   Case Study

Our case site was a Norwegian municipality with a population of approximately 40.000. The procurement was part of a larger project to comply with a directive of the Norwegian government which required message exchange of electronic health records (EHR) between all municipalities and public hospitals. A project group called "Message Exchange Group" was set up to determine how to comply with the directive. The group soon discovered that their present vendor could not add the message exchange functionality to the existing system. Consequently, the municipality established a new project group to procure an EHR system that included some members of the "Message Exchange group".

4.1   Case Narrative

In keeping with the usual practice in the municipality, the procurement project group consulted an inter-municipal procurement consulting entity and invited other municipalities in the regional network of municipalities to join the process. One smaller municipality decided to take part; however the process was led by the bigger municipality. The two municipalities applied tenders with negotiations as the procedure for this case.

Figure 3 depicts the timeline of the procurement process. As can be seen; the project commenced in April 2012. The municipality announced the upcoming tender and invited vendors to submit documentation for pre-qualification on issues such as financial capabilities and technical competencies. In parallel the project group finalized the requirement specifications, so they could invite vendors to submit offers. To do so, it borrowed a requirement specification from a neighboring municipality that had been through the same process less than 2 years before. The project group visited three neighboring municipalities that had used systems from three major EHR-vendors, to get insights to develop the specifications further. It also held a brainstorming session with a reference group of 16 super users to get further input.

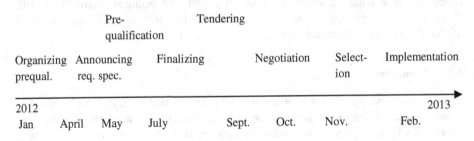

Fig. 3. Timeline of the procurement process showing the different stages

At the pre-qualification stage, three vendors expressed an interest in participating. We started our data collection with observation in the meeting where the project group opened the papers the vendors had submitted to establish their credentials. All three were found qualified and they were invited to submit offers. All of them did within the deadline, and were invited to take part in the negotiations.

The negotiations were carried out primarily through three day-long meetings with each vendor on scheduled issues. Each vendor got the same information prior to the meetings, and was given exactly a week between each meeting. The first meeting was meant to check whether there was a common understanding of the requirements and the software. The project group discovered that all vendors to some extent had ticked off incorrectly on whether their software met a requirement or not. Price and contract issues were on the agenda for the second meeting. In this meeting one of the vendors was told within minutes that they had to rewrite the contract terms and were sent home after approximately an hour. They submitted a new contract and were allowed to take part in the following negotiations.

In the third meeting the vendors were asked to demonstrate how the software could be applied in an assigned task. A group of super users was invited to this meeting, where they posed questions to the vendors on matters that concerned them. The procurement group leader led the session and ensured that the users did not focus on marginal issues. The project group also collected the opinions of the super users after the demonstration. After this round the project group carried on a short round of negotiation over telephone with two vendors before selecting the final winner.

4.2   Data Collection

We collected data through 15 interviews and observation in 7 project meetings. There were 10 telephone (Skype) interviews that lasted for 10 – 45 minutes and 6 face-to-face interviews that lasted for 60 – 75 minutes. We interviewed the project managers twice, 4 of the super users of the new system, the super user of the old system (who also was in the project group), one additional member of the project group, the procurement managers involved, and sales manager at the winning vendor. The meetings included 3 negotiation meetings with vendors and lasted for 2 – 7 hours. We also got access to memos from some of the meetings. We recorded all interviews and project meetings and later transcribed them. In our data analysis, we applied a hermeneutic circle [26] approach. We identified key stakeholders and their interests.

5   Findings

We began our analysis by identifying the various goals in the project and the stakeholders who were associated with these goals. Table1 summarizes our findings.

Table 1. Goals observed in the projects

Goal	Description	Evidence	Associated stakeholder(s)
1	Conduct a formally correct procedure	Extensive use of procurement consultants; careful organizing of the negotiation process.	Project group and procurement consultant
2	Select the system that meets their needs best	Considerable time spent by the project team on requirements specification; ranking vendors based on meeting specifications.	Project group, end users
3	Select a vendor within the deadlines	The project had tight deadlines, and the negotiations with the vendors were done over a 3 week intense period.	Project group
4	Implement message exchange	Government requirement; the requirement specification	Project managers, government
5	Acceptable contract terms	One of the vendors nearly disqualified as their contract terms not found acceptable	Project group
6	Avoid complaints	Project manager: *"If we disqualified them based on those criteria, they could have complained on the process"*	Procurement consultant
7	Keeping the old system	One stakeholder wanted to postpone procurement of the new system while waiting for new national requirements.	System owner of the old system, (s)he was a member of the project group
8	Migration of data from the old system	Note handed out in meeting; quotes from both project managers	System owner of both the old and the new system were members of the project group

We then used these goals and our interview data to conduct our dialectics based analysis to unearth the contradictions that existed in the project. We unearthed 4 contradictions which we describe next.

Contradiction 1: "Following regulations vs. satisfying system needs"

Thesis: The thesis arose from goal 1 (Conduct a formally correct procedure), and from goal 6 (avoid complaints). Right from the start, care was taken to ensure that procedures were followed strictly. The procurement consultant led the first few meetings of the project group, and gave the members precise instructions on how to run the process, e.g. the length of deadlines, the need to give the vendors equal access to information, and equal time to prepare in between negotiation meetings. He told them: *"We have to document that we do the procurement properly ...."*

Antithesis: The antithesis arose from goal 2 (Select the system that meets their needs best). In the brainstorming sessions, the reference group of users was e asked to "say something about what could be better in a new system", and "what we wanted as part of a new system", according to one of the members of the reference group. The group was further invited to take part in visits to municipalities that used software from the three main vendors. The project group spent a great deal of time and resources getting the requirement specification right.

Resolution: The thesis won. The project group went to great lengths to ensure that regulations were not violated. For example, to avoid complaints, it kept in one vendor who they considered for disqualification. The winning vendor essentially confirmed it thus: *"They are so afraid of doing mistakes, so a normal dialogue is not possible. You do not get a good solution. It`s all about fulfilling the requirement specification".*

Contradiction 2: "Change vs. persistence"

Thesis: The thesis arose from goal 4 (Implement message exchange). This was a government requirement. The project plan stated: "The goal of the project is to implement electronic messages between internal cooperating entities as well as to external collaborating partners", and it was clearly stated in the requirement specification.

Antithesis: The antithesis had its base in goal 7 (Keeping the old system). At the start it was not clear that the municipality needed to procure a new system to implement message exchange, but the understanding gradually evolved for the project leaders. However, not all group members shared this view. The project leaders were aware of this. According to the "Message Exchange project" leader: *"there was not agreement in the project group (on the need for procurement) ... one person knows the old system very well and it is probably a bit sad to replace such a system"*. . The procurement project leader conveyed the same story: *"nn (the system owner of the old system) suggested postponing it (the procurement) for a couple of years because of upcoming national requirements for a core record, and the risk of betting on the wrong horse"*. A quote from one of the members in the reference group goes the same way: "*I think we still do not understand what it means to lose some of the functionality we have in our current system*".

Resolution: The thesis won, the project was carried out according to plans, and the system was procured and installed according to the deadline.

Contradiction 3: "Revolutionary change vs. incremental change"

Thesis: The thesis arose from the implied goal of starting the new system from a clean slate. It required creating a new database with the old data being moved to an archive. The project leader and some members of the project group had the opinion that a part of the old data could be "garbage" and thus the new system could end up with dirty and unreliable data.

Antithesis: The antithesis arose from goal 8 (Migrate data from the old system). The owner of the old system (and the owner of the new system) wanted to migrate data from the old system and then do the needed conversion to the format of the new system. They argued that it would save a considerable amount of work. This led to very heated discussions with the proponents of a "clean slate" start for the new system. The question was not settled until after the contract was signed with the winning vendor. The project leader said: "*It (the disagreement on migration) has taken a lot of energy, … issues that were not decided …. focus remains there instead of on other issues that should have been discussed*".

Resolution: The result was a synthesis. The strategy was to postpone the decision till after signing the contract and basing it on the vendor´s recommendation. Some of the data from the old system was converted, but not to the extent suggested.

Contradiction 4: "Implementation as primarily technical vs. implementation as socio-technical change"

Thesis: The thesis was evident from the way the procurement project group scheduled activities such as training, without focusing on possible organizational changes or changes in work process. The procurement project leader said as an afterthought (after the installation), :"*we could have been better at describing our processes up front….. now it comes as are about to start the training*", implying that the software could have been "tailored" better.

Antithesis: The antithesis originated from one of the users who represented a unit that had specific interests. That unit took care of booking of different services such as home care and the existing system was vital to him and his group. He expressed serious concerns prior to the final selection as to whether the project group understood all the challenges: "*I feel that nobody on the management side has supervised us properly so that we understand the magnitude of the transition in changing system ….. ……..."The biggest challenges are coming, and they are related to us getting a new system …. It is a form of organizational change, quite a radical one, and I don`t think we properly understand this….*".

Resolution: The thesis won. After the implementation the project leader told us that they had really not understood this user and his unit´s needs: *"I don´t think one understands that changing a large system can have such large effects for some employees"* *"We have not understood well enough"*. *"The nn unit is suffering now"*. *"This "hit" us the other day"*.

6   Discussion

Table 2 summarizes our findings on the four contradictions that surfaced from our analysis. Two of these contradictions are related to stakeholders within the project group, none of them are across groups. Contradiction 1 is related to conflicting goals, whereas contradiction 4 is related to different perspectives of implementation.

Table 2. Overview and classification of the identified contradictions

Contradiction	Stakeholder related?	Conflicting goals	Continual or after a critical incident
Follow regulations vs. satisfying system needs	No. Related to conflicting goals within the project.	Conduct a formally correct procedure vs. select the system that meets their needs best	Continual, runs all through the process
Change vs. persistence	Yes, Super user on the old system vs. project leaders	Implement message exchange vs. Keeping the old system	Continual. The resistance took new forms (goal of migrating data, not meeting up on one occasion)
Revolution vs. incremental change	Yes. Project leaders vs. system owners.	Start the new system with a clean slate vs. migrate data from the old system	After. System owner of the old systems had to give in.
Implementation primarily as technical installation vs. Implementation as socio-technical change	Yes. Stakeholder related to user of the old system	Not goal related. Arose from different implementation paradigms	Continual.

Contradictions, 2, 3 and 4 are quite general in that they can be seen in almost all IS projects. Only contradiction 1 can be thought of as specific to public procurement although it can be argued that even private sector procurements are subject to some degree of regulation. However, public procurement, like any aspect in the public sector is heavily regulated, not only from the local and state level agencies, but also from international bodies (such as the EU in our case). As such, we view this contradiction to be biggest dilemma that public procurement of IS has to face. To deal with this contradiction, a number of strategies evolve. The type of tendering used in our case – tender with negotiation – itself represents such a strategy. This tendering procedure allows negotiation between the procuring agency and the vendor on matters related to system specifications and requirements while at the same time retain the transparent and fair process that regulations aim to ensure.

An intriguing feature of these contradictions is that they seem to be related. For example, contradiction 2 and contradiction 3 represent tensions between "cleaning house" from day 1 of a new system and retaining existing practices or gradually moving from institutionalized practices to new ones. An interesting analysis would be to map whether the same stakeholder or stakeholder group are responsible for multiple and related contradictions.

6.1 Future Research Directions

More research is needed to test the typology and to see whether the identified contradictions are generic and may be seen in other cases. A cross-case study will shed light into this issue. More research is also needed on issues such as the dilemma between adhering to procurement regulations and applying specific social goals. A related research focus would be on how public authorities can apply policy goals and how these goals influence different phases of the procurement process, especially the requirements specification phase.

End users is an important stakeholder group in all IS procurement. Their requirements may be contradictory to the project group's requirements. An important research questions is how end users should be involved in requirement specification. In our case, a reference group of end users was set up who were involved in requirements specification and in the selection. Whether this strategy of involving end users as a reference group instead of as members of the project group itself is an effective way is an interesting avenue of future research. Since decisions are made during a procurement process with long lasting effects, these issues may be time-sensitive.

References

1. Moe, C.E., Newman, M.: The Public Procurement of IS - A Process View. In: Proc. Hawaiian International Conference on System Sciences (HICSS), Big Island, Hawaii, January 6-9 (2014)
2. Markus, M.L.: Power, politics, and MIS implementation. Communications of the ACM 26, 430–444 (1983)
3. Howcroft, D., Light, B.: Reflections of issues of power in packaged software selection. Information Systems Journal 16, 215–235 (2006)
4. Sabherwal, R., Newman, M.: Persistence and change in system development: a dialectical view. Journal of Information Technology 18, 69–92 (2003)
5. Moe, C.E., Risvand, A.K., Sein, M.K.: Limits of Public Procurement: Information systems acquisition. In: Wimmer, M.A., Scholl, H.J., Grönlund, Å., Andersen, K.V. (eds.) EGOV 2006. LNCS, vol. 4084, pp. 281–292. Springer, Heidelberg (2006)

6. Bjerknes, G.: Dialectical reflection in information systems development. Scandinavian Journal of Information Systems 3, 55–77 (1991)
7. Robey, D., Ross, J.W., Boudreau, M.-C.: Learning to implement enterprise systems: an exploratory study of the dialectics of change. Journal of Management Information Systems 19, 17–46 (2002)
8. Soh, C., Kien Sia, S., Fong Boh, W., Tang, M.: Misalignments in ERP implementation: a dialectic perspective. International Journal of Human-Computer Interaction 16, 81–100 (2003)
9. Heiskanen, A., Newman, M., Similä, J.: The social dynamics of software development. Accounting, Management and Information Technology 10, 1–32 (2000)
10. Scholl, H.J.: Involving salient stakeholders Beyond the technocratic view on change. Action Research 2, 277–304 (2004)
11. Flak, L.S., Rose, J.: Stakeholder governance: adapting stakeholder theory to the e-government field. Communications of the Association for Information Systems 16, 642–664 (2005)
12. Rowley, J.: e-Government stakeholders - Who are they and what do they want? International Journal of Information Management 31, 53–62 (2011)
13. Flak, L.S., Nordheim, S., Munkvold, B.E.: Analyzing stakeholder diversity in G2G efforts: Combining descriptive stakeholder theory and dialectic process theory. E-Service Journal 6, 3–23 (2008)
14. Parliament, E.: DIRECTIVE 2004/18/EC on the coordination of procedures for the award of public works contracts. public supply contracts and public service contracts (2004)
15. Parliament, E.: DIRECTIVE 2004/17/EC coordinating the procurement procedures of entities operating in the water. energy, transport and postal services sectors (2004)
16. Bartle, J.R., Korosec, R.L.: A Review of State Procurement and Contracting. Journal of Public Procurement 3, 192–214 (2003)
17. Boyne, G.A.: Public and Private Management: What's the difference? Journal of Management Studies 39, 97–122 (2002)
18. Moe, C.E., Päivärinta, T.: Challenges in Information Systems Procurement in the Public Sector. Electronic Journal of e-Government 11, 308–323 (2013)
19. Myers, M.D.: Dialectical hermeneutics: a theoretical framework for the implementation of information systems. Information Systems Journal 5, 51–70 (1995)
20. Freeman, R.E., Harrison, J.S., Wicks, A.C., Parmar, B.L., De Colle, S.: Stakeholder theory: The state of the art. Cambridge University Press (2010)
21. Van de Ven, A.H., Poole, M.S.: Explaining development and change in organizations. Academy of Management Review, pp. 510–540 (1995)
22. Freeman, R.E.: Strategic Management: A Stakeholder Approach (Marshfield, MA: Pitman). FreemanStrategic management: A stakeholder approach (1984)
23. Clarkson, M.E.: A stakeholder framework for analyzing and evaluating corporate social performance. Academy of Management Review 20, 92–117 (1995)
24. Mitchell, R.K., Agle, B.R., Wood, D.J.: Toward a theory of stakeholder identification and salience: Defining the principle of who and what really counts. Academy of Management Review 22, 853–886 (1997)
25. Sæbø, Ø., Flak, L.S., Sein, M.K.: Understanding the dynamics in e-Participation initiatives: Looking through the genre and stakeholder lenses. Government Information Quarterly 28, 416–425 (2011)
26. Klein, H.K., Myers, M.D.: A set of principles for conducting and evaluating interpretive field studies in information systems. MIS Quarterly, 67–93 (1999)

Strategic Aspects for Successful E-government Systems Design: Insights from a Survey in Germany

Catherine G. Mkude and Maria A. Wimmer

Institute for IS Research, University of Koblenz-Landau,
Universitätsstr. 1, 56070 Koblenz, Germany
{cmkude,wimmer}@uni-koblenz.de

Abstract. The maturity of e-government implementation in research and practice has developed tremendously over the years. Nevertheless, the challenges encountered and the overall growth of e-government in different countries varies; studies by organizations such as the UN and World Bank evidence these variations. To successfully implement e-government, governments are required to deepen their understanding of aspects such as benefits, challenges and success factors. Contributing to this knowledge and understanding, the paper investigates factors framing successful design and implementation of e-government systems. The paper presents and analyses the literature and results from an e-government inquiry in Germany. The paper highlights important factors for successful implementation of e-government and also presents opinions on strategic aspects for e-government systems design with reference to Germany. It finally highlights the need for further research in the domain.

Keywords: e-government strategy, e-government design and implementation, benefits, challenges, success factors.

1   Introduction

Since their beginning, e-government research and practice have matured tremendously over the years, with governments opting to fully utilise the opportunities and benefits of implementing electronic government (e-government). Dynamic developments and resulting innovativeness of information and communication technologies (ICT) largely contribute to the way governments deliver their services to the public. With the increasing desire of realising good governance principles (see [25] for a definition of good governance principles) in e-government implementations, more and more countries transform their governments from traditional forms of paper-based and unconnected organisations to seamless and networked 'e-'governments. Through recognising the potentials of e-government to improve public service delivery and to achieve good governance principles, governments all over the world have initiated strategies to support e-government implementations. However, the pace at which governments mature in implementing e-government varies immensely. International studies such as an UN e-government survey [29] and a World Bank publication on ICT [33] evidence such variations as most developed countries mature far ahead of

M. Janssen et al. (Eds.): EGOV 2014, LNCS 8653, pp. 301–312, 2014.

developing countries in the up-take of e-government services. Therefore in addition to the enormous amount of available research, where principles for successful implementation of e-government systems are presented, it is imperative for further research to be conducted to determine the differences in approaches of implementing e-government with country-specific challenges and success factors. This will complement practices in different countries and help understand how these can be transferred from one country to another.

This paper aims to investigate strategic approaches and the understanding of e-government benefits, challenges, and success factors, which are important to successful design and implementation of e-government strategies with reference to Germany. An empirical research conducted among experts attending an e-government event investigates strategic aspects for e-government systems design. In particular, we aimed at receiving feedback and obtaining further understanding of strategic aspects for e-government systems design such as challenges and success factors, which need further investigations and particular attention. Prior to empirical investigations, relevant e-government literature was studied to gain an understanding of different factors influencing e-government development and implementation.

The remainder of the paper is as follows: the next section provides insights into current literature identifying distinct factors influencing e-government development and implementation. In section 3, we detail the research methodology for the study. The results of the survey are presented in section 4. We then discuss the findings with respect to the literature review in section 5 and conclude with final remarks and future research in section 6.

2   E-government Development and Implementation: A Literature Review of Strategies, Benefits, Challenges and Success Factors

Governments continue to initiate e-government strategies with the aim of successfully transforming public sectors into technology-savvy organisations in order to realise the benefits of ICT in public sectors. E-government strategies describe in detail the implementation of e-government by setting objectives, which are further elaborated into programs and subsequently in projects [23]. With the different and changing foci of e-government strategies, attributed by factors such as political interests and financial capabilities among others, it is inevitable also to understand the different approaches adopted by governments to implement their strategies. A study of e-government implementation approaches by OECD unveils the importance of a centralised approach, but - even more importantly - a relationship between centralised approach and coordination with decentralised actors. According to this study, "the e-government planning process within the central government helps to establish and diffuse the vision and to translate it into goals and targets. Goals serve not only to provide a direction for action and achievement, they can also be used to prioritise and even advance action. Government-wide planning and the setting of objectives can also improve co-ordination between government organisations, serve to establish criteria for *reconciling conflicting approaches and signal preferred approaches and shared resources for overcoming challenges"* [25].

Literature studies further unveil that the on-going efforts of governments initiating e-government strategies imply that the benefits of ICT in the public sector are increasingly acknowledged. Besides other resulting benefits of e-government, ICT is more and more viewed as a tool for seamless and improved interrelations among government organisations, among governments and businesses, and among governments and citizens. Literature study of e-government benefits identified the following: improved efficiency and effectiveness in public processes [2] [4] [8] [15] [17] [19] [22] [24]; cost-effectiveness in public service provision [2] [4] [19] [24] [27] [28]; enhanced quality of public services [2] [4] [19] [22] [24] [27] [28]; increased transparency and accountability [2] [4] [24] [27] [28]; integrated government processes [2] [4] [24] [27] [28] [32]; cost-effective access of public services [19] [22]; ease of access to information [6] [22]; creation of a more knowledgeable society [6] [21]; and reduced corruption [2] [4] [24] [27] [28], which is more reported in literature investigating benefits of e-government in developing countries.

In addition to investigating e-government benefits, the challenges encountered were studied. Many e-government implementation challenges are reported in literature, which are often classified as financial, economic, technological, social and cultural challenges [14] [17] [24]. In a recent study, we outlined thirteen e-government challenges from nine literature studies [23]. Similar to the different ways, in which governments realise e-government benefits as reported earlier, e-government challenges seem to vary in different countries, too. This implies that e-government challenges in respective countries and their ways of addressing these challenges need to be analysed.

Finally, factors contributing to successful implementation of e-government were investigated. Numerous studies have highlighted success factors (see e.g. [3] [10] [13] [15] [17] [19] [23]). Considering the extent of investments and commitment required for successful and sustainable development of e-government endeavours, most scholars point out the importance of political support to e-government implementation [1] [4] [7] [9] [12] [23] [24] [28]. The presence of legal and interoperability frameworks are also regarded as important factor, which should ensure seamless integration of processes and improved coordination among organisations [4] [15] [24] [26].

Based on the literature review studying aspects influencing and contributing to successful development and implementation of e-government, a survey was developed to collect insights on strategic aspects for successful design and implementation of e-government systems. The next section introduces the research methodology, followed by summarizing the insights of the inquiry in Germany (section 4).

3   Research Methodology

Based on the research objective outlined and the review of literature, a qualitative research approach was used to study e-government development and implementation aspects from German practitioners and academicians along an e-government event.

The objective of the study was to gain an understanding of e-government aspects from the perspective of German experts as outlined in the introduction. In such an exploratory study according to Flick et al., qualitative research is suitable to provide the basis of gaining such understanding and describe a phenomenon from the point of view of participants [11]. Germany was used in this study because one key country selected in the overall research works is Germany. The research method selected for this study was survey using a paper-based questionnaire as data collection method. The questionnaire was designed to capture relevant information and understanding of different aspects identified in literature (cf. section 2) and to gain insights from experts. The questionnaire consisted of eleven questions, with most questions being open-ended, which were assembled in five thematic parts with links and relationships among questions. The first part investigated demographical information of respondents, the second part investigated e-government benefits and challenges, the third part investigated development aspects of e-government, the fourth part investigated e-government supporting frames and the fifth part investigated recommendations for successful design and implementation of e-government systems. The questionnaires were distributed in person to respondents attending an e-government event in Koblenz, Germany. The attendees included e-government experts from academia, private and public sectors. Among 15 questionnaires distributed, 8 questionnaires were returned and used for analysis. Among the unreturned questionnaires, three respondents reported that they do not understand English well, one respondent reported that the questionnaire was too long and three respondents did not provide any feedback.

Qualitative data analysis was used to investigate insights from literature and from the answers to open-ended questions to determining similarities, differences and patterns in responses. The results of the inquiry are summarized in the next section.

4   Results and Insights from the Survey

The first part of the questionnaire aimed at investigating the background of responders necessary for analysing responses provided therein with respect to the influencing factors leading to the responses. Among 8 respondents, 5 respondents are ICT practitioners in the public sector with an experience in e-government ranging from 20 to 4 years. 3 respondents are academics with an experience in e-government ranging from 8 to 1.5 years.

Next, respondents were asked concerning the benefits of e-government implementation presented in literature, with respect to Germany. Further, the level at which the benefits are realised in Germany should be assessed. All respondents indicated that they are aware of the benefits of e-government implementation and they rated benefits of e-government as shown in Table 1. The assessment indicates the average rates of the level of realisation in Germany. All but one assessments were rather homogeneous. Reduced corruption yielded distinct assessments, with 2 respondents rating reduced corruption as a fully realised benefit of implementing e-government, 1 respondent rated it as not realised and 1 respondent indicated that reduced corruption is *"not among the most realised benefits of e-government"*.

The next part of questions investigated challenges encountered in developing e-government in Germany and possible ways of addressing these challenges. The literature review pointed out that e-government challenges are numerous but yet dissimilar in different countries. Therefore, the questions aimed at investigating what challenges are encountered from a German perspective and what solutions would be applicable. Respondents indicated diverse strategic challenges as listed in Table 2 (each mentioned once), and proposed possible solutions to these challenges (except for one).

Table 1. Realisation of e-government benefits
(N = 8; scale of rating: 1= not realised … 4=fully realised)

E-government benefits	Average rating
More effective processes	3
Accountability of public authority	3
Ease of access of information	3
Creation of more knowledgeable society	3
Enhanced quality of processes	3
More efficient processes	2
Cost-effective to the public authority	2
Cost-effective to access government processes	2
Transparent processes	2
Integrated services among public authorities	2
Reduced corruption	3

Table 2. Challenges for developing e-government and possible ways to address them

Challenges identified	Possible ways to address the challenges
Low interoperability at country level and EU level	Use of standards
Lack of legal frameworks and therefore restrictions in implementing e-government across organisations	Introduce legal and regulatory frameworks supporting e-government
Lack of user-friendly applications hence technology barriers	Develop user-friendly applications and integrate users and usability tests during development
Lack of awareness of the potential of e-government and therefore lack of interest in implementing e-government	Create and promote awareness of the benefits of e-government among citizens, politicians and government employees
Financial challenges	Coordinate efforts among agencies and ministries to reduce reinventing the wheel and promote create-once-use-frequently concept
Cultural challenges	Promote political changes and discussions among government and societies of the purposes of e-government implementation
Lack of concrete privacy laws	Enact and enforce international and national agreements of privacy protection
Lack of structured public procurement platforms	Developing and enforcing use for tendering platforms across the government
Lack of single point of contact to interact with the government at all levels	Developing service directive
Challenges in implementing electronic signatures	Develop and support validation infrastructures for online interaction with the government
Ineffective and inefficient public administration hence challenges in transforming to seamless and one-stop-government	Optimise internal administrative processes such as document management and workflow systems
Lack of cooperation among government organisations	No response

The objective of the subsequent question was to investigate the development and implementation of e-government frameworks in Germany with the basis of literature presented in section 2. Main focus in this study was whether the framework is developed at national level or whether many e-government frameworks exist at different levels and for distinct purposes. Respondents were asked whether they are aware of the presence of an e-government development framework at national level. Five respondents answered 'Yes' and they mentioned the following six different frameworks:

(i)   'Data exchange standards' to ensure interoperability[1],

(ii)   DOMEA[2] - an organisational concept for public administration work, especially workflow and archiving,

(iii)   'IT Planungsrat' – as a coordination framework involving the federal government and the 16 federal states in Germany to coordinate e-government works[3],

(iv)   V-Model XT of the Federal Government to ensure quality with a standard engineering approach in systems development[4],

(v)   SAGA - a standards and reference architecture guideline for e-government systems development in German public administrations[5], and

(vi)   E-government law - a newly introduced legal framework for the federal governments to implement e-government[6].

Further investigations were conducted to study and assess these frameworks and to get additional insights. One respondent answered that *there are many initiatives in federal states, cities etc. to standardisation* and another one stressed that no unique framework for e-government development exists at national level. The latter respondent also commented that the lack of such a unique framework resulted in uncontrolled and diverse (not interoperable) evolutions with isolated applications over the years. The five respondents aware of the frameworks were further asked to assess the adoption level of the frameworks among different government levels in Germany, and further to state the impact of the assessed adoption level – showing results in Table 3.

---

[1] KoSIT - Koordinierungsstelle für IT-Standards, http://www.xoev.de/

[2] Dokumentenmanagement und elektronische Archivierung im IT-gestützten Geschäftsgang (DOMEA), http://www.verwaltung-innovativ.de/DE/E_Government/orgkonzept_everwaltung/orgkonzept_everwaltung_artikel.html

[3] Introduced through German's constitutional law (GG) in art. 91c to foster collaboration in the development of public sector ICT, http://www.it-planungsrat.de/

[4] http://www.cio.bund.de/Web/DE/Architekturen-und-Standards/V-Modell-XT-Bund/vmodellxt_bund_node.html

[5] http://www.cio.bund.de/Web/DE/Architekturen-und-Standards/SAGA/saga_node.html

[6] http://www.bmi.bund.de/DE/Themen/IT-Netzpolitik/E-Government/E-Government-Gesetz/e-government-gesetz_node.html

Table 3. E-government development frameworks and their adoption level
(N=5; scale: 1=not adopted; 2=rather not adopted; 3=rather adopted; 4=fully adopted)

E-government development framework	Adoption level	Impact of adoption level
Data exchange standards	3	Minimised costs in public sector
DOMEA	2	No response
IT Planungsrat	3	Enhanced exchange of governmental services; Improved cooperation of the federal, federal state and local governments
V-Model XT	3	No response
SAGA	3	Availability and use of agreed and user-friendly technologies, methods and standards
E-government law	-	-

Four frameworks were rated as rather adopted. DOMEA was rated as rather not adopted. The e-government law was approved and entered into force only in mid-2013; hence, no indication and evidence of adoption or even impact exists so far.

Political support in the implementation of e-government is deemed in literature among most important factors to establish and sustain successful e-government systems. Therefore, respondents were asked to assess the existing political support in implementing e-government. Two respondents assessed the political support as fully supportive, five respondents assessed it as rather supportive and one had no response.

The response seems congruent with the introduction of CIOs or IT directors in federal, federal state and also larger local governments. The inauguration of the IT Planungsrat (cf. development frameworks above) also evidences political support for e-government developments in Germany.

Following the assessment of political support, respondents were then asked to assess whether the existing legal framework to support e-government implementation is sufficient. Literature review presented earlier revealed the importance of legal frameworks not only to provide an environment for integrated processes, but also for coordination among government organisations at different levels. Since the e-government law was only approved and entered into force in mid-2013, the assessment of the eight experts in regards to adoption level was equally distributed among 'rather sufficient' and 'rather not sufficient'. The impact of the legal framework could not yet be assessed due to the time-span of the e-government law being in force being too short.

As discussed above and in section 2, given the maturity of e-government developments, it is imperative to acknowledge the political, economic, socio-cultural, technological, environmental and legal differences in individual countries. With this regard, the subsequent part of the questionnaire asked for an assessment of selected principles, from literature, in their contribution to ensure successful implementation of e-government in Germany. Results are presented in Table 4.

In the following section, we discuss above findings with reference to presented literature in section 2.

Table 4. Assessment of the principles to ensure successful e-government systems design (N=8; scale of assessment: 1=not significant.....4=fully significant)

Principle to ensure successful design of e-government systems	Average assessment
Presence of national e-government strategy	4
Presence of political commitment	4
Presence of committed leadership	4
Presence of financial sources	4
Collaboration among government departments/agencies etc.	4
Digital literacy among government employees	3
Use of government enterprise architecture	3
Digital literacy among users of e-government systems	3
Presence of digital inclusion	3
Prioritisation of projects	3
Integration of processes among government departments/agencies etc.	3
Organisational interoperability	3
Legal interoperability	3
Semantic interoperability	3
Technical interoperability	3
Performance of risks management	3
Performance of change management	3
Implementation of small and/or pilot projects strategy	3
Presence of legal and regulatory frameworks	3
Promote e-government awareness across country	3
Generic approaches for re-usability in other areas	3

5   Discussion of Findings from Survey and Literature Review

The results and insights from the review of literature generally reveal that the knowledge of e-government development and implementation is immense. However, there is still a need of investigating and embracing the different approaches and perceptions in different countries. This will enable researchers and practitioners to fully collaborate in creating innovative e-government solutions while also tackling challenges in ways that take into account the different settings of particular governments.

The OECD study argues that a government-wide planning and implementation of e-government leads to more coordination among government organisations [25]. The survey results are congruent with the observation that the lack of such a 'framework' leads to isolated and un-interoperable e-government initiatives in the long run.

E-government benefits such as more effective processes, accountability of public authorities, ease of access of information, and enhanced quality of public services are among many benefits reported in literature. According to the results, the extent of realising these benefits is diverse. Such diversity highlights the need of not only understanding the benefits of implementing e-government in general, but also of more research into the extent, at which countries realise these benefits. Studies such as

[2] [4] [24] [27] [28] indicate that e-government contributes more to reduced corruption in developing countries. Results from the interrogation of German experts reveal a different view: On average, respondents view reduced corruption among other e-government benefits realised in Germany. However, results also reveal that reduced corruption is not yet among the benefits fully realised. This implies lack of common understanding of how e-government has impacted the level of corruption in public sectors, in developed countries such as Germany.

All e-government challenges that were indicated by respondents are challenges that are also widely documented in literature. The challenges indicated such as lack of political commitment, limited financial resources, cultural change and lack of interest, interoperability and legal challenges presents political, economic, social, technological, environmental and legal challenges categorised in literature [14] [17] [24]. In addition to the challenges identified by respondents, the National E-Government Strategy of Germany points out the following challenges[7]:

- *Global competition to ensure that Germany remains an attractive place to do business*
- *Ensuring Internet access, especially in rural areas affected by demographic change, growing shortages of skilled workers etc.*
- *Paying attention to and participating in the organisation of international processes and standards, to ensure Germany is with growing European integration*
- *Ensuring legal, organisational and technical modernisation to enable public administration to act and respond flexibly in technologically fast moving times*
- *Ensuring that standards and norms, especially when it comes to security and data protection, can be met also in the future*
- *Ensuring willingness to invest to promote innovation in the public sector, e.g. regarding service orientation and the capacity for innovation overall*
- *Ensuring greater agility and flexibility in public administration to make it easier to deal with difficult-to-control risks (such as financial and economic crises).*

Literature studies reveal that lack of evaluation and sustainability frameworks [20] and decline of citizen trust in e-government [5] [31] are among the significant challenges in e-government. However these challenges are not mentioned by respondents of our survey or the IT Planungsrat as important in the German context.

Political commitment and legal frameworks have been regarded as among important factors for innovative and sustainable e-government developments. The importance of political support is evidenced in a study by Furuholt and Wahid [12]. The authors determine lack of political support as one of the main failure factors of an e-government project in Indonesia. Similarly in a case of a developing country, Belachew suggests the need for Ethiopia to develop a suitable legal framework to ensure

---

[7] National E-Government Strategy, online
http://www.it-planungsrat.de/SharedDocs/Downloads/DE/Strategie/
National_E-Government_Strategy.pdf?__blob=publicationFile
(last access 2014/01/17)

seamless implementation of e-government services [4]. The responses gathered along the study here are deemed not to be sufficiently expressive, so further investigations will need to be made to confirm the impressions collected so far.

Implementation of successful e-government projects rely largely on lessons learned from previous projects and established knowledge of success principles from practice and research. All principles of success assessed by respondents are regarded as significant in e-government endeavours. On the one hand, the results from the survey confirm the success factors reported in literature. On other hand, as results highlight that principles such as presence of national e-government strategy, presence of political commitment and presence of financial sources are fully significant in Germany, literature informs that the same principles might not be fully significant in other countries. Likely, principles such as prioritisation of projects, digital literacy among users of e-government (citizens, businesses and NGOs) and interoperability might as well be fully significant while less significant in other countries. Therefore it is of utmost importance to note that the specific political, economic, socio-cultural, technological, environmental and legal settings of a particular country highly determine the 'right' approach and solutions for successful implementation of e-government.

6   Conclusion

Many approaches for designing and implementing e-government are documented in literature and in practice. The maturity of e-government over the years is reflected in continuous and innovative solutions of using ICT in public sectors. E-government is not only viewed as the use of ICT in public sector but more broadly, and even more significantly, as a tool for an integrated and better government. As far as e-government benefits are realised, also challenges are encountered and subsequently ways of tackling the challenges. In this study the researchers identified e-government challenges and solutions, which have long informed research and practice of the political, economic, socio-cultural, technological, environmental and legal factors, which highly influence the outcome and success of e-government implementation. Based on the analysis from the survey of experts and literature study, implementing and sustaining e-government systems requires a profound understanding of, first, the expected benefits of e-government. Therefore, the design of e-government systems should be geared towards achieving the perceived benefits of a respective country. Second, the particular e-government challenges encountered and the factors that influence the challenges have to be understood well at the country level. By investigating factors influencing the challenges, governments will be able to find solutions, which will work specifically in the country's settings. Third, the right approach of formulating and implementing e-government strategies at national level has to be identified and understood. Presence of a centralised strategy enhances coordination and collaboration of solutions at different levels of government. However, it is important that the strategy is adopted throughout the government at different levels for the purposes to be achieved. Fourth, the role of political support is highlighted in the study. Successful and sustainable e-government implementation requires profound political and leadership support at all governance levels. Fifth, formulation of legal frameworks supporting (and enforcing) implementation of e-government is also among the important factors for consideration when designing e-government systems.

Further research of the aspects investigated in this study will be carried out in a wider scope to deepen the understanding of different contexts and, hence, to contribute in theoretical perspectives of e-government research and in practical cases of successfully designing and implementing e-government systems.

References

[1] Allen, B.A., Luc, J., Gilles, P., Jeffrey, R.: E-Governance & Government on-Line in Canada: Partnerships, People & Prospects. Government Information Quarterly 18(2), 93–104 (2001)

[2] Alshawi, S., Alahmary, A., Alalwany, H.: E-government Evaluation Factors: Citizen's Perspective. Information Technology for Development - e-Government Initiatives in the Developing World: Challenges and Opportunities 15(3), 193–208 (2007)

[3] Baguma, R., Lubega, J.: Factors for Success and Failure of e-Government Projects: The Case of e-Government Projects in Uganda. In: Proceedings of the 7th International Conference on Theory and Practice of Electronic Governance, pp. 194–197. ACM, New York (2013)

[4] Belachew, M.: E-government initiatives in Ethiopia. In: Davies, J., Janowski, T. (eds.) Proceedings of the 4th International Conference on Theory and Practice of Electronic Governance (ICEGOV 2010), pp. 49–54. ACM, New York (2010)

[5] Bélanger, F., Carter, L.: Trust and Risk in E-Government Adoption. Journal of Strategic Information Systems 17(2), 165–176 (2008)

[6] Bertot, J.C., Jaeger, P.T., McClure, C.R.: Citizen-Centered E-Government Services: Benefits, Costs, and Research Needs. In: Proceedings of the 2008 International Conference on Digital Government Research. Digital Government Society of North America, pp. 137–142. ACM, New York (2008)

[7] Bhatnagar, S.: E-Government: From Vision to Implementation - A Practical Guide With Case Studies. SAGE publications, India (2004)

[8] Carter, L., Bélanger, F.: The utilization of E-government Service: Citizen Trust, Innovation and Acceptance Factors. Information Systems Journal 15(1), 5–25 (2005)

[9] Ebrahim, Z., Irani, Z.: E-government adoption: architecture and barriers. Business Process Management Journal 11(5), 589–611 (2005)

[10] Evangelidis, A., Akomode, J., Taleb-Bendiab, A., Taylor, M.: Risk Assessment & Success Factors for e-Government in a UK Establishment. In: Traunmüller, R., Lenk, K. (eds.) EGOV 2002. LNCS, vol. 2456, pp. 395–402. Springer, Heidelberg (2002)

[11] Flick, U., von Kardorff, E., Steinke, I.: What is Qualitative Research? An Introduction to the Field. In: Flick, U., von Kardorff, E., Steinke, I. (eds.) ACompanion to Qualitative Research, pp. 3–11. SAGE Publication Ltd., London (2004)

[12] Furuholt, B., Wahid, F.: E-government Challenges and the Role of Political Leadership in Indonesia: the Case of Sragen. In: Proceedings of the 41st Annual Hawaii International Conference on System Sciences, HICSS 2008, vol. 411. IEEE Computer Society, Washington (2008)

[13] Gichoya, D.: Factors affecting the successful implementation of ICT projects in government. The Electronic Journal of e-Government 3(4), 175–184 (2005)

[14] Gilbert, D., Balestrini, P., Littleboy, D.: Barriers and Benefits in the Adoption of E-Government. International Journal of Public Sector Management 17(4), 286–301 (2004)

[15] Gil-García, R.J., Pardo, T.A.: E-Government Success Factors: Mapping Practical Tools to Theoretical Foundations. Government Information Quarterly 22(2), 187–216 (2005)

[16] Heeks, R.: Information Systems and Developing Countries: Failure, Success and Local Improvisations. The Information Society 18(2), 101–112 (2002)

[17] Jaeger, P.T., Thompson, K.M.: E-Government around the World: Lessons, Challenges, and Future Directions. Government Information Quarterly 20(4), 389–394 (2003)

[18] Ke, W., Wei, K.K.: Successful e-government in Singapore. Communications of the ACM 47(6), 95–99 (2004)

[19] Kumar, V., Mukerji, B., Butt, I., Persaud, A.: Factors for Successful E-Government Adoption: A Conceptual Framework. Electronic Journal of E-Government 5(1), 63–77 (2007)

[20] Kunstelj, M., Vintar, M.: Evaluating the progress of e-government development: A critical analysis. Information Polity 9, 131–148 (2004)

[21] Layne, K., Lee, J.: Developing Fully Functional E-Government: A Four Stage Model. Government Information Quarterly 18(2), 122–136 (2001)

[22] Lee, S.M., Tan, X., Trimi, S.: Current Practices of Leading E-Government Countries. Communications of the ACM 48(10), 99–104 (2005)

[23] Mkude, C.G., Wimmer, M.A.: Strategic Framework for Designing E-Government in Developing Countries. In: Wimmer, M.A., Janssen, M., Scholl, H.J. (eds.) EGOV 2013. LNCS, vol. 8074, pp. 148–162. Springer, Heidelberg (2013)

[24] Ndou, V.: E-government for developing countries: opportunities and challenges. The Electronic Journal of Information Systems in Developing Countries 18(1), 1–24 (2004)

[25] OECD: The Case for E-Government: Excerpts from the OECD Report, The E-Government Imperative. OECD Journal on Budgeting 3(1), 61–131 (2003)

[26] Rashid, N., Rahman, S.: An Investigation into Critical Determinants of e-Government Implementation in the Context of a Developing Nation. In: Andersen, K.N., Francesconi, E., Grönlund, Å., van Engers, T.M. (eds.) EGOVIS 2010. LNCS, vol. 6267, pp. 9–21. Springer, Heidelberg (2010)

[27] Sæbø, Ø.: E-government in Tanzania: Current Status and Future Challenges. In: Scholl, H.J., Janssen, M., Wimmer, M.A., Moe, C.E., Flak, L.S. (eds.) EGOV 2012. LNCS, vol. 7443, pp. 198–209. Springer, Heidelberg (2012)

[28] Schuppan, T.: E-Government in developing countries: Experiences from sub-Saharan Africa. Government Information Quarterly 26(1), 118–127 (2009)

[29] United Nations: United Nations E-Government Survey 2012: E-Government for the People (2012), http://unpan1.un.org/intradoc/groups/public/documents/un/unpan048065.pdf (accessed January 17, 2014)

[30] Wang, Y., Liao, Y.: Assessing e-Government systems success: A validation of the DeLone and McLean model of information systems success. Government Information Quarterly 25(4), 717–733 (2008)

[31] Welch, E.W., Hinnant, C.C., Moon, M.J.: Linking Citizen Satisfaction with E-Government and Trust in Government. Journal of Public Administration Research and Theory 15(3), 371–391 (2005)

[32] World Bank: The Little Data Book on Information and Communication Technology. The World Bank Publications, Washington D.C (2013)

[33] Wimmer, M.A.: Integrated Service Modelling for Online One-Stop Government. Electronic Markets 12(3), 149–156 (2002)

Proposing an Entrepreneurial Process
for the Co-creation of IT Value

Hans Solli-Sæther[1] and Leif Skiftenes Flak[2]

[1] Aalesund University College, Norway
haso@hials.no
[2] University of Agder, Norway
leif.flak@uia.no

Abstract. Co-creation of IT value has received substantial focus from the IS research community over the past years. However, few if any have studied this phenomenon from a process perspective, and our understanding of the processes leading to successful co-creation is therefore limited. To address this shortcoming, we studied a complex, e-government case involving 38 government agencies intending to co-create value from a common IT platform. We used a mixed method approach, involving both qualitative and quantitative data. Data analysis was guided by two strands of theory, namely the theory of institutional entrepreneurship and the co-creation of IT value. Our findings suggest that neither theory is sufficient to provide a processual7 understanding of co-creation. Consequently, we propose a novel process for the entrepreneurial co-creation of IT value.

Keywords: IT value, co-creation of value, institutional entrepreneurship.

1   Introduction

The importance of realizing benefits from IT investments has been acknowledged by the IS community for many years [e.g., 1, 2] and a strand of IS research has explicit focused on the mechanisms behind the realization of such benefits. Most of this research has examined the relationship between investment and organizational outcome in one single firm. Given the centrality of the IT value question, researchers have expanded the agenda to also include the co-creation of IT value in multiple organizations [e.g., 3, 4]. In a special issue of MIS Quarterly on co-creating IT value, Grover and Kohli [3, p. 231] state that "co-creation represents one of the most important streams in the IT value research area that will gain greater importance as firms expand collaborative relationships with other firms." The idea of co-creation is intuitive and simple; i.e., integrating IT in the end-user environment to support inter-organizational work processes, improve end-user performance, and enhance overall organizational effectiveness in direct support of goals and strategies. Despite this, the process through which firms can successfully implement it is likely to pose several

M. Janssen et al. (Eds.): EGOV 2014, LNCS 8653, pp. 313–324, 2014.

challenges, e.g., partner selection, evolving relationships, and stages that need to be followed to co-create IT value.

Theoretical accounts of institutional entrepreneurship can be traced back to 1988 and the work by DiMaggio [5]. Stevenson and Jarillo [6, p. 23] define corporate entrepreneurship as *"a process by which individuals – either on their own or inside organizations – pursue opportunities without regard to the resources they currently control."* Recent advancements in institutional entrepreneurship suggest a theory in the form of a phase model to explain the *"process of institutional entrepreneurship from the emergence of institutional entrepreneurs to their implementation of change"* [7]. Battilana et al. suggest a three-phase model where a set of enabling conditions for institutional entrepreneurship leads to divergent change implementation that in turn results in institutional change. In this research, enabling conditions for the co-creation of IT innovations leads to co-creative change implementation that in turn results in the co-creation of IT value.

Contemporary public sector interoperability environments involve IT investments that are being made by multiple agencies that are cooperative, platform-based and relational arrangements, and where the objective is, e.g., to improve public services, promote democratic participation and improve public policy making (commonly referred to as e-government). The purpose is, according to Scholl and Klischewski [8] to achieve agility, customer focus, accountability, visibility and efficiency in public services. In order to create increased value, interoperability between independent information systems is essential. Information technology and systems have little or no intrinsic value, and therefore the introduction of technology must be done in the context of organizational development. New effects can arise when technology enables new ways of working. Hence, horizontal and vertical interoperability are regarded as one of the keys to realize the potential benefits. However, a recent review of the interoperability literature found that evaluations of such efforts are scarce, and that there is a need to develop a better understanding of the causes, behavior and effects of interoperability [9]. Thus, we have selected a public sector interoperability setting as the research base for our study.

Although the bureaucratic system has many positive aspects, it is not adapted to today's expectations for effective services, and it may be inadequate in relation to facilitating the necessary interoperability. Thus, there is a need to increase our understanding of what interoperability means in practice, how to improve it and what benefits increased interoperability can provide. To address these issues, this paper investigates the following research question: *How can organizations co-create IT value?*

In building our argument, we first review the literature on the co-creation of IT value and institutional entrepreneurship, focusing on the process perspective. Then, we present and analyze a revelatory case study concerning public sector interoperability, which serves as a basis for our conceptual framework. In the discussion section, we explore the theoretical and practical implications of our findings. The paper concludes with limitations and avenues for further research.

2   Conceptual Foundations

2.1   Co-creation of IT Value

Co-creation is the process during which consumers take an active role and create value together with the company [10]. By this view, the locus of co-creating value is at the firm level.

In a relational view firms establish inter-orgsanizational relationships to co-create relational value that cannot be created on their own. Dyer and Singh [11] defined relational value as mutual benefits that are jointly co-created by two or more firms. Thus, the relational view focuses on dyad/network routines and processes as an important unit of analysis for understanding the competitive advantage of partnerships. The relational view posits four determinants of relational value: relationship-specific assets, knowledge-sharing routines, complementary resources and capabilities, and effective governance [3, 11].

According to Kohli and Grover [12] the co-creation of value can be accomplished through two distinctive mechanisms: IT-based, and non-IT-based, value co-creation. In IT-based value co-creation, IT is used as the main tool for creating value, while in non-IT-based value co-creation firms collaborate in creating business value with less explicit attention to IT. Gnyawali et al [13] follow the distinction of IT-based and non-IT-based co-creation. They use the term co-development actions when firms undertake IT-based actions for the development of various applications based on core platform. They use the term relational actions when firms undertake non-IT-based actions to expand the breadth and depth of service offerings to the users.

2.2   Research Perspectives on the Co-creation of IT Value

According to Webster and Watson [14], a literature review is a sensible way of enabling theoretical progress and establishing a firm foundation for an emerging field. Webster and Watson not only suggest that more literature reviews should be published, they provide detailed guidelines for the practical work. In this study, we adopted their guidelines with the purpose of enhancing our understanding of and identify research gap on the co-creation of IT value. Major contributions are likely to be found in established journals. Consequently, we focused our first search on leading IS journals, i.e., the eight Senior Scholars' Basket of Journals[1] We used the ISI web of science, as well as databases like EBSCOhost. We applied the phrases "cocreation," "co-creation," "cocreating," and "co-creating" in all over searches. Then, we performed a backward search by reviewing the citations for the articles identified, and a forward search by using the Web of Science to identify articles citing the key articles identified in the previous steps.

The literature search in the journals resulted in 16 promising articles, which we checked manually for relevance. We sorted out papers that did not match our

---

[1] V. Venkatesh, "Rankings based on AIS Senior Scholars' Basket of Journals", online:http://vvenkatesh.com/isranking/

understanding of the above search terms. This procedure led us to base our analysis on a set of 13 articles.

All studies undertake actions characterized as IT-based value co-creation. The loci of co-creating values are at the firm level (five) and the relational level (nine). One of the studies is of public sector organizations. Different theoretical perspectives are used, but for the purpose of this study the relational view seems interesting. The issue of value co-creation from interoperability in the public sector undertakes co-development actions (common platform) and relational actions (new services to end-users).

The framework by Grover and Kohli [3] can be characterized as a descriptive integrative view of co-creation layers: relationship-specific assets, knowledge-sharing routines, complementary resources and capabilities, and effective governance. Sarker et al [4] identified alliance governance, collective strengths, and politics as the important mechanisms underlying value co-creation. Gnyawali et al [13] found that the engagement of third-party developers in their technology platform and formation of strategic alliances enhances their performance. Interfirm IT capability profiles of higher sophistication help co-create greater relational value [15]. Hadaya et al [16] demonstrates that the greater the partner-specific IT investments made by the firm, the greater its use of collaborative systems with those partners, the greater its benefits, through the generation of relational rents.

Dyer and Singh [11, p. 662] define *relational rent* as a supernormal profit jointly generated in an exchange relationship that cannot be generated by either firm in isolation, and can only be created through the joint idiosyncratic contributions of the specific alliance partners. We consider the logic of relational rent useful in the public sector context as well, but found it necessary to adapt two of Dyer and Singh's (1998) concepts to fit the new context. The term "profit" is replaced with the term "benefits" as public organizations do not exist to make profit. The term "firm" is replaced with "organization" as this is less context dependent.

The primary objective of the literature reviews was to identify gaps in the literature. We found that research has only investigated the co-creation of IT value to a limited extent, especially with respect to answering questions about how/when/why co-creation occurred. Rather, it addresses the "what" question, e.g., what are the characteristics of e-government interoperability? To address this research gap, we first examine (some) enabling conditions for the co-creation of IT value, and second we try to explore acts and processes of co-creation implementation. Last, we are trying to link antecedents, implementation and outcome. As the co-creation of IT value many times rely on organizational change, we used the theory of institutional entrepreneurship to investigate how the co-development actions and the collaborative actions lead to changes in relational rents.

2.3   Institutional Entrepreneurship

Battilana et al [7] propose a model of the process of institutional change. They present three different phases, and highlight challenges faced by the institutional entrepreneurs who attempt to create, mobilize, and adopt action that breaks with the existing institutions in a particular context.

The first part of the model describes the enabling conditions for institutional change. Different types of field-level conditions, as well as the actor's social position will influence the possible emergence of institutional entrepreneurship. Economic and political crises, technological disruption, competitive discontinuity, and regulatory changes, are examples that might disturb the field-level consensus and invite the introduction of new ideas. An actor's social position, whether they are an organization or an individual, is important because it may affect their perception of a field, as well as their access to the resources needed to engage in institutional entrepreneurship [7].

The second part describes divergent change implementation. Developing a vision encompasses activities undertaken to make the case for change including sharing the vision of the need for change with followers. Mobilization of allies includes activities undertaken to gain others' support for and acceptance of new routines. Implementing change that builds on existing institutions is challenging, but even more challenging if it challenges the existing institutional boundaries or stakeholder interests.

The third part of the model, institutional change, is a highly complex and uncertain process, and thus the outcome is difficult to predict. If one succeeds in implementing divergent change, it is likely that this in turn would influence the field characteristics and actors' social position.

3   Research Approach

This research has a mixed method approach with a literature review, an exploratory case study and a confirmatory field study. We covered various stakeholder groups with various techniques. In step 1 we conducted a systematic literature review of co-creating IT value research. In the exploratory case study in step 2, we highlighted the challenges faced by organizations that attempt to co-create, mobilize, and adopt actions that break with existing practices of creating IT value. In step 3, a survey was developed to further investigate the role of the co-creation process, and was followed up with interviews and a workshop.

3.1   Case Selection

We focused on a large interoperability project in the Norwegian government, as such projects are inter-organizational (or interagency), involving a number of stakeholders. Second, we were looking for relationships or projects that had an expressed interest in the co-creation of IT value. We selected a case involving 38 agencies which eventually included the association of municipalities.

3.2   Data Collection and Data Analysis

The exploratory case study was conducted through 2011-2013, and had two related parts. First, the important features of the co-creation of IT value in a large interoperability project in the Norwegian government were examined [17]. The second part of the exploratory case study consisted of an examination of how the co-creation of IT value influenced institutional change [18]. Data collection was done through a number of interviews, with questions addressing institutional entrepreneurship such as field level conditions, the actor's social position, vision for divergent change, mobilizing allies, and institutional change [7]. In addition, a large number of informal conversations with people from both the system owner and the two service owing agencies were held, and formal documentation of the benefits realization efforts were collected. See the overview of organizations and interviewees in Table 1.

Table 1. Organizations and Profiles of the Interviewees

Organizations	Brief description	Interviewee position/role
Brønnøysund Register Centre	System owner of common infrastructure launched in 2006. Today 38 service owners are operating on the common infrastructure.	10 interviews
Tax Authority	Among the largest service owners and one of the founding partners. Launched its first service back in 2006.	5 interviews
Register of Bankruptcies	Small service owner, which launched its first service in 2013.	5 interviews

We analyzed the data using two theoretical lenses, namely institutional entrepreneurship and the co-creation of IT-value. The first theoretical perspective allowed us to investigate the phenomenon from a process perspective, whereas the latter emphasized the objective of supernormal benefits as a consequence of collaboration.

4   Results: Case Description and Analysis

Brønnøysund Register Centre (BRC) was also responsible for coordinating 38 service owners (at the point of our study) that constitute the consortium of service owners using the Altinn platform. BRC had established integrated application architecture, standards, methods and tools for service development. Our study has shown that BRC's actions as an institutional entrepreneur within the Norwegian government to promote the co-creation of IT value has led to institutional change, especially within BRC's own organization, and also to some extent for agencies that currently provide, or want to provide services through the common infrastructure platform.

Battilana et al [7] propose that a set of enabling conditions for institutional entrepreneurship leads to divergent change implementation that in turn results in institutional change. We used the three phases in our case analysis, and we highlighted the challenges faced by case organizations who attempted to create, mobilize, and adopt action that breaks with existing practices and work processes in the government sector in Norway. The process model has a solid theoretical grounding, but seems to lack an empirical grounding.

4.1   Field Characteristics

Although the various entities involved in the Altinn federation in isolation appear highly institutionalized, the Altinn federation itself seems less institutionalized. Several issues support this perspective. For instance, the mandate from the Ministry of Commerce to monitor the benefits realization for services between government and industry requires new or additional tasks for BRC and the service owners. The mandate from the ministry in many ways echoes the political attitudes towards public sector IT in Norway; there is a need to document value for money. Further, Altinn has recently been rebuilt using new technology. New functionality will be added to enable more interoperability, and thus more sophisticated services with increased potential for benefits. As stated by a controller at BRC: *"There is an increasing political awareness of the need for effective and efficient services."* The planned functionality is not yet fully implemented but will enable service owners to develop services with a much higher degree of interoperability than before.

4.2   Actors' Social Position

The central actor for the co-creation of IT value at Altinn is BRC. BRC is responsible for Altinn and governs the Altinn federation. BRC´s formal position is therefore strong. The positive initiatives taken by BRC during the initiation and early years of Altinn also resulted in a strong social status where other agencies trust BRC to manage the federation in the best interest of the involved parties. However, three issues are threatening BRC´s social position. First, several delays in the development of the new Altinn platform have resulted in delays in functionality that are critical for the new services for other agencies. Consequently, a number of services are put on hold, and service owners are getting impatient. Second, BRC finds itself in a somewhat delicate position when reporting aggregated benefits delivered through Altinn. As the calculated benefit potential is high (ca. $ 2,6 billion), both political and public interest is considerable, and although BRC specifically underlines that it is the service owners that generate the benefits, confusion and misunderstandings around this are common. Such misunderstandings may seem trivial, but are certainly not. The popular press contributes to the confusion by publishing superficial stories of how Altinn generates benefits worth billions without describing the contribution of the service owners. Failure to credit the service owners invites at least two problems: 1) service owners are annoyed and less positive towards BRC and 2) service owners have problems when trying to get the necessary funding for service development internally to implement planned services in Altinn. As stated by an executive at BRC: *"Benefits realization in the public sector is a challenge, especially when the costs are taken by one agency, while the benefits are taken in another agency."* Third, no one questions BRC´s role regarding benefits realization in the intersection between government and industry. However, their role is less obvious regarding internal agency and citizen benefits, and BRC is concerned with their legitimacy in these areas.

4.3   Creation of a Vision for Divergent Change

Grover and Kohli [3] are framing the co-creation of IT value through four components: *the assets layer, the complementary capability layer, the knowledge sharing layer, and the governance layer.* In our context of e-government interoperability, each of the four determinants of value present a value creation layer, which is enabled, expanded or created by IT. For instance, the assets layer involves interoperability specific investments in infrastructure, or skills that enhance the relationship of the e-government project. Best practice arenas, common platforms, methods and standards for infrastructure, systems and data exchange can facilitate the knowledge-sharing layer. The complementary capability layer encompasses the unique IT skills shared by the partner organizations to enable common value configuration from cross-agency services for common end-users. Finally, the governance layer provides the effective management of the relationship through IT assets, such as common systems and methods for benefits realization. Considerable efforts were made by BRC to create a vision for change. The structures and processes that in sum constitute benefits realization at Altinn, as described in Section 4, are the results of a two-year effort, formalized in the form of a project. As stated by the project manager: "The project developed an infrastructure for benefits realization, a process model to be used, as well as a revised cost-benefit analysis for Altinn." Although some aspects of the model need further elaboration and fine-tuning, the vision for the desired change was explicitly and clearly described.

4.4   Mobilization of Allies behind the Vision

The mobilization of allies is considered critical to ensure the realization of vision. This is certainly the case in a complex effort such as Altinn. Our evidence suggests that BRC has had more success in some areas than others. Internally at BRC, the vision appears to be fairly well disseminated, and to a certain extent embedded in the organizational structure. A new unit within BRC is organized around the benefits realization process. Staff and management in this unit are very much aware of the vision as it is reflected in their daily tasks of facilitating the benefits realization for the service owners. Other agencies and service owners have been informed of the importance of the benefits realization effort. The interview with an account manager from BRC revealed the mobilization of the service owners: *"We contact all, existing and potentially new, service providers and assist them in the process of completing the cost-benefit analysis."* Although there seems to be a general consensus that benefits realization is sensible, BRC experiences varying degree of practical support. Few, if any, service owners experience that the benefits realization process adds value to them directly. Large agencies perform similar analyses independent of Altinn, and therefore experience the minimal additional administrative burden caused by the benefits realization regime. Smaller agencies, often with less experience with e-government, report an increased administrative burden. Neither reported the benefits of realization activities as directly useful for their agencies.

4.5   Institutional Change

The benefits realization process is embedded in the organizational structure of BRC, the governance layer. Thus, we found that there has been considerable institutional change within BRC caused by the ambition of realizing more benefits from e-government investments. Governance structures for Altinn and prioritization schemes are implemented resulting in new modes of operation. Service owners have also been subject to institutional change, as they are now required to follow BRC´s procedures for implementing services in Altinn in terms of pre-implementation analyses and post implementation benefits reporting. Although there is cooperation, there is still a ways to go, as stated by a service owner: *"If we want to increase the quality of benefits realization, we need even more assistance from BRC than today."* Finally, BRC experiences an emerging understanding of the mechanisms for benefits realization and the importance of interoperability at the government level. This understanding has yet to materialize itself in actions or organizational structures, but is considered promising. Despite the mentioned accounts of institutional change, planned changes are yet to be institutionalized in several areas. As stated by an executive at BRC: *"There is an ongoing political game of who should be responsible for benefits realization."*

4.6   Confirmatory Evidence from the Field Study

The field study included several types of data collection – a survey among all service owners, a follow-up workshop with a group of service owners, informal interviews and participant observations. Our survey was conducted during April – May, 2013. A questionnaire was sent to the 38 service owners and we received 22 complete answers. We had structured questions about enabling conditions, change implementation, and institutional change. In addition we had open-ended questions about benefits realization management in interoperability projects. We conducted a follow-up workshop with 7 service owners to discuss the results from the survey. In addition we had informal interviews and participant observations.

Results from the survey showed us that services ranged from 8 government-to-government services (G2G), 19 government-to-business services (G2B) and 17 government-to-citizen services (G2C). Service owners indicated an increasing complexity of services, as interoperability must be addressed at several co-creation layers: relationship-specific infrastructure, knowledge exchange, complementary resources and capabilities, and more effective governance structure. BRC's position among service owners was reputable regarding both coordination and mandate.

Related to the implementation of divergent change, service owners had invested in relationship-specific assets, and they had put some emphasis on knowledge-sharing routines. BRC had, to some extent, resources available for service owners with regards to application architecture, standards, methods and tools for new service development. The governance structure of the common platform was not well known or understood. The service owners stated that they were committed to co-create IT value both at the top management and the middle management level.

Change implementation was not very successful, as shown in Table 2. The service owner stated they were only able to create supernormal benefits in terms of improved services, benefits realization, and improved work processes to a small extent. The importance of the "improved entrepreneurial co-creation process" was emphasized.

Table 2. Antecedents and Consequences

Enabling conditions		Implementation of change		Outcome
Field	Social position	Creating a vision	Mobilization of resources	
G2G G2B G2C	Coordination (H) Mandate (H)	Effective governance (M) Complementary resources (M) Knowledge-sharing routines (M) Relationship-specific assets (H)	Commitment (H) Service owners (H)	Improved service dev. (L) Increased benefits (L) Improved work proc. (L)

H = high, M = moderate, L = low.

5   An Entrepreneurial Process for the Co-creation of IT Value

The model of the process of institutional entrepreneurship [7], has in this research been used as a framework for analyzing public sector interoperability in Norway. Based on our research, we propose a new model of the entrepreneurial process of the co-creation of IT value, as presented in Figure 1.

The first part of the model includes the enabling conditions in terms of system characteristics and the system owners' social positions. In our research different types of public sector field-level conditions, as well as the agencies' social positions, will influence the possible emergence of institutional entrepreneurship. Economic and political crises, technological disruption, competitive discontinuity, and regulatory changes are all examples that might disturb the field-level consensus and invite the introduction of new ideas. The system owners' social positions, whether they are organizations or individuals, are important because they may affect perception of the field. In addition, system owners have access to the resources needed to engage in the co-creation of IT value.

The next part includes the acts and processes that co-create IT value. Developing a vision encompasses the activities undertaken to integrate distinct co-creation layers, e.g., relationship-specific investments, knowledge-sharing routines, complementary resources and capabilities, and effective governance [3]. Mobilizing system owners include activities undertaken to gain others' support for, and acceptance of, new interoperable routines. Implementing change that builds on existing institutions is challenging, but it is even more challenging if it breaks with existing practices.

The co-creation of IT value is a highly complex and uncertain process, and thus the outcome is difficult to predict. If organizations succeed in co-creation and gain supernormal benefits [11], it is likely that this in turn would influence the field characteristics and the actors' social positions.

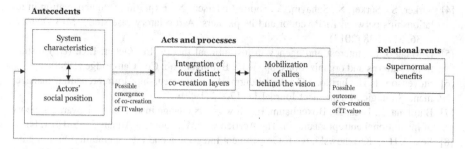

Fig. 1. Model of the Entrepreneurial Process for the Co-creation of IT Value, adapted from Battilana et al. [7]

6   Conclusion and Implications

This research was carried out to address the question "How can organizations co-create IT value?" By studying the phenomenon of the co-creation of IT value in a complex, public sector setting, we found that the existing theory was insufficient to provide an adequate analytical lens. Therefore, we adapted elements from two theories, the co-creation of IT value, and institutional entrepreneurship, and proposed a novel model of the entrepreneurial process for the co-creation of IT value.

Our research has several theoretical implications. The proposed model can be used for descriptive purposes when analyzing the complex co-creation of IT value in contexts similar to the one we studied. Further, our model introduces the concept of "supernormal benefits" as the objective of the co-creation efforts. We believe this is an important sensitizing mechanism that emphasizes the vast potential in co-creation versus creating alone.

We also consider our research to have practical implications. The above-mentioned concept of "supernatural benefits" is considered equally important for practice in terms of illustrating the value of joint efforts. Further, our model can give practitioners perspective and normative understanding for how to approach co-creation efforts.

Obviously, our proposed model needs further refinement and validation, and we would welcome studies with such objectives, in a variety of contexts. Further, the nature of supernatural benefits should be further explored and defined.

References

[1] Love, P.E.D., Irani, Z.: An exploratory study of information technology evaluation and benefits management practices of SMEs in the construction industry. Information & Management 42, 227–242 (2004)

[2] Ward, J., Daniel, E.: Benefits Management. Delivering Value from IT Investments. Wiley, Chichester (2006)

[3] Grover, V., Kohli, R.: Cocreating IT value: New capabilities and metrics for multifirm environments. MIS Quarterly 36, 225–232 (2012)

[4] Sarker, S., Sarker, S., Sahaym, A., Bjørn-Andersen, N.: Exploring value cocreation in relationships between ERP vendor and its partners: A revelatory case study. MIS Quarterly 36, 317–338 (2012)

[5] DiMaggio, P.: Interest and agency in institutional theory. In: Zucker, L.G. (ed.) Institutional patterns and organizations, pp. 3–12. Ballinger Pub. Co., Cambridge (1988)

[6] Stevenson, H.H., Jarillo, J.C.: A paradigm of entrepreneurship: Entrepreneurial management. Strategic Management Journal 11, 17–27 (1990)

[7] Battilana, J., Leca, B., Boxenbaum, E.: How actors change institutions - Towards a theory of institutional entrepreneurship. The Academy of Management Annals 3, 65–107 (2009)

[8] Scholl, H.J., Klischewski, R.: E-Government Integration and Interoperability: Framing the Research Agenda. International Journal of Public Administration 30, 889–920 (2007)

[9] Flak, L.S., Solli-Sæther, H.: The Shape of Interoperabiity: Reviewing and Characterizing a Central Area within eGovernment Research. In: 45th Hawaii International Conference on System Sciences (HICSS-45), Maui, USA, pp. 2643–2652 (2012)

[10] Prahalad, C.K., Ramaswamy, V.: Creating unique value with customers. Strategy & Leadership 32, 4–9 (2004)

[11] Dyer, J.H., Singh, H.: The relational view: Cooperative strategy and sources of interorganizational competitive advantage. Academy of Management Review 23, 660–679 (1998)

[12] Kohli, R., Grover, V.: Business value of IT: An essay on expanding research directions to keep up with the times. Journal of the Association for Information Systems 9, 23–39 (2008)

[13] Gnyawali, D., Fan, W.G., Penner, J.: Competitive actions and dynamics in the digital age: An empirical investigation of social networking firms. Information Systems Research 21, 594–613 (2010)

[14] Webster, J., Watson, R.T.: Analyzing the Past to Prepare for the Future: Writing a Literature Review, vol. 25, pp. xiii-xxiii. MIS Quarterly (2002)

[15] Rai, A., Pavlou, P.A., Ghiyoung, I., Du. Interfirm, S.: IT capability profiles and communications for cocreating relational value: Evidence from the logistics industry. MIS Quarterly 36, 213–262 (2012)

[16] Hadaya, P., Cassivi, L.: Joint collaborative planning as a governance mechanism to strengthen the chain of IT value co-creation. Journal of Strategic Information Systems 21, 182–200 (2012)

[17] Solli-Sæther, H., Flak, L.S.: Interoperability, maturity and benefits in e-government. In: Norsk konferanse for organisasjoners bruk av informasjonsteknologi(Nokobit), Universitetet i Nordland, Bodø (2012)

[18] Flak, L.S., Solli-Sæther, H.: Benefits realization in e-government: Institutional entrepreneurship or just hype? In: 46th Hawaii International Conference on System Sciences (HICSS-46), Maui, USA, pp. 2062–2071 (2013)

Developing Value-Centric Business Models for Mobile Government

Chien-Chih Yu

Dept. of MIS, National ChengChi University, Taipei, Taiwan
ccyu@nccu.edu.tw

Abstract. This paper proposes a value-centric business model (BM) framework and development process for building suitable business models to support the planning, implementation, operation, and evaluation of mobile government (MG) applications. MG stakeholders, values, systems, services, resources, costs, performances, as well as strategies and action plans are included as components to be specified in the BM framework. To achieve the objectives of creating value for all participating parties in the mobile government environment, four stakeholder and value perspectives taken into account are public beneficiaries, government internal organizations, government service chain, as well as society and nation. Based on the BM framework and value dimensions, a business model can be created by identifying and structurally linking values, objectives, systems, services, and performance measures for all stakeholders. To direct and facilitate the launching and evaluation of mobile government programs based on a value-centric business model, an adaptive balanced scorecard (BSC) with other methods and tools are used.

Keywords: Business model, value creation, mobile government, Balanced Scorecard, performance measurement.

1   Introduction

Mobile government (m-government, MG) can be collectively referred to as the adoption of mobile technologies to enhance e-government (EG) functionalities for enabling citizens, businesses, and agencies, with the use of mobile devices, to access government information and services, to exchange documents, knowledge, and experiences, as well as to participate and/or collaborate in government related activities [26,27,30]. Specific functional features of mobile networks and systems such as mobility, ubiquity, portability, accessibility, and localization provide new forms of connections, communications and interactions among stakeholders in the online government services environment. The aims are to eventually create added value and benefits for all MG participants. Value proposed and created for MG users and participating parties include convenience, efficiency, effectiveness, personalization, cost reduction, profitability, productivity, accountability, transparency, etc. [33]. Major identified MG service domains include m-communication (notice and mail), m-public services (transaction and payment), m-administration (internal operation and document

M. Janssen et al. (Eds.): EGOV 2014, LNCS 8653, pp. 325–336, 2014.

management), m-democracy (voting and participation), and m-communities (user generated content sharing and social networking) [4,30]. Business model (BM), on the other hand, has been defined as an architecture of the information, product and financial flows, including a description of the various business actors and their roles, a description of the potential benefits for the various business actors, and a description of the sources of revenues [25]. Commonly mentioned BM types in the e-business domain include business-to-consumer (B2C), business-to-business (B2B), and consumer-to-consumer (C2C), etc. In the e-government literature, identified BM categories include government-to-citizens (G2C), government-to-businesses (G2B), government-to-government (G2G), government internal efficiency and effectiveness (IEE), and overarching infrastructure (Cross-cutting) [14]. Similarly, in the m-government applications, adopted BM types include m-government-to-citizen (mG2C), m-government-to-business (mG2B), m-government-to-government (mG2G), and m-government-to-employee (mG2E) [18].

It has been noted that value proposition and creation are central tasks for the development and delivery of electronic/mobile business and government services. In the mean time, business models have been pointed out as proper means to illustrate the concepts and methods for value proposition, creation, capture, and assessment in business and government domains [1,5,11,12,16,18,24,31,33,34]. Therefore, e-/m-government related business modeling should focus on specifying values and their relationships with other structural components to facilitate value creation for all stakeholders through EG/MG services system development and operation. Developing and conducting suitable mobile business models are thus critical to the success in promoting and delivering mobile public services, creating mobile public values for stakeholders, as well as sustaining continuous operation of MG services systems. In recent years, although emerging issues regarding value creation and business model development for m-government have attracted increasing attentions, an integrated BM framework and process for guiding the construction of a value-centric MG business model are still lacking in the literature. This goal of this paper is to propose a value-centric business model framework and development process for building business models to support the planning, implementation, operation, and evaluation of mobile government systems and applications. The rest of this paper is organized as follows. In section 2, a brief literature review on value creation and business models is provided. In section 3, an integrated MG business model framework is presented based on value chain and value management concepts. In section 4, the development process of business model suitable for m-government based on design science is illustrated. Conclusion and future research directions are provided in the final section.

2   Literature Review

In both research and practices, previous works regarding value creation and business modeling for mobile government are still very limited. In this section, a brief literature review on value creation and business model for e-/m-business and e-/m-government is provided as a foundation for developing a value-centric business model framework suitable for mobile government applications.

2.1   Value Creation in e-/m-Business and e-/m-Government

In the e-commerce and e-business domain, value is defined as the amount buyers are willing to pay for what a firm provides them. It also refers to a preferred combination of benefits that services afford the end users compared with acquisition costs [2]. In the value chain and value management context, value proposition is a statement of what and how value is to be delivered to customers, or is referred to as an equation of the all positive factors that interest the individual and value chain partners. Value creation can be realized as the contribution of utilizing the final products and services to end users, as well as of attaining productivity and profit to the firm and other value chain participating parties. Value capture is defined as the difference between benefits/revenues and costs eventually retained by customers and the firm as well as other chain participants. Being considered as a cycle of value creation, communication, capture, and assessment stages, the value management process generally involves developing and structuring objectives for all stakeholders, establishing a value proposition, creating a value based measurement framework, developing briefs and specifications, designing and reviewing options, and assessing outputs and outcomes [3,7,9,10,18]. As for value model or framework in the e-business domains, Barber (2008) provides two frameworks based on the balanced scorecard (BSC) to incorporate both the tangible and intangible value aspects [3]. Keen and Williams (2013) propose a three dimensional value architecture to fit the dynamic nature of innovation and to sustain business growth [12]. For m-business specific value creation, Nah, Siau, and Sheng (2005) present a value-focused thinking procedure in which identify values, convert values to objectives, distinguish between means and fundamental objectives, and build means-ends objective network are listed as four consecutive steps [17]. Lariviere et al (2013), focusing on value in the mobile and social media environment, emphasize the concept of value fusion that aims at achieving value for the entire network of consumers and firms [13].

In the e-government domain, typical public and social values concerned in the public sector include equal opportunities, privacy, security, personalization, accountability, transparency, and participation, etc. Among previous works presenting value related framework, Hossain et al (2011) specify the measurement of EG system value in three dimensions including organizational efficiency, operational transparency, and public satisfaction [8]. Luna-Reyes, Gil-Garcia, and Romero (2012), aiming at creating value for government, citizens, and other end users, propose a three dimensional performance measurement model comprising EG determinants, EG characteristics, and EG results [16]. As for very few works addressing mobile government value models, Trimi and Sheng (2008) identify MG value-added advantages in various aspects including improving the delivery of government information and services, providing best solutions to Internet connectivity problems and digital divide issues, offering a more cost-effective choice for national networking, helping to avoid problems of corruption and low productivity, as well as increasing government employees' efficiency and effectiveness [27]. Yu (2013), considering value as tangible and intangible benefits perceived by and exchanged between stakeholders in the MG value chain, presents a three dimensional value framework encompassing functional features, user acceptance, and user benefits. The user benefits dimension is further classified into four specific constituent categories, namely, public beneficiaries, government officers and employees, participating parties of the government service chain, as well as society and nation [33].

It can be seen that since issues of value creation regarding mobile government applications are largely unexplored and no consensus in views and architectures of MG value exists, more research efforts in the direction of developing an integrated value framework for m-government are strongly demanded.

2.2   Business Models in e-/m-Business and e-/m-Government

Business model is widely used to depict the design of transaction content, structure, and governance for creating value through the exploitation of business opportunities [2]. To develop and implement an appropriate business model is a key to success and a crucial source of value creation for the firm, its customers, and all value chain participants. Commonly mentioned BM types include e-shop, e-marketplace, virtual communities, etc. when business functions are highlighted, or mobile portals, platform operators, wireless gateway and service providers, mobile application and content providers when mobile environment is involved.

As for component structures of e-business models proposed in the literature, Afuah and Tucci (2001) identifies value, scope, revenue sources, pricing, connected activities, implementation, capabilities, and sustainability as BM related elements [1]. Yu (2005) provides a business model framework with four value dimensions including market, supply chain, customers, and business organizations [31]. Osterwalder and Pigneur (2010) present an e-business model ontology that includes four component groups i.e. infrastructure, offering, customers, and finances [19]. As for the m-business domain, Schubert and Hampe (2006) adopt four main components including value proposition, product or service, value architecture, and revenue model to describe business models for mobile communities [29]. By adopting a design research perspective, de Reuver, Bouwman, and Haaker (2009) point out four domains (STOF), namely service, technology, organization and finance, for assigning common model components to build mobile business models [5]. To design mobile value co-creation services, Schmidt-Rauch and Schwabe (2014) adopt a user-centered design process (UCD) based on the design science methodology that emphasizes on a build-and-evaluate loop with five major steps [22].

As for BM component structures for e-government, only very limited efforts have been undertaken previously. Among these few works, Janssen and Kuk (2007) propose an EG-applicable BM framework that comprises six elements, namely, organizations in the public service network, service offerings, network coordination, business processes, shared resources, and network capabilities [11]. Towards developing a value-based e-government services framework, Yu (2008) proposes a

BSC-based business model to highlight four value dimensions including public beneficiaries, government organizations and processes, government service chain, as well as society and national/global environments. Model elements specified in each of the four BM perspectives include values, stakeholders, services, systems, and performances [32]. Peinel, Jarke, and Rose (2010), in their work of presenting a business modeling approach for e-government services, identify value chain, partners, object exchange, role, services, policy, and advantage/disadvantage as BM elements [21]. Panagiotopoulos et al (2012), focusing on evaluating ICTs in public engagement, adopt a business model perspective that consists of four dimensions including value proposition (effects), value network (actors), value architecture (resources), and value finance (costs) [20]. For m-government specific business models, it is still a relatively unexplored area. Some researchers treat m-government as a subset of e-government and simply present mobile characteristics within the aspects of conventional G2C, G2B, and IEE business model types [18,27]. By illustrating an example of m-government services project, Peinel, Jarke, and Rose (2010) use the similar approach as in e-government cases to identify options of value chain with public and private partners, as well as their relationships with individual advantages and disadvantages [21]. For addressing the m-government adoption with the focus on public-private partnerships (PPP), ITU (2011) describes a basic MG business model that contains a set of constructs including user groups of mobile services, specific benefit and value to user groups, revenue or benefit to the providers/partners, processes and activities, resources and competencies, costs, and suppliers of required resources [9]. To address the design issues of service platform and business model for mobile participation (MP), de Reuver, Stein, and Hampe (2013) adopt the STOF business model framework to the public domain aiming for creating MP services value [6].

The design and implementation of m-government specific business models, although considered as crucial to the success of m-government, are still less touched issues in the literature. Previous works discussing MG related business model framework, development process, and performance evaluation are extremely scarce in both research and practices. Therefore, more research endeavors are needed to explore mobile business model issues in the m-government domain.

3   Value-Centric Business Model Framework for M-government

By integrating different views from previous works and taking a value chain perspective, value in mobile government refers to functional features and acceptance characteristics of MG systems and services, as well as tangible and intangible benefits perceived and captured by MG stakeholders. To facilitate value proposition, creation, and management, MG users and stakeholders are further classified into four constituent groups including public beneficiaries, government agencies, government service chain participants, as well as society and nation. A value-centric business model framework for mobile government (MGvBM) can then be formed to structurally organize stakeholders, values, systems, services, performances, and associated resources, costs, functions, processes, and activities for all stakeholder groups and value dimensions. Figure 1 depicts the value-centric business model framework with major model components and their relationships. Key MGvBM components with related elements and factors are described below.

MG stakeholders: MG stakeholders are actors involve in the m-government services environment. For the four classified constituent groups mentioned above, potential MG stakeholders include (1) citizens, businesses, communities, and NGOs for the public beneficiaries group, (2) local authorities, internal organizations, and employees for the government agencies group, (3) wireless and mobile network operators, mobile content and application service providers, mobile device and software/hardware vendors, mobile payment and financial service providers, mobile security and trust service providers, horizontal and/or vertical integration of participated government agencies for the group of government service chain participants, as well as (4) other actors in the society and national environments for the society and nation group.

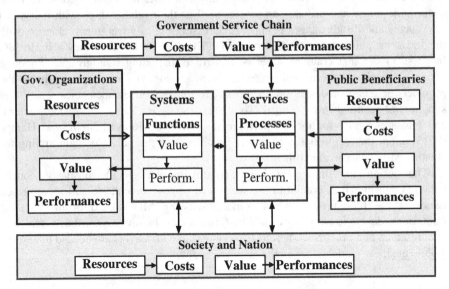

Fig. 1. A value-centric business model framework for mobile government

MG systems: MG systems involve mobile related networks, infrastructure, platforms, channels, devices and hardware/software that provide integrated functions for service providers to offer and maintain, as well as for users to access and utilize MG services in a secure and trust environment. MG system types include mG2C, mG2B, mG2E, mIEE, mG2G, etc, or m-gateway, m-cloud, m-tax, m-tourism, etc. System functions may include profile management, search and navigation, transaction and payment, personalization and collaboration, tracking and monitoring, community and social networking, voting and participation, etc. Functional features include mobility, ubiquity, portability, accessibility, personalization, localization, multimedia data handling, and GPS-capability, etc.

MG services: MG services are functional oriented and categorized value-added objects that are developed by government and associated service chain participating parties to enable users in accessing government information, exchanging personal experience and comments regarding government transactions, engaging with government agencies and/or service chain partners, and participating in government activities, etc. MG services are often classified as mG2C, mG2B, mG2E, and mG2G services, as m-information, m-transaction, m-payment, m-community, m-administration, and m-democracy services, or as m-tourism, m-taxation, m-healthcare, m-learning, m-agriculture, and m-police services, etc.

MG values: MG values refer to tangible and intangible benefits that are proposed to, created for, and captured by all MG stakeholders. Also identified as MG values include function, process and acceptance features of the MG systems and services. Specific MG values for stakeholder groups include citizen value, business value, and NGO value, employee value and organization value, service chain value, as well as society value and nation value. Value elements are specific functions and benefits corresponding to various value types in different services systems and stakeholder groups. For instance, value elements of systems and services value and public beneficiaries value in a m-tax services system include mobility, accessibility, localization, personalization, convenience, security, responsiveness, and ease of use, as well as being able to attain cost and time reduction, access location-based and personalized recommendation services, access cloud storage services, select m-payment methods, and report on user satisfaction, etc. Strategic objectives are specified goals transformed from the value elements associated with systems, services, and constituent groups.

MG performances: MG performances are actual outputs and outcomes generated and measured from implementing, operating, and controlling MG systems and services. Collected data of specified key performance indicators (KPIs) can be analyzed to reflect levels of objective achievement and satisfaction in terms of differences between proposed and created MG values for services systems and all stakeholders. For instance, some KPIs for citizen value of the m-Tax case afore-mentioned can be level of personalization, level of time and cost saving, level of satisfaction in ease of use and usefulness, etc. And subsequently the strategic objectives for MG performances can be set to achieve 90% and 85% for level of user satisfaction regarding ease of use and usefulness respectively.

MG resources: MG resources are financial and other necessary supports for MG development and operation. Major resources include budgets, equipments, human resources, technology infrastructure, management capabilities, and domain knowledge.

MG costs: MG costs are necessary expenditures for initiating and implementing MG programs, for managing and sustaining MG operations, and for accessing and utilizing MG services. Essential costs include expenses and charges on MG systems and services development, promotion, operation, maintenance, improvement, usage, feedback processing, as well as security and privacy control.

MG strategies and action plans: MG strategies and action plans are the specifications of strategic objectives, implementation processes, management functions and activities for building and operating MG business models, as well as for assuring value creation for all stakeholders in the MG environment.

Based on this MG business model framework, the planning and design of a suitable business model, the implementation and operation of the created business model in a proper way, as well as the evaluation and control of the performance outcomes for sustaining continuous improvement, can be carried out efficiently and effectively. The MGvBM framework incorporates concepts and methods in the fields of value chain, value management, strategic management and performance measurement. It takes into account all components of major previously presented EG and MG business models in the literature such as in [5,9,11,20,21,33], and enables a broader scope as well as flexibility for developing and using business models in the public domain. The MGvBM framework is applicable to different levels of MG programs/projects and applications. Foe validation purpose, a 5-year nation wide m-/u-government program, a few central government led m-taxation and m-tourism services systems projects, and a couple of local government launched m-marketing and smart city projects on mobile apps are reviewed for revealing the feasibility of adopting the MGvBM framework and for proposing BM restructuring and improvement suggestions for subsequent MG development.

4   The Development and Management of MG Business Models

To enhance the development and management of MG business models, we adopt the build-evaluate approach from design science technology and extend it to cover the whole process. The complete development and management process for MG business models contains planning, design, implementation, operation, evaluation, and control stages. Steps to be taken in the planning stage for building MG business models include (1) identifying MG stakeholders with roles and relationships, (2) identifying MG values for proposing to all stakeholder groups, (3) identifying MG systems and services for different user groups to create, deliver, and capture MG values, (4) identifying resources needed and available for MG project management as well as service system development and operations, (5) identifying costs required for conducting necessary development works and management processes to sustain continuous operation and improvement, (6) identifying performance indicators for evaluating MG effectiveness and success, and (7) transforming value into strategic objectives and formulating associated strategies. In the design stage, work steps include (1) specifying relationships between objectives, critical success factors (CSF), and actions, (2) selecting, classifying and weighting key performance indicators (KPIs) based on the ends-CSF-means relationships, and (3) setting up action plans with management functions and processes for achieving specified performances and goals. In the implementation and operation stages, action plans are implemented and operated with output data collected for all performance indicators. In the evaluation and control stages, performance outcomes associated with all stakeholder groups and the entire MG project/application are measured, the gap analysis is conducted, and necessary improvement actions are specified and taken.

To facilitate the MGvBM development processes through strategic planning, to performance measurement, a number of methods and tools are used in different stages including the balanced scorecard (BSC), strategy map (SM), ends-means analysis (EMA), critical success factors (CSF), analytic hierarchy process (AHP), and strategy gap analysis (SGA), etc. Specifically for the adoption and adaptation of the BSC method, four specified BSC perspectives representing MG stakeholder groups and associated value dimensions are the public beneficiaries perspective with citizen value and business value, the government internal organization and process perspective with employee value and organization value, the government service chain perspective with entire service chain value and values for all participating parties, as well as the society and national environments perspective with society value and nation value. Figure 2 illustrates the MGvBM-BSC perspectives with some major identified BM components and elements for m-government.

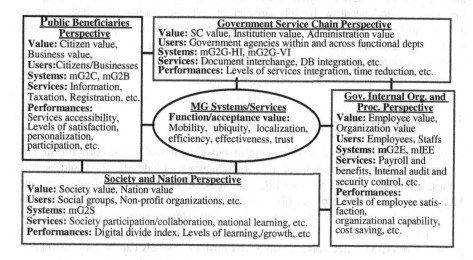

Fig. 2. The four MGvBM-BSC perspectives

Within each of the MGvBM-BSC perspectives, values, stakeholder groups, systems, services, and performance indicators related to MG projects and applications can be structurally linked and presented. For instance, in the public beneficiaries perspective, the MG user groups include citizens and businesses. The value types considered are citizen value and business value. The associated MG systems include mG2C and mG2B. The value-added MG services provided in mG2C and/or mG2B systems include m-information, m-taxation, m-tourism, m-registration, m-transaction, and m-payment services, etc. The MG value indicators for performance measurement include information and service accessibility, time and location convenience, cost efficiency, level of satisfaction, level of personalization, and level of participation, etc. For all the BM components in the BSC perspectives, more detailed specifications can be provided. For example, specific mG2C services identified for MG tourism applications may include (1) mobile information services for accessing government information about news, weather, traffic, and tourism events, (2) mobile notification and alert services for sending text message alerts about emergency conditions, and reminders about other environmental regulations, (3) mobile transaction and payment services for purchasing tickets to enter national parks or other sightseeing destinations, (4) location-based services for accessing GPS-enabled tour guides and road maps, nearby available perking lots, as well as restaurants and stores with price promotion in an acceptable distance range, (5) mobile community services for connecting friends to share information and experiences, (6) mobile reporting services for sending multimedia information to the authorities about real-time traffic conditions or accidents, and/or (6) other mobile tourism related services with personalized, collaborative, location-based, and context-aware features. Value proposition to all stakeholders is undertaken in the planning stage. In the implementation and operation stage, values can be created when systems are developed with sufficient functions and high acceptance, and services are delivered that match users' needs with high satisfaction. Whether values have been created, and/or whether the actual created values meet the pre-specified performance goals need to be assessed and analyzed in the evaluation stage. In the control stage, necessary actions for improvement are taken to ensure value capture and to sustain the continuous MG development and operations.

5   Conclusions

In this paper, we propose a value-centric business model framework for mobile government. Model components of the BM framework include MG stakeholders, MG values, MG systems, MG services MG resources, MG costs, MG performances, and MG strategies and action plans. MG stakeholders are classified into four constituent groups including public beneficiaries, government internal organization and process, government service chain, as well as society and national environments. Based on the proposed MGvBM framework, suitable MG business models can be built to support the planning, design, implementation, operation, and evaluation of various scales of MG projects and applications. An adaptive balanced scorecard with four stakeholder groups and value perspectives is created to facilitate the strategic planning through performance measurement processes of the MG development and management cycle. For any specific MG projects and applications, corresponding stakeholders, values, systems, services, strategic objectives, critical success factors, action plans, and key performance indicators can be structurally linked and presented with respect to each of the MGvBM-BSC perspectives. The contributions of this paper include (1) providing a value-centric business model framework that is taking a broader view, more flexible, and practically operable and measurable for guiding the development and utilization of MG business models, (2) incorporating value chain, value management, and design science concepts to take into account major issues such as creating values for all value chain stakeholders, managing the value proposition, creation, capture, assessment, and control cycle, as well as enabling design-build-operate-evaluate processes, and (3) creating a potential for adopting and adapting the proposed vBM framework and development process to fit the characteristics and needs of e-government and e-participation. Future works will include validating the proposed business model framework and development process by conducting empirical testing in a variety of MG application domains.

References

1. Afuah, A., Tucci, C.L.: Internet Business Models and Strategies: Text and Cases. McGraw-Hill (2001)
2. Amit, R., Zott, C.: Value Creation in E-Business. Strategic Management Journal 22(6-7), 493–520 (2001)
3. Barber, E.: How to Measure the Value in Value Chains. International Journal of Physical Distribution & Logistics Management 38(9), 685–698 (2008)
4. Criado, J.I., Sandoval-Almazan, R., Gil-Garcia, J.R.: Government Innovation Through Social Media. Government Information Quarterly 30(4), 319–326 (2013)
5. de Reuver, M., Bouwman, H., Haaker, T.: Mobile Business Models: Organizational and Financial Design Issues That Matter. Electronie Markets 19(1), 3–13 (2009)
6. de Reuver, M., Stein, S., Hampe, J.F.: From eParticipation to Mobile Participation: Designing a Service Platform and Business Model for Mobile Participation. Information Polity 18(1), 57–73 (2013)
7. Fong, P.S., Shen, Q., Cheng, E.W.L.: A Framework for Benchmarking the Value Management Process. Benchmarking: An International Journal 8(4), 306–316 (2001)
8. Hossain, M.D., Moon, J., Kim, J.K., Choe, Y.C.: Impacts of Organizational Assimilation of e-Government Systems on Business Value Creation: A Structuration Theory Approach. Electronic Commerce Research and Applications 10(5), 576–594 (2011)
9. ITU. Understanding m-Government Adoption: M-Government Mobile Technologies for Responsive Governments and Connected Societies. OECD Publishing (2011)
10. IVM. Value Management Techniques. Online document of The Institute of Value Management, http://ivm.org.uk/techniques (retrieved by April 2014)
11. Janssen, M., Kuk, G.: E-government Business Models for Public Service Networks. International Journal of Electronic Government Research 3(3), 54–71 (2007)
12. Keen, P., Williams, R.: Value Architectures for Digital Business: Beyond the Business Model. MIS Quarterly 37(2), 643–647 (2013)
13. Lariviere, B., et al.: Value Fusion: The Blending of Consumer and Firm Value in Distinct Context of Mobile Technologies and Social Media. Journal of Service Management 24(3), 268–293 (2013)
14. Lee, S.M., Tan, X., Trimi, S.: Current Practices of Leading e-Government Countries. Communications of the ACM 48(10), 99–104 (2005)
15. Leem, C.S., Jeon, N.J., Choi, J.H., Shin, H.G.: A Business Model (BM) Development Methodology in Ubiquitous Computing Environments. In: Gervasi, O., Gavrilova, M.L., Kumar, V., Laganá, A., Lee, H.P., Mun, Y., Taniar, D., Tan, C.J.K. (eds.) ICCSA 2005. LNCS, vol. 3483, pp. 86–95. Springer, Heidelberg (2005)
16. Luna-Reyes, L.F., Gil-Garcia, J.R., Romero, G.: Towards a Multidimensional Model for Evaluating Electronic Government: Proposing a More Comprehensive and Integrative Perspective. Government Information Quarterly 29(3), 324–334 (2012)

17. Nah, F.F.H., Siau, K., Sheng, H.: The Value of Mobile Applications: A Utility Company Study. Communications of the ACM 48(2), 85–90 (2005)
18. Ntalinai, M., Costopoulou, C., Karetsos, S.: Mobile Government: A Challenge for Agriculture. Government Information Quarterly 25(4), 699–716 (2008)
19. Osterwalder, A., Pigneur, Y.: Business Model Generation: A Handbook for Visionaries, Game Changers, and Challengers, 1/E. John Wiley & Sons (2010)
20. Panagiotopoulos, P., Al-Debei, M.M., Fitzgerald, G., Elliman, T.: A Business Model Perspective for ICTs in Public Engagement. Government Information Quarterly 29(2), 191–202 (2012)
21. Peinel, G., Jarke, M., Rose, T.: Business Models for eGovernment Services. Electronic Government: An International Journal 7(4), 380–401 (2010)
22. Schmidt-Rauch, S., Schwabe, G.: Designing for Mobile Value Co-creation - The Case of Travel Counselling. Electronic Markets 24(1), 5–17 (2014)
23. Schubert, P., Hampe, J.F.: Mobile Communities: How Viable are Their Business Models? An Exemplary Investigation of the Leisure Industry. Electronic Commerce Research 6(1), 103–121 (2006)
24. Teece, D.J.: Business Models, Business Strategies and Innovation. Long Range Planning (2009) (in press)
25. Timmers, P.: Business Models for Electronic Markets. Electronic Markets 8(2), 3–8 (1998)
26. Traunmüller, R.: Mobile government. In: Andersen, K.N., Francesconi, E., Grönlund, Å., van Engers, T.M. (eds.) EGOVIS 2011. LNCS, vol. 6866, pp. 277–283. Springer, Heidelberg (2011)
27. Trimi, S., Sheng, H.: Emerging Trends in M-government. Communications of the ACM 51(5), 53–58 (2008)
28. Varshney, U.: Business Models for Mobile Commerce Services: Requirements, Design, and the Future. IT Professional 10(6), 48–55 (2008)
29. Weinhardt, C., Anadasivam, A., Blau, B., StoBer, J.: Business Models in the Service World. IT Professional 11(2), 28–33 (2009)
30. Wu, H., Ozok, A.A., Gurses, A.P., Wei, J.: User Aspects of Electronic and Mobile Government: Results From a Review of Current Research. Electronic Government: An International Journal 6(3), 233–251 (2009)
31. Yu, C.C.: Linking the Balanced Scorecard to Business Models for Value-Based Strategic Management in e-Business. In: Bauknecht, K., Pröll, B., Werthner, H. (eds.) EC-Web 2005. LNCS, vol. 3590, pp. 158–167. Springer, Heidelberg (2005)
32. Yu, C.C.: Building a Value-Centric e-Government Service Framework Based on a Business Model Perspective. In: Wimmer, M.A., Scholl, H.J., Ferro, E. (eds.) EGOV 2008. LNCS, vol. 5184, pp. 160–171. Springer, Heidelberg (2008)
33. Yu, C.C.: Value Proposition in Mobile Government. In: Wimmer, M.A., Janssen, M., Scholl, H.J. (eds.) EGOV 2013. LNCS, vol. 8074, pp. 175–187. Springer, Heidelberg (2013)
34. Zott, C., Amit, R.: The Fit Between Product Market Strategy and Business Model: Implications for Firm Performance. Strategic Management Journal 29(1), 1–26 (2008)

Author Index

Adam, Frédéric   171
Alam, Muhammad Shahanoor   106
Albano, Claudio Sonaglio   181
Alexopoulos, Charalampos   230
Arendsen, Rex   120
Axelsson, Karin   59

Balta, Dian   194
Berger, Jesper Bull   17
Brooks, Laurence   106

Charapabidis, Yannis   230
Cognini, Riccardo   147
Corradini, Flavio   147
Crompvoets, Joep   72

De Araujo, Marcelo Henrique   242
De Groot, Manon   120
De Marco, Marco   159
Depaoli, Paolo   159

Eckartz, Silja M.   253

Fitzgerald, Ciara   171
Flak, Leif Skiftenes   313
Fu, Kai-Jo   96

Gil-Garcia, J. Ramon   47
Greger, Vanessa   194

Hellberg, Ann-Sofie   265
Hjalmarsson, Anders   277
Hofman, Wout J.   253

Janssen, Marijn   84, 230
Johannesson, Paul   277
Joia, Luiz Antonio   206
Juell-Skielse, Gustaf   277

Klievink, Bram   84
Krcmar, Helmut   194

Lee, Chung-Pin   96
Loukis, Euripidis   230
Lourenço, Rui Pedro   35

Madsen, Christian Ø.   17
Melin, Ulf   59
Mkude, Catherine G.   301
Moe, Carl Erik   289

Niehaves, Björn   218
Nijssen, Sjir   133

Palop García, Pau   218
Phythian, Mick   17
Pieterson, Willem   120
Polini, Andrea   147

Re, Barbara   147
Reinhard, Nicolau   181, 242
Rudmark, Daniel   277

Sandoval-Almazan, Rodrigo   47
Scholl, Hans J.   1
Sein, Maung Kyaw   289
Serra, Leila   35
Snoeck, Monique   72
Soares, Carla Danielle Monteiro   206
Solli-Sæther, Hans   313
Sorrentino, Maddalena   159

Thapa, Basanta   218

Van Cauter, Lies   72
Van den Boer, Yvon   120
Van Engers, Tom   133
Van Veenstra, Anne Fleur   253

Wimmer, Maria A.   301
Wolf, Petra   194

Yu, Chien-Chih   325

Zuiderwijk, Anneke   84, 230